Cambridge Studies in Social Anthropology

General Editor: Jack Goody

20

PEOPLE OF THE ZONGO

OTHER TITLES IN THE SERIES

CAMBRIDGE PAPERS IN SOCIAL ANTHROPOLOGY

People of the zongo

The transformation of
ethnic identities in Ghana

ENID SCHILDKROUT
Assistant Curator
American Museum of Natural History

WITHDRAWN

Cambridge University Press

Cambridge
London   New York   Melbourne

Published by the Syndics of the Cambridge University Press
The Pitt Building, Trumpington Street, Cambridge CB2 1RP
Bentley House, 200 Euston Road, London NW1 2DB
32 East 57th Street, New York, NY 10022, USA
296 Beaconsfield Parade, Middle Park, Melbourne 3206, Australia

First published 1978

Printed in the United States of America

Library of Congress Cataloging in Publication Data

Schildkrout, Enid.

People of the zongo.

(Cambridge studies in social anthropology)

A revision of the author's thesis, Cambridge
University, 1969.

Bibliography: p.

Includes index.

1. Kumasi, Ghana – Foreign population.
2. Mossi (African people)
3. Ethnology – Ghana – Kumasi.
4. Ghana – Emigration and immigration.
5. Upper Volta – Emigration and immigration.
I. Title.

DT512.9.K8S34 1977   301.32'6'09667   76–47188
ISBN 0 521 21483 1

To my parents and L. P.

Contents

Tables, figures, and maps

Tables

Tables, figures, and maps

Figures

Maps

Preface

Like many books that were originally dissertations this one has gone through
numerous revisions since it was presented to Cambridge University in 1969. In that
year, a considerable body of literature appeared on the subject of ethnicity and,
since then, a number of important works on several issues relating to migration and
trade in West Africa, the Asante, and the Mossi have been published. Over the last
five years, partly as a result of these publications, my views on a number of issues
raised in this book have changed, and indeed are still changing. But there comes a
point at which one has to accept the somewhat patchwork quality of one's endeavor
and the knowledge that interpretations inevitably change as one's awareness of facts
and their implications grows.

My debts in writing this book are many and go back for such a long time that it
is possible to mention only the most important ones. First, I want to acknowledge
my enormous gratitude to the people in Ghana and Upper Volta whose lives I have
tried to understand. In the text, all names have been changed, except those of persons whose positions as public officials are so well known as to make this caution
meaningless. There are points in a book such as this when one is uncertain whether
one is writing anthropology or history, or indeed if that is a meaningful distinction
at all. At these moments the decision as to whether or not to change names becomes
difficult. The present procedure was adopted after consultation with members of
the Kumasi zongo community in New York, who are related to characters in this
book. It is far from an ideal solution, but it appeared appropriate, given the juxtaposition in these pages of very public and very personal information.

This research, and the publications which have resulted from it, would never
have been possible without the trust, interest, and affection bestowed upon me by
al-hajj Rahman and his entire family. Before I met him, in 1965, the political situation in Kumasi was tense, and ethnicity seemed non-existent – at least, overt expressions of it were rare. In the last days of the Nkrumah regime, the Mossi and
others were in no position to openly admit strangers into their confidence. Meetings
and activities organized on an ethnic basis were banned by the government, and,
although a community existed, it functioned underground. I knew this, knew a fair
amount about it, but also realized that I could not do fieldwork in these circumstances. I had just about decided to give up the attempt to work in Kumasi when

the coup occurred, and al-hajj Rahman returned to Kumasi, following several years of local deportation. For some reason, he trusted me and was sympathetic to the aims of my research. He agreed to give me a room in his house and to help with my attempts to learn the Hausa language, if I would help him to learn English. My association with him and his family developed into much more, and I am quite certain that, without them, I would never have gained the trust of many others in the Mossi community and the rest of the zongo.

There were others who became especially important to me in the two years I lived in Kumasi. Baba Yisa and the Mossi elders were forever patient with my interference. Despite naming me Sarkin Tambaya (Chief of Asking), their indulgence seemed infinite. Al-hajj Rashide Shaban, who has himself written a book in Arabic on the Mossi in Kumasi which I hope to help publish someday, gave me mines of information and shared his insights with me most generously. His family, too, deserve special mention for their warm hospitality. Baba Ahmadu "Cushionmaker's" infallible memory provided an amazing validation of archival sources. Besides teaching me a great deal about the Mossi, I remember hours of fascinating conversation when he told me about his experiences in Burma, about Mossi traditions, and about his insights on world politics. Al-hajj Ahmadu Baba, the other zongo headmen (particularly the Mamprusi, Busansi, and Dagomba leaders), and Hajia Billa were all, as I believe they know well, extremely helpful. In New York, Ibrahim Abu Sahlaga and Safia Adam patiently went over many points of fact and interpretation with me. My assistant, Musa, who spoke six languages and taught me much of what I learned about how to do fieldwork, and Barimuda, who helped to carry out the house census, will, I hope, see this book and know what a big part they had in it.

Among the many other people in Ghana and Upper Volta whose help was important, the cooperation of the late Asantehene, Sir Osei Agyeman Prempeh, and Dr. Alex Kyerematen stand out. Among the staffs of the regional and municipal governments, the Kumasi Cultural Centre, and the National Archives of Ghana in Kumasi, the Cocoa Marketing Board, and the Department of Sociology, Legon, were many individuals who helped in many many ways. Thanks are especially due to Professor K. E. de Graft Johnson, Mr. J. Reindorf, Mr. S. Gyandoh, Mr. David Acquah, Mr. W. de Borde, Mr. P. K. Y. Boatchie, Mrs. Otelia Mensah, Dr. Carlos Salles, Mr. Joe Appiah and Mrs. Peggy Appiah, Miss Joyce Addai, and Mr. Peter Dagate. Dr. Victor Kabore, then Upper Volta's ambassador to Ghana and Monsieur Y. Tiendrébéogo, the Larhalle Naba of Ouagadougou, were of great help and have also published significant works on the Mossi which I have been fortunate to be able to cite.

In Ouagadougou, M. Tahiru Yarse and his family generously provided accommodations for several weeks. The people of Rakai also generously allowed me to ask many questions about their absent relatives. In Ghana, I worked in several other areas which have been mentioned only briefly in this book. There are many individuals who helped time and again in the following places: Obuasi, particularly the Mossi chief; Bawku, particularly the Mamprusi chief and his family; Pokokrum, the Mossi headman; Anyinasa, Amoaman, and Accra. It is to individuals in all of these places, and especially to those in Kumasi, that I feel most responsible for any errors in this book, and it is for them that I most hope I have understood what they tried to teach me.

There are some people whose assistance has been significant for such a long time that by now they have probably forgotten how helpful they have been. Without the patient encouragement, guidance, and stimulation over the past ten years of my supervisor, Professor Jack Goody, I might never have gone to Ghana, completed this research, or written a dissertation. Professor Meyer Fortes has also encouraged and inspired me with his vast and insightful knowledge of Ghana. He also generously allowed me to consult his own unpublished material on Kumasi, work done as part of the Ashanti Social Survey. Dr. Audrey Richards was much more than an examiner and critic of my Ph.D. dissertation: she has been a very significant intellectual and personal influence on me from the beginning of my graduate career at Newnham College, where she first supervised my studies. Dr. Esther Goody first introduced me to field work in Africa, in 1964, and has remained a valued teacher and friend over the years. Professor Peter Lloyd, in examining this book, as a dissertation, in 1969, offered many helpful suggestions which, I hope, have been reflected in this rewriting. Others to whom I feel special intellectual and personal debts, for their generosity in sharing their knowledge of Ghana with me and, in some cases, for reading parts of this work, include Drs. Susan Drucker Brown, Phyllis Ferguson, Keith Hart, Polly Hill, Christine Oppong, Sandy Robertson, Niara Sudarkasa, Ivor Wilks, and Malcolm McLeod, and John Dunn. Discussions over the years with Drs. Abner Cohen and Elliott Skinner have also been stimulating and helpful. Although my first excursions into anthropology were some time ago, Dr. Irving Goldman's encouragement, when I was still an undergraduate, also deserves mention here.

In the years since I left Cambridge, others have read and criticized parts of this book. Drs. Myron Echenberg, Nancy Foner, and John Stewart, and Douglas Midgett, Lani Morioka Sanjek and Mary Falk Horwitz offered valuable suggestions and encouragement. Dr. Roger Sanjek kindly read through the entire manuscript in its final stages, suggesting many important changes in style and, more importantly, in interpretation. Dr. David Thomas helped me to rescue the sections where I have used quantitative analyses, but, like others who have helped, bears no responsibility for any errors that remain. Vita Dalrymple and Carol Slotkin painstakingly typed the manuscript, Nick Amorosi and Luciano Pavignano helped prepare the diagrams, Marcia Darlington helped with the bibliography, and Carol Slotkin labored over the index.

One's most personal debts are perhaps hardest to describe. There is no way to adequately acknowledge all the practical assistance, moral support, and actual labor Luciano Pavignano contributed to this work through practically all stages of the field research and writing. Very special appreciation also goes to my parents, Drs. Herman and Mollie Schildkrout, who not only read and criticized the thesis, but who from a distance always seemed to trust that I would finish something I'd begun, even when I most doubted it myself.

Over the last ten years this work has been supported by a number of institutions

Preface

in many ways. Financial aid has consisted of a National Institute of Mental Health predoctoral fellowship and research grant, a Wenner-Gren Foundation for Anthropological Research postdoctoral fellowship, two University of Illinois faculty summer fellowships, and a grant from the African Studies Center of the University of Illinois, Urbana. The African Studies Centre at Cambridge University (particularly Jane Whiter and Frances Klein) and the Department of Anthropology of the American Museum of Natural History have provided many crucial forms of support without which this book would not have been completed.

E. S.

New York
October 1977

Glossary

For practical reasons diacritical marks have been omitted in the text; they appear in the glossary below. The following abbreviations have been used: A., Arabic; H., Hausa; M., Mossi.

alhaji	H.	one who has done pilgrimage to Mecca (from A. al-hājj)
ʿAshūrā	A.	Muslim festival celebrated on the tenth day of Muḥarram
aure (pl. aurarraki)	H.	marriage
ba (pl. barãmba)	M.	father
babissi	M.	lit., father's brothers; minimal lineage
būdu	M.	collectivity of objects with something in common; race, family, lineage
budkasama	M.	lineage head
dakyia	M.	relative-in-law of the same generation, with whom one carries on a joking relationship
ʼdan ƙ'asa (pl. ʼyan ƙ'asa)	H.	stranger who has lived for a long time in an adopted locality; in Kumasi, second- and third-generation immigrants
Dapore	M.	palace servants of the Mogho Naba, believed to be descendants of captives
dim (pl. dimdamba)	M.	lit., "submit only to god"; king's son
doaghda	M.	family, descendants of a common male or female ancestor (from doghem, birth)
dogari	H.	bodyguard; policeman
ʿīd al-fiṭr	A.	festival following the fast of Ramadan
ʿīd al-kabīr	A.	Muslim festival of the sacrifice
ijmāʿ	A.	consensus; agreement
kāfir	A.	unbeliever, infidel
Kambonse	M.	guards of the royal household among the Mossi
kari	H.	bridegroom's gifts to his bride after consummation of marriage

kombere	M.	district chief, minister to the Mogho Naba's court
kyẽma (or chema)	M.	older brother
maigida (pl. masugida)	H.	householder, landlord
malam	H.	learned person
Mogho Naba	M.	title of the ruler of the Mossi of Ouagadougou
Naba (pl. Nanamse)	M.	chief, ruler
Na'ib	A.	deputy Imam
Nakomce	M.	children of a Naba, people of the Mossi ruling estate
nam	M.	chieftainship; power inherent in an office reserved for royals
pogsiourdse	M.	wife given as a gift to a chief, or by a chief to a subject
sadaka	H.	alms
sadaki	H.	formal marriage payment
saka (pl. saghse)	M.	section of a village
samari	H.	young men; term of address for those younger than oneself
sãmba	M.	father; msama, my father
sarki (pl. sarakuna)	H.	chief
sondere	M.	patronym
swẽya	M.	witch
Talse	M.	commoner; collective name for many non-royal peoples in Mossi society
tarīqa	A.	Sufi brotherhood
teng	M.	earth
tengsoba (pl. tengsobadamba)	M.	earth priest, also called tengnaba
Tijāniyya	A.	Sufi sect founded by Aḥmad al-Tijānī
'ulamā'	A.	learned men, especially in Muslim law and traditions
'urf	A.	custom
yāba (pl. yābrãmba)	M.	grandparent; ancestor
yagenga (pl. yagense)	M.	sister's son; child of female lineage member
yao	M.	younger brother
yasaba (or yésba; pl. yésrãmba)	M.	male uterine relative, *e.g.,* mother's brother, maternal grandfather
yiri (pl. yiya)	M.	household; house
yirisoba (pl. yirisobadamba)	M.	head of household
zaka (pl. zaghse)	M.	interior courtyard
zakāt	A.	tax; legal alms

Part I

Ethnicity and migration

I

Introduction: conceptual approaches to the study of ethnicity

Confronting the consequences of centuries of massive migration all over the globe, anthropologists are now recognizing that their task is not only to study culture, but also, and perhaps more urgently, to study how people with different cultural backgrounds behave towards one another: how they attempt to preserve, annihilate, exaggerate, or ignore their similarities and differences. One aspect of this concern, amply demonstrated in the literature in the past few years, is an interest in ethnicity – that is, in the ways in which people conceptualize and utilize symbols of cultural distinctiveness.

This book is about the changing meaning of ethnicity among first- and second-generation Voltaic immigrants in Ghana. It is an attempt to study ethnicity independently of the processes of migration and urbanization. As valuable as many studies of ethnicity in Africa have been, their wider applicability has sometimes been limited by a lack of analytic separation of these variables. In hindsight – having written the rest of this book before completing this introduction – the distinction between the study of migration and the study of ethnicity has enabled me to reconsider the relationship between ethnicity and cultural variation. Models of ethnicity based only on the study of first-generation migrants – as are many derived from Africa – tend to obscure important aspects of ethnicity, because they confuse the consequences of migration and urbanization with the nature of ethnicity. This study deals with only one cluster of communities in Ghana, but, in focusing on changes in concepts of ethnic identity over several generations, I have tried to develop a model which is applicable to situations where ethnicity is significant but not dependent on continued migration, where it does not necessarily express the perpetual confrontation of many cultures.

Migration and the study of ethnicity

Africans have, over the centuries, devised many ways of dealing with strangers and incorporating migrants into their societies. In the precolonial period, methods of accommodating cultural differences and population movements were many and varied, depending upon the type of contact and the cultural and structural features

3

of the groups involved (Smith 1969; Cohen and Middleton 1970). In precolonial Asante, for example, the government regulated the number of immigrants admitted as war captives, slaves, refugees, or merchants, so that the influx of aliens never surpassed the state's ability to cope with them (Wilks 1975). In other areas, as among the Mossi, migration and the political incorporation of culturally distinct groups was continuous, intimately connected with the expansion of the state itself (Kohler 1972). People moved in search of fertile farmlands and pasturage, so that population density was controlled by the capacity of the environment to sustain it. When strangers came as conquerors, as they did in many parts of the continent, their numbers were frequently small. Conquest usually led to intermarriage and to the cultural incorporation of the intrusive population into the host society.

The nonincorporation of very large numbers of strangers or aliens is a modern phenomenon in Africa (Skinner 1963; Sudarkasa 1975). Since the end of the nineteenth century, the overall pattern of migration in Africa has changed. Precolonial migrations were primarily migrations of persons, usually involving resettlement. The migrations of the colonial period were, on the whole, migrations of labor (Amin 1974). They were temporary and usually involved seasonal or short-term shifts of labor from relatively undeveloped rural areas to cities and plantations directly linked to export production and the world economic system. Many of the long-range problems created by massive temporary labor migration were ignored in the colonial period, for the African laborer was seen as a necessary asset to development, while the home areas of the migrants – Upper Volta being a case in point – were allowed to stagnate through loss of labor and lack of capital.

During this period the political status of the migrant was determined by the colonial government, and strangers and hosts were equally impotent vis-à-vis the colonial powers. The inability of African hosts to determine stranger policy, as well as a great increase in the number of strangers, disrupted those processes of incorporation which previously regulated migration. With the cessation of direct colonial rule a new situation was created. No longer equally impotent before an alien administration, hosts and strangers had to face complex questions about who had the power to control the situation: demographically, economically, politically, and socially. The tensions, ethnic conflicts, and expulsions of aliens typical of many areas in the postindependence period were causally linked to shifts in the locus of power to regulate these matters.

Besides these changes in political structure, other factors have altered the status of strangers. The rapid growth of African cities, shifts in the location and scale of economic activity, unequal development within and between regions, and the creation of national states with rigid boundaries have all deeply affected relationships between strangers and hosts. Perhaps the most significant change, however, is that in many areas of Africa today most migration is no longer temporary and periodic. As in the precolonial period, most migrations today, even though they are still migrations of labor, involve permanent resettlement.

Despite the intentions of migrants to return home, many migrants today are, in fact, immigrants. In the area of West Africa considered in this book, the largest

4

movement of population follows a precolonial pattern, from the northern savannah
to the coastal forest belt. Trans-Saharan trade routes and the slave trade linked these
ecologically distinct regions before and during the early colonial period. In this
century, however, the pattern of migration has changed, as the north has become a
vast labor reserve for the relatively prosperous industries and cocoa farms of the
south. Today, therefore, settled labor migrants take their place beside those who
have continued a precolonial pattern of migrating to trade, those who have set up a
diaspora of stranger communities along long-distance trade routes. Together, these
two categories of immigrants – traders and laborers – are creating the settled immigrant communities of the type described in this book. These stranger communities,
known as zongos, and similar in some ways to the Sabon Gari of Ibadan described
by Cohen (1969), are not based totally on trade. In urban areas, from small towns
to large cities, besides the independent self-employed merchants, they also include
artisans, service employees, and a very large proportion of the unskilled, uneducated
urban proletariat. In rural areas, northerners are more scattered but they nevertheless constitute the mass of the rural labor force: as sharecroppers, wage laborers,
jobbers, and, occasionally, settled tenant farmers.

For many years people from the Northern Region of Ghana, Upper Volta,
Nigeria, Mali, Niger, Dahomey, and Togo have moved into southern and central
Ghana on a temporary basis to work in industry or cocoa farming, returning home
to carry on meager subsistence farming in the rainy season. Some observers have
described this as an "ideal" adaptation to seasonal climatic variations, enabling the
migrant to enjoy the best of both worlds. Increasingly, we have realized that this
pattern is neither ideal, nor generally followed. Many migrants do not return to
their homes, and the costs for the rural population of temporary or permanent
migration often far surpass the benefits. In the long run, this obviously affects both
the areas of immigration and emigration, as it leads to an inevitable reliance on the
importation of food. Massive temporary labor migration thus is based on and perpetuates a pattern of unequal development. Permanent labor migration, when it is a
result of underdevelopment in the rural areas, reflects a situation of increasing
regional inequality.

The notion of an ideal seasonal pattern of migration and a concentration by
scholars on first-generation, rural-born migrants has influenced the analysis of migration, urbanization, and ethnicity in Africa. These have tended to focus on the problems of the migrants' adaptation to seasonal and ecological variations, rather than on
their adaptation to an unequal, man-made distribution of economic opportunities.
In urban areas, migrants' behavior has been viewed as an adaptive response to
modern, Western institutional structures. There has been a tacit assumption in many
of these analyses that there is an equation between traditional and rural society on
the one hand and modern and urban society on the other. Ethnicity has been seen
by some as a link between these two hypothetically distinct contexts, as a kind of
transition or bridge, drawing inspiration from traditional culture but functioning in
the modern context.

Now that we have recognized that most contemporary migration is indeed permanent, a reevaluation of the concept of ethnicity is appropriate. Recently, a number of writers have begun to note that migration in West Africa today is not simply a temporal process, but rather is a structural situation (Amin 1974; Cohen 1974: xiv). The dichotomy between hosts and strangers is not a temporary phase of interaction. Immigrant or stranger status is often more or less a permanent identity, persisting over generations and reflecting the degree to which certain groups can or cannot achieve full incorporation into the host society on a local or national level[1] (Fortes 1975). Obviously, long-term changes of status and identity sometimes occur, and individuals cross boundaries. Strangers become citizens, and people sometimes are able to change from one ethnic identity to another. But the timing, direction, and frequency of these changes vary with the demographic and structural relationship between hosts and strangers and with the provisions made in law or custom by the host society for the accommodation, absorption, or rejection of strangers.

This book is about one particular stranger community in Ghana: Kumasi zongo. This community includes immigrants from a number of areas of northern Ghana and the surrounding countries (see Map 1), but this study focuses primarily on one sector of the zongo: the Mossi from the Republic of the Upper Volta. In concentrating on the Mossi, I did not limit this research to a study of urban immigrants, although most of the material presented here is based on work done in Kumasi, the capital of the Ashanti Region, and the traditional capital of Asante. Links between rural and urban Mossi migrants are important, however, and also give us some clues

Map 1. West Africa: national boundaries and approximate locations of ethnic groups.

about how ethnicity operates in different structural contexts. In focusing on one ethnic community I was able to follow these rural/urban links within Ghana and to compare these different contexts. This has helped me to abstract the significance of ethnicity from the urban context. Both urban and rural Mossi are immigrants and strangers, whether they were born in Upper Volta or in Ghana. For both, ethnicity is often significant, although its manifestations and its meaning are quite different. For the Mossi living in rural Asante, the possibility of losing Mossi cultural identity is frequently perceived as a threat. It implies cultural absorption and social incorporation into the host society, sometimes in a status analogous to that of the slave in an earlier period. For the urban Mossi in Kumasi, ethnicity does not depend upon the maintenance of cultural boundaries. Despite cultural and social integration[1] into the multi-ethnic zongo, Mossi identity remains an expression of social status (in the sense of rank) in a community where stratification is, in part, still based upon ethnic categorization.

The view of ethnicity which I attempt to develop in this book emerges out of a comparison of ethnicity in a number of different contexts. While all of these are in West Africa and provide the ethnographic background for the generalizations I have drawn, this study has wider relevance for situations in other places where ethnicity remains structurally significant, even though, as in Kumasi zongo or in parts of the United States, it has lost much of its cultural basis. In the second chapter of this book, I have analyzed the meaning of ethnicity in traditional Mossi society. In later sections of the book, I have compared notions of ethnicity held by rural and urban Mossi immigrants in Ghana and discussed how the meaning of ethnicity changes in these different contexts. Throughout, I have compared the differing perceptions of ethnicity among first- and second-generation urban immigrants. This comparative approach has enabled me to separate analytically the strands of ethnicity, migration, and urbanization and to arrive at conclusions which are less dependent upon a particular ethnographic example than might otherwise be the case.

In the past two decades, an inevitable trend has become apparent in the anthropological literature on Africa: there has been a movement away from the writing of ethnographies of "tribal societies" to a concern with "complex societies" and contemporary problems of social, economic, and political development.[2] In the period around independence, anthropologists, political scientists, sociologists, and others began to take into account the national context in which African societies existed, much more so than many writers had done during the colonial period. A number of publications appeared in the late 1950s and early 1960s which dealt with the transition from "tribe" to nation, and ethnicity was often seen as a phase or aspect of this process.[3] Other studies considered ethnicity in relation to migration and urbanization. Most important among these was the work in Central Africa done by Epstein (1958), Mitchell (1956), Gluckman (1961), and others; by Richards (1955, 1966) in East Africa; and by Mayer (1962, 1963) in South Africa.[4] The major writings on ethnicity in West Africa included Banton's work on Freetown (1956, 1957, 1961, 1965), Little's work on voluntary associations (1957), and Rouch's (1956, 1960) studies of migration.[5] All of this work, without exception, was about ethnicity and urbanization or ethnicity and migration. All of it was concerned with the pressing problems posed by labor migration and the rapid growth of African cities.

In 1969, the year this study was presented as a dissertation, a number of works focusing more directly on ethnicity were published. Many important insights have been put forth in these publications and they have, of course, affected the way in which I have rewritten this book. Among the most important of these studies were Barth's *Ethnic Groups and Boundaries,* Cohen's study of the Hausa of Ibadan, Kuper and Smith's *Pluralism in Africa,* Gulliver's edited collection on tribalism in East Africa, and Suzanne Bernus's study of ethnicity in Niamey.[6] In the next year, Cohen and Middleton's volume on processes of incorporation and Gutkind's collection, *The Passing of Tribal Man in Africa,* were published. All of these books, with the exception of Cohen's and Bernus's monographs, are edited volumes. Taken together, they represent a growing concern on the part of many scholars with ethnicity, not necessarily in its urban manifestation.

Despite all of the publications just cited, very little has been done on urban-born immigrants in Africa. There is still only one book (Pauw 1963) and one brief article (Rouch 1961) on the second generation. This omission is explicable in two ways: first, in East, Central, and South Africa most migrants are still rural-born, and most do maintain ties with home, often returning when they are not employed. Those born in cities were often children at the time these studies were done. Secondly, this omission reflects the persistence, over time, particularly in the older towns of West Africa, of a distinction between strangers and hosts, indigenes and immigrants.[7] The structural stability of this dichotomy justifies classifying the urban-born as immigrants, but classifying first- and second-generation immigrants together as strangers also leads observers to ignore important differences between first-generation migrants and immigrants born in the areas, rural or urban, to which their parents have emigrated. These generational differences have much to teach us about ethnicity, for they provide a time depth which is absent when only first-generation migrants are considered.

Toward a definition of ethnicity

As soon as one begins to talk about ethnogenesis, ethnocide, integration, assimilation, or acculturation, one is dealing with complex processes of sociocultural change. In this book I try to show how the people described here conceptualize ethnic identity, how these concepts develop, why they persist and change, what functions they serve, and how they are expressed. In chapter 4, on the growth of the zongo community in Kumasi, and chapter 8, on the political history of the zongo, I have presented chronological accounts of changes in the social and political context in which ethnicity operates. Chapter 2, on ethnicity in traditional Mossi society, and chapter 3, on migration, also deal with change, but from a different perspective: these sections set out parameters of change in space and time, in order to show how Mossi migrants were likely to have conceived of ethnicity on their arrival in Ghana.

Conceptual approaches to the study of ethnicity

The remaining sections on domestic organization (chapter 5), kinship (chapters 6 and 7), the social organization of the Mossi immigrant community (chapter 9), and Mossi politics (chapter 10) are also concerned with changes in the significance of ethnicity but are considered from the perspective of generational time (Fortes 1971: 2). Throughout, I have made comparisons between recent migrants, settled immigrants, and immigrants born in Ghana. These three categories represent stages in a process of integration into the stranger community, which is described in detail throughout the book (see also Schildkrout 1975a). The comparison between these categories of immigrants, like the comparison I have drawn in chapters 4 and 5 between old and new neighborhoods, points up trends which, while described synchronically, occur diachronically. These are not stages in a developmental cycle which repeats itself as one generation follows the next, for a cycle presumes a certain stability in the physical and social environment over time. In this case, the event of migration is the starting point of a series of unrepeatable and irreversible occurrences in the lives of the migrants and in the society in which they live. For this reason, the description of change using synchronic comparisons has been supplemented by descriptions of change in a diachronic sense.

The comparison of ethnicity among first- and second-generation immigrants has led me to question the centrality of the concept of culture in models of ethnicity. In his discussion of the epistemological status of the concept of ethnicity, Mitchell (1974: 20ff.) cautions us not to confuse the analyst's constructs of culture and structure with the actor's categorizations and perceptions of ethnic variation. In other words, it is important not to confuse ethnography (the study of cultural variation) with the study of ethnicity (the attribution of symbols of cultural distinctiveness). The description of ethnicity as a kind of folk ethnography has served thus far as a brief working definition. However, this definition, with its emphasis on the subjective, actor's view, that is, on the emic aspects of ethnicity, is not entirely adequate, either from an observer's or an actor's point of view. This is particularly apparent when ethnicity among second- and third-generation immigrants is considered. For them, ethnic categories remain important cognitive constructs even when ethnic groups are no longer perceived by these immigrants as culturally distinct. After extensive periods of cultural integration, traditional symbols and values may have been reinterpreted (Cohen 1969), new symbols of ethnic identity may have been adopted, or symbols of ethnicity may no longer be descriptions of cultural diversity at all, but may simply be markers of membership in distinct social groupings. From an observer's, analytic, or etic point of view, groups claiming a common ethnic identity may persist even when cultural differences between populations disappear.

If one studied ethnicity only in culturally plural societies, then a definition of ethnicity as the attribution of symbols of cultural difference would suffice. However, in societies in which multiple processes of cultural integration are occurring, second- or third-generation immigrants may no longer be cognizant of or concerned with differences in the values and behavior of members of different ethnic groups. In Kumasi, because cultural integration into the zongo community is so

9

extensive, and so deliberately emphasized by the actors, cultural differences between ethnic groups are frequently denied by urban-born immigrants. This is so,
even though, in particular social situations, these same individuals emphasize the
importance of ethnicity as a form of social differentiation. Thus, ethnic categories
remain important in the second or third generations and correspond to actual
social groupings; but the symbols used to distinguish these categories are not
necessarily, and often cannot be, descriptions of cultural differences. Urban-born
immigrants admit that, at some time in the past, members of different ethnic
categories did form distinct cultural communities, with distinct local origins. Today, however, ethnic categories are defined simply by a rule of descent which
confers eligibility to membership in a particular social category and/or group.
This, some might argue, represents the disappearance of ethnicity as a consequence of cultural absorption or integration. However, the study of second-
generation immigrants demonstrates that the persistence, on an etic level, and the
attribution, on an emic level, of cultural differences are not necessary conditions
for ethnicity to persist as an aspect of social structure.

The view of ethnicity that has just been outlined derives from viewing ethnicity in diachronic perspective. It is, in a sense, a conclusion reached after the com-
pletion of this study. At this point it is appropriate to set out in greater detail
the conceptual and methodological orientation with which I approached the study
of ethnicity in the field and in the analysis of field data. In the considerable
literature which has appeared on ethnicity in the past few years, a number of
points have been made which are relevant to this discussion and, where possible,
I have cited these. It is not, however, my intention to present an exhaustive critical review of the literature, but rather simply to set out the basic premises with
which I approached the study of ethnicity in Ghana.

Ethnicity is a set of conscious or unconscious beliefs or assumptions about
one's own or another's identity, as derived from membership in a particular type
of group or category. These beliefs may affect social behavior and may influence
relationships and interaction in a number of social fields: economic, political,
domestic, or religious.[8] Ethnic categories are frames of reference which affect
people's perceptions of events, relationships, and other persons or groups. They
have a descriptive content, stereotypes, and a normative content consisting of
values and/or moral imperatives about behavior. Although these values may not
differ from those held by members of other ethnic groups, as is often the case
after long periods of cultural assimilation or integration, they do consist of rules,
expressed as moral imperatives, which distinguish expected intragroup behavior
from behavior to outsiders. Stereotypes consist of ideas, prejudices, and expectations about the ways members of particular groups should and do behave. They
may be accurate perceptions of the stereotyped groups' characteristic behavior or
may bear little relation to what the stereotyped group is really like and simply
express aspects of the relationship between groups (Levine and Campbell 1972;
Schildkrout, forthcoming). Many discussions of ethnicity describe only one ethnic
group, focusing on its internal organization, but this is always in the context

of a larger system. Even if one does not employ the concept of pluralism, and thereby presumes to describe an entire society, it is impossible to describe an ethnic group in isolation. This is why in this study I have embedded a description of the Mossi community in the larger stranger community, the zongo, and this, again, in the context of Kumasi and Ghana as a whole. In defining the context in which ethnicity operates, some writers focus on the city, others on the state, and others only on interpersonal relations. But in trying to define an ethnic group, all inevitably face the issues of incorporation/exclusion – the boundary problem and that of the relationship between ethnic communities and the larger society of which they are a part.

This problem, in my view, is identical, whether the society is defined as a city, a nation, a tribe, a town, or whatever unit is selected for analysis. In the comparison I have drawn between Kumasi zongo and the Mossi community in Upper Volta, it emerges that ethnicity operates in similar ways in both situations. In both, ethnicity is a means of determining the allocation of socioeconomic and political roles, the criterion for inclusion in particular social networks, and the allocation of status and prestige. The notion that one could carve up precolonial Africa into culturally distinct "tribes" has long since been abandoned by all but the most naive observers. Although ignored in much ethnographic literature, which, for analytic purposes, employs the model of the tribe (Cohen and Middleton 1970: 4), ethnicity has been significant in many African societies for centuries. Ethnicity is, admittedly, not important in all societies, and is perhaps more obvious and easier to study in the bounded context of a nation or a city,[9] but it emerges as a variable[10] in most situations – traditional or modern, rural or urban – where once-distinct groups are brought into juxtaposition through processes such as migration, warfare, intermarriage, or trade. More rarely, ethnic categories evolve after a population splits, and the segments develop differently, each exploiting different ecological niches (Barth 1969: 17ff., Schein 1975: 91). Members of these communities then relate to each other with the presumption that they have diverse origins, histories, and cultural heritages.

Discussions of the significance of ethnic boundaries have been complicated by two other related issues: the situational nature of ethnic identity and the possibility of individuals opting to assume or repudiate ethnic group membership. Situationality refers to the fact that individuals may belong to a number of ethnic communities which exist on different levels and with which they can identify in different social situations. Ethnic categories are always based on some notion of a common place of origin (Barth 1969: 13). Even when other characteristics are more important in ascribing ethnic identity, some notion of common provenance can be invoked. For example, race, class, and culture are more important than provenance in defining the ethnic identity of American Blacks or Jews, but at various times, among both of these groups, ethnicity has expressed itself in Zionism or Back to Africa movements of one kind or another. Among recent migrants the geographic component of ethnic identity is likely to be more significant than among American Jews and Blacks, to the extent that their migration is more immediate.[11] It expresses itself in the formation of a series of increasingly inclusive communities defined, at least in part, in geographical terms. The Mossi in Ghana, for example, form groups based on hometown locality, on northern identity, on Mossi identity, and on Voltaic identity. In relation to Europeans, Africans may be seen or may see themselves as an ethnic category. Each of these identities may be invoked at different times, and the analysis of any social situation should reveal why a particular level of identity is relevant.

Situationality also refers to the fact that individuals may, in some situations, have a degree of choice about whether or not to invoke their own or others' ethnicity. However, ethnic identity is often determined by one or more rules which preclude an individual's opting to be in or out of an ethnic category. When a strict rule of descent or a racial classification determines ethnic identity, an individual cannot easily choose not to be identified, at least by others, as a member of a particular category. The person may not necessarily identify with groups formed on the basis of this categorical ascription, however.

The importance given to ethnic-group membership varies according to a number of factors, including other aspects of personal status, such as age, sex, generation, and socioeconomic or class position. It also varies with respect to the context of interaction and the intentions of the actors – that is, their perceptions of the possible benefits or liabilities which may come from invoking their own or another person's or group's ethnic identity. Describing ethnicity as a person's basic, most general identity (Barth 1969: 13) can obscure the importance of situationality. Ethnicity is not always an inevitable basis for identity. It is a special sort of identity which may be an asset or a liability in respect to furthering individual or group interests.

The situational importance given to ethnicity is not simply a matter of individual choice. I have mentioned the limits on optation in the case of certain types of ascription, such as race or descent. The nature of the social structure in which ethnicity operates determines the parameters within which individual choice, in invoking or ignoring ethnicity, can operate. Thus, in many stratified societies ethnicity is an important means of expressing and maintaining the boundaries between strata. The classic example of ethnicity operating throughout a system to determine the allocation of status is, of course, the Hindu caste system. However, ethnicity may be significant only as a means of identifying minorities which are excluded from political or economic power or it may provide the criteria for identifying and restricting membership in a ruling elite. Ethnicity is negotiable only to the extent that the social structure allows mobility across the boundaries that are used to define ethnic categories.

In Kumasi (see Map 2), there is a basic economic, social, and cultural distinction between the indigenous Asante population and all of the northern strangers. In the long run, this is the most important social and cultural cleavage now developing in Kumasi and in many other areas of Ghana as well. This regional classification cross-cuts the distinction between citizens and aliens and between Muslims and non-Muslims.[12] It is, in a sense, an emerging ethnic cleavage, while northern identity is

12

Map 2. Ghana: regions and towns mentioned in text.

13

an emerging ethnic identity. Regional identities are not, strictly speaking, rooted in notions of common ancestries, although origin myths linking the ancestors of various northern groups are often cited. Nor is this identity perpetuated by a notion of descent or filiation, criteria which in Kumasi are associated with ethnicity. Increasingly, however, this important cleavage resembles, and perhaps supersedes, other cleavages which are unquestionably ethnic.[13] As the nation becomes a more important economic and political arena, regional identities may be expected to assume greater importance. In Kumasi, northerners claim common provenance vis-à-vis the Asante and southern Ghanaians, many of whom make no distinctions within the ascription "northerner." (See Map 3 for the distribution of the population of Ghana as a whole.) In the zongo, an ideology of kinship, that of Islamic brotherhood, unites immigrants from many different localities. Although ethnic groups within the zongo are more highly organized than these regional communities, the dichotomy between the northern stranger community as a whole and the local Asante population provides the background, the setting, and in many ways the explanation for the manifestations of ethnicity within the zongo which are described in this book.

Within the stranger community in Kumasi there are many different ethnic categories, and many different communities and groups formed on the basis of these categories. The boundaries between them do not consistently reflect traditional cultural, linguistic, or political divisions which, in any case, were rarely clearly bounded or isomorphic. The emphasis in the literature on first-generation migrants has obscured this fact and led to the assumption that ethnicity can be explained in terms of the persistence of tradition. Traditions or historical events may be used by the actors as explanations for the existence of ethnic categories or as explanations of interethnic relations. But these are rationalizations, not explanations adequate for the level of analysis we are seeking here. Rouch (1956: 31, 134) has spoken of "supertribalism" as "fidelité à l'histoire," while Mitchell has maintained that hostility among groups on the Copperbelt can be traced to traditional relations between groups (1966: 52). However, the number of historic scores to settle may be infinite: more interesting is how these historical "facts" are used as symbolic expressions of interethnic relations. Traditions and historical relations between groups may help to explain the content of stereotypes which are used to express ethnic boundaries or intergroup relations; they do not explain the definitions of ethnic boundaries or the causes of interethnic hostility or friendship.

These things are rooted in the contemporary situation in which ethnicity operates as a behavioral variable. Were this not the case, we would have no way of explaining the emergence of new ethnic categories or changes in the definition of old categories. The cleavage between southerners and the Asante, on the one hand, and northern strangers, on the other hand, and the corollary of this – the zongo identity which is superseding other divisions among northerners – provide examples of emergent ethnicity which can be explained only in terms of contemporary economic, political, and social facts.

I have stated that ethnicity is a distinctive type of communal identity. In Kumasi

14

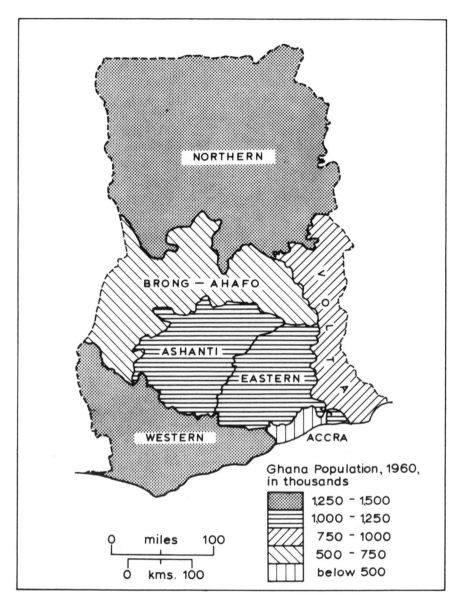

Map 3. Ghana: population by region, 1960 (based on the *1960 Ghana Census*).

zongo, ethnic categories are defined according to two basic notions: provenance and kinship. The boundaries of ethnic categories change over time: new categories emerge, and others disappear, merging into larger, more inclusive units. But in all cases, these two notions are used by people in Kumasi to explain membership. This is true, even though other characteristics such as race, language, dress, particular customs, traditions, or printed membership cards may be used as symbols of distinctive identity. While all of these may be used to define communities (Paden 1970), it is the co-occurrence of the notions of kinship and provenance which distinguishes ethnicity from other forms of identity (Shibutani and Kwan 1965: 47). Individuals may demonstrate ethnic identity by adopting all kinds of symbols of ethnic distinctiveness, but membership is ultimately explained in terms of ascription through a real or fictitious kinship link. The way in which the element of kinship is expressed may vary. For example, when race and ethnic identification coincide, a filial link is usually assumed to exist, based on phenotypic "evidence." When biological attribution is less clear, a strict rule of descent may determine the ascription of ethnicity according to patrilineal or matrilineal principles. In other cases, the notion of kinship may be only a metaphor used to describe the brotherhood linking all members. However, the use of the metaphor in this minimal sense constitutes an aspect of ethnicity only when, at the same time, recruitment consists of ascription at birth on the basis of other criteria such as race, religion, natal language, or place of residence.[14]

This book is primarily about how ethnicity operates in the domains of kinship and politics. The second section is about the relationship between kinship and ethnicity among first- and second-generation immigrants. Among rural-born immigrants kinship is often fictive, while for the urban-born, bilateral networks of biological kin exist. These often include members of several ethnic communities. Nevertheless, in both generations ethnicity is expressed through the idiom of kinship. The third section of this book is about ethnicity and politics. Among first-generation immigrants political life is closely connected to controlling and protecting the corporate organization of the ethnic group, for this offers migrants many important kinds of support. Politics among second-generation immigrants is not so closely involved with the formal organization of ethnic communities, but ethnicity is still used as one among several bases of support in the politics of the zongo as a whole.

There are both empirical and theoretical reasons for this emphasis on kinship and politics. The empirical one is simply that these two fields of behavior were the ones through which immigrants in Kumasi most often expressed their concern with ethnicity; ethnicity is relevant and necessary in explaining behavior in these two fields. It is somewhat less relevant, in Kumasi, for explaining economic behavior, because of the significant economic cleavage between the zongo and the Asante community and because no ethnic group within the zongo has ever been able to attain a monopoly of any sphere of trade.

The theoretical rationale for discussing ethnicity as an aspect of kinship and political relations follows from the model of ethnicity which I adopt in this book. Ethnicity, as I see it, as well as having the attributes already mentioned, is the conceptual link between these two domains. It is based on a notion of kinship and is used to define a person's membership in a political community. It is the link between what Fortes (1969) describes as the familial and the politico-jural dimensions of social structure. The fact that ethnicity is rooted in familial and kinship relations (real or fictive) accounts for the moral imperative associated with ethnicity, particularly in societies where morality and kinship relations have always been intimately connected. The extension of ethnicity into the politico-jural domain accounts for the corporate expressions of ethnicity and also for the fact that ethnicity so often becomes a means of allocating status in a stratified society.

2

The Mossi: ethnicity in Voltaic society

While the Mossi view themselves as a single ethnic unit when they are in contact with others, Mossi society itself is internally divided into a number of different subcategories, none of which identifies itself simply as Mossi. The unity apparent to outsiders reflects the fact that members of these various Mossi collectivities have more in common with one another than they have with non-Mossi. This unity is the result of a long and complex process of incorporation which has been characteristic of Mossi society since its beginning in the fourteenth or fifteenth century (Fage 1964; Illiasu 1971).

Although the distinctions between ethnic communities within traditional Mossi society are not of great importance to the organization of the immigrant Mossi community in Kumasi, the process of incorporation that has characterized the growth of the Mossi state is relevant. In a number of significant ways the processes of integration taking place in both communities are similar. In the Kumasi immigrant community and in Mossi society in Upper Volta, ethnic communities have increasingly lost their cultural individuality as they have been incorporated into larger sociopolitical units. At the same time, ethnic categories have become elements of the social structure of the larger community, wherein they are a means of expressing status distinctions between groups and allocating distinctive social, political, and economic roles.

In Mossi society,[1] as among immigrants in Kumasi, ethnic categories are perpetuated through patrifiliation. This principle generates an ideology of ethnicity which divides the population into communities which are differentiated according to the social roles they perform, their political status, and various attributes which confer differential prestige upon their members. Societies which, in at least some contexts, recognize a principle of unilineal descent tend to allot complementary ritual, political, or economic functions to different groups or communities on the basis of this principle. All of the states in the Voltaic culture area, as well as the Hausa and Gonja, two groups which in nonpolitical contexts have bilateral kinship systems, use patrifiliation as a means of recruitment to political office and as a means of determining political status. On this basis nobles and commoners are dis-

18

tinguished in these states, and, although individuals may occasionally move from one category to another, the ideology of ethnicity remains to express distinctions between social strata and to define political statuses.

In Mossi society ethnic categories are distinguished, in theory at least, according to their place of origin (see Map 4). There are numerous myths describing the origins of each ethnic unit, its entrance into Mossi society, and its relationships with other ethnic communities. These myths symbolize certain aspects of the political structure, and their symbolism, in many cases more than linguistic or cultural differences, demonstrates the existence of boundaries between different strata. These strata correspond to ethnic communities within Mossi society, while the ideology of ethnicity forms the cognitive basis of a system of stratification. In the next section some of these myths are discussed, in order to show how the Mossi conceptualize their social structure. Following this, actual differences in political and economic status between these communities are discussed. The effect of ethnic differentiation on migration from Mossiland is examined in the subsequent section.

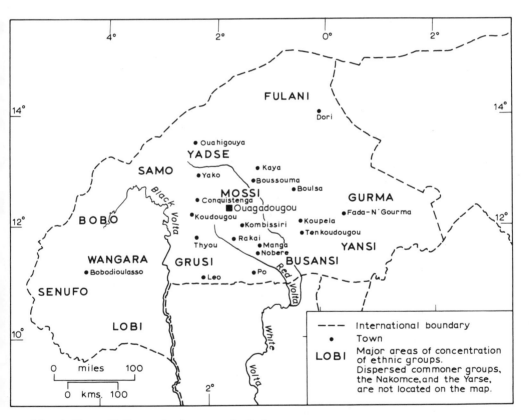

Map 4. Upper Volta: major towns and ethnic groups.

19

Ethnicity and migration

The origin myths

A study of Mossi origin myths does not unequivocally establish who the Mossi are, or even who they think they are. Nevertheless, many writers have taken the myths to be either historical or symbolic descriptions of Mossi social structure. After examining one or more versions of the myths, various writers have identified one or another group within Mossi society as the "real" Mossi. However, since the discrepancies in the myths center around precisely this point – the identification of the Mossi – the answer seems to lie, not in a single myth, but in the total body of myths. A comparison of conflicting versions, all of which must be assumed to have some meaning for some part of the population, leads one to conclude that within Mossi society the Mossi cannot be identified with any one ethnic category to the exclusion of the others. The myths demonstrate this, for in them the primary identity of all the actors attributed with the founding of the Mossi state is always something other than Mossi. It is the interaction between the individuals and groups described in the myths which creates Mossi society, a new polity which then incorporates them all.

There are many versions of the myth which explains the origin of the Mossi state. The most well known are the Nakomce (royal) myths which validate the political power of the ruling group, according to a story of military conquest. These myths have been interpreted as historical accounts by some writers, including the French colonial administrators, Tauxier and Delafosse, and by a number of contemporary writers, among them several members of the Nakomce group. Members of the royal estate in all the centralized Moré-Dagbane states place particular emphasis on oral history, for stories of conquest may be used to legitimize claims to political office. There are, however, other myths which express the views of commoners (collectively known as Talse [s. Talga] in the Ouagadougou kingdom and as Foulse [s. Fulga] in the Yatenga kingdom), blacksmiths, Muslims, especially the Yarse (s. Yarga), and others. These nonroyal myths do not emphasize conquest; they portray the Mossi state as composed of a number of interdependent and equal groups. Some Yarse myths refer to conquest but describe the Yarse as important participants in it. The major discrepancies in different versions of the myths concern the ethnic identity of the various actors in the myth.[2] As all of these myths explain the origin of either Mossi society or the Mossi state, the different versions may be used by different local groups to legitimize their claims to have played a part in the founding of the state. In this sense, the variations in the myths reflect the incorporation of distinct local communities and cultural groups into Mossi society, while the myths, as a whole, reflect the persistence of ethnicity in the Mossi ideology of stratification.

In various versions of the royal, or Nakomce, myth, the origin of the Mossi state is attributed to the journey of a Mamprusi princess, Nyennenga, northwards into the area which subsequently became incorporated into the Mossi state system. After her marriage to a local hunter, her son, Ouedraogo, becomes the first Mossi ruler and he and his descendants become founders of the several Mossi kingdoms.

After a visit to his Mamprusi grandfather, Ouedraogo returns to Mossi country with a group of Mamprusi and Dagomba horsemen who proceed to conquer the indigenous populations and expand the political hegemony of the Moré-Dagbane royal lineage.

After their visit to Mamprusi, Ouedraogo and the Dagomba horsemen marry the indigenous Nionossi, Kibissi, Busansi, and Foulse women. These groups have since come to be considered commoners (collectively known as Talse) in the Mossi state. The offspring of these marriages are generally said to be the first Mossi people – a new "race" formed from the intermarriage of the invading Dagomba horsemen and the autochthonous women – while the Mossi royals are the patrilineal descendants of Ouedraogo and his Dagomba followers. The major Mossi chiefs, the Mogho Nanamse, and their sons, the Dimbissi, are all said to be lineal descendants of Ouedraogo, while the district chiefs of Mossiland, the Kombere, are Ouedraogo's collateral descendants. In Mossiland, the lineal descendant of any hereditary chief ultimately claiming descent from Ouedraogo is a Nabiga (pl. Nabissi), while ordinary members of the royal group who claim to belong to distant branches of the royal lineage are Nakomce.

A debate has ensued in the literature on the Mossi over the question of whether or not the term Mossi should be applied to royals alone or whether it refers to the "mixed race" created by the intermarriage of the horsemen and the local women. The question is, of course, meaningless if significance is given to patrifiliation, since all members of this mixed group would be royal. The Nabissi theoretically belong to a single lineage, all of whose members claim to be descendants of Ouedraogo, while the Nakomce claim royal status because the Dagomba horsemen, from whom they descend, were royal. But Ouedraogo himself claimed his royal status through his mother. If his children did the same, ignoring the principle of patrifiliation, the royal group would obviously disappear. In one version this problem is resolved by an incestuous marriage between two of Ouedraogo's children (Moulins 1909, quoted in Tauxier 1912: 454). Ultimately, however, the emphasis in the myths on this point demonstrates that, once the kingdom was founded, descent became a major principle of structural differentiation and a means by which ethnic identities are preserved.

Izard and Izard-Héritier (1959: 47) and Zahan (1961, 1967) maintain that, strictly speaking, today the name Mossi applies to the nobility, the Nakomce. Zahan adds that it is also applied to state officials and their descendants who were not originally Nakomce. He states that "the term Mossi refers to a concept which may best be envisaged in the form of a pyramid" (1967: 156). The pyramid consists of Nabissi at the top (numerically the smallest group), followed by Nakomce, who are non-office-holding royals, then the Talse, and, finally, at the bottom, the Zemba (assimilated foreigners), and slaves. The pyramid does not restrict the term Mossi to royals, but there is a suggestion that the royals do regard themselves as "more Mossi" than the others.

This same ambiguity about the use of the term *Mossi* is illustrated in the work of Hammond, who uses the term in two different ways (1966: 16):

Ethnicity and migration

Two ethnically separate groups inhabited the region of Yatenga prior to the Mossi immigration. One appears to have remained and to have assimilated Mossi culture, the other evidently fled. The Mossi refer to this first group as Nyonyose. . . . Through most of the country, however, the people known to be their descendants usually are referred to as the Mossi.

Izard and Izard-Héritier state that theoretically the most correct usage is to call only the Nakomce "Mossi," but they also claim that calling the descendants of the Dagomba and commoner women "Mossi" is ethnologically accurate (1959: 47). Here they seem to be contrasting the restrictive ideology of ethnicity with the realities of social and cultural assimilation. All of these interpretations reflect the problem of ideologically restricting membership in the royal group, and thus restricting eligibility to political office. Some versions of the myth, as well as some interpretations of them, attempt to do this linguistically, by equating the notion of real Mossi with either royals or commoners. However, there are actually two boundaries that are difficult to maintain, for reasons that will become clearer below: that between office-holding royals (Nabissi) and Nakomce and that between Nakomce and commoners. The myths are used by the Mossi and by interpreters of Mossi culture in an attempt to maintain and explain the persistence of these categorical boundaries in the face of the sociocultural assimilation of diverse groups in Mossi society.

Several Nakomce authors maintain that the word Mossi refers exclusively to commoners. Delobsom (1932: 1) says that Mossi means "those who are uncircumcised" and "impure," and that since royals, and not commoners, are circumcised, the term refers to the latter. Kabore (1966: 19), following Delobsom, claims it is an insult to call a royal *moaga*, since this is actually the Dagomba word for the "savage, uncircumcised 'ninissi,' and, by extension, the mixed-blood children issuing from the union of the 'Dagombas' with the daughters of the conquered."

The theory of Mossi social structure which is expressed in various versions of the Nakomce myth stratifies the society into royals and commoners. Taking this as their starting point, a number of writers have described all other groups in Mossi society as strangers, despite the fact that in the past several centuries these groups have been politically and culturally incorporated into the society. There are other myths, not royal ones, which describe the entrance of these stranger groups in Mossiland and present them as founders of the state, along with the Nakomce, who could also, in a sense, be regarded as strangers vis-à-vis the autochthonous peoples. Some of these myths are told as moral tales and are not regarded as history by the Nakomce or by those who would give a literal interpretation to the Nakomce myths; but for others, particularly for the members of the groups concerned, they describe the structure of Mossi society no less than do the Nakomce myths. Delobsom (1932: 118–23) records a story which is interesting from this point of view. He says that it is intended to explain why the blacksmiths, the Yarse, and the Fulani do not perform the customary Mossi greeting (*kantisse*) when they meet Mossi chiefs.

In the story, God (Wende) created four brothers and four bags of miracles.

Each brother is told to choose a bag and goes with his bag to build a house in a different part of the country. Each brother then goes to sleep, and when he wakes up he finds that he has become a different type of person. The eldest has become a blacksmith; the next has become a Fulani herdsman; the next is a Yarse trader; and the youngest (the last to come into the world) has become a chief. The eldest goes to find his younger brothers, and when the three oldest finally arrive at the place where the youngest has settled, they discover that he has much land and a beautiful palace. The three eldest brothers then decide to stay in the youngest one's country, each agreeing to contribute his special talent to the others. Governing, like smithing, herding, or trading, is seen as a vocation, and the Mossi state is established by the voluntary cooperation of collateral branches of a single sibling group. Birth order, rather than migration or conquest, is used to establish the relative chronology of each group's appearance in the country. (See d'Hertefelt 1964 for a discussion of similar myths in Ruanda.)

Stratification in Mossi society

In trying to specify who the Mossi are, most authors look for answers by using two types of data: the myths, which express Mossi theories of social structure, and empirical data about the degree of cultural differentiation between groups. Early writers, Marc and Moulins, for example, regarded the conquerors and their descendants – the "metissage" – together as "la race Mossi." Tauxier and Binger noted some cultural differences between incorporated groups but nevertheless emphasized the cultural homogeneity of Mossi society. Tauxier (1912: 452) states:

The Mossi actually form a perfectly homogeneous race in their customs and their language, but this homogeneity is only an end product. The Mossi masses actually result from the fusion of a conquering population (the Mossi, properly speaking) and a conquered population which was probably related very early to the Habe, Kipirsi, Gourounsi, Boussanse, etc. [Author's translation.]

Binger (1892: I, 491), with his interest in Muslims and trade, conceptualized the society differently, emphasizing the Yarse presence and ignoring other distinctions:

One can divide the population into two races. The most numerous, not Muslim, is so ancient that one might consider it up to a certain point as autochthonous; one distinguishes its subjects under the name of Moro'o and Mossi. The other, of Mande origin, came from the shores of the Niger. . . . It is called by the Moro'o: *ai de r'a* [yaraga, or Yarga; pl. Yarse].

The discrepancies in the myths and their interpretation, over the ethnic identity of the actors, the meaning of the term *Mossi,* and the relationship between ethnic groups in Mossi society, all point to the problem of evaluating the significance of ethnic categories in a culturally and politically integrated society. If Mossi society has become relatively homogeneous culturally, why is it that observers, and the Mossi themselves, continue to ask who the "real" Mossi are, and why do the myths, particularly the royal myths, so often deal with the distinctions between ethnic categories?

The answer seems to lie in the nature of the Mossi political system. Theoretically, Mossi society is stratified, although questions may be raised about the sociological and economic basis of this stratification. Despite the difficulty many observers have had in evaluating the significance of stratification "on the ground," the Mossi and those who have discussed them usually conceptualize the society in terms of a hierarchical model in which members of different ethnic categories, distinguished by their diverse origins, have different roles and statuses in the political system. Chiefs are theoretically members of the royal (Nakomce) group who trace their origins to the south. Commoners, originally descending from a number of distinct, supposedly autochthonous ethnic groups, are collectively referred to as "Talse" when they are viewed in opposition to royals. If the ideology of ethnicity were not maintained, it would be difficult, in view of the extent of cultural assimilation that has occurred, to justify the very important distinction between the ascribed statuses of ruler and subject.

The ideological basis of the political system contains the notion that the Nakomce have the exclusive right to possess *nam*, the power to rule or govern. *Nam* is connected to an office and is conferred on an officeholder in an installation ceremony. However, it is not only Nakomce who can succeed to office, and *nam* is not the only kind of power, *panga*, which the Mossi recognize. *Tenga* is power derived from the earth (and is the earth), and the Tengsoba (earth priest), who is always a member of an autochthonous group, has power, because he controls earth shrines and mystical forces associated with the earth. The Ninissi, or Nionossi, another indigenous group, have yet another kind of power, since they are believed to control the rain. Thus, the guardians of natural forces are members of autochthonous groups, while the guardians of political power are members of the conquering Nakomce group. Royal and commoner groups possess complementary forms of power and perform complementary roles in the political and ritual system.

While this is the ideology behind the political structure, it does not preclude individual mobility. Given the fact that new groups are constantly being incorporated into Mossi society, cultural differences often disappear, even though distinct origins remain important criteria for the assignment of political and ritual roles. Cultural assimilation, however, makes mobility of individuals from one category to another a very real possibility, although social and political mobility is, in the final analysis, a function of economic and demographic conditions in Mossi society.

Early European writers, Tauxier for example, were pleased to find an "aristocracy." This made the society comprehensible in European terms and was also useful for the purposes of colonial administration. Thus, Tauxier (1912: 573) wrote:

One must note carefully the existence of an aristocracy among the Mossi; one does not often find this among the blacks in West Africa, only in populations which were formerly conquerors. There is a degree of complexity or of superior social development here, in a word, a superior level of civilization.

Kabore (1966: 127) later expresses what would seem to be the Nakomce view, saying that "the Nakomce distinguish themselves from other Mossi by their comportment, their level of life, their mentality and their culture. It is the reigning aristocracy." But he goes on to say that they do not form

a social class in the strict sense. If they have a real social awareness ["conscience sociale propre"], if they have a sense of superiority about their group, this is not on the basis of economic advantage. The economic criterion does not establish any hierarchy here. . . . Despite their superior social condition (the political chiefs come from this group), the nakombse live in perfect harmony with the other Mossi and form a homogeneous group with them, thanks to a solid political organization.

Arguing from an economic point of view, Hammond (1966: 211) claims that Mossi society is not stratified. This, he says, results from the "relative unproductivity of Mossi technology and the accompanying economic system which inhibits the private accumulation of whatever surpluses there are." On the other hand, he does recognize that chiefs had more wives,[3] larger fields, more slaves, the benefits of their subjects' labor, and the right to *pogsiourse* (wives presented to chiefs by their subjects).[4] However, because most of a chief's wealth was redistributed, he argues that these benefits did not lead to substantive economic or political stratification.

The answer to all such arguments depends, of course, on what criteria one adopts to evaluate stratification. On close examination there does seem to have been considerable variation in wealth, in terms of control over labor and land, in Mossi society. Izard and Izard-Héritier (1959: 88, 95) note that gradations in wealth could be observed in any village, according to the distance of peoples' farms from their homesteads. The Tengnaba (village chief), Tengsoba (earth priest), and other long-settled families had larger and more productive farms than did newcomers, whose farms were in the bush. However, this situation could be corrected by moving to new areas where homes could be established near the village. Two crucial points, however, are that differences in wealth did not necessarily correspond to ethnic divisions and that differences in wealth were not always inherited from one generation to the next, as they depended so much on access to a fluctuating labor supply. Wealth in Mossiland depended upon land and labor, so that the economic significance of political power was that it provided access to labor. Officeholders had access to their subjects' labor, and, through increased production, might purchase slaves. Successful traders, generally Yarse, were able to use the proceeds of trade to purchase slaves. By the colonial period families who had a number of young men at home were more fortunate than those whose young men had all migrated to Ghana or Ivory Coast. In any one year some Mossi would offer their labor services to their neighbors in exchange for needed grain, but the following year they were likely to find their neighbors working for them. Thus, despite inequalities in wealth, it is not clear that a stable class system existed or that the inequalities which did obtain corresponded to ethnic divisions.

Ethnicity and migration

Despite the factors inducing a certain economic levelling and despite the general poverty of the area, chiefs and other officeholders did have certain benefits and privileges. People who were recognized as Nakomce, whether by birth, the attainment of office, or by the simple adoption of Nakomce patronyms, might claim some privileges which ordinary Talse lacked. For example, they received more lenient sentences for crimes, and crimes against them were more seriously punished than were similar acts committed against commoners (Marc 1909: 165; Tauxier 1917: 364ff.). By being able to command labor, in particular through their ability to obtain more wives, as well as their ability to exact tribute, they had a kind of economic insurance that others, who had to rely on the protection and benevolence of chiefs and kin, might lack.

While theoretically only Nakomce could rule in Mossi society, others, in fact, might come to possess *nam,* not to speak of *panga,* such as that possessed by the Tengsoba. Since *nam* is conferred on an officeholder in an installation ceremony, members of nonroyal groups may come to possess it. Thus, one Mogho Naba (Mossi king) who reigned for seven years was a Fulani who usurped the throne (Mogho Naba Motibi). Many traditional court officials are not Nakomce, and the same is true of some Mossi village chiefs. In villages where there are people of several ethnic groups, a Nakomce is generally the headman, the Tengnaba. In villages consisting entirely of members of one ethnic group, such as Yarse, Busansi, Foulse, or others, a member of this group becomes the Tengnaba. They are traditionally approved and installed by the District Chief, who is usually a Nakomce. Often, the Tengnaba is the first man to have settled in a particular place or a descendant of the first settler. A Tengnaba who is not a Nakomce passes his office on to his sons exactly as would a Nakomce Tengnaba.

Despite the theory of stratification which restricted political power to the Nakomce group, one of the most important means of political incorporation in Mossi society was the distribution of offices among members of different ethnic groups. Besides some village chiefships, these included many offices that were associated with the central government. Many officials in the Mogho Naba's court were commoners, but by virtue of holding titles they could become assimilated to the ruling group, at least in terms of their right to exercise the powers associated with royal status. They were not entitled to succeed to offices reserved for Nabissi, but this was also the position of many Nakomce whose immediate forebears had not held office. Many of the officials in the Mogho Naba's court, including some of the highest ministers, were not royals. Their children usually inherited their offices, although they might not succeed to other offices reserved for royals. Since they were originally appointed by the Mogho Naba or brought into the court through relationships of patronage to the king, they were more directly dependent on the Mogho Naba than royal officials may have been.

There is disagreement in the literature on the Mossi about the origin of many officials, probably because this became somewhat irrelevant, in view of their high official status. The ministers, Kougzidba (s. Kougzida), were officials attached to the Mogho Naba's court who also controlled provinces, which were, in the traditional context, noncontiguous geographical areas under the control of Kougzidba. District chiefs (Kombere) and individuals could approach the Mogho Naba only through the Kougzida in charge of the province in which his district was located. These ministers came from several different ethnic groups; most were not royal, although there is disagreement in the literature about the ethnic affiliation of some of them (Kabore 1966: 46; Tiendrébéogo 1964: 91; Tauxier 1917: 356). In Ouagadougou one official, the Panzani Tengnaba, was indisputably a commoner. He represented the commoners in the court and performed sacrifices to the earth shrines for the Mogho Naba.

There is also uncertainty about the ethnic affiliation of some of the less important officials. For example, the *samand'kamba* (pages) were said to be either "ancient freed slaves" (Kabore 1966: 44), the sons of *pogsiourse* – women whom the king had given to his subjects as wives (Tiendrébéogo 1964: 103) – or individuals from any "courageous" family (Tauxier 1917: 356). The Dapore were another class of palace attendants who were either of slave or commoner origin, but whose identity is uncertain. Some Dapore were supposedly captured in war, and others were purchased slaves. They are regarded as a group with distinct origins, and, like other such statuses, this identity is inherited. The Kambonse, traditionally warriors who guarded the palace, may have been of Akan origin. They are regarded as a nonroyal group coming either "from the south" or "from the west" and having a distinct political status and role. According to Izard (1971: 1), in Yatenga the Kambonse are said to be of Bambara origin. The Bengere, also palace attendants, are said to have been slaves of Fulani origin who either were captured or voluntarily sought asylum in the Mogho Naba's court. Many of these attendants could attain positions of considerable power in the court, since they served the king and also acted as intermediaries between the Mogho Naba, the Kombere, and the subordinate chiefs. Thus, the Dapore Naba and the Bengere Naba were accorded respect as chiefs, despite the fact that they were theoretically slaves.

Although the ideal that the Nakomce form a descent group which has the exclusive power to govern is conceptually an important part of Mossi social structure, nonroyals could actually raise their status as they gained access to political power. Skinner (1964: 17) says that they could never become noble, although they might become chiefs and gain political power; Zahan (1967: 156) says that commoners, freed slaves, and "foreigners" could be given Mossi patronyms, and thereby become assimilated into the royal group.

Such mobility also went "downwards," in that the possibility of claiming noble status could be lost. The sons of Mogho Nanamse, Dimbissi, and the sons of chiefs, Nabissi, were able to claim higher status than ordinary nobles or Nakomce because they were likely to gain political office. If they were unable to reinforce their claims to status through the actual attainment of office, Nabissi, Dimbissi, and their descendants would become untitled members of the Nakomce group. Eventually, Nakomce families who had not held office for several generations became indistinguishable from Talse (Skinner 1964: 16). They could no longer assert claims to office on the basis of descent. Nakomce who violated taboos also became commoners (Kabore 1966: 123).

These possibilities for status mobility were a consequence of the way in which the Mossi state developed – through the gradual incorporation of diverse ethnic groups. The mechanisms of political incorporation and integration just described were accompanied by linguistic and cultural assimilation, intermarriage, and economic interaction. All these were means through which strangers could be integrated into Mossi society. The result of this policy of incorporation is the heterogeneity and ethnic diversity within Mossi society today. Noting this, Izard and Izard-Héritier (1959: 47) have remarked that "more than any other African group the Mossi group is the least precise in its contours. . . . The interethnic relations within the Mossi group are good. The policy of incorporating minorities seems to have always been characterized by tolerance."

Although the Nakomce myths about the origin of the Mossi state describe Mossi expansion in terms of military conquest, this can only have played a minor part in the development of the state. Ecological conditions also account for much of the expansion, for the Mossi were constantly moving into non-Mossi areas in search of new and better farmlands. In the beginning of this century Marc (1909: 129) was able to observe the "conquest" of the Kipirse which, according to the myths and to the date generally accepted for the founding of the state, had begun four centuries earlier:

At the moment of our penetration into their country, the Mossi were in the process of conquering the Kipirse. They had divided the country into large areas over which the chiefs of Lalle, of Conkizitenga and of Yaco had reserved rights for themselves. They would often send expeditions to pillage in this direction. But at the same time a gradual push brought the Mossi fields and villages a little further west every year, and Mossi customs were substituted, little by little, for those of the autochthones.

This process of migratory expansion must be seen in the light of the high density of population in Mossiland. A 1969–70 publication (*Africa 1969/70, Jeunes Afriques Editions,* Rome, 1969) states that in Mossi country the density varies between 130 and 190 persons per square mile in the west. A more detailed study of Upper Volta, as a whole, published by O.R.S.T.O.M. (Savonnet 1968) shows that 37 percent of the population live in areas having between 35 and 75 inhabitants per square kilometer. Traditional methods of farming are based on shifting cultivation, and no prepared fertilizers are used. After several years a plot must be left fallow, often for twenty years and sometimes for as many as fifty years. This, combined with high population density, forces the Mossi to resettle frequently. The demographic basis for migration was noted in the early part of the century and has since been amplified by other observers (for example: Capron and Kohler [1975]; Hammond [1966: 73]; Izard and Izard-Héretier [1959: 66]; and Kohler [1972]). Marc observed (1909: 115):

One can walk for two days in these regions without losing sight of houses for a

28

A Mossi commoner's compound, Upper Volta

A district chief's compound, Upper Volta

single instant. . . . It seems that the population has already attained the maximum density that the soil can support with the methods and tools in use. This mass of population naturally extends in the direction where the soil is most fertile and in their constant need to expand, they are liable to accomplish considerable amounts of work.

Migration within Mossiland is one of the most frequent occasions of lineage fission (Finnegan 1976). Junior branches of lineages move to new areas to start new farms. This partially accounts for the short duration of most Mossi lineages. Office-holding royals can recite long genealogies, since these may be used to legitimize claims to office, but Mossi commoners and Nakomce who do not hold office rarely can recite genealogies of more than four or five generations. In some cases this may account for gradual changes in ethnic-group membership. In this way geographical mobility facilitates social mobility. Freed slaves and commoners may claim to belong to Nakomce lineages by adopting Nakomce patronyms when they move. Nakomce who have lost their royal status by not obtaining offices for many years may try to regain their noble status or may become known as commoners.

Most Mossi, with the exception of Nakomce officeholders and the Yarse, do not know their clan patronyms (*sondere*). Some may know them but still may be unable to cite a genealogy to "prove" their relationship to the clan, or even the lineage founder. Tauxier noted that when he asked Mossi for their clan names they often recited names which were associated with different ethnic categories, depending upon the context in which the question was asked. He remarked (1917: 337) that:

In fact this ancient parentage amounts to nothing, creates no serious bond or definitive obligation between members of the same clan. Most of the time, the Mossi themselves, as well as the Foulse and other blacks of Yatenga, do not even know to which clan they belong. When one asks them their *sondere,* they laugh, most of the time giving *sondere* that they invent out of their imagination, suggested to them by the order of the chief of the village. The Mossi give Foulse *sondere,* if they are in a Foulse village, and the Foulse, in a Mossi village, give the same *sondere* as that of the people around them.

Among migrants in Ghana the same loss of genealogical memory occurs. A common explanation for people's unwillingness to mention their *sondere* is their fear of witchcraft. It is said that, in order for a witch (*sweya*) to do harm, he or she must know one's *sondere.* In Ghana, the inability to recall the *sondere* may also reflect the irrelevance of the traditional ethnic statuses. As I will show later, the importance of the Mossi subgroups are minimized as all immigrants become merged into a single Mossi community.

As Mossi migrate towards the borders of Mossiland they often settle in villages which are inhabited by members of different ethnic groups. It is in these areas that the gradual process of cultural integration takes place and the basis for an undifferentiated Mossi identity is created. Non-Mossi become politically incorporated as they accept the authority of Mossi chiefs and, in some cases, assume political offices. Intermarriage occurs, and ties of economic interdependence are created, all of which are factors contributing to the integration of diverse ethnic communities in Mossi society.

The importance of intermarriage in integrating different groups into a single cultural system has been noted often (e.g., Merton 1964: J. R. Goody 1970). Partly through this process, most of the distinct ethnic communities in Mossi society have lost their original languages, with only dialectal differences remaining. But, despite extensive cultural assimilation, several distinct subcategories have been formed through the intermarriage of Mossi and non-Mossi. These are not necessarily distinct cultural units, but they are regarded as ethnic categories, since their origin differs from that of all other groups. This again points to the Mossi emphasis on origin: no one is simply Mossi in the context of Mossi society; everyone must have a distinct status identity based upon his group's provenance. The Silmi-Mossi are the descendants of Mossi men and Fulani women. The Maranse are the offspring of Mossi and Songhai. And, as we have seen, the Nakomce and many Mossi commoners are the offspring of unions between Dagomba men and indigenous women.

The Mossi call the child of a Mossi woman and a stranger *gananga* (pl. *gananse*), which literally means "a person whose language you don't understand." When such a child is brought up in Mossi society with its mother's family, it becomes Mossi by cultural assimilation. If it were to be brought up in its father's group, it could no longer be regarded as Mossi.

The most common form of out-marriage is between Mossi men and non-Mossi women. This practice, as Izard and Izard-Héretier (1959: 38) observe, is linked to Mossi expansion, since patrifiliation confers Mossi identity on the children. In Yatenga,

If a Mossi voluntarily takes a woman from a stranger group, he does not voluntarily give his women to outsiders; this marriage policy is evidently favorable to Mossi expansionism, but it is perceived with hostility by certain populations (the Samo in particular). We note however that marriages between Mossi are the most numerous . . . that for each ethnic group [in Yatenga] there is a stronger tendency towards endogamy than towards exogamy.

As I will show below, in Kumasi the Mossi also discourage their women from marrying men of other groups, since they claim that this "will make the tribe lose" – that is, it will diminish the number and strength of the ethnic community. Among the Mossi in Kumasi different ethnic subgroups (Nakomce, Talse, Yarse, and others) intermarry freely, since these categories have very little relevance in determining status in the immigrant community.

The idea that female out-marriage diminishes the numerical strength of the community would seem to conflict with a strict interpretation of the idea that patrifiliation determines ethnic identity. Thus, some Mossi claim, in seemingly contradictory fashion, that, in terms of preserving ethnic identity, it does not matter what group their wives come from, although it does matter whom their daughters marry. This demonstrates that, although legally ethnicity is, in Mossi theory, determined by patrifiliation, ideas about kinship and inheritance do not entirely support this political ideology. More general kinship concepts, such as that of *doaghda* – which implies common birth, including uterine kinship – affect Mossi ideas about ethnicity. The importance given to uterine ties unites in kinship ethnic categories in which membership is, for jural purposes, determined by patrifiliation. At the most general level, kinship through both parents is important in determining identity and conferring various rights. Mossi believe that physical and spiritual qualities are inherited from both parents, and they recognize that environment can influence a person's ethnic identity. Thus, a child brought up by its mother's group may identify itself with her group and eventually claim rights there that are ordinarily conferred through patrifiliation. For this reason, Mossi in Ghana hesitate to marry Asante women, claiming that their children, if raised with their mother's family, will "become Asante" – not just by virtue of the Asante rule of matrilineal descent, but also through socialization. It is, however, mainly when ethnicity becomes a means by which recruitment to political status is determined that the concept of descent must be distinguished from nonunilineal kinship. In both Upper Volta and Kumasi ethnic identity affects political status, and in both areas descent is politically significant.

The political importance of descent is demonstrated by the stereotyped kinship and marriage relationships which are said to exist between ethnic groups within Mossi society and between their ancestors, the founders of the various Moré-Dagbane states. These relationships are described in the origin myths which symbolize the political relationships between groups in terms of kinship. Not only are all Nakomce related to each other by descent from a common ancestor, but all Talse are metaphorically described as mothers' brothers, *yesramba* (s. *yasaba* or *yesba*) of the Nakomce, since the original union of the two groups was supposedly derived from the marriage of Nakomce men and Talse women. Similar myths exist about the Fulani and the Mossi to explain the origin of the Silmi-Mossi. The Yarse are also included in this symbolic kinship system, through intermarriage, since they claim that their men marry Talse women and that they are, therefore, also *yangse* (s. *yagenga*) (sisters' sons) to the Talse. Metaphorical kinship relationships based upon mythical and actual intermarriages also exist between the various ruling groups of the different Moré-Dagbane states. The Mossi regard the Mamprusi rulers as their *yasaba*, since their ancestress, Nyennenga, was the daughter of the chief of Gambaga. According to some myths and informants' statements, the Dagomba are regarded as siblings, or as cross-cousins, since they are descendants of Nyennenga's brother. Since the ideology of unilineal descent preserves ethnic identity despite intermarriage, these groups remain conceptually distinct even when they are no longer culturally differentiated. As cultural differences disappear, ascribed status differences replace them to distinguish symbolically one group from another. The ethnic subgroups within Mossi society are theoretically ranked, and statements each group makes about its marriage policy reflect the Mossi theory of stratification, despite the fact that in practice the ideal rules are frequently violated. The marriage rules, like the origin myths, are means of demarcating and symbolizing the boundaries of ethnic categories. The categories are broadly ranked, both in the literature and from informants' statements, in the following way: Nabissi, Nakomce, Yarse, Talse, Fulani, and blacksmiths. The marriage policy each group claims to follow shows that each one tries to maintain or improve its ranking by contracting only hypergamous or endogamous marriages. Thus, the Nabissi are theoretically exogamous, since they are said to belong to a single lineage, that of the descendants of Oubri, Ouedraogo's eldest son and the first Mogho Naba. In fact, Nabissi women marry members of the Nakomce group, collateral descendants of Oubri, but they claim that their women do not marry men who are not royals. The Nakomce are not exogamous, but they also claim to be hypergamous, allowing their women to marry only Nakomce or Nabissi men. The Yarse also claim that their men will marry Talse women, although their women never marry commoner men. Mossi kings are said to be given Yarse women as wives (Izard 1971: 216), and even immigrant Yarse cite this to demonstrate the superiority of Yarse to Talse in Mossi society. The Talse likewise claim to forbid their women marrying blacksmiths and Fulani. These two groups constitute an endogamous caste. A joking relationship exists between them, and they occasionally marry each other, while both claim that they would not permit their women to marry members of other Mossi groups.

Several factors which have assisted the integration of stranger groups in Mossi society have been mentioned, including migration, intermarriage, and political incorporation. It is also important to note economic integration, for many of the incorporated groups in Mossi society perform distinct and complementary economic roles. Although almost all Mossi are agriculturalists, many are also specialized in nonagricultural tasks. Different groups consequently exchange goods and services, including agricultural labor and locally manufactured goods, such as pottery, tools, and cloth. Chiefs and other officeholders receive gifts, taxes, and labor from their subjects and redistribute produce on ceremonial occasions. Earth priests receive grain at the beginning of each harvest, and kin regularly exchange produce and labor. Members of different ethnic groups specialize in certain craft activities, purchasing or exchanging their products with other groups. Yarse trading activity benefits not only their own group, but all others in Mossi society, since they are largely responsible for the development of the major Mossi markets.

The most economically specialized groups are the Fulani and the blacksmiths, and it may be that their preference for endogamy is related to the necessity of preserving specialized knowledge and a monopoly of certain skills. Although culturally they remain the most distinct group, the Fulani are highly integrated into the economic system. Several types of contracts between Fulani and Mossi exist, in which the Fulani care for the cattle or manure the fields of Mossi farmers. In return the Fulani receive milk, young animals, and grain. Even the sedentary Fulani in Upper Volta seldom grow sufficient grain, so they consequently sell milk products in the markets to purchase the deficit.

Blacksmiths make tools and ornaments, and their women manufacture clay pipes for sale. The Maranse are specialized in cloth dyeing in Yatenga, while Yarse, besides being traders, specialize in weaving and tailoring. Members of all of these groups also farm and, unlike the nomadic Fulani, are therefore forced to enter into permanent social and political relationships with the other Mossi around them. Economic integration entails other kinds of noneconomic interaction and eventually implies linguistic and cultural assimilation. Perhaps one indication of whether a group has been incorporated into Mossi society is whether, when faced with members of a different society, individuals identify themselves as Mossi. Members of all the groups just mentioned invariably claim to be Mossi in Kumasi, with the exception of the Fulani, who sometimes identify themselves as Mossi and sometimes as Fulani.

To illustrate how economic interdependence entails other forms of sociocultural assimilation, the Yarse will be considered in more detail. Since the Yarse are in many respects the most important Mossi group in Kumasi, this account provides background to an understanding of their role in Ghana.

The Yarse

Writers who have discussed the Yarse (with the exception of Tauxier, Binger, and, recently, Izard 1971) have primarily stressed their role in spreading Islam in Mossiland (e.g., Skinner 1958, 1966; Levtzion 1968). Although attempts to convert the Mossi to Islam through conquest or direct proselytization failed, the Yarse, having achieved an important position in the society through their economic contribution, were gradually able to convince an increasing number of Mossi – including some chiefs – of the values and benefits of Islam.

Binger, and Marc who followed him, claimed that the Yarse entered Mossiland in the mid-eighteenth century. Binger (1892: II, 394) stated that the Yarse moved into Mossi country following wars among the Mande rulers. Tauxier (1912: 465) took the view that 150 years would have been insufficient for the Yarse to lose their language and, following Moulins, estimated that they entered Mossi country at the end of the thirteenth or the beginning of the fourteenth century, the period of the greatest Mossi expansion. Delobsom (1932: 203ff.), Tiendrébéogo (1964; 112) Levtzion (1968: 164), and Izard (1971: 216) place the Yarse movement after the beginning of the sixteenth century, although both Mossi authors date the penetration of Islam to the time of Naba Doulougou, who reigned from 1783 to 1802, and is credited with appointing the first Imam and building the first mosque in Ouagadougou. The earlier date coincides, however, with the period of the greatest expansion of Malian trade, and it is probable that the Mande traders who became known as Yarse entered Mossi country in this period – in the early sixteenth century. This date is supported by Yarse legends which describe the Yarse role in the expansion of the Mossi state.

Tauxier, concerned with the question of stratification in Mossiland, placed the Yarse in an interstitial position between the "aristocracy" and the "Mossi masses" (1912: 441):

Politically, the Yarse are subordinate to the Mossi. In effect, in installing themselves among the Mossi, our Yarse found themselves in a vast centralised empire. . . . If they have benefitted by their commerce . . . on the other hand they have had to give up all hope of establishing, little by little, their political power in the area. . . . Our Mande have had to content themselves with holding their place, still privileged, in this great black kingdom, beneath the chiefs and the nobles, but above the mass of Mossi (which, in fact, despite its name, descends for the most part from a conquered population and is not pure Mossi).

There are many close links between the Yarse and Mossi royals. Not only do the Yarse claim to have helped in founding the state, but also, it is said, are responsible for the introduction of circumcision among the royals and the conversion of a number of Mogho Nanamse to Islam. Kings and other royals marry Yarse women, and their children, although royal, are often raised as Yarse by their mother's patrilineage. The Yarse quarter of Ouagadougou has close links with the Mogho Naba's court, and some of the palace retainers, the Nayirdamba (literally, chief's house people) are Yarse. The YarNaba, the chief of the Yarse in Ouagadougou, plays a role in the installation of a Mogho Naba and acts as an advisor to him. Tauxier (1912: 569) ranked the YarNaba just below the five most important ministers. Although the main Imam of Ouagadougou belongs to another Mande Muslim group – the Bagayugu – the first mosque in Ouagadougou was built by the Yarse. Their trading activities also necessitated cooperation with the Mossi chiefs who controlled the markets.

The Yarse have maintained their adherence to Islam, although in many other ways they have completely absorbed Mossi culture. They have lost most distinctive Mande characteristics, including the language. Many examples could be cited to show how they often adopt Mossi customary law, rather than strictly following Qur'anic law. Some Yarse have, however, ceased to be Muslims. Tauxier describes Yarse pagans, and Alexandre (1953: II, 465) defines the Yarse as a fraction of the Mossi people of Mande origin, who are distinguished by their commercial occupations and who are sometimes Muslims. Izard (1971: 220), in his study of the Yarse of Yatenga, points out that some Yarse lineages are of Mossi (presumably, Talse or Foulse) or Maranse origin. Having become traders, members of other groups adopt Yarse patronyms and usually become Muslims.

The Yarse still have exogamous patriclans which are more significant than are clans among other Mossi, with the exception of the Nabissi. Yarse clans can be etymologically linked to Mande patronymic groups. There are said to be twelve clans, although few informants can name twelve, and some claim there are more. There are seven major clans, whose members generally disagree about how these are ranked, if indeed they are ranked at all. The Kwanda clan (Kunate in Mande) regard themselves as superior to the others, because the Ouagadougou YarNaba is from this group. The Sanfo regard themselves as "stronger," because they claim to be more numerous and the first to enter Mossiland. This competition for rank within the Yarse group extends to Kumasi, although it is not always evident there. On one occasion a Kwanda man told me about a dispute he had had with a Yarse who belonged to the Sang clan. He concluded by saying, "However, inside the Yarse I pass him because I am Kwanda, and he is only Sang. I told him that 'a wolf with nothing in his hands is more than a goat with a bow and arrow.'"

Certain clans are clustered in particular areas of Mossiland, usually around large market towns which the Yarse have developed. All the clans are dispersed, partly because they are exogamous, and also because of trading activities and migration to new farmlands. It is likely that the persistence of the Yarse clan organization is related to the trading networks which join market centers within and outside of Mossiland (this point has also been made by Izard 1971: 217). In Kumasi, clan ties among the Yarse are still sufficiently strong so that migrants and itinerant traders seek out members of their own clans for lodging and assistance.

The markets in Mossiland were important junctions on the precolonial trade routes connecting the Sahara and the southern trading centers. Caravans from Timbuctoo, Jenne, and Hausaland bringing goods from across the Sahara met in Mossi country and exchanged products with caravans coming north from the Asante forest and the coast. Some caravans made the journey southwards through Mossiland to the markets just north of the forest, and primarily to Salaga, which was for some time Asante's major northern outpost. At other times Kintampo, Techiman, Wenchi, Yendi, and other towns were important junctions where traders from the savannah and the forest exchanged goods. In the eighteenth and nineteenth centuries, and perhaps even earlier, some of the caravans from Mossiland and Hausaland went as far south as Kumasi and as far north as Timbuctoo. In 1839 Freeman noted two Mossi in Kumasi (1843: 51), and Bowdich (1819: 180) remarked that while he was in Kumasi he learned that "five journies [sic] from Yngwa [Dagomba] is Mose. . . . A more warlike but less visited kingdom, it consists of many states but the superior monarch is named Billa and the capital Kookoopella." Kookoopella, now known as Kupela, is immediately adjacent to the important trading center of Puitenga, along the route connecting Hausaland and what is now northern Ghana.

There were many different items of trade on these early caravans, but the most important were slaves, kola nuts, salt, and cattle. These products originated at different points along the trade routes and were exchanged at several places in the trading cycle. The caravans from Mossiland left for the south with slaves, cattle, sheep, goats, donkeys, cotton woven and dyed by Yarse and Maranse, leather products, shea butter, and other goods, mainly salt, which were purchased in Timbuctoo, Jenne, and other northern markets. The donkeys, raised in Mossiland, were sold or were used to take back to Mossiland the kola which was purchased in Salaga and other Asante markets. Slaves could be obtained in Mossi country for salt slabs which were purchased in the northern markets with kola from the forest. In the colonial period, after the French demanded that taxes be paid in coin, these traders began dealing in currency. Yarse traders would purchase hundred-sou pieces from the Songhai and resell them in Mossi country at a profit. According to Tauxier (1912: 423), their skill in this compared unfavorably with that of the Hausa.

36

The Mossi: ethnicity in Voltaic society

The caravans which Binger described as Mossi were undoubtedly composed mainly of Yarse, although they were probably regarded as Mossi by the Hausa and others. Yarse traders were sometimes sent as representatives of important Mossi chiefs, with whom they maintained a special mutually beneficial relationship. The Yarse were exempt from taxation in grain, and instead were expected to give regular gifts to the Mogho Naba and other chiefs. Caravan leaders informed the chiefs of their movements and regularly brought gifts to the chiefs.

The slave trade, in particular, necessitated cooperation between the Yarse traders, the Mossi chiefs, and the Zabarama slave dealers. The Mossi chiefs received a tax for every slave sold in a Mossi market. Most of the Mossi who joined the Zabarama in raiding the noncentralized peoples around Mossiland were Nakomce, but there were some Yarse among them. Usually, however, the Yarse bought their slaves from the Zabarama and resold them or used them on their farms as laborers or in their caravans as carriers.

The more the Yarse specialized in trade and in craft activities, particularly weaving, the more they became dependent on other groups in Mossiland for access to trading supplies, food, and services. They were known to hire Mossi (Talse) as carriers on their expeditions and also employed them as gravediggers and masons. They purchased tools, jewelry, pottery, and pipes from the blacksmiths and relied on slaves for much agricultural labor. Those Yarse who traded exclusively were forced to buy grain in Mossi markets, but most Yarse also did some farming. For some families, trading was only a dry season activity; and some did not trade at all.

The next chapter deals with patterns of migration followed by the various Mossi groups which have just been described. Despite broad variations in migratory patterns and economic activities observable among the different Mossi groups, migration to Ghana, like migration within Mossiland, leads to social mobility (Fortes 1971). This is not so much because individuals can "pass" from one category to another, but because the importance of the traditional ethnic categories is minimized in the new context. In Ghana the ethnic groups which become part of the operative status system consist of those "super-tribal" categories, of which Mossi is one; the ethnic categories which are important within Mossi society become quite irrelevant in the heterogeneous immigrant communities of Ghana. Outside Mossiland, the common identification of these traditional ethnic groups as Mossi is based upon both ascription and self-identification. The common place of origin of all of the Mossi vis-à-vis non-Mossi, their common language, and the traditions of cultural integration and political incorporation which have always characterized relationships between ethnic categories within the Mossi state are all important factors in accounting for the irrelevance, in Ghana, of subdivisions within the category of Mossi. The persistence of the category of Mossi itself, however, is based on quite different factors. These pertain less to the situation in Upper Volta, whence the Mossi have emigrated, than to the social, economic, and political situation in which they find themselves in Ghana.

3

Migration and settlement of Mossi in Ghana

In descriptions of migration among the Mossi a distinction is often drawn between short-term, seasonal migration and the permanent emigration of individuals or families for the purpose of settling in new areas (Deniel 1968; Izard and Izard-Héritier 1959; Kohler 1972; Rouch 1956). The first involves the migration of labor, and is primarily a consequence of European colonization,[1] while the second is a more traditional movement of population which occurs as people redistribute themselves according to the availability of resources. Seasonal and short-term migration mainly involves young men working for wages in the towns of Upper Volta or in the cocoa farms, coffee plantations, and industrial centers of Ghana and the Ivory Coast. Permanent emigration involves resettlement of families in response to poor soil fertility, dense population, and a relatively underdeveloped agricultural technology. As noted in chapter 2, this type of migration has been part of Voltaic life for centuries.

There are numerous differences between these two types of migration, including differences in the motivations and intentions of the migrants, the sex and age profiles of the two groups, and the effects of these two types of movement on the development of the economies of the Upper Volta, Ivory Coast, and Ghana. The incentives leading to both types of migration are economic, but the seasonal migrant is entering the urban or rural wage-earning economy – usually at the lowest level – while the permanent emigrants are resettling, in order to continue subsistence farming. The seasonal migrant intends to return home, while the emigrant quite consciously moves his home. Seasonal migration selects out a restricted segment of the population – primarily males between the ages of fifteen and thirty-five – so that every family living in Upper Volta has some young men away at any one time, and many have lost practically all of their able-bodied young men. The two types of migration also have different consequences for development: permanent rural emigration being a traditional means of maintaining the subsistence level of production of the Upper Volta, while temporary migration to the south is an intrinsic part of the differential development of the forest and savannah regions.

Ideally, according to some writers (most obviously Berg 1965), seasonal migration to Ghana and the Ivory Coast fits into an ecological complementarity of the southern forest and the northern savannah. According to this view, the seasonal migrant is in a fortuitous position – able to fulfill his agricultural responsibilities in Upper Volta during the farming season, between April and November, and also able to earn money and contribute to the developing economy of the south in the dry season. This argument is based on two suppositions. One is that most migration is seasonal or short-term, and the other is that this has no ill effects on the home economy. In short-term migration, according to Berg (1965: 170ff.), men can still periodically clear new fields every few years, while women do most of the annual labor, in any case, and therefore do not miss their men![2] Critiques of this view are many and cogent and need not be repeated here (Amin 1974; Songre, Sawadogo, and Sanogoh 1974). They suggest strongly, as Skinner has noted (1965) that, even if the ideal pattern of seasonal or short-term labor were followed by Voltaic immigrants, the effects on the home areas are negative, sometimes disastrous, involving a lowering of production, as well as numerous unfortunate social consequences.

We are only beginning to get large-scale scientific studies of Voltaic agriculture which contribute hard data to the debate about the effects of migration on Voltaic agricultural productivity.[3] But one need not even resort to this data to dismiss this theory, for the "ideal" pattern of seasonality is increasingly not followed today, and there is evidence that it was often not followed in the past. Rouch (1956: 56), for example, noted that the Mossi tended to remain in Ghana for long periods. Migration which begins as seasonal may end up being permanent, and no count of returning migrants at the borders of Upper Volta, Ghana, and the Ivory Coast will tell us how many do not come back. Amin (1974: 74ff.) has estimated the cost to Upper Volta of this migration, by using regional and national censuses, and his study indicates that seasonal migration has steadily decreased in the last twenty years. Kohler (1972: 41), studying western Mossiland, where most foreign migration is to the Ivory Coast, reports an increasing tendency for migrants to remain away for long periods or simply to remain in the Ivory Coast. Even more striking is his observation that the rate of migration to Ivory Coast and Ghana actually rises during the agricultural season (p. 43).

In terms of a study of Mossi immigrants in Ghana, the distinction between seasonal and permanent migrants is of very limited use. The fact that all of the migrants in Ghana probably intended to return home is relevant only to a study of their attitudes towards their lives in Ghana. Like those who have moved to find new farms, they have resettled in search of better opportunities. Some did not return because they were, at least initially, too unsuccessful economically to go back; others did not return because they were too successful. For individuals in both of these positions the significant fact is that they have often broken their ties with people in Upper Volta, retaining only a deep sentimental attachment to their original homes. They may continue to talk about "home" long after they have married and perhaps even acquired property in Ghana, while their families in Upper Volta may continue to count them among the absentees for many years. The retention of these affective ties is not difficult to explain. The move for the migrant who remains in Ghana or the Ivory Coast differs from permanent emigration within Upper Volta in that it is complicated by international boundaries and cultural discontinuities; Mossi who colonize relatively underpopulated areas of Upper Volta achieve some level of cultural integration with the autochthonous population, while the Mossi immigrant in Ghana is an expatriate, a stranger. In terms of citizenship, the migrant in Ghana is an alien, and while this made little difference in the colonial period, since independence it has been of critical importance (Schildkrout 1974a). Socially and culturally, migrants often remain strangers vis-à-vis the indigenous populations of Ghana and the Ivory Coast. These aspects of stranger status may last, regardless of how completely a migrant is integrated into an immigrant community in Ghana. There are different levels on which social and cultural integration can occur, and few migrants become part of the local or national society in all senses.

On a statistical, or even a conceptual, level, then, the distinction between temporary and permanent immigration is not useful for a study of the Mossi population in Ghana today. Rural, rather than urban, migration is likely to be seasonal, and this has steadily decreased in Ghana, as in the region in general (Amin 1974: 74ff.; Hart 1974: 330). The decrease in seasonal migration to Ghana, in particular, is due to a number of factors, including restrictions on transferring currency between the two monetary zones, fluctuations in the state of the cocoa industry and in Ghana's general economic situation, and, more recently, restrictions on the entry and movement of aliens in the country (Adomako-Sarfoh 1974; Songre, Sawadogo, and Sanogoh 1974). The decrease in seasonal migration means that the Mossi community in Ghana is increasingly stable, with more and more of the immigrants born in Ghana. In 1960 the Mossi were still the largest group of immigrants in the country, numbering, according to the *1960 Ghana Census,* 106,140 persons.[4] Four-fifths of these were still enumerated in rural areas, and a third of them were in the major cocoa and timber area, the Ashanti region (see Map 5). It is impossible to say how many of these fit the idealized seasonal pattern, but my own observations, confirming the earlier work of Rouch (1956), suggest that the great majority had been in Ghana at least two or three years, and many for much longer periods. Almost a third (28 percent) of the Mossi enumerated in the 1960 census were born in Ghana. This means that, if many parents of children in this group are considered, the number of permanent migrants is much higher and probably comes to at least half of the total migrant population. A further indication of the degree to which the Mossi have settled in Ghana comes from noting two additional points brought out in the 1960 census. Hill (1970b: 50) calls our attention to the fact that the census does not indicate the larger numbers of settled Mossi living in the north, although nearly a quarter of all Mossi immigrants were enumerated in the northern region. In 1966, during a few weeks of field work in the Bawku area I found that there are large numbers of Mossi families in the north who emigrated to Ghana around the turn of the century, very often to escape forced labor and taxation by the French. Many of these brought their families, but others married local northern women. Another interesting point, noted by Hill (1970b: 64), is that if one subtracts the number of Mossi of foreign origin[5] from the total Mossi population, there are approximately eleven thousand Ghanaian Mossi, according to the census. With the exception of

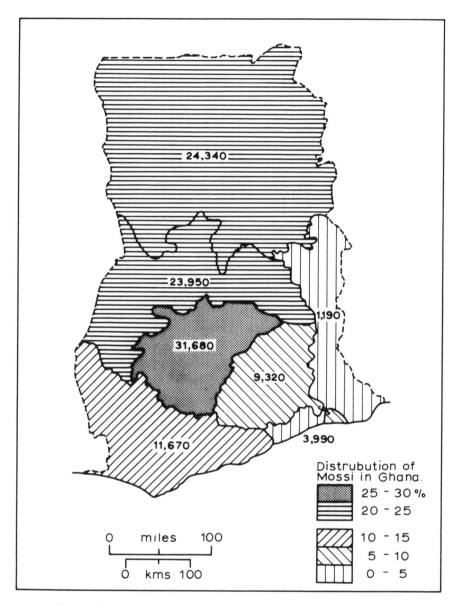

24,340

23,950

1,190

31,680

9,320

11,670

3,990

Distrubution of
Mossi in Ghana.

25 - 30 %

20 - 25

10 - 15

5 - 10

0 - 5

0   miles   100

0   kms   100

Map 5. Ghana: distribution of Mossi by region (based on the *1960 Ghana Census*).

ethnic groups whose home areas straddle Ghana's borders, the Mossi have the highest proportion of Ghanaians of any foreign group listed in the census.

The Mossi population in urban areas is more stable than in rural locations, although in both there are many who have settled down with families and acquired property. Some indication of this is given by examining the relative rural/urban sex ratio, since one may assume that communities with a more equal sex ratio contain fewer single, temporary migrants. According to the *1960 Ghana Census,* in rural areas there are approximately three Mossi men to one Mossi woman, (308.6 : 100), while in urban areas the proportion is slightly over two to one (212.8 : 100). If one also notes that there are very few adult women who remain unmarried, and that many Mossi men marry non-Mossi women, one can conclude that a sizable majority of urban men are married and that at least a third of the rural migrants are married. Since married men do not migrate as frequently as do unmarried men, this means that many migrants marry in Ghana or return to Upper Volta to obtain wives. This enhances the tendency to stay and discourages the seasonal pattern.

Rural-urban migration of Mossi within Ghana is frequent, and almost all Mossi living in urban areas have had previous rural experience. Many have also lived in small towns before moving to the larger cities. One can gain an idea of how stable Mossi urban communities can be by looking at the figures from Kumasi. Of a sample of 446 Mossi men and women who were born in Upper Volta (see chapter 5 for details of this sample), 63 percent (279) had been in Kumasi for over ten years, and only 9 percent had been there for less than five years. Forty-five percent had been there for over sixteen years.

At the time this study was done, between 1965 and 1967, many Mossi in Ghana had little intention of returning to Upper Volta in the foreseeable future. But this changed drastically at the end of 1969, when Busia issued the compliance order requiring unregistered aliens to leave the country. At this time the citizenship laws in effect defined as aliens those of foreign birth or parentage. Many of the temporary migrants, and many others who could have been considered to be on the borderline between seasonal and permanent status, abruptly changed their view of prospects in Ghana and returned to Upper Volta.

It is extremely difficult to make an accurate quantitative assessment of the effect of the compliance order on the Mossi population in Ghana. According to the U.N. Economic Commission for Africa's 1970 survey in that year, migrants from Niger surpassed the number from Upper Volta, while the reverse had been true in 1960 (Songre, Sawadogo, and Sanogoh 1974: 389). In the country, as a whole, it was officially known that 213,750 aliens had left by June 1970, six months after the order went into effect (Adomako-Sarfoh 1974: 138). This is 26 percent of a total foreign population of 830,000 (including 290,000 born in Ghana), according to the 1960 census (*Special Report E*: 48). Among the Mossi, however, many migrants who left returned soon afterwards. Their commitment to living in Ghana was apparently greater than their inclination to resettle in Upper Volta. Ghanaians also had something to do with the return of the Mossi, for soon after the effects of the order began to be felt by the cocoa farmers, delegations of farmers began appealing to the government to make exceptions for rural laborers. Although the cocoa industry suffered immediately after the expulsions, it is doubtful if the events of 1969–70 had long-term economic effects on the cocoa industry or on the position of Mossi laborers within it (Adomako-Sarfoh 1974: 41). The compliance order may have discouraged further rural migration, but as this had been declining in any case, the order in itself probably did not have a long-term effect on the size of the Mossi population in Ghana. Thus, despite the dramatic events of 1969–70, the trends toward permanent settlement and the decline of seasonality in Mossi migration observed in the mid-1960s are still accurate observations for the mid-1970s.

The poor condition of the economy of the Upper Volta, based on factors such as a high density of population relative to agricultural productivity, poor soil, irregular and infrequent rainfall, and the paucity on nonagricultural economic opportunities, is at the basis of the extremely high rate of Voltaic migration. Economic factors are also primary "causes," as expressed in the motivations and aspiration of migrants (Kohler 1972; Skinner 1965). From the beginning of the century, however, political factors, in the form of colonial policies of forced labor and taxation, contributed greatly to labor migration. When one interviews Mossi elders in Ghana, almost all can recount stories about why they left. In the beginning of the century the policies of the French administration are seen as direct causes. Forced labor for the government or European firms and the imposition of taxation, in a society where labor was the most valuable economic commodity and where there was no source of cash income, were the reasons for almost all of the early migration. The Gold Coast seemed a land of opportunity in relation to the difficulty of meeting French demands. Mossi informants in Upper Volta and Ghana often said that it was preferable to run away to Kumasi than to endure the "shame of being tied up in the sun" by the French or by the chiefs who were appointed by the administration. Many of the Yarse who migrated in the early part of this century claimed that they had had slaves who helped with trading and farming.[6] These were taken from them by the government-appointed chiefs, and even relatively well-off men were reduced to poverty such that they saw no choice but to migrate to the Gold Coast in hopes of improving their positions. As a result of these imperatives, even those who did not leave felt that the migrants pursued an honorable and inevitable course.

The Mossi have become resigned to accept migration as a normal and, perhaps, unavoidable pattern. When a migrant leaves, neither he nor his family may know if the move will be permanent. For many years a person's room will remain empty; often it will fall to ruins, rather than become a home for someone else. Most migrants maintain little communication with their families, and those left behind usually know only when a particular person left and the general direction in which he or she went – to Kumasi or to Abidjan. Sometimes, they have heard that a migrant has died, or married, or been in difficulty, but they seldom know details about the migrant's experiences.

This pattern differs markedly from that found in some other groups. The typical Tallensi migrant, for example, no matter how many years away, may return to the north in old age. There, he may be able to claim lineage land, sometimes even political office, and prestige. The more successful he has been in the south, the higher the payoff when he returns home. Very often he has left wives and children at home and has visited them frequently. But, even if he hasn't, his ties are seldom entirely broken. When there is a crisis situation, the Tallensi migrant is likely to turn to his lineage kin and his ancestors for support. Migrants in the south regularly return north for funerals and major festivals (Hart 1974: 328ff.). Many Yoruba migrants also maintain close ties with their hometowns, sending money back and investing in property in Nigeria. The same may be said for the Ibo, whose hometown organizations help keep up ties and link the rural and urban areas together.

Among the Mossi the situation is very different. As we will see in chapter 9, the social organization of immigrant Mossi is not closely linked to hometown ties and reflects the break that the migrants make with their families in Upper Volta. The Mossi migrant who has been away a long time is likely to experience shame, rather than pride, on his return. In the case of those who were not Muslims before, they have usually converted to Islam and have stopped making sacrifices to their ancestors. Although those left behind may be sympathetic with the migrants' reasons for leaving, if the migrant remains away too long and fails to maintain regular ties with those at home, it becomes increasingly difficult to return.

Since the justification for migration is economic, all migrants feel that they must justify their trip by distributing gifts upon their return. Many do not reach this goal after one year and try to stay on to save more money. Then, of course, they feel the obligation to bring back even more when they return. But wages are low, currency conversion is extremely difficult, customs duties at the border are considerable, and purchases are expensive. All of these factors induce the migrants in Ghana to invest their meager savings there, rather than trying to take them home. The response to the question, "Do you plan to go back to Upper Volta?" by Kumasi migrants who have been in town for anywhere from one to twenty years invariably is, "If I get money."

Those who have stayed away a long time claim that they would feel like strangers if they went back. One of them explained to me that, no matter how successful he might be in the south – he was in fact a Mossi headman and quite wealthy – if he went home he would feel like the "same small boy" he was when he left, fifty years before. Among the Mossi, then, the gain in status a migrant may make in the south is not transferable to the north. Accepting stranger status in an alien society can often be easier than accepting it in one's own.

Two examples illustrate the attitude of Mossi migrants who have been away for many years. The late headman of the Kumasi Mossi community and the headman of the Obuasi Mossi community were both deported by the Nkrumah government for their refusal to support the Convention People's Party. The Kumasi headman came from the predominantly Yarse village of Rakai, about forty miles from Ouagadougou. At the time of his deportation he was over seventy and had been in Ghana, without going back to Rakai, for almost fifty years. When he was deported he moved with some members of his family to Ouagadougou and died there two years later, never revisiting Rakai. The Obuasi headman remained at the border town of Po, about seventy miles from his hometown. He never visited his hometown and claims that he waited at the border for the day of Nkrumah's overthrow. He, too, was over seventy at the time. After the coup in 1966, he immediately returned to Ghana and resumed his headship of the Mossi community in Obuasi. When asked why he had not gone to his hometown, he replied that, had he gone, nobody would have remembered him. "In Ghana I am something. So, why should I go where I am nothing? Besides, I knew that Nkrumah would not last long."

Yet the attitude of the migrants who do not return remains ambivalent because of the emotional attachment they retain for their homes. A story about the former Mossi headman of Kumasi illustrates this point. Sometime before his deportation, he sent his eldest son, who was born in Ghana, to the town of Thyou in Upper Volta to return a sum of money belonging to the family of the deceased previous Mossi headman, whose property he had been entrusted to sell. During this journey, the son decided on his own initiative to visit Rakai to see his father's birthplace. He went alone, explained who he was, and was greeted warmly by most of the villagers. After two weeks there, he returned to Kumasi and told his father about his trip. He recounts how his father wept for joy and bought him a beautiful new *batakari* (gown) when he learned that his son had seen Rakai.

Delobsom expressed another aspect of this situation when he noted that Mossi expatriates changed so drastically in their way of life and their attitudes that if they were to return they would find it difficult to identify with their Mossi kin. He wrote (1932: 187):

Whenever a Mossi expatriates himself, establishes himself definitively in a foreign country whether to trade, or to study the precepts of Islam, he is obliged to abandon his habits, . . . he also loses his personal status. If he wishes to embrace Islam he changes his surname, his first name, and if by chance he should return to his village of origin, he could not stand to be compared to the Moaga with whom he shares neither customs nor beliefs and whom, he considers, besides, to be quite inferior.

This is not to say that all Mossi migrants inevitably lose contact with kin in Upper Volta. Some men return to marry after several years away, and some families in Ghana foster younger siblings or siblings' children. But these children grow up in Ghana and usually remain there, just as if they had migrated themselves. They, too, often lose contact with their parents in the north. A few people send their children to school in Upper Volta, and others make regular visits, particularly if they are involved in trade. Women who had been divorced or widowed in Upper Volta sometimes have children remaining with their former husband's family, and they may try to maintain contact with these children. But the vast majority of migrants who settle in Ghana or who remain away for more than about ten years eventually lose effective contact with their relatives in the north. Also, as Delobsom states, most change their names, so their families cannot even locate them if they try.

A frequent grievance of Mossi who are settled in Ghana concerns demands by relatives in Upper Volta upon the property of Mossi who have died in the south. The Mossi claim that when a man dies, relatives from Upper Volta with whom he has not maintained contact sometimes hear of the death and come to Ghana to take his property and his children. During 1966–7, at least four such cases came to the attention of the Kumasi Mossi headman, while others were handled through the Upper Volta Embassy in Accra. The Mossi in Ghana generally fight these claims with the help of their headmen. They resent the attempts of distant relatives to take the property and children (sometimes from a remaining widow), and they claim that the traditional Mossi law which gives members of a man's patrilineage such rights is inapplicable in Ghana. In some cases the widow has never seen the relatives, and Mossi in Ghana claim that they are too distant to have rights of inheritance, even according to Mossi customary law. These cases occasionally reach the courts, and if the wife is Ghanaian, the relatives from Upper Volta generally lose. But if the wife is also Mossi, the disputes can drag on until either the widow agrees to relinquish the children or the husband's family gives up. Mossi headmen in Ghana almost always are in favor of leaving the children in the place where they were born, especially if there are Mossi relatives or guardians to look after them, but they are not always successful in obtaining this resolution.

At this point, it is essential to ask why the Mossi who stay away for more than five years break their ties with their homes. A complete answer entails a comparative study of the economies of Ghana and the Upper Volta, which is beyond the scope of this book. However, a few major points may be noted. The migrants in Ghana are involved in a situation replete with contradictions. In Ghana, the pay of seasonal and short-term migrants is so poor, and customs duties at the border are so high, that they are unable to send or bring money home. If they stay long enough to take advantage of the relatively greater opportunities in Ghana, they have made a commitment and investment which prevents them from returning. This commitment involves leaving wage labor (rural or urban) and becoming involved in trade, farming, real estate, or other forms of entrepreneurial activity. Virtually all the Mossi who have done well in Ghana have accumulated assets in the form of houses or farms, none of which are transferable to Upper Volta. The idea of shame on the part of the migrants who have not prospered or those who have not regularly remitted money to their kin in Upper Volta, and the attitude of resignation to their loss on the part of those who have remained in Upper Volta, reflect this situation.

The seasonal or short-term migrants, far from bringing the benefits of the south to the north, make a significant contribution only to the developing economy of the southern regions. Neither their families in Upper Volta nor the economy of the Upper Volta profit from this. Migrants recognize these facts and often decide to seize whatever opportunities they can find in Ghana, rather than return home with so little.

An unfortunate overemphasis on the seasonality of migration has led observers to ignore the way migrants form commitments to their lives as strangers in Ghana. In order to understand Mossi social organization in Ghana, we need to place the migrants in the context of Ghanaian social structure, rather than viewing them in the context of the migration process itself. Before continuing this theme in the remainder of this book, however, we must look at one further aspect of Mossi migration: the extent to which migration patterns vary among the ethnic subcommunities of Mossi society. According to Kohler (1972), in the western area of Mossi settlement there is no difference in the rate of migration of different groups today. He observes that members of all ethnic categories migrate at the same rates and for the same economic reasons. The fact that migration lessens the importance of the traditional ethnic divisions is also suggested by a study of Mossi communities in Ghana, where these distinctions no longer are used to confer status. Nevertheless, viewed in historic perspective, there do seem to be some variations in the migration patterns of different categories of Mossi. These differences were far from absolute, even in the past, however, for there were Nakomce and Talse on nineteenth-century caravans, just as some Yarse were primarily farmers and became rural laborers as migrants. The variations that did exist can still be discerned only among older migrants, in the distribution of occupational roles and leadership positions among them.

Migration of Nakomce

The migration of Mossi royals into northern Ghana was complicated in the early part of the century by their collusion with the British, in the latter's attempt to pacify the area. Raiding areas outside the limits of Mossi political control had been a traditional pattern and had been intensified in the late nineteenth century by the collaboration of Mossi royals with Zabarama slavers. After the Anglo-French border was drawn in 1898, raiding continued and, indeed, was encouraged for some time by the British, who were actually enlisting the followers of Bukari Koutou, the former Mossi king who had entered the Gold Coast to escape the French. In 1898, a British officer (Morris) began recruiting the Mossi who were retainers of the ex-king of Mossi (who resided at Zongoiri) into a cavalry corps known as the Moshie Horse (*Annual Report, Northern Territories,* 1903). These men, mostly Nakomce who had their own horses, were used in expeditions against the Tallensi and the Dagomba. They gained a reputation as excellent fighters and horsemen, and in 1900, Morris reported that "without their most valuable assistance these expeditions could not have been brought to so successful an issue."[7]

After their dismissal from the British force, some of these men continued raiding the area. At the point when the British were trying to impose a peace on the area, these men became a problem for them, and an example was made of one of them, a man named Asana Moshie, who had been Morris's flagbearer. Asana had continued the raiding he had done in British service and even claimed that he was still a member of the West African Frontier Force. In 1907, Asana and some of his associates were convicted of murder in the Bolgotanga area and were publicly hanged in Gambaga. The British intended to use this as a deterrent to others and to impress the local population with their protective role.

Following this period some Nakomce migrated further south, often in attempts to become chiefs in areas of new Mossi settlement. They migrated as laborers, like commoner Mossi, but eventually sought leadership roles in the new communities.

Ethnicity and migration

Although these offices were not traditional, some of the benefits of chieftainship could still be had in the southern immigrant communities. Since these chieftainships were far outside the Mossi territory, the immigrant chiefs could never become part of the traditional political structure; they were not formally installed by Mossi chiefs in Upper Volta, and only rarely were they even acknowledged as chiefs by the traditional Mossi rulers; and they could also never hope to attain higher offices in Upper Volta by virtue of holding chieftainships in Ghana. It is difficult to estimate the number of immigrant chiefs who actually were Nakomce, since many claimed to be from this group when they were not. When Mossi attain the title of Naba they often claim that they are entitled to it by tradition and by birth. In Ghana, they are more likely to do this in rural areas than in towns, for in towns the dominance of the Yarse makes claims to royal descent virtually useless.

Nakomce who could not claim traditional office in Upper Volta or who were not in a relatively advantageous economic position migrated to Ghana as seasonal laborers in the same way as nonroyals. In Kumasi there are very few people who seriously claim to be Nabissi, and some who do are said to be "telling lies." Some people claim that their mothers were Nakomce, or even Nabissi, but this has no effect on their status in the immigrant community. Others are called "Nabiga," but this usually is a nickname, often for people of slave origin and, again, not a description of actual status in town. There are probably relatively few royals in Ghana, but, since they are also a minority of the Mossi population, as a whole, it is difficult to tell whether they migrate at a significantly lower rate than commoners. Except for Kohler's study of Western Mossi, the relevant statistical data are not available for Ghana or Upper Volta.

Leadership positions in Ghanaian Mossi communities are, then, never reserved for royals, and they receive no special respect or privileges. In Ghanaian towns, royals are actually the victims of considerable verbal abuse, especially if they are known to be involved in exploitative activities within the Mossi community. Nonroyal Mossi, who often have considerable hostility to those who claim superiority on the basis of noble status, accuse the royals of spoiling the Mossi name and they remind them that their ancestry means nothing, once they have migrated to Ghana. At times the behavior of certain individuals, and particularly their exploitation of new migrants, is explained in terms of their pretensions to noble status. Some Mossi feel that the Nakomce are less amenable to control than are nonroyals and that, because they believe themselves immune from the law, they are likely to put the whole community in trouble.

Migration of Talse

In considering the migration of commoners we must count all nonroyals, including variously named local groups, blacksmiths, Silmi-Mossi, and others, but not the Yarse, who do show a distinctive pattern because of their association with Islam and trade. At least initially, most Mossi commoners migrate as agricultural laborers. Many blacksmiths, Maranse, or Silmi-Mossi give up their traditional craft occupations

48

and work as agricultural laborers. Those who do not return home after a few seasons may move to towns and resume smithing, but in a new way, manufacturing ornaments rather than tools.

Before the advent of motor transport, many migrants passed through Kumasi on their way to rural areas in Asante. By the 1920s, when lorries came into use, the new migrants were often led from one point to the next in their journey by "collectors," men who received a commission for organizing the traffic of migrants and goods. These collectors had contracts with lorry drivers, prospective employers, and landlords in town. They received a commission for their services from some, or even all, parties, although, strictly speaking, they were entitled to collect only from the person offering to transport, employ, or house the migrant. Collectors were settled immigrants who might be of great assistance to newcomers, but who also were known to exploit the inexperienced *yiri moaga* (literally, Mossi from home). Today, migrants making the trip for the first time have gained by the experience of their predecessors and head directly for rural villages where they have relatives or friends. Many, afraid of exploitation, avoid the major towns, particularly Kumasi, on their southward journey and stop there only to buy gifts on their way home.

According to the *1960 Ghana Census,* there were 38,380 Mossi farm laborers in Ghana in 1960 (see also M. Dupire 1960, on rural Mossi in Ivory Coast). This amounted to 66 percent of the Mossi men who were classified by occupation. More than seven thousand of these had their own cocoa farms or worked for Asantes on the *abusa* system, a sharecropping system in which the laborer receives a third of the farm owner's crop or profit. A number of other kinds of contracts also exist between Mossi laborers and Asante employers. Some migrants work on a yearly contract, earning between twenty-five and forty Ghanaian pounds per annum (in the late 1960s) and receiving food or a plot of land on which they are allowed to make their own food farm. Some work "by day," at a rate of four shillings plus food for a morning's labor. Groups of migrants, usually friends and sometimes kin, go from village to village on this basis. Some do piecework, contracting to do a specified job for an agreed sum. Le Moal (1960) describes the *kotokuano* system, where the laborers get a commission per bag (Twi, *kotokuo*) of cocoa, but this is not very common in the Kumasi area. Dayworkers rent rooms in villages where they stop and may do both daywork and piecework at the same time for different farmers in the village. Some regard this as the most advantageous way of working, in that it avoids the entanglements of having a single constant employer, but it is also less secure. On the other hand, laborers who work on annual contracts sometimes claim that if the season is poor they are not paid, and there is little they can do in such cases. The only sanction is that the following year the Asante employer is apt to remain without labor. Any migrant who stays in the same rural area for two years or more is likely to make his own food farm there. He easily gets permission and a plot of land from his employer or the local Asante chief, on payment of a bottle of schnapps (liquor), the customary Asante thanking gift.

Since 1938 there has been a labor department through which farmers and migrants may get together, but only a very small proportion of laborers pass

A cocoa farming hamlet in the Ashanti Region

through the official channel. Those who do are usually people who have been in Ghana for some time and who are looking for urban employment. Most migrants to rural areas get jobs on the spot, and the official farm contract, which is made through the labor department, is rarely signed. Mossi farm laborers find jobs through other migrants and through collectors, headmen, or landlords (Hausa, *masugida,* s. *maigida*) in the urban areas. These men have established contacts with Asante employers, who come to them regularly in search of workers. The settled immigrants serve as an unofficial labor exchange and receive commissions from employers and occasionally from employees as well. Sometimes, employees of the labor department actually send men who are looking for jobs to these *masugida,* and some of the *masugida* make sure that contracts are signed. Very often, a lorry driver who has not been paid brings the migrant to the headman or *maigida.* This man then pays the migrant's fare, cares for him, and finds him a job, deducting his expenses from an advance the new employer gives the laborer.

Asante employers on the whole admire the Mossi as laborers and say that, despite their quick tempers, they work hard. They admire the fact that, like themselves, the Mossi have respect for chiefs. The Asante considers this an admirable quality which makes the Mossi amenable to law and reason. Employers consequently encourage hard-working Mossi laborers to stay on their farms. In order to induce their laborers to stay, Asantes sometimes offer them land for cocoa farms as well as for food farms. Since cocoa takes several years to produce, the Asante whose employee makes his own cocoa farm feels assured of his services for a long period. Some Asante also say it is shrewd business policy to offer a good laborer a wife, who is often an older, widowed, or divorced daughter. The children of the marriage are regarded as Asante by the employer, but the Mossi will often attempt to convert his wife to Islam, so that he may claim the children under patrilineal Islamic law. However, it is recognized that, having grown up in an Asante community, these children rarely become Mossi. This type of marriage is denigrated by many Mossi who regret the loss of social and legal paternity. The majority of Mossi in towns and villages maintain contact with each other, in order to maintain their ethnic identity and obtain the benefits they feel derive from this identity. They are critical of those who are isolated in rural areas and who lose contact with other Mossi. They say that such men forget who they are and are likely to be harmed by the Asante. They tell stories about how northerners have disappeared in strange and inexplicable ways and are quick to blame all sorts of misfortunes on the Asante. These Mossi regard marriages with non-Muslim Asante employers (who are often women) or their employer's daughters as a form of slave marriage and note that the status of the children is identical in both cases. Despite this attitude there are migrants in rural areas who have been socially incorporated into Asante society, who have little sense of Mossi identity, and who are unconcerned with the fears of the urban migrants. However, this usually happens in places where there are few Mossi or other northerners in the area. There is, of course, also an assimilated category of people of northern origin, including Mossi, who are the children of unions between Mossi and Asante or the descendants of northern slaves.

Commoners can become chiefs or headmen of Mossi communities in Ghana. Wherever there is a sizable community of Mossi, one of the first settlers is likely to become the chief, or Naba. He may be resident in a large Asante village and claim to be the headman for the Mossi in all the surrounding hamlets and scattered farm cottages. The villages under his jurisdiction usually, but not always, correspond to those that are under the jurisdiction of the Asante chief in the village where he resides. The Mossi headman is sometimes ritually installed by the Asante chief and is thereby incorporated into the Asante chieftancy hierarchy. On behalf of all the Mossi in the area, he usually gives an annual gift, such as a sheep, to the local Asante chief. These Mossi headmen are not recognized by the Mogho Naba or any other chief in Upper Volta, although there was one occasion during the early 1960s when one Mossi headman in Ghana publicly went to greet the Mogho Naba. This had much more to do with competition between two rival Mossi headmen in Ghana and their attempts to secure any and all forms of recognition than it did with any normal procedure wherein the Mossi headmen in Ghana are incorporated into the Upper Volta chieftancy hierarchy.

In some areas where the Mossi are the most numerous northern immigrant group and where other northern groups are sparsely represented, non-Mossi may come under the jurisdiction of the immigrant Mossi headman. He then acts as a leader for members of other Voltaic groups, such as the Gourma, Tallensi, Kusasi, Builsa, and Busansi. The Mossi are able to cite traditional precedents for this, claiming that in the north their group claims hegemony over these others. It is only when the number of immigrants in these groups becomes sufficiently large for them to require internal leadership that they appoint their own headmen. The Mossihene, as a Mossi headman is called by the Asante, is responsible for arbitrating disputes among northerners and representing their interests to the Asante chiefs. When a Mossi laborer in the area has a problem with his employer, the Mossi headman is usually asked by the laborer to plead his case. The headman is sometimes called to court to stand bail for the laborers in his area, and he is responsible for taking care of such matters as the inheritance of deceased migrants' property, the jurisdiction over their children, and disputes over marriage payments, divorce, debt, and other matters.

In urban areas, the Mossi can be divided into several occupational categories: the self-employed traders and craftsmen and the wage-earners. With other northern migrants, the latter constitute a very significant proportion of the unskilled labor force, including most of the underground mine labor.[8] The vast majority of these workers come from various Mossi commoner groups. They are watchmen, latrine carriers, household servants for educated Africans and Europeans, and manual laborers. In the country, as a whole, most of the Mossi are part of a rural proletariat; according to the 1960 census, 66 percent of employed Mossi were engaged in farming. Eleven percent were laborers, and the rest – under 5 percent for each category – were in mining, crafts, transport, service, and professional occupations. Table 1 shows this distribution in detail. In urban areas, although many Mossi are unskilled laborers, a significant proportion are, in fact, skilled or self-employed. In Kumasi

Table 1. *Major occupations of Mossi in Ghana*

	Male		Female	
	No.	%	No.	%
Total, classified by occupation	56,120	99	3,510	100
Professional, technical, and related workers	450	1		
Administrative, executive, and managerial	60	0		
Clerical workers	90	0		
Sales workers	1,760	3	1,560	44
Farmers and farm laborers	38,430	68	1,480	42
Fisherman, forestry	2,170	4		
Miners and related workers	1,800	3	30	1
Transport drivers	570	1		
Craftsmen and production process workers	2,400	4	310	9
Laborers (not elsewhere specified)	6,030	11	60	2
Service, sport, and recreation workers (police, guards, cooks, maids, etc.)	2,460	4	70	2

Source: 1960 Census of Ghana, Special Report 'E': Tribes in Ghana.

this is even more marked, for the community is older and includes many immigrants who have graduated from unskilled wage labor to entrepreneurial activity. Some are in an intermediary stage, holding salaried jobs and beginning to invest in trade or to practice craft occupations at the same time. According to my own survey of 412 men of all Mossi ethnic categories in Kumasi in 1967, 28 percent were unskilled laborers, 21 percent were skilled laborers or craftsmen, 10 percent were drivers, collectors or otherwise engaged in transport. The remaining 20 percent were Arabic teachers and malams, repairers of one sort or another (electricians, watch or bicycle repairers), farmers, or unemployed (Table 2). This distribution can be compared to that of other groups in Kumasi. Most of these show much clearer patterns of clustering either in unskilled occupations (as with some northern Ghanaian groups), skilled jobs and professions (Akans), or trade (Hausa, Songhai, Yoruba) (Table 3).

Many, although certainly not all, of the Mossi craftsmen in Ghana come from groups which specialize in craft activities in Upper Volta. The Yarse are tailors in

Table 2. *Occupations of Mossi adults in Mossi-owned houses*[a]

Occupation	Men		Women[b]	
	No.	%	No.	%
Landlords (Masugida)	39	9	16	8
Trade	51	12	184	92
Cattle *maigida*	3			
Sheep and livestock	21			
Kola	20			
Wholesale food	1			
Flour			15	
Cloth			20	
Oil and shea butter	2			
Chop bar			1	
Medicines	2			
Manufactured articles	2			
Other, unspecified			148	
Transport	44	10		
Driver	23			
Driver's apprentice	2			
Collector	12			
Fitter	1			
Rents bicycles	3			
Caterpillar tractor driver	3			
Crafts and skilled jobs	87	21		
Tailor	50			
Mason	3			
Watch repairer	2			
Cushion-maker and mattress-maker (also sells)	19			
Shoemaker	3			
Blacksmith	6			
Wanzam (barber)	3			
Cook	1			

53

Table 2 (*cont.*)

Occupation	Men		Women[b]	
	No.	%	No.	%
Unskilled and semi-skilled jobs	*115*	28		
Steward boy	2			
Watchman	46			
Garden boy	3			
Laborer, city council	5			
Laborer, firm or government agency	19			
Laborer, w.o.s.[c]	18			
Railway worker	6			
Prison warden	1			
Store boy	13			
Sanitary inspector	1			
Carrier (*kaya-kaya*)	1			
Farming	*27*	7		
Cocoa farm caretaker	1			
Farming, w.o.s. (not cocoa)	26			
Religious and educational	*30*	7		
Arabic school teacher	11			
Malam[d] (divination, medicines)	15			
Sells Arabic books	2			
Imam or assistant Imam	2			
Other	*19*	6		
Butcher	2			
Pot maker	1			
Chief's assistant	1			
Beggar	2			
Musician	3			
No occupation	5			
Old person, unemployed	5			
Total	412		200	

[a]Thirty-three houseowners and fourteen other people who have specified more than one occupation are listed twice. Three people are listed three times. However, many others also engage in more than one occupation. Night watchmen, for example, often trade or have businesses (e.g., tailoring) or hold laboring jobs during the day. Some have farms.
[b]Many women did not list their occupations, and considerably more are engaged in trade than those listed.
[c]w.o.s. = without other specification.
[d]This word is Hausa and is commonly used as a title for any man educated in Arabic. Not all malams "do malam work."

both places, the Maranse dye cloth, the blacksmiths make tools and ornaments. But in Kumasi these traditional divisions are often overlooked, since many people who were farmers learn crafts in town, and many traditional crafts, such as weaving or sewing traditional Mossi cloths, are rarely practiced. New ones, however, have often replaced them. It is common practice for a father to apprentice his sons to various

Table 3. *Occupations of male residents in Mossi-owned houses*

	A		B		C		D		E		F		G		H		I		J		K		Total
	No.	%	No.	%	No.	%	No.	%	No.	%	No.	%	No.	%	No.	%	No.	%	No.	%	No.	%	
Landlord	20	5					1	2									1	2			1	25	22
Transport	38	10	3	4	5	9	12	20	5	7	2	6	1	4	3	18	22	50	5	45			70
Trade	88	23	11	14	3	6	30	51	6	8	16	42	19	83	4	24	5	11					204
Crafts/skilled	62	16	9	11	32	59	1	2	2	3	11	33	3	13	5	29	2	5					130
Services	59	15	12	15	3	6	2	3	13	17	1	3					11	25	4	36			96
Unskilled (laborers)	57	15	33	44	5	9	8	14	48	63					3	18			1	9			168
Farming	24	6	5	6	1	2	1	2													1	25	32
Religious and educational	34	9	5	6	5	9	4	7	2	3	3	9			2	12	3	7	1	9	2	50	61
Total (100%)	382		80		54		59		76		33		23		17		44		11		4		783

Key: Ethnic Groupings
A. Mossi. B. Upper Volta, non-Mossi. C. Akan and Southern Ghanaian. D. Northern Ghanaian centralized (Mamprusi, Dagomba, Gonja, Wala). E. Northern Ghanaian uncentralized (Frafra, Kusasi, Kanjaga, Grusi). F. Hausa and Northern Nigerian. G. Songhai. H. Kotokoli and others from northern Togo and Dahomey. I. Yoruba and Nupe. J. Ibo. K. Wangara (not from Upper Volta).

friends (usually of the same ethnic group) or relatives, so that the son can learn a trade. Seldom will all the sons end up in a single trade, or necessarily in the trade of their father. Tailoring in Western and Islamic styles is the most common craft occupation of the Mossi in towns, but there are also shoemakers, mattress-makers, masons, mechanics, cooks (for Europeans and Indians), gardeners, watch repairers, potters, barbers, bicycle repairers and renters, electricians, musicians, and others. In Kumasi the Mossi began the mattress- and cushion-making business and practically monopolize it today. They sew covers with bright colored imported cotton cloth and stuff them with kapok and straw. They have a center in the main market, where an elderly Mossi man, the founder of the industry in Kumasi, acts as head. Most of the workers are Mossi, but members of other groups are sometimes admitted when the leader approves. There are two Calabar mattress-makers and several Silmi-Mossi and Fulani who come at certain seasons each year to help sell the mattresses. There are now two centers of mattress-making in the town, since in the early 1960s the group split into two factions on the basis of political party affiliation. The CPP faction, led by a son of the man who was the CPP-appointed Mossi headman, moved from the central market and opened another shop in the Asafo market (then known as the Kwame Nkrumah market). In both these areas each man works for himself, making and selling his own products, but they all cooperate in buying materials, setting prices, and maintaining the work area.

The Mossi in Ghana still practice smithing with traditional techniques, but they no longer make tools. Using the lost-wax method they manufacture brass trinkets which are purchased by Zabarama traders and sold in villages throughout southern and central Ghana. Blacksmiths, more often than not, migrate permanently, perhaps because of their relatively low status and poor economic position in Upper Volta. Inquiries in one village in Upper Volta revealed that a great majority of the young men had left, and all had lost contact with their families. Those left in Upper Volta had heard only that some of their men were working as smiths in Ghana or the Ivory Coast. They knew that others were engaged in other activities, but they knew nothing about some of their migrants.

The Mossi smiths in Kumasi are organized similarly to the cushion- and mattress-makers. They share a workshop, although each man works for himself. The group in Kumasi includes four men who came from traditional blacksmith families, one Maranga, two Yarse, two Fulani born in Upper Volta (who spoke Moré), and two Ninissi. The elder Fulani is referred to as the head of the group.

In Kumasi there are also several members of Talse groups who perform traditional divining and curing. Some of them travel north regularly for herbs, while others specialize in sand or cowrie divining. Their clients come from all ethnic communities and include many Asante and many northern Muslims, who approach these practitioners, as well as others who use Islamic magic and medicine. They diagnose physical and emotional problems and provide cures. Some use herbs, and others make traditional Mossi charms which involve sacrifices, ritual, and the preparation of medicine. These preparations may be to help a person recover from an illness, become wealthy, be successful in love, or virtually anything else. During the period

56

around Ghanaian independence when members of opposed political parties were fighting in Kumasi, some of these men did extremely well, providing war magic, including bullet-proof vests and amulets to make the wearer invisible. Their techniques differ from those of the Muslim practitioners, but the problems they deal with are more or less the same. Despite the importance of Islam in Kumasi and the prevalence of Muslims who perform similar functions, these men do well, and most have large clienteles.

A number of Mossi in Kumasi keep what they call Sunday farms, small plots on the outskirts of town where they grow corn and vegetables. There are several full-time farmers who sell vegetables to Africans and Europeans, but most of the Mossi who farm are also wage-laborers. Seven percent of Mossi in the Kumasi sample of 412 men listed farming as their main occupation, but many more would be included if these Sunday farmers were counted. In every one of 89 Mossi-owned houses, which were studied in four neighborhoods in Kumasi, at least one man did some farming, but there was no one who subsisted entirely off the products of his own farm.

Although quite a few Mossi commoners engage in trade, this will be considered more fully in the discussion of Yarse migration, since, once they begin trading, the pattern of their activities does not differ significantly from that of the Yarse, except that it is more likely to be done on a part-time basis.

Migration of Yarse

The dispersion of the Yarse in Mossiland indicates that permanent migration for the purpose of trade and settlement may be considered a traditional phenomenon in this group. Such migration was never contained within the boundaries of the Mossi state, and present Yarse migration to Ghana can be regarded as an extension of this precolonial pattern.

The Yarse in Ghana come from all over Mossi country but mainly from the main trading centers, where they have traditionally been clustered – towns such as Rakai, Sarabtenga, Kaya, Puitenga, and Yako. From these towns many Yarse followed the nineteenth-century caravans into the Gold Coast, and some originally settled in the northern trading center of Salaga and other towns just outside metropolitan Asante. The Yarse were the first Mossi to settle in Kumasi and began coming in large numbers in the beginning of this century. In many ways Yarse trade still follows traditional patterns. Kola, timber, and manufactured goods are exported from Kumasi and the south to Upper Volta, while cattle and livestock are imported into Ghana. The Yarse deal more with livestock than cattle, although many settled Yarse immigrants are *masugida* who accommodate cattle traders and act as middlemen in the sale of the cattle. A few of them are cattle dealers, buying animals from Mossi and Fulani transporters and selling them to butchers, who are mostly Hausa (Hill 1966, 1970a). For most Yarse in Kumasi, however, the outlay of capital this involves is more than they can afford.

Since only a small minority of Yarse migrate seasonally, the break that most of them make with their families in Upper Volta is usually very great. In order to illustrate the extent to which ties are broken and the type of homes these Yarse come from, we may examine several compounds in the Yarse village of Rakai, about forty miles from Ouagadougou. This village was the home of the former Kumasi Mossi headman; I worked there briefly in 1967 with the headman's son, who, as I have mentioned, had first visited it a few years before. At least fifteen other members of the Mossi community in Kumasi come from this town, and, although they identify with one another in Ghana on the basis of provenance and kinship, none of them has maintained contact with relatives in Rakai.

Yarse villages, or Yarse sections (*saka*) of Mossi villages, are almost always composed of segments of one or more extended patrilineages. In Rakai the majority of the people are members of the Sanfo clan and claim descent from the first Sanfo man to enter Mossiland – supposedly a hunter who settled in Rakai. There is also one *saka* of the Dere clan and an abandoned compound which once belonged to a Hausa family. One member of this family lives in Kumasi in the house of the late Mossi headman. There are many other ruined and abandoned dwellings in Rakai, testimony to the volume of emigration which the village has undergone. Many other surviving compounds contain abandoned and empty rooms. These ruins stand amidst inhabited dwellings as monuments to the extensive emigration which has taken place.

In each compound described here the head (*saksoba*) was able to list many men who had left permanently. Their accounts are summarized in Figures 1–3. In the listing of absentees, there were large numbers of migrants who were described as brothers' sons. The result of this pattern of migration is that those who remain in a compound are very often lineal descendants of a single man. Compound A (Figure 1) is headed by the lineage head, the *budkasama,* of all the Sanfo in Rakai, including those living in other compounds. He is the oldest man in the Rakai Sanfo lineage, and it is on this basis that he claims his position. He is *saksoba,* by merit of his being the oldest male member of Compound A. Compound B (Figure 2) is headed by the Yarnaba, the village chief, or Tengnaba, of Rakai, who is also a member of the Sanfo clan. He is not the oldest man in the village but claims genealogical seniority among the Sanfo. Since he is Tengnaba, he has some limited authority over the non-Sanfo in Rakai as well. Besides the Dere lineage mentioned above, wives of Sanfo men are also from non-Sanfo lineages and from other towns. A few of them are Talse. Figure 3 illustrates a relatively complete compound, that of the family of Adamu, headman of the Kumasi Mossi community until his deportation in 1957.

Figures 1, 2, and 3 show three compounds as they were in March, 1967. The lists accompanying them show the migrants that the compound head could name, with all the information he could give about them. These lists and the paucity of information about individual migrants clearly show how completely ties are broken and how communication practically ceases, once a migrant has stayed away more than five years. Other compounds, such as those of the blacksmiths, not illustrated here, show the effects of migration even more dramatically, with more abandoned rooms and more absent kin.

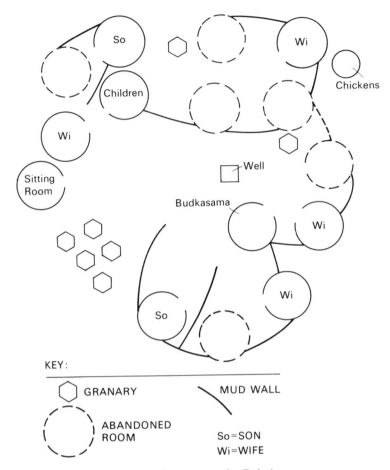

Figure 1. Sanfo Budkasama's compound – Rakai.

Relatives absent from Sanfo Budkasama's compound
1   Budkasama's brother: went to Ghana twenty years ago.
2   Budkasama's brother's son: went to Ghana more than twenty years ago.
3   Budkasama's brother's son: went to Ivory Coast about twenty years ago.

Very few people who were still in the village had left for any length of time, although many had been away on short trading expeditions. The YarNaba himself had been away for a few years in Senegal, where he had gone to study with a renowned Arabic scholar.

Since the Yarse were the first Mossi to settle in the towns of the Gold Coast, they now occupy the most important leadership positions in the immigrant Mossi communities. Many of them are among the most successful traders and landlords. In Kumasi and other towns they are often the Mossi headmen. The criteria for leadership in these immigrant communities are length of residence, wealth, and

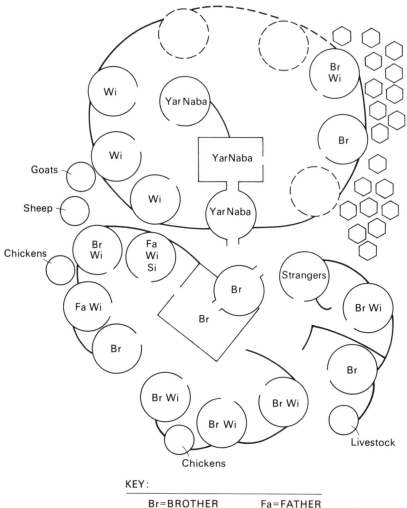

KEY:
Br=BROTHER   Fa=FATHER
Wi=WIFE   Si=SISTER

Figure 2. YarNaba's compound – Rakai.

Relatives absent from YarNaba's compound

1   YarNaba's sister's son: went to Kumasi ten years ago.
2   YarNaba's brother: left twenty years ago, destination unknown.
3   YarNaba's brother: left twenty years ago, destination unknown.
4   YarNaba's sister's son: went to Obuasi twenty-seven years ago.
5   YarNaba's younger brother: went to Tumu (northern Ghana) with his wife in last ten years.
6   YarNaba's son: went to Ghana eight years ago. They heard he took another man's wife, was discovered, and lost the woman. They know nothing else.

60

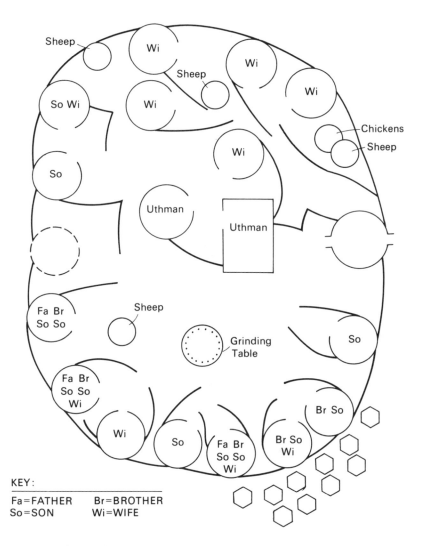

KEY:

Fa = FATHER   Br = BROTHER
So = SON   Wi = WIFE

Figure 3. Uthman's compound – Rakai.

Relatives absent from Uthman's compound

1   Adamu: Uthman's father's brother's son became Mossi headman in Kumasi.
2   Braimah: Uthman's father's brother's son.
3   Ali: Uthman's father's brother's son.
4   Uthman: Uthman's father's brother's son.
5   Ahmadu: Uthman's father's brother's son.

All of these left over forty years ago, and none has ever returned, although the sons of two, Adamu and Ahmadu, returned for short visits. All said they were going "to Kumasi," but none ever met in Ghana.

Islamic education and orthodoxy – all qualities in which the Yarse, in general, surpass the other Mossi groups. In Kumasi the religious criterion is one of the most important, and it becomes increasingly so among second-generation immigrants, who are usually more orthodox than their parents.

For the Yarse, becoming educated in Islam does not involve as great a change in value orientation as it does for other Mossi. It is well known that conversion to Islam among West African migrants assists in the social and psychological adjustments which migration entails. For the Yarse, most of whom already are Muslim, the adoption of Islam does not in itself imply abandoning customary forms of behavior. The Yarse already follow Muslim food prohibitions, profess to deny the existence of witches, deny the mystical powers of ancestors or the necessity of making sacrifices to ancestor spirits, circumcise their young men, and incorporate Islamic ritual into naming, marriage, and funeral ceremonies. For non-Muslim Mossi, giving up each non-Islamic belief and practice can be difficult. This puts the Yarse, in a sense, a step ahead of other Mossi in acculturating to the norms of the Islamic immigrant communities in Ghana, in that most of them already accept the basic values on which Islam is based.

In Kumasi the version of Islam which is practiced is strongly influenced by Hausa culture. Since the Yarse are leaders among the Mossi in terms of the adoption of Islamic practices, they are often accused by other Mossi of attempting to become Hausa. Many of them have studied Arabic and Islamic law with prominent Hausa scholars. In Kumasi many follow the Hausa in joining the Tijaniyya *tariqa,* even though many belonged to the Quadiriyya *tariqa* in Upper Volta, if they belonged to any *tariqa* at all.[9] In their trading activities they cooperate with the Hausa, and they generally speak Hausa better than other Mossi. They are neither powerful nor numerous enough to compete seriously with the Hausa in some areas of trade, so they must cooperate or risk being driven out of the market. This is particularly true in the kola trade, but it happens in other areas as well. They admire the Hausa for their Islamic knowledge, wealth, and trading ability, and for the Yarse, more than for other Mossi, the Hausa form an important reference group. First-generation Yarse migrants usually wear the long Hausa gown, rather than customary Mossi dress, while other Mossi migrants maintain their traditional dress much longer. Most of the marriages contracted between Mossi and Hausa are made by Yarse.

Despite this, there is ambivalence in the attitude of many Yarse towards the Hausa. Most Yarse still cannot, and perhaps would not, choose to, "become Hausa," even if such conversion were possible. The Yarse are occasionally challenged by the Hausa for their "pagan" practices, although in many instances, "pagan" simply means non-Hausa. This happens more frequently in rural areas than in town, where the pressure to conform to a Hausaized version of Islam is greater. Thus, one Yarse man living about sixty miles from Kumasi was berated for burying a corpse beneath his house. He was a well-known malam who had a reputation for being especially good at curing mental illness by using a combination of Islamic and pagan medicine. He refused to give up this method of burial, because he regarded it as a diacritical sign of his Mossi identity.[10]

Migration and settlement of Mossi in Ghana

In most contexts the Yarse in Kumasi today identify themselves as Mossi, and a number of them have devoted themselves to teaching other Mossi the precepts of Islam. Some have started to write the Mossi language in Arabic script, in order to elevate the status of the language. While the Hausa serve as a reference group for the Yarse, the Yarse, in turn, serve as a reference group for other Mossi and, by identifying themselves as Mossi, the educated Yarse feel that they raise the prestige of the Mossi group, as a whole.

Their attitude towards Mossi and Hausa identity depends on the context in which they are acting. Occasionally, when an orthodox Yarse malam is in conflict with members of the Mossi community, he may express the feeling that he is held back by the pagan Mossi. At other times, when he is in some way rejected by the Hausa community, he may express hostility towards the Hausa and emphasize his Mossi identity. A solution to this dilemma which works in many situations is to deny the importance of ethnic identity altogether, on the basis of one possible interpretation of the Islamic ideology of brotherhood. This is, of course, but another variation of situational ethnicity, since to deny identity based upon traditional ethnic divisions, he must accept an identity based upon something else – in this case, on Islam and his status as a stranger in Ghana.

Part II
Kinship and community

4

The growth of the zongo community in Kumasi

The northern Ghanaian and non-Ghanaian immigrants whose descendants are today referred to as members of the zongo community began to settle in Kumasi just before the beginning of this century, around 1896, when the British placed a Resident in the town.[1] The word *zongo,* a Hausa term meaning the camping place of a caravan, or the lodging place of travellers (Abraham 1962: 967), was used by the British to refer to the section of the town where Muslim traders lived. It was used interchangeably with "Hausa settlement," "Mohammedan settlement," and "strangers' quarter." The term *Hausa* was itself "a generic term used to refer to all up-country traders" (*Annual Report, 1906–1907*). In this chapter the history of the settlement of the zongo is described, and the several current usages of the term zongo are clarified.[2] First, something must be said about the position of Muslims in Asante before the British conquered it and made Kumasi the administrative center of the Ashanti Crown Colony in 1901. In many ways there is a significant pattern of structural continuity in the position of strangers in the two periods. The British, and the Chief Commissioner in particular, replaced the central authority of the Asantehene, but the strangers remained in Asante under the patronage of the governmental authority in both the colonial and the precolonial periods. Their settlement was encouraged, for as strangers they had no traditional authority and were dependent on the government for permission to remain in the town and, even more, for any rights and privileges they acquired.

Northerners in Asante before 1874[3]

Until the centralized power of the Asante state was broken by the British victory in Kumasi in 1874, the activities and movements of strangers within Asante territory were strictly controlled. At the height of Asante power, between the consolidation of the state at the end of the seventeenth century and its defeat almost two centuries later, a strict immigration policy controlled the passage of non-Asante through the forest and prevented the establishment of direct links between northerners and traders on the coast. Road wardens (*nkwansrafo*) collected tolls, prevented the export of arms to the north, controlled the movements of traders, and

67

informed the government of the movements of strangers in Asante territory (Wilks 1967: 218).

At the same time the aim of traders from the north was precisely to create such links, in order to trade directly with the coast and to avoid Asante taxes and the supervision of Asante officials. Thus, in 1881, after Asante control in a major northern market, Salaga, was broken, a British officer wrote: "The Ashantis would like to obtain control over all roads leading from the interior. Let this but happen and no more trade from the interior will get beyond Ashanti; the flow of the interior trade will all be directed to Coomassie." (Lonsdale, quoted in Johnson: I, SAL 41/3).

During the period when the Asante did effectively block the link between the north and the coast (from about 1744 to 1874), most trade with northerners was carried on in commercial centers in the outlying part of Asante, first in the northwest and later in Salaga and Yendi. Rebellions against Kumasi authority in the northwest in the beginning of the nineteenth century led to a decline in trade in this area and a shift to the center and the east (Wilks 1961: 24; Goody and Arhin 1965). In the various trading towns Hausa and Mossi caravans exchanged slaves, cattle, leather goods, and cloth for gold dust, salt, and kola nuts from Asante and the south. Although some caravans did reach Kumasi, most trade was carried on outside metropolitan Asante, where the King's authority was enforced by the appointment of royal ambassadors. These were responsible for maintaining Asante rule, as well as for collecting tribute, a large part of which consisted of slaves.

Kumasi itself was established on an ancient north-south gold route (Wilks 1962), and trade was always an important factor in its development (Nyarko 1959). Contemporary sources note the presence of northerners there soon after the Asante campaign against Dagomba in 1744 (Romer 1760, quoted in Wilks 1961: 21). While there were only two northerners in Kumasi in 1750, by the beginning of the next century there was a community of over a thousand who came mainly from the tributary states of Gonja and Dagomba (Wilks 1966: 319ff.). By the time Bowdich and Dupuis came to Kumasi in 1816 and 1820, respectively, these Muslims played an important role in Asante government by performing numerous services for the king. They served as court scribes, keeping accounts and records in Arabic; acted as ambassadors for the king on foreign missions; advised the king on matters of trade and war; served in the army; and performed magical and religious services. They also acted as hosts for visitors from distant countries in the north, including Mossiland, Hausaland, Timbuctoo, and North Africa.

The position of the Kumasi Muslims changed under various kings (Wilks 1967, 1975), but in general they were welcomed and protected so long as their services could be utilized. They had considerable religious influence on a number of rulers, and on the population at large, through the sale of amulets, by training Asante children in their Arabic schools, and by intermarrying with Asante. At some time around 1860 an Imam al-Bilad, a personal Imam to the King, was appointed. Today, this office still exists, and members of the present-day Asante Nkramo community (Asante Muslims) trace descent to these early immigrants. By the time the British arrived, these Muslims had already become sufficiently incorporated into Asante society so that, in the wars of 1874 and 1900 with the British, they were loyal to the Asantehene.

The cessation of Asante control in the north in 1874 led to a mounting influx of northerners from Mossi and Hausa country into Asante and the areas further south. A British officer noted that, "No one who has been for some years on the coast can fail to be struck by the increasing Mohammedan infiltration." (entry of 22 April, 1880, C.O. 96/131, 1880 May–Sept., Vol. II, Public Record Office [P.R.O.], London). In Salaga, news of the British victory in Kumasi led to a revolt against Asante authority in which many Asante were killed. Trade between Salaga and Kumasi temporarily ceased, and new routes from the north to the coast were opened which, for the first time since the creation of the Asante state, were out of Asante control. By 1892, the year of the civil war in Salaga, the commercial importance of that northern town faded still more, and Kintampo, Kete Krakye, and many smaller towns became important market centers and absorbed many Salaga Muslims originally from Hausaland, Mossiland, and elsewhere in the north. When Kumasi was finally reopened to trade in 1896, northerners from these towns moved into the zongo.

Northerners and the British in Kumasi

Two sources of population contributed to the early Muslim stranger community in Kumasi in the colonial period: northern soldiers recruited by the British to fight against the Asante and northern traders and laborers who were able to enter Kumasi freely, once Asante power was broken. Thus, the settlement of the zongo depended upon British support and was a development which was directly linked to the destruction of the Asante empire. This undoubtedly affected the type of community which emerged, and it contributed in a minor way to its increasing social and cultural differentiation from Asante society.

Both the British and the Asante employed northern soldiers, but the former, in promising to free trade routes to the coast from Asante control, attempted to play upon long-standing ambitions to gain recruits. Before 1874 soldiers were recruited in Nigeria to be used in the 1869 and 1874 campaigns against Asante. Most of these men returned to Nigeria, but many remained and joined the Gold Coast Constabulary in the north, eventually to return to Kumasi. In 1880 a movement was started to recruit a permanent Hausa force in the northern Gold Coast, since the British had found that it was cheaper to keep African soldiers than to employ West Indian troops, as had been the practice before. Consequently, an African officer was sent to Salaga to recruit troops. He was followed by the British officer, Lonsdale, who was told to explain to the local chiefs "that this Government has so high an opinion of the natives of the Houssa country that it employs a military force recruited entirely from people of that district" (Lonsdale, in Johnson: Vol. I, SAL 59/1). The British were impressed with the way the recruits fought, and the records are full of praise for them. For example, one report states: "My observations of the

Hausas lead me to believe that if fanatical they are faithful and well behaved. . . .
They are fierce and intractable in warfare and look with contempt on Pagans"
(*Half-yearly Report on the Gold Coast Constabulary,* 25 March 1880, ADM 1/470).
The British attitude towards Mossi recruited in Gambaga was similarly compli-
mentary. Major Morris, the head of the force, wrote: "I cannot speak too highly
of these horsemen. . . . They are excellent riders and display a great deal of dash
and gallantry" (Morris to Colonial Secretary, 24 February 1900, ADM 56/1/1).

Asante armies, on the other hand, are known to have consisted of special
regiments of northern troops as early as 1817 (Bowdich 1821a: 52, quoted in
Wilks 1967: 227 and Dupuis 1824: 124, xxxvii), while the Kumasi Muslims were
also expected to perform military services for the king (Dupuis 1824: 98; Wilks
1966: 329). In 1879 the Asante were training northerners along British lines. Some
of these soldiers were gathered from the slave population (Dudley to Hay, 25
March, 1879, ADM 1/642), but others were paid to desert the British forces. In
1880 Mensa Bonsu, the Asantehene, offered soldiers double pay to desert (Wilks
1967: 215).

The British force actually included soldiers from many ethnic groups, including
Hausa and Mossi, but also Yoruba, Zabarama, Grusi, and others from the Northern
Territories of the Gold Coast and the surrounding countries. According to government counts in the Northern Territories, Mossi formed the largest number of
recruits in any single year in the first decade of the century and constituted about
a quarter of the force (*Annual Reports, Northern Territories, 1902, 1903, 1904*).
When the Constabulary (later renamed the West African Frontier Force) moved to
Kumasi it was divided into companies on the basis of ethnic affiliation. This
heterogeneous army of men, who had fought together under the British, formed
a significant segment of the early zongo population.

The number of "Hausa" soldiers with the British in Kumasi during the 1900
rising was over seven hundred (Hodgson 1901: 195). The "Lagos Hausas" (Hausas
recruited in Nigeria) were joined by recruits from the north, including the Mossi
horsemen. Soldiers were also gathered from the civilian Zongo which had developed
just outside Kumasi after 1896. A story is told of a Kotokoli woman who ran a
house of prostitution in Kumasi and received a commission from the British for the
recruits she gained among her clientele. In 1899 the British built new cantonments
for the soldiers, mainly with Asante convict labor, but in 1900 these buildings, as
well as the civilian Zongo, were burned by the Asante. The northern soldiers and
civilians took refuge in the British fort.

Hostilities between Asante and northern soldiers did not end immediately after
the war, at least according to British reports. By 1901 the British had subdued the
Asante, and about five hundred Kumasi residents who were being punished for the
rising were forced to build new quarters for the northern soldiers (*Report on
Ashanti, 1901*). In the following years relations between northern soldiers and
Asante civilians were said to be poor, the northerners reportedly sometimes taking
advantage of their position as allies of the governing power (*Annual Report,
Ashanti, 1905*). As late as the First World War, when the British attempted to

recruit Asantes, they were hindered by the Asante unwillingness to join "an alien and hated body of men" (C.C.A.'s Confidential Diary, 29 January, 1917, NAG, Kumasi). Whether or not these reports accurately reflect Asante attitudes, there is no doubt that subsequent actions on the part of the government did little to dispel hostility, and in fact perpetuated it (Schildkrout 1970b).

The British actively encouraged the development of trade and believed it to have a "civilizing and peaceful influence" (*Departmental Reports, 1908-1909*). But, from the British point of view, the economic benefits of trade were undoubtedly more important reasons for encouraging it, for, "Mohammadanism leads to desire for European goods: cloth, kettles, beads, sewing machines, etc." (*Report on the Northern Territories, 1906*). The governments in the north and in Asante had to pay their own administrative expenses, and officials in the beginning of the century were preoccupied with finding sources of revenue. A major source was the caravan tax, which the British actually believed was welcomed by traders, who were usually strangers in the area and in need of protection. The British rejected the idea of direct taxation, finding it unworkable in the north and impolitic in Asante. They noticed the resentment engendered by the French head tax and found that other means of indirect taxation, like road tolls and market taxes, were detrimental to trade. "Impositions of fines in Salaga and Gambaga," it was noted, made traders "prefer going to Kumasi for goods" (*Annual Report, 1906*). They therefore decided that the caravan tax was the best solution and managed to justify this in moral terms (ibid.):

The caravan tax presents to all who pay it substantial advantages in that once in possession of the Government piece of paper, which is looked on by the majority of people with the respect generally accorded to fetish, they are immune from extortion or robbery on the road. . . . Another point that should not be lost sight of in this connection is that for the most part it is paid by strangers to the country as the majority of traders come from Sokoto, Kano, or are French subjects from Moshi and the country beyond.

Caravan taxes formed the largest single item in the revenue of Asante and the Northern Territories until 1908, when they were abolished. In that year Asante suffered a loss of revenue of ten thousand pounds (*Annual Report, 1908*). The tax was abolished, because, once a regular trade pattern was established, the traders no longer seemed to "desire" this form of protection. It was hoped that the abolition of the tax would increase trade through Kumasi, which by 1908 was competing with a route through German Togoland (*Annual Report, Northern Territories, 1908*).

Cattle was the largest import from the north in the beginning of the century, as it is today. In the first decade of the century, people from the Northern Territories had not yet started bringing cattle to Kumasi, and the market was monopolized mainly by Hausa and Mossi traders. The large animals from Mossiland were more likely to withstand the walk to Kumasi than were the smaller cattle from the Northern Territories. The British, however, encouraged their subjects to bring cattle south, and by 1910 Gold Coast northerners began making two trips each season with their cattle. Today, the two types continue to share the cattle market in Kumasi (Hill 1970a: 96–132).

Cotton grown in Mossiland was another major import in the early part of the century. The *Annual Report, 1905* noted that in the Northern Territories there "is a good deal of cloth making . . . but the cotton is all purchased from Moshie traders who get it from French Territories." Thus, although Mossi traders had come south before the British arrived, often as far as Salaga, the colonial government's encouragement of trade led to an increase in activity. This coincided with the strict measures used by the French to recruit labor and collect taxes. Consequently, the Report of 1908 on immigration noted that, "A developing feature of this [north-south] movement is to be found in the number of Moshies that now come to Coomassie. . . ." (*Annual Report, 1908*).

In the beginning of the century, caravan traders still came south to purchase salt from Ada on the southern coast and kola nuts from the Asante forest. Asante paid for four-fifths of its imports from the north in kola, and enough was exported to pay for all imported cattle and livestock. Virtually all this trade was in the hands of northerners who were almost always Muslims – Hausa, Yarse, and other Muslims from Dagomba, Gonja, Wa, and Mamprusi. Most of the trade followed traditional routes, although new zongos and roads were being built all the time. When the route from Salaga to Kumasi was reopened soon after 1900, new towns developed along this road (*Annual Report, Northern Territories, 1908*):

Markets with permanent Hausa traders are growing up in towns which a few years ago were considered unsafe even to go to owing to the probability of having their loads looted from them en route. . . .The increasing number of zongos which exist to supply the caravans with food . . . point to the increasing trade which is passing through the Protectorate.

The British also encouraged Asante entrepreneurial activity, but this developed mainly in the rural sector. In 1907, large quantities of cocoa seed were introduced into the Kumasi District. This and the development of mines and public works led to a growing demand for northern labor. Asante farmers were willing to pay wages for farm laborers which were double those paid in the north. In 1914, for instance, wages in Asante were one shilling and sixpence, compared with ninepence in Salaga, per day (*Annual Reports for the Northern Territories, 1902, 1903, 1904*). Asante chiefs preferred hiring northern laborers to fulfill the government's demands for road-building and construction workers, rather than risk unpopularity with their subjects (over whom many of the government-appointed chiefs had no traditional authority) by demanding "voluntary" service (*Annual Report, Eastern Province of Ashanti 1929–30: 3*).

Before the formation of the government labor department in 1938, political officers in the Northern Territories actively assisted in the recruitment of labor for both government projects and commercial firms, especially the gold mines (Thomas 1973). This formal labor recruitment supplemented an informal system of recruitment which had developed in the zongos in Asante. The government, as well as the Asante farmers, preferred hiring northerners to using Asante labor.

The growth of the zongo community in Kumasi

As the British noted in their *Annual Report, Ashanti, 1931,* "Ashanti farmers do not now work their farms with their own families but hire laborers from the Northern Territories." When the government hired 450 Asante laborers to work on the Accra-Kumasi railway, they "showed little aptitude for work and arrangements were made to obtain laborers from the NTs [Northern Territories] indentured for service for six months" (*Annual Report, Ashanti, 1920*).

Most migrants came for only a few months, but many drifted to the towns and stayed several years or indefinitely. By 1920 these had become a second tier in the zongo population. Unlike the earlier migrants, these were not primarily traders. Many came from traditionally uncentralized societies of the Northern Territories and Upper Volta, and they were often not Muslims. When they came to town many were destitute, unskilled, and unemployed. Their plight depended very much upon worldwide economic conditions, and particularly on the fluctuating price of cocoa. In certain years, for example, during the 1929 depression, very few laborers were paid, and many of them failed to return north. Health problems in the larger towns became serious (*Reports, Eastern and Western Provinces of Ashanti 1930–31: 17*):

In Kumasi the sick pauper is a problem. A large number of the natives of the Northern Territories come south for the cocoa season. Generally speaking they are dirty, lousy, ill fed, and of very poor physique. They are veritable museums of helminths of all descriptions, yaws and guinea worms.

A high number of these people arrive in Kumasi and are unable to work. They cannot obtain food and arrive at the hospital in semi-dying conditions. Consequently they have to be admitted and the hospital is over-crowded with these poor starving creatures. . . .

This had important consequences for the political development of Kumasi zongo, since the British soon began seeking African assistance in meeting this problem.

The growth of the zongo in Kumasi

The development of Kumasi zongo may be viewed in terms of the expansion caused by these successive waves of northern migration: first that of Muslim traders, second that of labor migrants. Although both types of migration continued simultaneously, many of the first settlers, the traders, established themselves permanently in the town, acquired property, and built houses. They soon dominated the zongo economically and politically and often controlled the fate of new migrants. It is significant that they came mainly from certain traditionally centralized states outside the Gold Coast, including the Hausa, Yoruba, and Mossi kingdoms. The labor migrants, on the other hand, came mainly from the noncentralized communities of the Northern Territories – Frafra (Tallensi), Grusi, Kanjaga (Builsa), Kusasi, and others. Few of these migrants were Muslims before they came to Kumasi, while many of the traders had a long tradition of Islam, a factor which gave them an advantage in the Muslim community in Kumasi, where Islamic knowledge and orthodoxy conferred prestige. The division between these two categories of migrants was mitigated by several factors: that some of the soldiers recruited by the British came from the non-Muslim groups which later provided laborers; that most ethnic communities had subgroupings, some of which were traditionally traders and Muslims, while others were labor migrants (for instance, the Yarse and the Talse among the Mossi); that both types of migration continued simultaneously; and that social mobility was possible in the stranger community, so that an individual could become a Muslim, a trader, and a *maigida,* regardless of his origins. Furthermore, the ethnic identity of many of the Muslims was open to question and would sometimes change when they came to Kumasi. While some of the Muslims in the Moré-Dagbane-speaking states of Dagomba, Mamprusi, and Mossi were converts to Islam, others were of diverse origins, mainly Dyula and Hausa. In Kumasi these people could often choose whether to identify themselves with other Moré-Dagbane–speaking people or with Hausa or Wangara, on the basis of their more distant history. Such mobility occurred particularly with migrants who were born in trading towns, including Kumasi and Salaga.

The physical development of the stranger neighborhood reflected a growing tendency for migrants to remain in town, the expansion of the economy, and British policy. The first neighborhood in Kumasi known as a Zongo in the colonial period consisted of Muslim traders and camp-followers who came to Kumasi with the British forces around 1896.[4] By the time of the Asante rising against the British in 1900, there was a sizable Zongo just north of what was then the town, in an area known as Mmoromu, or Zongo Tuni, after a Malam Tuni who is said to have been the first settler, and now known as Mbrom. During the 1900 rising, the Asante burned this Zongo, but it was soon rebuilt by the Muslims in the same place.

After 1900 the British encouraged the reconstruction of Kumasi. A large swamp was reclaimed in an area that is now the center of the city, and the Central Market was started (see Map 6). In 1901 the town limits were set at one mile's radius from the British fort. Within this area, which did not include Mmoromu, the British confiscated land, thus deriving a substantial amount of revenue from the collection of ground rents for plots which were leased at one pound to twenty-four pounds per annum, depending upon the size of the plot and the identity of the lessee.[5] In 1905 the government moved the Muslims from Mmoromu into the town, to the area now known as Old Zongo, or Yelwa (a Hausa term meaning abundance or plenty), thereby benefiting from the collection of rents. *The Annual Report, 1905* noted "the demolition and repartition of the Hausa Zongo. . . . It has been divided up into plots which are leased out to settlers at from £4 to £1 per annum according to size. Over 150 plots were already in occupation at the end of the year."

Kumasi was by no means an Asante town in terms of its ethnic composition. The stranger population almost equalled the Asante population, and, if transient traders were counted, probably far surpassed it. In 1905 there were 3,650 permanent Asante residents and 2,265 permanent non-Asantes, classified as Fantis,

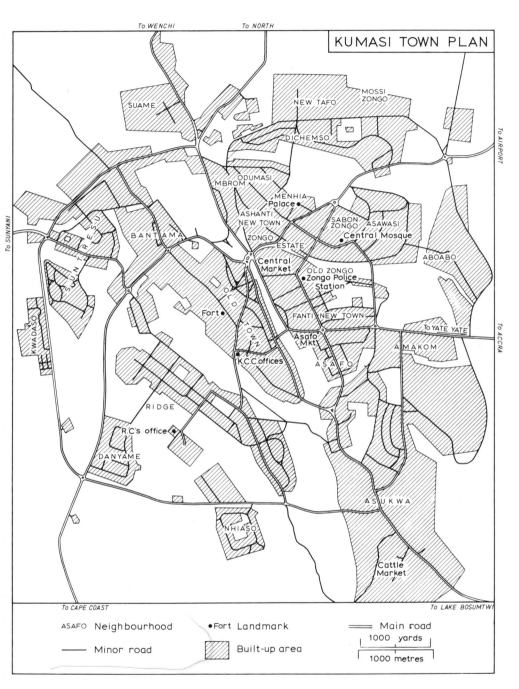

Map 6. Kumasi: town plan, 1960.

Mohammedans, and "other" (*Annual Report, 1905*). As far as the British were concerned, the rate at which strangers moved into the town was an index of its growth: "The town is developing with surprising rapidity and the eagerness with which building plots are sought after by strangers . . . is a sign of the prosperity and popularity of the town" (*Annual Report, 1906-1907*). A large part of the town revenue was, in fact, derived from strangers. Until 1928 there were no town rates in Kumasi, and the major sources of revenue were the ground rents, slaughterhouse taxes, and market taxes. One-third of the ground rents came from the zongo, and the strangers paid a large part of the slaughterhouse and market taxes.

The government also benefited from the strangers by utilizing their labor. Headmen in the zongo, whose role will be discussed in detail later, were able to provide the administration with voluntary labor, since they often sheltered unemployed and newly-arrived migrants. The headmen promised migrants jobs, shelter, and food, and while migrants were waiting for their jobs, the headmen were able to offer their services to the government. In return, the headmen received political support from the British, even though they were not officially chiefs, since in the colonial period, recognition as a chief entailed recognition by the Governor of the Gold Coast Colony.

Between 1905 and 1924 the Old Zongo (Yelwa) had expanded northwards into the area now called Zongo Extension. These two neighborhoods are today known as the Zongo. In 1924 Kumasi was struck by a serious plague, most severely in the overcrowded Zongo. In the next year the Public Health Board was formed, replacing the former Kumasi Council of Chiefs as the main organ of local government.[6] As described in the *Annual Report, 1924-1925* (53):

The Board immediately undertook the demolition of unsanitary areas at Kumasi rendered imperative by the outbreak of plague, and the remodelling of the Hausa Zongo and construction under mass production methods of housing accommodation for the dispossessed. Accommodation for 1700 people in substantial concrete houses at a cost of about £17 per head was provided in less than six months.

In 1929 a second portion of the scheme was opened at a cost of twenty thousand pounds. This was a considerable financial saving for the government when evaluated against what the cost would have been if "voluntary labor" (i.e., "mass production methods") had not been provided by the strangers. After the plague, the headmen were required to organize weekly town-cleaning (known as grass-cutting) sessions in the Zongo and on the outskirts of the town. This relieved the Health Board of the necessity of providing paid labor for a substantial part of the sanitation and development of Kumasi (Medical Officer to President, Kumasi Public Health Board, 16 January 1928. File 12/60, *Zongo Affairs,* NAG, Kumasi).

The new houses were built in an area now known as Sabon Zongo, or New Zongo, and were modelled after the houses in the Old Zongo. Rooms were rented to individuals and families on a monthly basis by the Health Board, originally at six shillings a month and, in 1966, at fifteen shillings. In 1948 a second government housing project, Asawasi, was started. Today, both areas are predominantly occupied by northerners.

The boundaries of the areas inhabited primarily, though not exclusively, by northern immigrants have expanded as the population of Kumasi has grown. Suburbs, where Asante and immigrant landlords built houses for residence or hire, were gradually incorporated into the town, so that today Kumasi includes areas which were formerly villages outside it, such as Aboabo, Ayiga (called YateYate by Muslims), Ahinsan, Nhiaso, and others.

In Kumasi today (according to the 1960 census), the stranger population has grown to the point that the Asante constitute less than half (42.7 percent in 1960) of the population of approximately 220,000. Other Akans constitute 17 percent, although these, like the Ga-Adangbe (3 percent) and the Ewe (5.3 percent) are also strangers vis-à-vis the Asante. Approximately one-third of the total population consists of northern Ghanaians and non-Ghanaians (Table 4). Aliens, including those born outside of Ghana and those born in the country (38 percent of Kumasi's aliens were born in Ghana) numbered 40,245 in 1960, or 18 percent of the population. Only a small number of aliens (2,100) were counted as non-Africans – Europeans, Indians, or Lebanese. There is also a very large population of transient northerners – traders and people en route to rural employment or towns further south.

Although there has never been any ordinance enforcing a separation between the Asante and strangers, or between Europeans and Africans, the British policy of allocating special areas to strangers encouraged clustering on this basis. A number of neighborhoods, Amakom and Dichemso, for example, settled mainly after 1930, contain many northerners amidst a predominantly Asante and southern Ghanaian population (Table 5). Many Asante have also bought houses as investments in mainly stranger neighborhoods. Although most of these are nonresident landlords, some live in their houses and rent some of the rooms to tenants. Furthermore, in the beginning of the century, when housing in Kumasi was scarce and when there were fewer northern landlords, many Asante chiefs and entrepreneurs rented rooms in their own houses to migrants, often benefiting from the labor services of their tenants.

The acquisition of land by strangers

Traditional methods of acquiring land in Asante have been described in detail by Rattray (1929: 340–67). Strangers, like Asante migrating from one area to another, were able to lease land from the local chiefs by paying a small fee, nowadays in the form of a bottle or two of liquor or schnapps. During most of the colonial period the British, having confiscated Asante lands, became responsible for issuing leases. In Kumasi, until 1943, when the Kumasi Lands Ordinance was passed, the government, as represented by the Public Health Board, gave out leases to plots in Kumasi. No special provisions were made for people indigenous to Kumasi, with

Table 4. *Ethnic groups in Kumasi municipal area*

	Major group	Subgroup	%
Kumasi municipal area: total population	218,170		100
Not classified by tribe	2,050		
Akan	130,530		59.7
Nzima		1,850	
Anyi-Bawle		500	
Twi-Fante (Fante)		23,450	
Twi-Fante (Twi)		104,610	
Akan, n.e.s.[a]		120	
Ga-Adangbe	6,590		3.0
Ga		4,380	
Adangbe		1,220	
Ga-Adangbe, w.o.s.[b]		990	
Ewe	11,460		5.3
Guan	3,560		1.7
Gonja		2,100	
Other Guan		1,460	
Central Togo tribes	110		–
Yoruba	9,800		4.5
Ibo	1,430		.7
Gurma	1,860		.9
Kotokoli (Tem)	1,500		.7
Moré-Dagbane	20,690		9.6
Mossi		5,150	
Dagomba		3,830	
Wala		970	
Mamprusi		520	
Nankanse, Gurensi, Frafra (Tallensi)		4,750	
Dagati		2,330	
Builsa (Kanjaga)		2,140	
Kusasi		990	
w.o.s.		10	
Grusi	5,350		2.4
Sisala		1,011	
Kasena		70	
Grusi, w.o.s.		4,270	
Lobi			
Songhai	3,780		1.7
Songhai		2,010	
Zabarama		1,770	
Mande	7,110		3.9
Busansi		5,010	
Wangara		2,100	
Hausa	8,010		3.7
Fulani	1,780		.8
Kru	70		
Others	2,490		1.1
from Ghana		60	
from Nigeria		980	
from other African countries		1,450	

[a]n.e.s. = not elsewhere specified. [b]w.o.s. = without other specification.
Source: 1960 Population Census of Ghana, Special Report 'E'.

Table 5. *Kumasi population, by census enumeration area and country of origin*

Enumeration area	Total population	Country of origin									
		Ivory Coast	Liberia	Mali	Upper Volta	Togo	Da-homey	Niger	Nigeria	Other	Ghana
Kwadaso	10,386	9	–	13	461	235	11	2	133	23	9,466
Ridge Area	3,719	3	34	11	99	81	18	11	111	14	2,710
Amakom	19,742	47	5	57	1,002	1,286	201	103	1,134	13	15,694
Technology area	5,245	18	2	6	130	410	3	8	147	21	4,321
Fanti New Town/Asafo	24,423	23	4	213	556	578	54	354	1,354	57	21,068
Odum/Lake Road	11,159	77	31	417	639	262	17	51	271	17	8,833
Suntresu	15,055	24	11	163	393	289	9	13	136	34	13,975
Ashanti New Town	25,590	51	3	941	595	393	22	37	1,296	25	22,092
Zongo	25,466	150	6	711	1,972	449	43	301	6,262	39	15,516
Aboabo	15,567	46	3	538	1,441	689	50	149	6,292	8	7,351
New Town Extension	15,992	17	–	73	482	337	58	49	400	11	14,548
Suame	8,098	41	–	85	837	101	26	75	569	1	6,319
Tafo	10,909	30	4	94	991	449	121	6	458	5	8,746
Northern outskirts	13,385	38	1	64	410	156	70	25	386	14	12,209
Southern outskirts	13,236	65	13	93	515	191	155	5	184	146	11,793
Total	218,172	639	117	3,479	10,523	5,906	858	1,189	19,133	428	173,841

Source: 1960 Population Census of Ghana, Special Report 'E'.

the exception of permitting Asante chiefs to pay lower rents. The fact that the Asantehene had lost control over Kumasi lands remained a bitter issue when the Confederacy was established in 1935, and it was not until 1943 that lands were again vested in Native Authorities (Tordoff 1965: 363ff.; Triulzi 1972: 100). The Kumasi Land Ordinance of 1943 provided Kumasi natives[7] with the right to acquire free plots. Everyone who was not a Kumasi native could still obtain a lease from a Kumasi native: the lessee was then under obligation to pay ground rents, and this was divided between the Ashanti Traditional Authority and the Town Council. The 1943 law was modified by the Administration of Lands Ordinance of 1962, which vested lands in the president of Ghana and gave financial responsibility to the Ministry of Lands. The president could now also lease land, but Kumasi natives were still entitled to their free plots, at a nominal rental of one shilling per annum.

These facts indicate two things which are important to this study: first, that after 1943 northerners and other non-Asante could obtain land by appealing to Asante chiefs, just as they had in the precolonial period. Second, that after independence, during the CPP period (1957–66), the national government took authority away from the chiefs and dealt directly with the strangers, just as the British had done before 1943. This pattern is significant, because it replicated developments in the political sphere.

To get some idea of how a stranger settles in Kumasi and how a new neighborhood is developed we can take the area known as Mossi Zongo as an example. This is the newest neighborhood to be settled around Kumasi and does not appear on 1960 government maps, since it was not yet incorporated into the city. The land on which Mossi Zongo has developed is owned, according to customary law, by the Tafo royal family – that is, the Tafo stool. In the early 1960s, the Tafohene appointed a caretaker, Panin Asante, to look after the land. Panin's nephew, a schoolteacher, wrote an account of the settlement which shows the events from an Asante's point of view:

Haruna, an aged Mossi laborer, erected a hut on his own initiative at the site. When asked, he said he could not afford hiring a room in Kumasi. People who saw him at first thought he was mad, yet with courage he alone stayed there.

He started rearing fowls and making cassava and corn farms near his hut. During one of Panin Asante's rounds he saw him. Panin cautioned him and even threatened him to stop making farms without authority. Haruna apologized and promised to see him later [that is, with a gift].

Another Mossi man, Braihmah, was attracted to the site, erected a hut, and also started farming. These two men saw Panin with £2 each, the cost of two bottles of schnapps. . . .

In 1962 Panin Asante discovered that thirty other northerners including Grunsis, Sisalas, Busansi, had joined the chorus, so the amount paid as rum was increased to G£7 per head. The need for a surveyor to make a modern layout plan arose. The money collected was used to engage a surveyor to demarcate plots in 1962 even though they had already put up queer thatched houses. The surveyor never wanted to discourage them so most of their huts were allowed to stay or were not affected by the layout. The plan has already been submitted to the Kumasi City Council for approval.

The growth of the zongo community in Kumasi

At the moment [1966] there are about fifty Mossis with house plots. . . . Others apart from the Mossis are Busansi, Grunsis, Sisalas, and Nigerians, not to mention all.

This developing village needs modern amenities such as latrines, water, a motorable road to the village, and so on. Owing to high cost of materials the development is slow. The inhabitants work voluntarily on Sundays.

In 1967 Haruna Mossi, the first settler, was installed as headman of Mossi Zongo by the Tafohene. It is significant that he was installed by the Asante chief, and not by the Mossi headman in Kumasi, who did, however, send a delegate to the ceremony. He became responsible for giving out plots and he keeps a pile of sticks on hand for demarcating boundaries. He receives the "rum money," which he says now amounts to thirty-four pounds per plot, and gives this to the Tafohene who in return gives him a thanking gift (a "dash") of about four pounds. The Tafohene keeps a list of plot-owners, but Haruna says he knows the names only of the Mossi. The others, he says, "are not my family."

In the older neighborhoods the houseowners and the majority of tenants are predominantly from the early migrating groups, including many Hausa, Yoruba, Mossi, and Wangara (Table 6). The oldest neighborhood, Yelwa, is regarded by the strangers as an almost wholly Hausa area, and, in fact, it does have the greatest proportion of Hausa landlords and residents. The Hausa themselves claim that they were the first landlords in Kumasi, and this appears to support their claim. This situation is not entirely unambiguous, however, since in the beginning of the century many migrants who were not Hausa were identified as Hausa. In subsequent generations many of their children have continued to identify themselves as Hausa.

There were many non-Hausa traders and soldiers in Kumasi early in the century, but not many of them seem to have acquired property until after the 1920s. In the first quarter of the century most Mossi migrants were still oriented towards Upper Volta. They were more interested in saving to return to their homes in the north than in investing in property in Kumasi. Many Mossi were wage laborers, rather than traders. Since ownership of houses was generally associated with accommodating itinerant traders, and with trading activity itself, the Mossi were slower than the Hausa in realizing the economic benefits of house-building. In retrospect, the Mossi say that members of their group did not have the sense to build houses until the 1930s, when there was no more land available in the Zongo. At that time many Mossi and even more Yoruba started building in Aboabo, which was just beginning to develop. Many of them continued to hire rooms in the Zongo for their own families and rented out their new houses to more recent migrants and itinerant traders.

Very few members of the northern Ghanaian non-Muslim groups have built or bought houses in the neighborhoods which were developed before the 1940s. Most of these migrants still intend eventually to return north, and comparatively few of them make investments in immovable property in Kumasi. Other groups, the Gao for example, migrate seasonally and do not invest in property, although even in these groups there are always a few settled migrants who play a part in running the groups' activities in the town. In contrast to these patterns, many

81

Table 6. *Ethnic groups of houseowners in three neighborhoods in Kumasi in 1966*

	Old Zongo		Zongo Extension		Aboabo	
	No.	%	No.	%	No.	%
Muslim or Hausa name, precise ethnic identity not known	27	16	14	10	125	26
Not known	4	2	9	6	16	3
Hausa	43	25	29	20	84	17
Yoruba	16	9	14	10	69	14
Mossi	5	3	10	7	42	9
Asante	29	17	28	20	50	10
Northern Ghanaian, centralized[a]	4	2	3	2	12	2
Northern Ghanaian, uncentralized[b]	9	5	6	4	14	3
Gonja and "Salaga"	8	5	9	6	19	4
Fulani	3	2	6	4	16	3
Songhai[c]	6	3	8	5	6	1
Kotokoli	1	1			9	2
Dogon[d]	2	1	1	< 1		
Busansi			1	< 1	4	1
Gurma	1	1			4	1
Lebanese	3	2	1	< 1	1	< 1
Laraba[f]	2	1	1	< 1	3	1
Banda	1	1			1	< 1
Wangara	7	4	4	3	10	2
Total	171	100	144	< 101	485	99

[a]Mamprusi, Dagomba, Wala.
[b]Frafra, Kanjaga, Sisala, Kusasi, Grusi, and Dagati. The Grusi group includes one or more "Kantoshies," an incorporated group of Dyula Muslims.
[c]Including Zabarama, "Gao," "Djougou," Dendi (Westermann and Bryan, 1952: 76).
[d]Includes Kibisi and Kado (Westermann and Bryan, 1952: 60ff.).
[e]Includes Chamba (Westermann and Bryan, 1952: 67).
[f]North Africans are called "Laraba," regardless of precise ethnic classification.

Hausa originally came with the intention of settling permanently. From the beginning of the century they seized opportunities to acquire buildings, recognizing this as a form of investment which directly benefited their trading activities.

All neighborhoods are ethnically heterogeneous, and today all ethnic groups are scattered throughout the town. The *1960 Ghana Census* does not show the ethnic composition of each neighborhood but it does give the population of areas, according to the inhabitants' countries of origin. The largest percentage of aliens is in Aboabo (53 percent), and the Zongo follows with 39 percent of its population listed as alien. If the large numbers of northern Ghanaians are added, these two neighborhoods are shown to have the highest concentrations of northern immigrants in Kumasi. Sixty-four percent of Nigerians are in Aboabo and Zongo, and another 20 percent are in Amakom, Ashanti New Town, and Fanti New Town. One-third of all Voltaics in Kumasi are in Zongo and Aboabo, and another third are in Amakom, Tafo, Suame and Odum (see Table 7). It should also be clear that

Table 7. *Distribution of major national groups in Kumasi (in percentages)*[a]

Enumeration area	Country of origin			
	Nigeria	Upper Volta	Togo	Mali
Kwadaso	1	4	4	0
Ridge Area	1	1	1	0
Amakom	6	10	22	2
Technology/including Ayiga	1	1	7	0
Fanti New Town/Asafo	7	5	10	6
Odum/Lake Road	1	6	4	12
Suntresu	1	5	5	5
Ashanti New Town	7	6	7	27
Zongo	32	19	7	20
Aboabo	32	13	12	15
New Town Extension	2	4	6	2
Suame	3	8	2	2
Tafo	2	9	7	3
Northern outskirts	2	4	3	2
Southern outskirts	1	5	3	3
Total	99	100	100	99

[a]Only groups with over 3,000 persons are included.
Source: 1960 Population Census of Ghana, Special Report 'E'.

in the oldest neighborhoods one finds the greatest proportion of immigrants who were born in Kumasi, known by the Hausa term *'yan k'asa* (s. *'dan k'asa*), literally, sons of the town, or by the Moré term *rogoweogo*, literally, born in the bush. This partially coincides with ethnicity, since most of the early immigrants come from certain groups, particularly those active in trade. In the country, as a whole, more Nigerians are second- than first-generation immigrants, and a third of Voltaics in Kumasi were born in Ghana (Table 8). The greatest majority of adult *'yan k'asa* among the Mossi, Hausa, Yoruba, and other early migrating groups live in the older neighborhoods of Zongo and Aboabo.

In interpreting the high percentage of Hausa in the oldest neighborhood, it is essential to note the high value placed upon being Hausa among most Muslim groups, the fact that, to some extent, ethnic identity in Kumasi is voluntarily assumed, and the effect of population growth on the differentiation of ethnic groups in the stranger community. The criteria by which prestige is measured among the Muslims in the zongo are mainly wealth and Islamic knowledge and orthodoxy. Place of birth and length of residence in Kumasi also makes some difference when eligibility to political office or political leadership is being considered. In the early part of the century, Hausa migrants became known both as wealthy *masugida* and as educated Muslims. They controlled many sectors of trade, opened more Arabic schools, and built more houses than did members of other groups. Although both wealth and Islamic orthodoxy could be achieved, they came to be associated with the status of being Hausa. Consequently, many of the first migrants from poorly

Table 8. *Persons of foreign origin in Kumasi municipal area, by country of origin, country of birth, and sex*

	Country of origin									
	Ivory Coast	Libe- ria	Mali	Upper Volta	Togo	Daho- mey	Niger	Nige- ria	Other (Afri- ca)	Non- Afri- can
Born in Ghana										
Male	139	14	252	2,056	918	136	105	5,073	57	219
Female	147	17	256	2,086	947	140	111	5,054	53	175
Born abroad										
Male	244	57	2,733	4,860	2,352	365	915	5,140	235	1,119
Female	109	29	238	1,521	1,662	217	58	3,866	83	596
Total										
Born in Ghana	286	31	508	2,142	1,865	276	216	10,127	110	394
Born abroad	353	86	2,971	6,381	4,014	582	973	9,006	318	1,715

Source: 1960 Population Census of Ghana, Special Report 'E'.

represented ethnic groups identified themselves as Hausa and were successful to the extent that their children were accepted as Hausa. Muslims from trading towns like Salaga, who came from the centralized and partially Islamized states of Mossi, Mamprusi, Dagomba, Wa, and Gonja often identified themselves as Hausa, rather than as members of the kingdoms from which they had come, claiming that they were originally of Hausa descent. Insofar as the Hausa controlled certain sectors of trade, becoming a Hausa could present distinct economic advantages for the individual. Admitting to their community successful non-Hausa who were willing to assimilate and identify themselves as Hausa may also have been one way in which the Hausa actually preserved a preeminent position in certain fields.

However, as the population of Kumasi increased, distinctions in status within the Hausa group developed, based upon whether or not an individual or group was "pure" Hausa, Hausa *sosai*. These distinctions were, as in the case of the Mossi, based on place of origin, rather than on traditional statuses. Thus, being of Fulani background was not as important in defining Hausa identity in the context of the zongo, as a whole, as was simply coming from a Hausa-speaking area of northern Nigeria. The rejection of a group of immigrants as Hausa would lead to its reidentification as a separate ethnic group.[8] Thus, in 1933 a group of people from Salaga proposed a candidate for the office of Hausa headman. Rejected by the other Hausa, the Hausa *sosai*, on the ground that he was not real Hausa, the Salaga people then attempted to join the Asante Nkramo community, basing their claim on the fact that Salaga was in Asante's former tributary state of Gonja. They asked to serve the

Asantehene directly, through his Imam and through the Nsumankwahene, the court official responsible for the Asante Nkramo community. This request was refused by the Asantehene and the Asante Nkramo Imam, on the ground that these Salaga people were recent migrants to Kumasi and that as strangers they were part of the zongo. After this, the group identified itself as the Gonja community and installed a Gonja headman, although in the eyes of the Asantehene and the British the Gonja were still under the authority of the Hausa headman. They were, however, given permission to perform their own marriage ceremonies (*District Record Book 1926–1951*, June, 1933, and September, 1934, ADM 51/5/6).

Without detailed investigations into individual case histories it is difficult to tell whether many of the Kumasi-born Hausa in the oldest neighborhood, Yelwa, are Hausa by virtue of their parents' assimilation or by descent. This ambiguity is evident in the population of all areas but is particularly obvious in the older neighborhoods, where the number of generations of settlement is greatest and where the residents are descendants of people who migrated to Kumasi when the zongo was just starting. At that time, when the main socio-political opposition relevant for the zongo was between all the Muslim strangers and the local Asante population, ethnic differentiation within the stranger community was in some ways less marked than it was to become. The growth of the zongo has led to internal segmentation, so that by the 1930s many people who formerly might have identified themselves as Hausa became Mossi, Grusi, Gonja, Dagomba, and so on. Individuals who had succeeded in one way or another as Hausa no doubt maintained that identity, but many others sought to raise the status of their own groups instead. In a heterogeneous community such as Kumasi zongo, where ethnic identity is an aspect of social status and individuals tend to rank groups hierarchically, ethnic communities that become too large begin to lose their effectiveness in conferring status or prestige (see chapter 11). If membership is not restricted, they are not able to express the distinctive identity and interests of their members. It is, then, not surprising that every ethnic community with more than five hundred members has appointed a separate headman (Table 9).

The meaning of the term "zongo"

It should already be clear that the term *zongo* as used in Kumasi has different meanings which vary according to the context in which it is used and the identity of the speaker. In the beginning of the century the term was used to describe a neighborhood and, by extension, it was applied to the inhabitants of that area (and later of other areas) who were regarded as members of the zongo community. From the Asante and European points of view, the zongo community included all northerners who were recent migrants, and who therefore were strangers vis-à-vis the Asante. It did not include northerners who were incorporated into the Asante Nkramo community or former slaves of northern origin, all of whom were, for some purposes at least, regarded as Asante. Nor did it include southern Ghanaian migrants.

To an outsider – an Asante, a southerner, or a European – the zongo community

Table 9. *Rank order, by size of immigrant groups in Kumasi*

Ethnic group[a]	Population
Yoruba	9,800
Hausa	8,010
Mossi	5,150
Busansi	5,010
Frafra	4,750
Grusi, w.o.s.	4,270
Dagomba	3,830
Dagati	2,330
Kanjaga	2,140
Gonja	2,100
Wangara	2,100
Songhai (Gao)	2,010
Gurma	1,860
Fulani	1,780
Zabarama	1,770
Kotokoli (Tem)	1,500
Sisala	1,010
Kusasi	990
Wala	970
Mamprusi	520

[a] All of these groups had a headman in Kumasi in 1966, with the exception of the Dagati, who were about to install one. The only other immigrant headman in Kumasi is the leader of the Yadse (s. Yadiga), who are included with the Mossi in the census.
Source: 1960 Population Census of Ghana, Special Report 'E'.

often appears to be culturally unified, if not homogeneous. On some levels this unity is real, and among second- and third-generation immigrants a common immigrant culture is emerging. This unity is expressed by the use of Hausa as a *lingua franca,* by the adherence of most immigrants to Islam, by residential clustering in neighborhoods and houses predominantly inhabited by northerners, by the similar Muslim dress and behavior of many migrants, and by their common involvement in trading activities and unskilled jobs. The fact that all northerners and aliens are regarded as strangers by Asantes and other southern Ghanaians also adds to their apparent unity.

Nevertheless, today, when the zongo includes first-, second-, and third-generation immigrants, short- and long-term residents, and members of many groups acculturated to the life of the immigrant community in varying degrees, there is still no single set of characteristics which describe all persons who may, at some time or another, be identified and identify themselves as members of the zongo. Cultural characteristics, like place of residence, are not absolute criteria indicating that a person is part of the zongo community, yet these factors all, at different times, may be crucial components of an individual's identity. Membership in the zongo, like ethnic identity, is defined situationally. Both are types of identities but ethnic identity is associated with both a common place of origin and the idea of a kinship link uniting the members. Only the first could apply to the zongo, since they all consider themselves to be northerners. A Frafra (Tallensi) may be regarded as part of the zongo by an Asante but not by a Hausa – in the first case, because he is a northern migrant; in the second, because he probably is not a Muslim. Moreover, a group may identify with the zongo community in some situations and not in others. Thus, in a 1968 dispute over the succession to the Imamate of the central mosque (Schildkrout 1974a), most Dagombas maintained that, as Ghanaian citizens, they were not part of the zongo, which they defined in this situation as a community of non-Ghanaian strangers under the informal ritual leadership of the Hausa. (The Hausa had always provided the Imam of the central mosque.) The Dagomba candidate for the Na'ib, the office of the Imam's assistant, attempted to identify himself with a national Ghanaian Muslim community and tried to disqualify the Hausa candidate on the grounds of citizenship, claiming that the Hausa were indisputably aliens, since their place of origin was outside Ghana. A few months earlier the headman of the Dagomba community had petitioned the government on another matter as a member of the zongo, with the Hausa and others who were regarded as aliens. Yet, in one phase of the dispute over the mosque he found it advantageous to repudiate this identification and regard himself simply as a Ghanaian. He was then operating in a national, not a local, context in which he was a northern Ghanaian, not a stranger in Asante.

The zongo community is in no sense a bounded unit. Most Asante and southern Ghanaians think of it as the community of northern strangers, from northern Ghana and the savannah zones of the surrounding countries. They assume that it is a Muslim community, since many of the immigrant leaders are Muslims, but they will often speak also of non-Muslim northerners as members of the zongo. From the viewpoint of orthodox Muslim immigrants, non-Muslim northerners may be strangers in Kumasi, but they are not necessarily part of the zongo either, since the Asante Nkramo, the Ahmadiyya, and the Lebanese and Pakistani (usually Ahmadiyya) Muslims are not included.

The use of a common language also does not accurately demarcate boundaries to the zongo community. While most immigrants from the north or from outside Ghana speak Hausa, many do so only in particular situations when they are speaking to members of other ethnic groups. First-generation immigrants from the same home area almost always use their own language with each other. Most headmen conduct informal courts and deal with members of their own communities in their own language, even though they consider themselves to be part of the zongo. Second-generation immigrants often speak only Hausa, but they sometimes form clubs with the purpose of learning their parents' language.

Occupational activities also do not distinguish the zongo, as a whole, from other Kumasi communities. Although the zongo is regarded as a community of traders, many immigrants do not trade. There are large numbers of unskilled and semiskilled wage earners, craftsmen, and the unemployed. Also, many important traders are not immigrants, but Asante or Lebanese. This is true even in such traditionally northern-dominated activities as the cattle trade and the long-distance transport business. The zongo is, however, characterized by the negative distinction of having few members of professions who are literate in English. Consequently, for many purposes the zongo residents must rely upon Asantes and southerners who are government officials, lawyers, Western-trained doctors, firm managers, and so forth.

Thus, one main characteristic that all members of the zongo have in common is that they are neither Asante, southern Ghanaian, European, Lebanese, or Indian – the other main groups in the town. The zongo exists in conceptual opposition to these other categories. Its existence depends on the maintenance of the distinctions between strangers and indigenes, aliens and citizens, Asante and non-Asante, and northerners and southerners. These distinctions are manifested socially, culturally, economically, and politically and exist on both local and national levels. Locally, strangers do not easily become assimilated into the Asante ethnic community, and nationally, legislation prevents large-scale absorption of immigrant aliens into the state. Since the category of stranger as well as other ethnic categories is defined situationally, no stable boundaries can be drawn to define the zongo community, but the fact that the category exists makes the realization of social groupings based upon it a constant possibility.

Given the fact that zongo, as the name of a community, designates a category, similar in many ways to other membership categories, including ethnic ones, we have still to examine its concrete manifestations. What are the cultural coefficients of zongo identity? And what are the political, economic, and social consequences of the existence of this category?

To begin with the second question, we may note that during two brief periods in the history of the zongo, it was formally recognized as an administrative unit. This occurred under the British, between 1927 and 1932, and under the CPP government, between 1958 and 1961. In both periods the government formally recognized a Hausa leader as Sarkin Zongo (Chief of Zongo) and diminished the informal authority of the unofficial headmen of other immigrant ethnic groups (Schildkrout 1970b). These periods were the only occasions when the immigrants were formally incorporated into local government, yet at all other times immigrant leaders have been unofficially acknowledged as representatives of their respective ethnic groups. The government's attempts at centralization failed in both periods because, even though the Hausa had prestige and influence with other immigrants, members of other groups were unwilling to grant them formal political hegemony.

As the zongo has grown, the number of ethnic groups asserting their autonomy and competing for prestige and status has increased. Most groups, including all the Muslim ones, in one way or another appoint headmen who represent them to outsiders and who informally govern their own communities. Each community insists on the equal status of its headman with the others. They are willing to call the Hausa headman Sarkin Zongo but they deny that this implies that he has authority over all immigrants in the zongo. They recognize neither his right to rule non-Hausas nor to appoint other headmen; nor are they willing to allow him to monopolize the channels of communication which each headman develops with officials outside the zongo. Thus, in 1927, when the Sarkin Zongo was granted a tribunal with authority over "those persons of African descent who ordinarily reside in or resort to the Kumasi Zongo, such persons not being natives who owe allegiance to the Kumasi-hene,"[9] riots ensued. The government was operating on the assumption that the apparently homogeneous Islamic culture in the zongo implied that ethnic divisions were insignificant. The Sarkin Zongo was supposed to apply Muslim law, rather than "customary law," to all members of the zongo community, regardless of their distinct origins. The characteristics of being non-Asante, of living in predominantly stranger neighborhoods, and of being Muslim all contributed to this definition of the zongo community. The boundaries of the community remained unclear, however, and it was only after repeated protests from the Kumasihene[10] that jurisdiction over Ga and Fanti immigrants was removed from the Sarkin Zongo. Before these separate jurisdictions were defined, many strangers from southern groups, particularly the Muslims among them, brought cases to the Sarkin Zongo's court.

Despite the reluctance of non-Hausa to grant a Hausa leader authority over them, the Hausa headman was, and still is, accorded some ritual recognition in the stranger community. The non-Hausa headmen are informally consulted upon the election of a Sarkin Zongo and when they personally get along with him, they often meet to discuss affairs that concern the zongo as a whole. On the important Muslim festival days all the leaders in the zongo follow the Sarkin Zongo in a procession to greet the Asantehene and government officials. Disputes between two or more immigrant groups are often brought to the Hausa headman for arbitration. But the important point about all these activities is that they are voluntary. They are not based upon the formal political authority of the Hausa headman, but rather upon the prestige and importance of Islam and Hausa culture.

In all of these informal political activities the Muslim headmen are most likely to participate. They are the ones who meet with the Hausa headman to discuss the affairs of the zongo as a whole, such as problems concerning the central mosque, or petitions to the government for a Muslim court, or formal representation on government councils. Gatherings of these leaders always open and close with Arabic prayers, and the more orthodox the headman, the more he may participate in this aspect of the zongo political system. Among the traditionally non-Muslim and non-centralized Moré-Dagbane–speaking communities, like the Tallensi, Kusasi, Builsa, and Dagati, pressure to appoint headmen has generally come from the few Muslims in these groups. The Muslim headmen who have been appointed have been more successful in participating in the informal zongo political system than have their pagan or Christian counterparts, although these may do very well in handling the day-to-day problems of first-generation migrants.

In the same way, when a headman is not as orthodox as other members of his own ethnic group, the more religious leaders become more prominent in the zongo political system than the headman himself. By adopting behavior which is highly valued by all Muslims, many leaders are able to gain followers outside their own ethnic communities. This sometimes applies to headmen, but it is even more true of urban born malams, landlords, and traders. The acceptance of common norms, of a common cultural code, enables those *'yan k'asa* to appeal to members of many groups for support. This explains the increasing importance of other leaders besides the headmen in Kumasi, a development reflected in the growing role of multiethnic Islamic associations in zongo political life. With the exception of the Hausa headman – the only one who, in the mid-1960s, was born in Kumasi[11] – most headmen concerned themselves mainly with the affairs of first-generation immigrants of their own groups. Second-generation leaders, on the other hand, more often concerned themselves with the affairs of the zongo as a whole. They may have used their ethnic communities as a basis for support, but their political interests and ambitions involved the wider Muslim immigrant community.

Clearly then, incorporation into the zongo political community, for immigrants of all generations, is brought about through the adoption of Islam. By providing a common value system and prescribing common ways of behaving, Islam, albeit a Hausa version of it, facilitates sociocultural integration in the zongo. Although it must be learned and consciously adopted by many immigrants from traditionally non-Muslim groups, it becomes the common denominator which makes it possible for strangers with traditionally distinct cultures and political systems to form, on one level, a single community.

There can be no doubt that part of the reason for the high status of the Hausa in the zongo is the fact that Islamic and Hausa culture are often thought of as a single body of tradition. On many occasions people are unable to distinguish "pure" Islam (an abstraction in any case) from Hausa culture, or from what they think of as Hausa culture. For example, the groups which have had headmen the longest and those which are most Islamized have given many of their elders Hausa titles, as shown in Table 10. Some of these titles, such as Waziri, are known to be of Arabic derivation. Installing a Waziri is regarded more as a sign of Islamic orthodoxy than as a sign of Hausaization, although both interpretations could easily be made. Since Islam is transmitted through Hausa culture in Kumasi, the prestige of the former easily becomes attached to the latter.

Chieftainship is only one institution which has become simultaneously Islamized and Hausaized. The same process can be observed in many other areas, such as the manner in which funerals, naming ceremonies, and marriages are performed. In virtually all of the public status passage, or life-crisis, ceremonies Hausa custom provides a model and increasingly establishes norms. For example, the Mossi, including the Yarse, traditionally circumcised boys just before puberty in large circumcision camps where many boys were both circumcised and initiated into adult status at once. Now, as among Kumasi Hausas, it is done at the naming ceremony, seven days after birth.[12] In marriage, too, Hausa customs prevail. The most orthodox Mossi Muslims in Kumasi will now allow patrilateral parallel-cousin marriages, while even Yarse traditionally prohibited them. The Hausa custom of giving one's daughter as a *sadaka,* or alms (Trimingham 1959: 74, 100ff.; M. Smith 1954: 99–100, 151–4), is frequently followed by the wealthier members of all groups. In this type of marriage, known as *auren sadaka* in Hausa, a man demonstrates his status and his generosity by giving his daughter to a friend, a client, or occasionally to a relative and forgoes the marriage gift (also called *sadaka*) customarily given by the bridegroom. The bride's father also pays the *sadaki,* the formal marriage payment otherwise given by the husband to the girl's guardian, or *wali,* and he usually provides a dowry as well. Many such *sadaka* marriage arrangements are publicly announced in the mosque during the important Muslim festival concluding Ramadan, known as Tukuru in Hausa. Among wealthy Muslims, especially those born in Kumasi, men attempt to gain respect, influence, and prestige through gift-giving. This is justified in religious terms, since a *sadaka* is a gift of alms, a voluntary gift which pleases God. In Kumasi the recipients are generally not the poor – except when they are the donor's clients. They are usually prominent men whose favor is valued. In all marriages, whether bride price is paid or not, second-generation immigrants and others demonstrate their social status by providing a large *sadaka,* including many cloths, veils, sandals, gold jewelry, and enamel pots for their daughters in the case of an *auren sadaka* or for their own and their son's wives in other marriages. Many people display these gifts in the mosque during the marriage ceremony to be counted with the money given as *sadaka* and with the formal payment, the *sadaki.* At one time, the Mossi Imam ruled that these gifts must not be displayed, since this practice made the poor feel they could not get married. When this was described I was told, "Only the Mossi have done this, because everyone is becoming too much like the Hausa."

While traditional Mossi marriages entailed very little bride price, that paid in Kumasi is sometimes considerable. The Mossi (Yarse) husband traditionally went to his bride's house with his friends and finalized the marriage by throwing a homespun cloth (*pend lobere*) over the girl's shoulders, after which she was brought to her husband's house. In Kumasi, although the Muslim ceremony is performed either in the bride's house, if there is a mosque there, or in a mosque near the house of the headman of her group, the husband does not go to "capture" his bride.[13] The standard ritual followed is almost entirely Hausa, including the series of payments given to the bride's family, the custom of covering the bride's hands and feet with henna (Hausa, *lalle*), bathing the bride, and other details. While first-generation immigrants who are not Hausa do maintain a few of their traditional practices, including dancing, drumming, and joking after the Muslim ceremony, among the second-generation these practices are quickly disappearing.

Since the prestige-conferring qualities of Islam are achieved through education and practice, it is not surprising that, in general, town-born immigrants are more thoroughly incorporated into the zongo community, in terms of their sense of identity and their way of life, than are their parents. Among the Mossi and some other groups, this sometimes leads to considerable intergenerational conflict, mitigated only by the persistence of ethnic identity among town-born immigrants. In many situations ethnicity is an important basis for association among urban-born migrants, and numerous formal organizations exist to perpetuate the interests of

Table 10. *Titles of elders of various ethnic groups in Kumasi*

Hausa[a]	Meaning of title	Yoruba	Mossi
SARKI	Chief or emir	*SARKI*	*Naba* or SARKI
WAZIRI	Chief advisor to the emir on legal matters	*WAZIRI*	WAZIRI
SARKIN FADA	Title given to emir's most trusted servant, outside his family (Padan 1973: 434)		*SARKIN FADA*
GALADIMA	Important pre-Fulani title usually reserved for son or brother of emir.	GALADIMA	*GALADIMA*
MAGAJI	Katsina title. Word also means heir or elder brother (Bargery 1934: 743)		
MAJIDADE	Servant or companion to emir (Last 1967: 190)		MAJIDADE
SARKIN ASKI	Chief barber		*WANZAM*
IMAM	Leader of prayer	*IMAM*	*IMAM*
NA'IB	Assistant to Imam		*NA'IB*
SALAMA	Traditionally, a title held by a slave of the emir of Kano (Bargery 1934: 889)	SALAMA	*SALAMA*
MAGAJIA	Chief of women, as used in Kumasi. Traditionally associated with the *bori* (spirit possession) cult		*MAGAJIA*
MADE WAKE	Same as *madaki,* a Hausa title of importance in Kano, Zaria, Yolawa, and elsewhere		
CHIROMA	A title usually given to a son of the paramount chief (emir?) (Bargery 1934: 166)		
			SAMARE
			Wid 'naba
			Balm 'naba
			Bi 'naba
			Timboco 'naba
			Sama 'naba
			Rud 'naba

[a]There are several other titles used in the Hausa community, but not replicated in the others. These include, Sarkin Dawake (official in charge of horses), Sarkin Fawa (chief butcher), and Sarkin Dogari (chief of palace police).

Key:

    Upper case: Titles in Hausa language.

    Lower case: Titles in ethnic group's own language.

    Italics: Office filled at time of fieldwork.

    Roman: Office has been filled in the past.

               Adjacent titles are said to be equivalent.

Dagomba	Mamprusi	Gonja	Busansi	Kusasi	Frafra
Na *Wilana*	*Naba* *Wulana*	*SARKI* *WAZIRI*	*SARKI* *WAZIRI*	Na *WAZIRI*	Na
Kpanarana	Kpanarana	*SARKIN FADA*	*SARKIN FADA*		Kwadarana
Gundana		*GALADIMA*	GALADIMA		
			MAGAJI		
		MAJIDADE	*MAJIDADE*		
WANZAM *IMAM* *NA'IB*	*IMAM* Pegina	*IMAM* *NA'IB* *SALAMA*	*IMAM* *NA'IB* *SALAMA*		*IMAM*
MAGAJIA	*MAGAJIA*	*MAGAJIA*	*MAGAJIA*		
		MADE WAKE			
		CHIROMA			
SAMARE	*SAMARE*		*SAMARE*		
Lu Na					
Yima Na					

second-generation migrants of the same ethnic group. But the persistent importance of ethnicity as a basis for social action does not entail the continuity of the traditional cultural systems. Second-generation Mossi immigrants know that Mossi culture exists, but they also recognize that, although they are Mossi, they are rarely familiar with the norms of traditional Mossi culture. *'Yan k'asa* from other ethnic groups are rarely conversant with any body of custom other than that of Kumasi zongo. For some time, in Kumasi, one group of town-born *'ulama'* (Muslim scholars) from a number of ethnic groups formed a committee which legislated a set of rules they called the "Kumasi constitution."[14] In the name of Islam they stipulated such things as the limit on marriage payments, the prohibition of the ceremony of washing the bride, the prohibition of dancing and joking at funerals and weddings. Insofar as such rules are enforced and obeyed, they constitute part of the culture of the zongo. They provide a model for the cultural adaptations which immigrants from different ethnic communities must make in town. Whether or not the existence of this Kumasi constitution indicates that Kumasi zongo actually has a distinct culture is not the point; people believe that it does and that this is in some ways different from other zongos or from the traditional culture of particular ethnic groups in the zongo. This sense of common culture forms the basis for the existence of what I describe as the zongo community. As Nadel (1942: 17) has written, ". . . There is not *one* community, but a complex hierarchy of communities. The consciousness of a uniform culture defines the widest, loosest unit in the hierarchy of communities – potential rather than 'actual' common life. One turns easily into the other."

From another point of view one could define the zongo as a social unit using the concept of a network, insofar as peole who identify themselves as members of the zongo have many more social relationships with each other than with outsiders, with whom, most typically, they interact only economically and sometimes politically. Relationships within the zongo include those of kinship, affinity, friendship, and common ethnicity, which transcend the boundaries of particular neighborhoods and which may be informal or formal, as in the case of some of the ethnic associations. They also include many relationships formed on a neighborhood basis, including those between coresidents in a house, people who worship together at local mosques, children who attend the same neighborhood Arabic schools, and patrons and clients who work at the same business. There are, as well, many important institutionalized manifestations of the reality of the zongo, including the central mosque, at which all Muslims congregate on Fridays and on the major Islamic festival occasions, and the Islamic associations which unite immigrant Muslims from all ethnic groups and all neighborhoods. There are many different such associations, which are usually formed on the basis of age, generation (town-born versus first-generation immigrants), and neighborhood. Each generation of adolescents forms new associations which eventually become identified as the associations of the *'ulama'*. Both formal multiethnic associations and the ethnic associations, which exist concurrently, set down codes of behavior for members and penalize infractions of these rules. Except in the case of some first-generation migrant associations which attempt to enforce the customary mores of particular ethnic communities, these rules are expressions of the Islamic norms which govern life in the emerging zongo community and which are explicitly intended to transcend traditional, ethnically specific codes of behavior.

The process of incorporation into a culture of Kumasi zongo implies an increasing polarization between the strangers and the Asante community.[15] The process of assimilation going on in the zongo has not been towards the local Asante culture but towards a very different cultural model influenced more by the Arab world than by Asante traditional culture or by Western Europe. While the Asante become increasingly Westernized, and therefore increasingly able to participate in modern government on the national level, the zongo Muslims continue to change, but in a very different direction. Time has intensified the dichotomy between the zongo population and the Asante, for, while many strangers formerly lived in Asante houses, learned to speak Twi, and married Asante women (particularly in the pre-colonial period, but also during the first quarter of this century), the growth of the zongo has meant a decrease in such interaction. Migrants today seldom learn Twi and very rarely marry Asante women, unless the women are Muslims. Everyday contacts between the immigrants and the Asante, with the exception of the Asante Nkramo, are increasingly restricted to business, although in the urban area, where Asante do not regularly employ northerners for any purpose, even these contacts are few. There are many factors which have led to this polarization between the host and stranger communities, including the size of the zongo, the economic position of the immigrants as unskilled laborers and traders, the common cultural background of many migrants, and the importance of a Hausaized version of Islam as a cultural model for the strangers. All of these factors have been reinforced over time by the divergent educational systems in the two communities and the way in which these relate to their position in Ghanaian society in general.

Although they live in a large cosmopolitan city where education would seem to be more accessible than in many rural areas, very few migrants have, in fact, sent their children to government or mission schools where they might become literate in English. The number doing so is much greater now than in the past, and many town-born immigrants who had no English schooling themselves are beginning to send one, and occasionally more, of their children to English schools. Some send their children to night school to learn English while they continue to attend Arabic schools in the daytime.

A brief survey done in all of the neighborhood schools around the areas where strangers lived showed that in 1966 one-third of the primary, and only one-fourth of the middle-school, pupils were northerners and non-Ghanaians, although the neighborhoods around the schools were almost entirely inhabited by these people (see Table 11). There is no deliberate policy of sending children to schools in neighborhoods distant from their homes, and only a small minority of migrants send their children "home" to the north to school.[16] Certainly the settled Hausa and Mossi immigrants do not send their children back to Nigeria and Upper Volta and they, too, are poorly represented in the local government schools. On many occasions the Muslims have requested the government to help them, by integrating Arabic and English schools, but little has been done. During political campaigning various parties have made promises to this effect, and there are a few schools, such as the Ahmadiyya secondary school and the Muslim Mission school, which do have government support, but most of the Arabic schools are not approved by the government, have no government support, and do not conform to the curriculum in government schools.

On the other hand, the standard of Arabic scholarship is high in Kumasi, according to the Muslims themselves, and most immigrants do send their children to local or even distant Arabic schools. The most conscientious sometimes send them outside to study with famous teachers as far away as Senegal, northern Nigeria, and

Table 11. *Ethnic identities of school children in five primary and two middle schools in Asawase, Aboabo, Zongo areas*[a]

Ethnic category	Primary schools	Middle schools
Asante	1,308	198
Fanti	527	48 (1)[b]
Ga	78	9
Ewe	166	13
Nzima	31 (4)	2 (1)
Krobo	6 (3)	1 (1)
Akwapim	15 (3)	4 (1)
Adangbe	7 (1)	
Ada	8 (1)	
Kwahu	45 (2)	7 (1)
Brong/Ahafo	3 (2)	
Sefwi		1 (1)
Agona	5 (2)	
Busansi	76 (4)	
Banda	1 (1)	
Basari	1 (1)	1 (1)
Dagomba	20 (4)	8
Dagati	3 (2)	
Frafra	25 (4)	3
Fulani	1 (2)	1 (1)
Gao (Songhai)	1 (1)	
Gonja	5 (3)	
Grusi	19 (3)	2
Gurma	5 (2)	
Hausa	260 (3)	22
Ibo	108 (2)	5 (1)
Kanjaga (Builsa)	5 (2)	
Kotokoli (Tem)	9 (1)	
Kusasi	3 (3)	9
Mossi	49	2
Mamprusi	1 (1)	
Wala	2 (2)	
Wangara	20 (3)	2 (1)
Yoruba	181 (3)	45
"Nigerian"	142 (3)	
Sisala	12 (1)	
Zabarama (Songhai)	3 (1)	
"Togolese"		6 (1)
Arab		1 (1)
Northerner	165 (1)	
Niger Republic (Songhai)		1 (1)
Dendi (Songhai)	1 (1)	
Chokosi	3 (1)	
Total northerners and non-Ghanaians	1,121 (33.5%)	99 (26%)
Total Akans and southerners	2,199 (66.5%)	283 (74%)
Total all tribes	3,320 (100%)	382 (100%)

[a]This survey was conducted in all schools near the main centers where strangers live – in the Zongo, Aboabo, Asawase, New Tafo, and Sabon Zongo. The Local Authority primary schools were Asawase, New Aboabo, Adukrom Presbyterian (in Aboabo), New Tafo, and Akurem (in Aboabo). The middle schools were Asawase and New Aboabo.

[b]Numbers in parentheses indicate that this group was not specified in all schools and show the number of schools in which the ethnic category appeared. When a group was not specified there were no students in this category or, in a few cases, students in this group may have been counted in another related group. Ethnic labels are those given by students and teachers.

even, in one or two cases, the United Arab Republic (Hodgkin 1966; Wilks 1968). Boys and girls both go to Arabic schools, and although many only memorize the Qur'an, others gain considerable competence in Arabic and Islamic literature and law. Yet this education has only rarely been supplemented with training in English. In the past, immigrants refused to send their children to government or mission schools, on the ground that there they were induced to abandon Islam, become Christians, and "become Asante." In the view of many immigrants, this was clearly a threat. The alternative educational system of the Muslims seemed to offer prestige and even a limited but real basis for economic and political power in the zongo. At least until Ghanaian independence, when the issue of citizenship made the immigrant aliens' position tenuous,[17] this identification with a distinctive stranger community seemed to present advantages in terms of participation in supranational networks of trade and social relations. However, the expression of this identification in the reluctance of the Muslims to send their children to English-language schools was, in many ways, ultimately disadvantageous, in that it precluded the possibility of full participation in the national political arena, leaving the strangers vulnerable to vicissitudes in the national political and economic situation.

Many of the strangers have dealt with this precarious position by attempting to maintain as many options as possible. This has by no means always been possible, as, for example, in 1969, when all unregistered aliens were asked to leave the country. However, during those periods when attitudes and official policy towards strangers are most tolerant it is useful to be able to identify oneself with a number of communities defined in different ways: according to nationality, religion, ethnicity, or place of birth. This was demonstrated after independence, when national identity became important. No doubt partly because of fear that Ghanaian nationalism might lead to their exclusion, national associations such as the Upper Volta Union and the Nigerian Community flourished among the immigrants at this time (see chapter 7). For those who had broken kinship ties with relatives in their countries of birth and for those born in Ghana, this identity was expressed by carrying membership cards and paying dues into formal organizations. These organizations include immigrants from many different zongos throughout Ghana. Like the older, and still significant, trading, religious, ethnic, and kinship bonds, these national associations link strangers throughout the country, and even outside it, into vast supranational networks. Immigrants are able to move from one zongo to another with ease; marriages are often made between strangers of different zongos; trading relationships are easily established; and politics is barely comprehensible without taking account of such links. Thus, although Kumasi zongo has its particular local character, its specific ways of performing funerals, of greeting the Asantehene and the administration, its patterns of speech, and so on, it forms part of one or more larger stranger communities whose boundaries extend far outside Ghana. These communities are defined in many ways, according to different and coexisting principles of identification. These alternative bases of identification are valuable, for they offer multiple sources of support and, sometimes, protection to strangers, not only in Kumasi itself, but also in Ghana and West Africa generally.

5

Ethnicity and the domestic context

The emergence of a sense of community and a common set of values among zongo people results from multiple processes of sociocultural integration which take place in all fields of social life. In politics, economics, in their marriage and kinship relationships, immigrants from varied cultural backgrounds learn to cooperate, accept each other's differences, and discover areas of common interest. Frequent interaction in these different domains leads to the development of new values which characterize and guide life in Kumasi zongo, and which differ from the traditional values of each immigrant group. The dynamics of these processes of integration are most easily observed in the domestic field, which is also the primary context for the development of a sense of common identity among the immigrants in Kumasi.

The typical dwelling unit in Kumasi zongo can be regarded as a microcosm of the zongo community itself, for each house is composed of unrelated individuals from many ethnic communities, who live together in a confined area. In this chapter the factors which affect household composition, the kinds of relationships that develop between coresidents, and the ways in which these contribute to social integration are described. Because very few dwellings are self-contained social units in any sense, it is also necessary to consider relationships which link individuals who live in different houses and different neighborhoods – links of kinship and common ethnicity.

There are two complementary processes which contribute to integration in the domestic field. One is the coresidence of unrelated individuals of heterogeneous background within the context of the house; the other is the dispersal of kin and members of the same ethnic category in different houses and neighborhoods and the formation of social networks reuniting these individuals. Coresidence of unrelated individuals and small clusters of kin creates what one could call bounded networks within the context of the house; however, they are bounded only in the sense that the house itself provides the criterion of inclusion. The dispersal of kin and coethnics in different houses and neighborhoods could likewise be analyzed in terms of unbounded, ego-centered networks. These analogies refer to two aspects of a single social process, for, as kin disperse and move out of houses, non-kin move in.

Ethnicity and the domestic context

The heterogeneity of houses is maintained by the operation of certain principles of residence which continually separate kin. Most important are a prevalent pattern of virilocal marriage and the residential separation of adjacent generations. Historical and demographic factors have led to crowding in some neighborhoods, which, in turn, has often led to the residential separation of spouses and kin. Economic individualism also results in the dispersal of kin and the consequent aggregation of non-kin within the house, for houseowners often have their eyes on profit as much as on any obligation to support parasitic relatives.[1]

Although the house may be taken as a unit for study, it is by no means a bounded social entity. It is a physical structure within which people meet and perform certain daily tasks. The residents of a house do not form a household in any functional sense. As I am using the term, a household is a group which provides and prepares food together and which may be coresident. All residents in a house seldom belong to one household, and all members of a household may not always sleep or eat in the same house. The house in Kumasi cannot be defined in terms of any single criterion. There are three elements to be considered: the physical unit of the house; its composition, that is, the persons who meet and live together in it; and the activities they perform there, including sleeping and preparing and eating food. These may be combined in many different ways, producing different kinds of houses and households, and no variable alone can be used to define these units.

The material on which this section is based is derived mainly from a survey of Mossi-owned houses in four neighborhoods in Kumasi. For the purposes of our survey, house of residence was defined as the house where a person sleeps, at least part of the time, except in the cases of two men who had wives in two houses in the sample; these men were counted in only one house. The neighborhoods were selected because they were all settled at different periods. In order of age, they are Zongo Estate and Old Zongo (referred to here simply as Zongo), Aboabo, YateYate, and Mossi Zongo. The average age of houses in these neighborhoods varies from well over twenty-five years in Zongo to less than five years in Mossi Zongo. Most of the houses in Zongo were built approximately forty years ago, for by 1925 this area was completely settled. All of the present houseowners in this neighborhood have either inherited or bought their houses, and a very large proportion of them were born in Kumasi. In Aboabo most houses are about twenty-five years old, and all but three of them are over fifteen years old. The neighborhood of Aboabo is really a combination of two areas, Aboabo No. 1 and Aboabo No. 2, but I have not distinguished them in this chapter. Aboabo No. 1, nearer the Zongo, was settled first, while Aboabo No. 2, near the Accra Road, is slightly newer. Both sections are considerably older than YateYate and younger than Zongo. The houses in YateYate were built between five and fifteen years ago, in most cases by their present owners. Two were built less than five years ago. In Mossi Zongo, two houses are between five and ten years old, and the rest are five years or less. In both new neighborhoods (YateYate and Mossi Zongo), the majority of owners and adult residents are first-generation immigrants.

I describe and compare data from these four neighborhoods and suggest that

99

certain trends of development may be observed in this way. For one thing, it is
of historical interest to note the differences between these neighborhoods, all of
which represent different sectors of the contemporary immigrant community.
At the same time, the behavior observed in the oldest neighborhoods among adults
who are born in Kumasi may eventually be characteristic of the children of first-
generation migrants who are now living in the newer neighborhoods. This is suggested by the structural similarities between the houses in all four areas. Immigrants
born in Kumasi have quite different attitudes towards ethnic identity than their
parents. There is no traditional cultural basis to ethnicity among the *'yan k'asa,*
and their sense of identity, their attitudes towards their own group and towards
others, is developed first of all within the context of the house and the neighborhood. In all neighborhoods, houses are ethnically heterogenous, and in all of them
intergenerational differences between those who were born in Kumasi and their
parents, born in the north, are obvious. But these differences become less important in the older neighborhoods, where a majority of residents were born in town.
This variation between the neighborhoods depends upon the continuation of a
current trend: that of new migrants acquiring houses in the new areas, while the
population of the older neighborhoods maintains itself, not by immigration, but
simply through the cycle of life and death. The trend so far has been that after an
initial influx of population, migration subsides, and the demographic balance is
maintained by births, deaths, and internal changes of residence from one house to
another.

The number of houses studied in each neighborhood varies, depending upon the
size of the households, and the total number of Mossi-owned houses in each
neighborhood. I had hoped to include all Mossi-owned houses in each neighborhood, but this proved impossible, since some houseowners who were not living in
Kumasi could not be contacted.[2] The houses that were studied are typical of most
of the others in the same neighborhood. One rather unusual house was studied
intensively in still a different neighborhood, but it does not appear in the tables.
It was an instructive case, because it was the only house I discovered which was
made up entirely of a single set of kin.

Houses with Mossi owners were selected for several reasons. First, it was hoped
that this would provide information about the economic activities of the Mossi in
Kumasi, particularly about their investments in property. Second, houseowners
fulfill a key leadership role, since most owners are in a position to act as patrons
in a variety of ways. A detailed study of the roles of houseowners has therefore
provided data about patron/client relations and about the basis of authority in the
zongo. Third, a selection of Mossi-owned houses provides information about the
ethnic distribution of the immigrant population in the zongo. Although ethnic
groups do not dominate territorial areas, this detailed house census indicates that
there is some clustering of ethnic communities within particular houses, at least
among the Mossi. Mossi constitute just under 50 percent of the population in
Mossi-owned houses. If this clustering is typical of houseowners of other groups,
as I suspect it is, then this is one way in which members of the same ethnic com-

Table 12. *Characteristics of Mossi-owned houses in four zongo neighborhoods*

	Zongo	Aboabo[b]	YateYate	Mossi Zongo
Average age of houses (in years)	45	25	10	3
Average number of rooms per house	15[a]	13.5	12	8
Average number of persons per house	40[a]	38	26	14
Number of houses studied	13	26	19	31
Total number of houses owned by Mossi	15	42	25	45
Total neighborhood population	476	959	495	442

[a]These figures would be slightly higher, had not two houses been included in which only half the house was owned by a Mossi, and only that half was enumerated. They were included because they provided data on the relationships between residents and owners.
[b]Actually a combination of two neighborhoods, known as Aboabo I and Aboabo II.

munity have more contact with each other than they have with others. Still, almost all houses include members of several ethnic categories, and most are surrounded by houses owned by members of other communities. If the composition of these neighboring houses also shows such clustering, this means that the neighbors of Mossi immigrants are mainly members of different ethnic categories.

Significant differences emerge in many points of comparison of the four neighborhoods. Basic differences which underlie the following discussion are summarized below. In the tables, the population in each neighborhood refers to the total population in the houses studied in that neighborhood. Table 12 shows immediately that the older houses have more rooms and contain more residents.

The neighborhood

The house is a physically bounded structure but it is very much a part of the neighborhood in which it is located. The main entrance of a house may be closed during the night as a barrier against thieves, but it is open all day, and people enter freely, without comment or introduction. Individual rooms are private places and often are locked during the day in their occupants' absence, but the house itself, particularly the central courtyard, is not the private domain of any individual resident, even though it is only slightly more private than the outside space between houses; it is most unusual for a resident, or even the houseowner, to attempt to prevent someone from entering or leaving this area.

In all the neighborhoods except Mossi Zongo, the newest, houses are arranged in lines opening onto long streets. Some of these are paved roads for motor traffic; others are simply unpaved spaces where children play, people walk, women sell cooked food, cigarettes, soap, and other small items, and men sit around talking and praying. Houses are numbered and appear on city council survey maps, and the paved streets have names, but the residents do not use these to indicate directions; rather, they mention the name of an important person who owns a house nearby.

Kinship and community

Houses are large square structures built only a few feet from one another on each side, and facing each other in rows ten to twenty yards apart. In the older areas of the town, building has gone on at such a rapid pace that there are no vacant spaces between neighborhoods. Zongo runs into Ashanti New Town on one side and Fanti New Town on the other. Sabon Zongo and Asawasi are contiguous and run into Aboabo. The character of a neighborhood changes gradually from the center to the periphery, where it blends into that of the next area. This is important when predominantly northern, Muslim areas are adjacent to neighborhoods inhabited almost entirely by Asantes or southerners.

Within neighborhoods there are many meeting places for informal interaction among coresidents. For children, ethnically heterogenous Arabic schools are important. Among adults, local mosques are meeting places for worship and for the discussion of everyday affairs. Many houses have their own mosques or praying grounds where neighbors and coresidents congregate. Mosques and schools, however, do not foster a sense of neighborhood solidarity or exclusiveness, because of the extraneighborhood extension of individual social networks, but they are important centers where members of many different ethnic communities interact frequently. Like children's playgroups, adult religious congregations are informal groupings formed among peers on a neighborhood basis, irrespective of the ethnic and kinship affiliations of their members.

There is a mosque known as the Mossi mosque and another called the Yoruba mosque, but these names merely refer to the ethnic identity of their builders. Today, both mosques draw their congregations from people who live and work nearby. At only one time of the year do they serve members of a single ethnic category exclusively. During the last week of Ramadan, religious leaders of each ethnic community conduct daily readings in Islamic literature and law (the Qur'an and Tafsir). They read the entire Qur'an in their own languages and attempt to encourage and teach members of their communities to obey the rules of Islam. On the last and most important night, known as Tukuru, all the men gather in the mosque to read the Qur'an in Arabic and in their own languages, and the women cook and send food to the men in the mosque, to the houses of kin, and to important members of their ethnic community who live in the same neighborhood. This is, therefore, a ritual occasion which symbolizes the persistence of the ethnic unit within the Islamic community. Nevertheless, except on the final evening, the notion of separatism is deemphasized, almost as if there is a feeling that this contradicts an important value. Before and after these segregated readings there are daily prayers at the central mosque and at neighborhood mosques attended by all Muslims, regardless of ethnic affiliation.

Neighbors often have other occasions to express their friendships in ritual, particularly on the Muslim holidays of 'id al-fitr and 'id al-kabir. On these days and also at marriages, naming ceremonies, and funerals, gifts of cooked food and portions of sacrificed animals, as well as baskets of kola nuts, are sent from one house to another. Over the years, relationships between neighbors may become very close, indeed. They may exchange children for fostering or hire rooms in each others' houses for members of their families.

During the day, children move freely from one house to another, although they usually eat and sleep in the houses of their own parents, of foster parents, or in the houses of kin who live nearby. Adolescents may sleep in their friends' houses, especially if there is a boys' room or girls' room in one house. Children form play-groups with neighbors and other children from the same house, and adolescent boys form social clubs and sports clubs. In time, these informal neighborhood associations become more formal Islamic organizations uniting neighbors of all ethnic communities; common interests and coresidence in a house or neighborhood form the basis for early friendships, many of which last throughout life.

Clubs and associations, especially sports clubs among youth, are formed among town-born children and sometimes compete with one another on a neighborhood basis. For example, the Wonderful Boys Club is a Zongo group with members from at least thirteen ethnic categories. This club holds dinners at which the sisters and girl friends of members cook, high-life records and the radio provide music, and the members (all males) demonstrate their dancing skills. It also participates in football matches with other neighborhood clubs, such as the Flamingo Club (New Tafo), Red Lions (Old Zongo), Ghana Stars (Ashanti New Town), Bantama Black Bombers (Bantama), Real Madrid Club (Asawase), Eleven Wise (Yelwa), and others. Among adults, neighborhood associations are primarily seen as religious groups. None of these have become very important, however, since the most important religious organizations, such as the Muslim Community, draw their membership from all neighborhoods.

Even among adolescents, there is a constant attempt to merge neighborhood clubs into more inclusive units based on the common interests of all Muslim immigrants. Thus, in 1968 a group called the Muslim Youth Association, but commonly known as the OAU, was formed. This was a federation of fifteen different clubs in all neighborhoods with a high proportion of Muslim immigrants. There were four clubs from Zongo and Ashanti New Town, three from Aboabo, one from Asawase, three from Sabon Zongo, and four from more outlying areas. No clubs formed on an ethnic basis were admitted into the OAU, although many members also belonged to other associations based on ethnic and national identity. All members of the OAU addressed each other as "brother," attended and contributed to each other's marriage payments and other personal events, and, as in most other formal associations, set out rules of proper behavior for members. There was considerable discussion during the organizational meetings about whether the club should approximate the model of the Organization of African Unity or the United Nations General Assembly. Finally, each member club sent two representatives to a central committee, and one chairman was elected. The stated purposes of the club included the promotion of unity and solidarity among members, the celebration of Muslim festivals, mutual aid, and the promotion of "international cooperation," that is, cooperation between members of different neighborhoods and different ethnic communities. This group, like the member clubs, from time to time took stands on major political issues affecting the immigrant community, such as national and local elections and the dispute over the central mosque. When some of the elders in the Muslim Community refused to consider a reconciliation with members of yet another group, the Muslim Mission, during the 1969 dispute over the Imamate of the central mosque, the OAU, claiming to represent zongo youth, began to negotiate with the elders of the Muslim Community to encourage them to compromise, in the interest of brotherhood and unity in the zongo. They explicitly emphasized that conflicts among Muslims made the community, as a whole, vulnerable to pressure and exploitation by outside politicians.

There are a number of important reasons why neighborhood clubs never become highly competitive, or really focus competition for power or socioeconomic status. For one thing, there is a great deal of mobility between neighborhoods in the sense that many people live in several different areas in the course of their lives, and some live in more than one neighborhood at a time. This happens with some polygamous families, in which one or the other spouse changes houses every few days. It also occurs when members of adjacent generations in the same family eat in one house and sleep in another. Thus, ties of kinship and affinity, friendship and common ethnic affiliation, cut across neighborhoods and minimize the importance of neighborhoods as bases of personal and communal identity. Because of these factors, and because of the pervading structural opposition between strangers and the local population, class differences do not differentiate the various northern immigrant neighborhoods from one another. Within the stranger community people do not attain a particular socioeconomic identity through residence in a particular neighborhood (as occurs in some other African towns like Kampala, as described by Parkin 1969). In Kumasi, as a whole, Europeans and African professionals and civil servants, many of whom are southern Ghanaians or Asante, live in more luxurious neighborhoods and in spacious single-family "bungalows"; the zongo community itself is not differentiated in this way. The residents in the older areas sometimes express feelings of superiority over people living in the newer areas, because many of the former are born in Kumasi, are successful traders, and are educated in Arabic and in urban ways. All these attributes confer prestige, according to the values of the *'yan k'asa,* but they are not perceived as deriving from place of residence. Wealth, education, length of urban residence, birthplace, and ethnic identity – not place of residence – are the criteria which enable individuals within the zongo to rank each other, to decide who is a "big man," who has influence, followers, contacts, and, therefore, power. While "big men" may be clustered in the older stranger neighborhoods, simply living in one of these neighborhoods does not confer any kind of distinctive identity. Moreover, to some Kumasi residents, particularly to some who are Westernized Christians and possess a minimal degree of Western education, northern Muslim immigrants and the neighborhoods they inhabit are generally stereotyped as "low class." This occurs, despite the obvious wealth and Arabic education of many of the strangers.

Ethnicity and the domestic context

The heterogeneity of neighborhoods and the frequency of interaction among neighbors means that children's play groups, adolescent clubs, and adult associations formed on a neighborhood basis ignore considerations of ethnic identity. Yet, by late adolescence, ethnic associations which draw their membership from all neighborhoods become important.[3] Immigrant neighborhoods, being multiethnic, unbounded, and undifferentiated in terms of socioeconomic level, are, as I have explained, unable to focus competition for status and for economic and political power. Ethnic associations, on the other hand, are discrete units in which the common interests and aspirations of members may be expressed. Ethnic ties cut across neighborhood ties and become a basis for association among immigrants who feel they have common interests and problems. People feel that they may be able to raise their status or simply protect their interests through cooperative efforts in ethnic associations. However, because immigrants who are born in Kumasi form their first significant social relationships in an atmosphere in which ethnicity is irrelevant, that is, in the context of the multiethnic house and neighborhood, ethnic associations must always coexist with other, more inclusive formal and informal associations. Islamic ideology is learned in the neighborhood context and emphasizes the brotherhood of all Muslims. Thus, the socialization of second- and third-generation immigrants in an atmosphere that is in many ways "atribal" limits the extent to which the divisive tendencies of ethnicity can operate in the zongo community.

The structure of the house

The construction materials used in house building reflect the time period in which sections were built, as well as the affluence of the houseowner. In the older neighborhoods a patchwork variety of construction materials attests to the cumulative building of several decades. Rusted and shiny-new corrugated tin roofs are combined with old packing crates, straw mats, and cardboard, as walls and roofs are added to the original structure, which may be made of clay and earth, wood, concrete, or a combination of all these materials. Whole rooms made of packing crates or concrete may be added, so that the original rectangular structure is barely a skeleton in a complicated maze of rooms. Fancy iron screens, glass windows, and linoleum tile floors adorn some rooms, while others are patched together with cardboard. Tenants, particularly young married couples, sometimes take considerable pride in making decorative additions to their rooms, both inside and out. There is also much variation in the standard of improvements made by different houseowners.

Despite additions and modifications the basic physical structure of the house is identical in all neighborhoods. A set of rooms – usually twelve to sixteen – forms a rectangle around a central courtyard. Most houses have an entrance room which resembles the *zong,* or entrance chamber, in northern Ghanaian and Hausa houses, but this is seldom used in the traditional manner. It often becomes a workroom for

Zongo dwelling, Kumasi

women's industries, such as flour grinding, or a store room for grain, fruit, or vegetables. Sometimes it becomes a tailor's shop or an Arabic school; or it may be used as an extra room for visitors.

A house is never completed. Over the years additions continue to be made. In the older neighborhoods most houses have additional rooms built onto the outer wall of the house. These rooms have separate entrances which lead outside but have no entrance into the central courtyard. They may be hired as shops or living quarters. People who rent them may have little contact with others whose rooms face the courtyard, and the fact that they inhabit the same house may be of little social importance. In one house four outside rooms were rented to Asante crafts-men as shops. People living inside, including the houseowner, would send them meat from any ritually sacrificed animal, demonstrating their incorporation into the domestic unit. In the older neighborhoods, where rooms are scarce – since these areas have more amenities (particularly electricity) and are nearer the central market – the houseowner has an opportunity to select tenants. Outside rooms are sometimes rented to people who would not be especially welcome inside: to non-Muslims, to prostitutes, or to temporary migrants such as the Gao, who tend to hire one room for many single men.

Zongo dwelling, Kumasi: inside view with kitchen area on left

Rooms may also be added onto the original rectangular structure inside the courtyard. Sometimes a whole inner rectangle of rooms is added, so that every room becomes a "chamber and hall." A veranda opening onto the courtyard may be added first, and walls may be filled in later, so that the veranda becomes an inner set of rooms which are then rented for higher sums. Most additions are made gradually but ultimately raise the value of the house.

The central courtyard contains a roofed, sometimes walled, kitchen. Each woman has her own clay cooking stand inside the kitchen area or, if space is insufficient for the number of tenants, she sets up a charcoal stove outside her room. Most houses have very few amenities. There is always at least one enclosed bathing space which drains into the open gutters that flow between the houses. Very few houses have latrines, but in all neighborhoods except the newest, there are public latrines maintained by the City Council. A few houseowners in the older neighborhoods have had water taps installed inside the courtyards. These are usually locked most of the day to avoid waste, and each woman has a large tin drum in which she stores water for bathing and cooking. Some houses in Zongo and Aboabo have electricity, and tenants may pay to have outlets installed in their rooms.

The architectural design of the house inevitably leads to social interaction between coresidents. Rooms are poorly ventilated, for very few have more than one tiny window and a door opening into the courtyard. Therefore, people spend most

107

of their time in the courtyard and in the spaces outside which separate one house from another. "Big men," that is, men who are important enough so that they can stay home and wait for others to call on them, usually have an habitual resting place outside the house where they sit, talking to friends and praying. When they are not trading in the market, women spend most the day working, talking, or entertaining visitors inside the courtyard. Children play, help their mothers, and are bathed there early every morning before the main activities of the day begin.

Women cooperate in many chores, even when they are not kin. They share the cooking area and help one another prepare food. They look after each others' children and share food among themselves and between their children. They must divide the work of cleaning the courtyard, either on a rotational basis or by dividing the yard into areas of responsibility. The former arrangement is more common and is preferred, since it is less likely to lead to arguments.

Kinswomen very often cook together or divide the work according to the seniority of their husbands. When a married man still lives with his father, his wife may do most of the hard labor for the senior man's wives. When two or more brothers live together, the wives take turns cooking for the whole kinship group, or the wives of the youngest brother may do the heavy work all the time. Cowives may help each other voluntarily, or the junior wife may cook for all. Usually, each wife cooks on those nights when she sleeps with her husband. There is considerable variation in the arrangements made by the wives of the same man or of related men, so that it is difficult to generalize. Many of these arrangements between wives and in-laws depend upon whether or not the women are living in the same house. Cooperation is more likely when they are, but in some cases it extends to women who live in different houses. Unrelated women seldom cook for each other, even when they are living in the same house, since the source of their food is different. But friends and coresidents help each other on the basis of an informal exchange of favors, not from any sense of obligation. Old women often receive cooked food from the houseowner's wife or from other women in the house.

Cooperation among women, even among cowives, is limited by the tendency of women, especially those born in town, to insist on their independence and equality. A junior wife, especially once she has children, may refuse to work for her senior cowives. Women born in the north are less insistent about this, but senior wives still find it difficult to enforce what many regard as their traditional rights. In one case, a Mossi (Yarse) man attempted to force his two junior wives to work for the senior wife, while she spent her time making money by selling rice in the market. He soon found himself with only one wife; the junior wives said they would return to him only when he "stopped trying to put Mossi law into Kumasi."

Women cooperate a great deal in caring for each other's children, both through formal fostering arrangements, and simply on a day-to-day basis. Almost all women in Kumasi trade and spend some or most of their time in the market. When they have young children they usually ask other women in the house to look after them. They leave money for the children's food or a friend feeds them, in expectation of the eventual return of a similar favor. Women who have kin in Kumasi often leave their children with relatives for the day, but many first-generation immigrants must rely on the friendships they form with coresidents and neighbors.

These arrangements are facilitated by the ease with which food may be obtained at any time of the day. Every few yards there are stands where women sell food ranging from snacks, such as fried plantains, peanuts, fruit, or chewing gum, to complete meals sold in "chop bars" with tables and benches. Women usually use their own money to buy their own and their children's midday meal, while their husbands use their own money or give money to their wives to buy their meal outside. The husband's obligation is to pay for the evening meal, and the wife's is to cook it, but in many cases the wives also make some contribution to this meal. When husbands are better off they give their wives enough money to pay for the midday meal as well; still, few women cook during the day unless they are doing it on a commercial basis. In a sense, most women regard the daytime as a period to work for themselves and their children, not for their husbands. In fact, husbands whose wives cook food for sale may buy their midday meal from their own wives if they happen to be near the place where she is selling food.

Eating arrangements vary from house to house and are dependent on many variables, including the kinship relationship between residents, economic relationships, including clientage, between kin and non-kin, and ethnic and religious affiliation. In one house in Zongo, for example, one family ate alone, while all the others sat together on one side of the courtyard. This was said to be because the excluded family was not Muslim. Despite the fact that they had lived in the house for over twenty years, and that the man's father had occupied the same room before, the religious barrier remained. It is surely this kind of pressure that forces many pagans to convert to Islam in Kumasi.

It is unusual for a man to eat his meal alone in his room. He may eat in the courtyard or on the verandah with all or some of the coresidents. Clients generally eat with their patrons, and kin eat together when they all contribute to the household economy. Economically independent kin rarely live in the same house. Sometimes, especially in the afternoons, people eat in the meeting places outside their houses, outside the mosque, or in the market. Food then is passed around and shared between neighbors, friends, and work mates.

Contact between coresidents is close, and quarrels are infrequent. In general, coresidents cooperate in most matters of daily living. If there is a quarrel the houseowner may exercise a jural role, for if he is respected the tenants will bring their problems to him. For first-generation immigrants, the houseowner may become a kind of paterfamilias. On one occasion a Hausa man quarrelled with his Gonja wife. She wanted to bring the case to the Gonja headman, but the husband prevailed upon her to take it to the houseowner "for respect." The case was settled in the house as if it had been a "family matter," and the husband later presented the houseowner with a gift of kola. This was something he regularly did, even when there had been no quarrel, but on this occasion the amount was unusually high.

The houseowner may also perform social services for his tenants, such as caring

109

for the sick or arranging naming ceremonies, marriages, and funerals. But he is not expected to do these things, and whether or not he defines his role in this way depends upon many personal factors, such as the relationship he has with his tenants, his income, and his political ambition. The more he does, the more will his tenants come to assume the role of his clients. The houseowner's role also depends upon his choice of tenants. Some houseowners reserve rooms for clients who help in their business; most of the important *masugida* have built up their businesses in this way. Other houseowners prefer to rent their rooms to unknown people of different ethnic categories, since they claim it is easier to collect rent from them or to evict them if they don't pay. These are usually houseowners who do not also use their houses as trading establishments; the income they derive in rents is their primary interest in the house. In these cases the houseowners take little or no personal interest in their tenants: the less involvement, the better, as far as they are concerned. Still other landlords may give many of their rooms to kin, sometimes in exchange for services of some kind, and at other times merely to fulfill what they perceive as an obligation. The role a landlord assumes also depends upon whether or not he lives in the house. Nonresident owners generally have less contact with tenants, although sometimes they, too, are called in to arbitrate disputes.

Whatever the kinship or business relationship between landlord and tenant, his status as a landlord confers respect from his own tenants and in the community. Tenants formally greet resident houseowners every morning and evening; they inform him if they are travelling; if they are performing a ceremony which involves sacrificing an animal they may ask him to perform the sacrifice. This occurs especially if the tenant is a first-generation immigrant with no senior kin in Kumasi. Even if the landlord does not perform the sacrifice, he is usually given a generous portion of any animal killed. In some cases, when men have wives in several different houses, they attempt to place their wives under the jural control of the houseowner. The idea is that the wife will feel as if she is a kinswoman of the houseowner and will be under his authority. The husband's expectation is that this will help him control his wife in his absence. This is symbolically expressed in Muslim ritual during the festival of *'id al-fitr.* During this ceremony each houseowner buys a large sack of millet or corn, known as *zakat* (Arabic, tax or alms). He measures out a quantity equivalent to four handfuls for each dependent. The measures, *muddu* (Hausa, after *mudd,* Arabic, a measure), traditionally in the Western Sudan represented an obligatory tax paid to the state by the head of each family in the name of each family member old enough to pray.[4] In Kumasi the grain is then given as *sadaka,* a gift of alms, to some unrelated person – theoretically to a deserving pauper, but most often to an influential malam. In this way the houseowner not only extends his influence by distributing his largess strategically throughout the community, but he also is said to have obtained the protective blessing of Allah for everyone in whose name he has given *sadaka.* Any family head may perform this ritual, but it is noteworthy that certain houseowners include as their dependents unrelated tenants in their houses, such as elderly women, dependent foster children, and the wives of men who have specifically asked the houseowner to perform the ceremony on behalf of their wives.

Another example of this is the ritual which occurs in the month of Safar, on the day the Hausa call *laraba gana* (bad Wednesday). The Muslims in Kumasi believe that Safar, the second month of the Islamic calendar, is the "bad month" in which everyone's fate for the coming year is determined. In this month, it is said, God gives the angels (Hausa, *malaika*) instructions about what fate to deal out to each person in the coming year. In Kumasi, houseowners who are able to write Arabic and who know the proper prayers perform a ritual for each person in their house to ensure their good fortune during the year. They pray four times[5] and then write a specific passage of the Qur'an on a writing board. Following Qur'anic instructions (according to informants), the ink is washed in water in which onions have been cut up into small pieces. The final potion of water, onions, and ink is known as *faida* (Hausa), and it must be drunk by each person. On the one occasion when I witnessed this ritual, the houseowner prepared the potion, said the prayers, and distributed the drink to each person in his house, both kin and unrelated tenants.

A houseowner has the right to expel a tenant from his house, and this is some-times done for nonpayment of rent. Someone who quarrels frequently or who is accused of being a witch or using bad "medicine" (*juju*) may be asked to move. These accusations are seldom made publicly, since admitting fear of witchcraft is tantamount to admitting belief in pagan spirits, but they are nevertheless common. Coresident women without children, who are of different ethnic groups, are ac-cused most often. Muslims also accuse each other of doing supernatural harm by hiring a malam, whose use of Islamic magic can cause damage equivalent to that caused by witchcraft. These accusations can also lead to residence changes.

Kin who make no contribution to the economy of the household may be asked to move. Political differences may also provide a landlord with an excuse to dismiss a tenant. During the period around Ghanaian independence, when the CPP and MAP were in conflict, changes of residence were frequently based upon party differences. Also, during the 1969 dispute over the Imamate of the central mosque, some Mossi houseowners asked their Dagomba tenants to leave. Others, however, said that it was wrong to bring politics into the house. The outcome of these dis-putes depended upon other elements in each relationship. In general, relationships between resident landlords and tenants are complex. This makes the dissolution of the relationship more difficult the longer the tenant remains in the house, and it also means that simple landlord/tenant relationships easily become patron/client ones and eventually become phrased as pseudokinship relationships.

The close proximity of immigrants from many ethnic communities leads even-tually to the abandonment of traditional cultural patterns and to the adoption of new values and customs which more adequately fit the conditions of urban life. In these heterogeneous houses immigrants observe others' ways of behaving and ad-just their own behavior to conform. Language is the most obvious area in which this may be observed. Hausa is almost always spoken by women and children in the house.

Kinship and community

When marriages are made between first-generation immigrants of the same ethnic community, spouses may speak their own language with each other and encourage their children to do the same. But in most houses this is a losing battle for the parents, since it is always necessary to communicate with people who do not speak the same language. Children born in the zongo learn Hausa first, if not from their own mothers, then from other women in the house and from their peers. If they learn their parents' original language at all, they do so much later, well into adolescence, at the same time that concepts of ethnic identity are developed and ethnically based associations are formed. Although second- and third-generation Mossi immigrants have formed a club, one of whose explicit aims is to teach members Moré, only a small minority of the members are sufficiently fluent to teach or even speak it.

Like language, other distinctive aspects of traditional culture disappear as sociocultural integration occurs. In cooking together, women exchange recipes and learn to cook foods that were traditionally associated with particular ethnic categories, modifying them to the ingredients of the region. One woman once said that it took her a year before she would eat yams and other forest products, instead of the traditional Mossi guinea corn porridge. Now she cooks all kinds of foods in a great variety of ways. The result of this exchange is that zongo cooking is known for its richness and variety. Asante, who otherwise pay few compliments to northerners, often come to Zongo and Aboabo to buy cooked food. One man said he did this surreptitiously, so as not to offend his Asante wife.

House ownership

The acquisition of an estate – land in rural areas or a house in town – marks the endpoint in a transition from the status of migrant to that of immigrant. Although the change in attitude may come about slowly, building a house may be regarded as a symbolic expression of the transformation. It may be considered a kind of rite of passage. It is an expression of the fact that the migrant's attitudes to such basic issues as lineage membership, citizenship, and religion have changed.

When a Mossi builds or buys a house in Kumasi he admits to himself that he is unlikely to return to the north and that the most significant close kinship relationships he has are those with his affines, his children, and, occasionally, with a few siblings in Kumasi. He admits that if he were to return to Mossi country he would be unable to claim land or property there and that whatever status he has achieved in Ghana can no longer be transferred back to his original home.

For those migrants who were not Muslims before leaving home, integration into the urban community often implies becoming a Muslim and abandoning many beliefs and practices associated with traditional religion. Islam specifically disallows ancestor worship, and, although belief in the power of ancestors may not entirely disappear, public practices expressing this cease. This means that not only is the urban migrant unable to placate his own ancestors without resorting to traditional practices, which he may do clandestinely, but also that there is no obvious assurance that his own descendants will remember him after his death. Moreover, the Muslim law of inheritance stipulates the division of property among all siblings, men receiving twice the amount as women. This means that property holding corporate lineages, also traditionally associated with ancestor worship in many areas of northern Ghana and the Voltaic savannah, do not develop in town. For these reasons many migrants quite explicitly regard houseownership as a kind of guarantee of immortality. As long as at least one descendant keeps the title deed to a house, it continues to be known by the name of its original owner. Migrants who have no children often adopt orphans or the offspring of relatives in Upper Volta, so that these children may inherit their property and keep their names. Every houseowner I knew who did not have children adopted at least one child.

The acquisition of property also gives a person a sense of being a citizen in the immigrant community. Some regard this as a precondition not only for gaining positions of power but also for political participation. For example, when the Zabarama were electing a headman, the late Hausa headman commented that Zabarama migrants who had no property in Kumasi had no right to influence the selection. And when the Dagomba attempted to put forth a candidate for the Imamate of the central mosque, people commented that, just because this man and a few others owned property in Kumasi, they should not think that this entitled them to run for a traditionally Hausa office. When the Yanga (pl. Yana) people, a subgroup of the Mossi from the Tenkodogo area, wanted to appoint their own headman, instead of remaining under the jurisdiction of the Mossi headman, a group of Yarse commented that, since there probably were not more than ten Yana people owning houses in Kumasi, they had no business calling themselves a separate "tribe." All headmen and most titled elders, with some exceptions in the traditionally noncentralized groups from northern Ghana (e.g., the Kusasi, Builsa, and Tallensi), own at least one house, and important leaders often own several. It is a symbol of affluence, as well as an indication that these leaders are committed to remaining in Kumasi.

Houses represent a reliable and important source of income, a safer form of investment than transport. The most wealthy men in Kumasi own many houses; the Hausa headman, for example, owned twenty-six. In the Mossi-owned houses included in this survey only three houses out of eighty-nine did not have rooms hired to tenants. Two houses had all rooms hired; nineteen had more than ten rooms hired; thirty-eight houses had between five and ten rooms rented; and twenty-seven had between one and four rooms rented. Monthly rents between £G1 and £G2.10 per room were charged.

Many houses have rooms reserved for strangers – itinerant migrants, either traders or laborers, who usually do not pay rent but who represent economic assets in other ways. These migrants receive free hospitality, including food and lodging, from a *maigida* in town. The *maigida* may receive a gift from the stranger when he leaves and he also derives income from commissions on trade. Some commissions are fixed: five shillings per cow, one shilling per sheep, for example. Commissions are also paid on other items such as loads of wood, clothing, and kola nuts. The *maigida,* as a middleman, receives a commission from the seller for every transaction which takes place while the stranger is in his house. Some landlords serve as middlemen between Asante cocoa farmers and rural laborers and receive commissions from the Asante employer, and sometimes from the laborer as well, leading to the frequent accusation that they are engaged in "selling people."

The role of a houseowner as a middleman in trade or in the provision of jobs is also politically important. Being a *maigida* is a way of building up a following of dependent clients and grateful acquaintances. Wealthy men are able to dispense hospitality, jobs, and information to new migrants and at the same time to provide Asante farmers and, formerly, government officials, with laborers. They then are in a key intermediary position dispensing the services of migrants to influential members of the local community and helping migrants who come without kin, money, or knowledge of the urban scene. Since landlords so easily build up clienteles in this way, it is not surprising that virtually all of the important leaders in the zongo were originally *masugida.*

Clients frequently are of the same ethnic category as their *maigida* and often become partially integrated into the landlord's kinship network. This happens when, after many years of service, the client is provided with a wife. The *maigida* either pays the brideprice (*sadaki*) for the woman or gives the client a woman he has been given as *sadaka*. The fictional kinship relationships which then develop may last for more than one generation. Clientship is an important way in which metaphorical kinship relationships are created among members of the same ethnic community. Since clientage operates mainly, although not exclusively, within ethnic communities, it is a means of intensifying interdependence between members of one community to the exclusion of others. Clientage also operates between immigrant leaders (as clients) and important patrons outside the zongo, but these relationships are never expressed in kinship terms and involve only the exchange of political support and, occasionally, economic services.

The specific characteristics of the Mossi houseowners in the four neighborhoods vary in ways that may be expected from what has already been said about the differences between the neighborhoods and the early migration of Yarse to Kumasi.[6] More of the houses in the newer neighborhoods are owned by first-generation immigrants. The latter are mainly Yadiga or from various commoner groups who migrated as wage laborers, rather than traders. Correspondingly, most houses in the older neighborhoods were inherited by their present owners. This data is summarized on Tables 13 and 14.

In keeping with the pattern I have described earlier, in which the zongo was settled first by Muslim traders, ex-servicemen, and Arabic teachers (malams) and later by labor migrants, it is not surprising that in the two older neighborhoods a much higher proportion of male houseowners are traders than in the newer ones (25 percent, as opposed to 8 percent are traders, while 11 percent, as opposed to 58 percent are laborers). Houseowners who are malams are found only in the older areas, and full-time farmers are found only in the newer ones.

Since houses provide a safe and productive source of investment, many owners

Table 13. *Birthplaces of Mossi houseowners, by neighborhood*

	Zongo		Aboabo		YateYate		Mossi Zongo		Total	
	No.	%	No.	%	No.	%	No.	%	No.	%
Kumasi	22	85	16	52	1	5	1	3	40	37
Upper Volta	3	12	14	45	18	95	29	94	64	60
Northern Ghana	1	3	1	3	0		1	3	3	3
Total	26	100	31	100	19	100	31	100	107	100

Table 14. *Mode of acquisition of house, by neighborhood of houseowner*

	Zongo		Aboabo		YateYate		Mossi Zongo		Total	
	No.	%	No.	%	No.	%	No.	%	No.	%
Built	0		18	58	18	95	30	97	66	62
Bought	2	8	1	3	1	5	1	3	5	4
Inherited	24	92	12	39	0		0		36	34
Total	26	100	31	100	19	100	31	100	107	100

attempt to build or buy more than one. This is a factor which leads to numerous houses with absentee owners. Other reasons for absentee landlordism are the virilocal marriages of female owners, the occasional uxorilocal marriages of male owners, and the absence of the owner when he chooses to live elsewhere, near his place of work or with other kin who also own houses. In several houses in the sample the owners were living in Zongo, close to their businesses and the central market, while they owned houses in other neighborhoods. Some landlords, then, chose to live as tenants in one neighborhood, while they rented out their own houses in another.

In houses with absentee owners, at least one room in each house is given to someone, free of rent – usually a relative or a client who acts as caretaker for the house. If the houseowner is not resident, the caretaker may select tenants, collect rent, maintain the house, and even assume some of the moral and jural roles often assumed by houseowners.

Houses in the sample with nonresident owners are found in all four neighborhoods, but most are in Aboabo, since quite a few landlords there also have inherited houses in Zongo, where they continue to live. They usually place adult children in the Aboabo houses as caretakers. In the older neighborhoods there are some houses with both resident and nonresident owners, since when these houses are inherited by groups of siblings, one or more of the siblings may move to a different house, still maintaining his or her right to collect rents in the inherited house. In Zongo

Table 15. *Sex and residence of houseowners, by neighborhood*

	Male	Female
Zongo		
Resident	12	4
Nonresident	3	7
Aboabo		
Resident	15	3
Nonresident	8	5
Yate Yate		
Resident	16	0
Nonresident	2	1
Mossi Zongo		
Resident	25	0
Nonresident	6	0

most of the nonresident houseowners in the sample were women. Since many of the women have inherited their rights in property, and since most of these live virilocally, it is not surprising that most absentee owners who have inherited their houses are women (12 out of 13), while most male absentee owners (16 out of 19) have built their houses. In the total group of 107 houseowners, owning 89 houses among them, 33, or approximately 30 percent, of the owners were not living in their own houses. Table 15 summarizes this data.

All nonresident landlords whose houses are not jointly owned by resident kin appoint caretakers to superintend their property. A comparison of the four neighborhoods on this point brings out some of the changing kinship patterns which immigrant families experience over time. In the twenty-four houses with caretakers, half of the caretakers are kin of the owner, but a higher proportion in the older neighborhoods are kin. Since the owners in Zongo usually come from families which have been in Kumasi longer, they have more kin available to act as caretakers, and the kin who do act as caretakers tend to be lineal descendants – children, and siblings' children, rather than siblings, as is the case in the newer neighborhoods. In three cases in Zongo and Aboabo, however, the caretakers are clients who do not pay rent. One is an Asante who has known the owner for many years. Unlike the other clients, his relationship with the owner does not formally involve working for the owner in any other capacity. This particular owner is, however, one of the main labor suppliers for Asante cocoa farmers, and entrusting his house to an Asante is a way of maintaining contacts with Asante employers. All the other caretakers who are not kin of owners worked for the landlord in his trading business before becoming caretakers.

If there is no resident owner this may affect the composition of the house, particularly when the caretaker is not a relative. The number of kin in the house then tends to be lower. In the one house in which an Asante was appointed as caretaker, none of the rooms was rented to the owner's kin, and all were rented to Asantes.

There are twenty female houseowners in the sample, but only seven of these are resident in their own houses. Seventeen of the women have inherited their property; four of these actually live in it, and the others live with their husbands. Several women who have inherited the rooms in which they live (three out of four) have husbands living with them. All these men have wives in other houses as well, so that they are only partially resident in their wives' houses.[7] Three women (two in Aboabo and one in YateYate) have built their own houses. The woman in YateYate is a widow who runs a "chop bar"; the divorced woman in Aboabo was formerly a brewer of pito (millet beer); and the married woman in Aboabo lives with her husband, a farmer, in her own house.

This last woman, known as Hajia, made her fortune trading cloth, built two houses, and visited Mecca. Her second house, in Tafo, is superintended by a foster son whose parents are in Upper Volta. Like the other women who have built houses, she was born in Upper Volta; she is the most active in maintaining her ties with kin in Tenkodogo and she has adopted and fostered numerous siblings' children. On one occasion she returned from Tenkodogo with a brother's daughter and presented this girl to her husband as a second wife. Most of the housework is done by this wife, who defers to Hajia and calls her "mother." Hajia plays an important part in the Mossi women's association. Like men, women may assume prominent leadership positions in Kumasi through their role as houseowners. But unlike a man, the successful woman does not always find it difficult to revisit her kin in Upper Volta. This is due in part to the way in which many women migrate. Hajia, like other women who did not run away from their husbands or elope, was able to claim that she remained in Ghana because her husband was there. Following an established pattern of virilocal residence, her absence did not imply that she was deliberately abandoning her kin in the north. Furthermore, although she has made money in Ghana, it is not assumed that she has abdicated responsibility for dependents in the north.

According to Maliki Muslim law, a man's daughters receive half as much property as his sons. When houses are inherited in Kumasi, the units of inheritance are individual rooms, so that many houses have multiple owners. Almost all the houses (sixteen out of eighteen) that have been inherited are jointly owned. As expected, almost all of the jointly owned houses are in the older neighborhoods, where houses have been obtained most frequently through inheritance (see Table 16).

Since houses and rooms may be sold separately, it is not uncommon to find joint owners who are not kin and who may even be members of different ethnic communities. There were two houses in the sample which were owned jointly by Mossi and non-Mossi owners, in one case a Dagomba, and in the other an Asante. Individuals may sell their rooms to their kin or to outsiders. In time, the ownership of a house may become so fragmented that the house, as a whole, is no longer an economic investment for any owner. The few rented rooms may barely pay the upkeep and taxes for the house as a whole.

Table 16. *Single or plural ownership and mode of acquisition of houses, by neighborhood*

	Built	Inherited	Bought	Total	%
Zongo					
Joint ownership	0	9	1	10	69.2
Single ownership	0	2	1	3	30.8
Aboabo					
Joint ownership	0	7	0	7	26.9
Single ownership	18	0	1	19	73.1
Yate Yate					
Joint ownership	0	0	0	0	0
Single ownership	18	0	1	19	100
Mossi Zongo					
Joint ownership	1	0	0	1	3.3
Single ownership	29	0	1	30	96.7
Total	66	18	5	89	

The expression *joint ownership* does not imply that extended families with joint interests in property are developing. This may appear to be the case when there are many heirs, but in fact it seldom is. In one house in Zongo the original Mossi owner had left two widows and many children and grandchildren. So long as the widows were alive, the inheritance was not divided, and the rents from the few rooms not occupied by kin were used to pay the expenses of the house. When the widows die, however, some of the heirs are likely to sell their parts to others. If they do not, they will retain rights to single rooms. It is difficult to say what happens after three generations, since there were only a few such examples in the sample. In one house in Aboabo, the original owner died and left the house to two daughters, one of whom died, leaving her five rooms to three young children. It is impossible to predict what the next division will be, but clearly the assets will have to be turned into cash, through either rent or sale.

When a house consists of twelve rooms or more, four owners can still realize some profit from their property; but after several generations, fragmentation is so great that if a profit is to be realized, some of the owners will have to sell their rights, or all the owners can rent and then divide the income proportionally. If neither of these alternatives is adopted, a joint property-owning kinship group develops. But, given the fact that kin so often disperse and use their rooms as investments to gain cash, this rarely occurs. The principle of individual ownership seems to be too firmly accepted for this to ever become a general pattern in Kumasi. There is one unusual case of corporate ownership among the Mossi immigrants. This house, built in the 1930's and inherited by the present owners (three brothers, two of whom live in the house), is exceptional, as it is the only house which consisted entirely of kin. All but one person (a Hausa wife of one owner) are Mossi (Schildkrout 1969:

173–5). This is the only house in which Moré is spoken, and today the third generation in this family still speaks it fluently, with Hausa as a second language. It seems likely that Mossi custom determined the inheritance of this house when the original owner died. According to a common Mossi practice, the eldest son inherits the father's immovable property in trust for his siblings, the estate theoretically being the joint property of a group of siblings who are descendants of one man. This house in Kumasi is corporately owned by all of the original builder's children, and it is impossible to specify which son owns each room, as can easily be done in most other houses. Since, however, none of the rooms are rented, the precise division of inheritance is unimportant.

Even so, some segmentation in the kinship group has taken place, since this one house could never have accommodated an expanding polygynous family over several generations. The original owner married five times and had many children, but the only children still resident in the house are those of his first wife, who still lives there herself. All of the other kin have moved away and lost contact with the remaining relatives. This dispersal of kin is strikingly reminiscent of the pattern described in chapter 3 for Upper Volta. After some years away, these siblings lose their effective rights in property and no longer visit each other.

It is interesting to note the social consequences of this unusual pattern of residence and inheritance. The members of this family are regarded as "different" and "strange," and there are frequent expressions of resentment towards them – reflecting both jealousy of their knowledge of Mossi traditions and language and also suspicion about their lack of social integration into the wider community.

As the discussion of joint ownership has shown, adult siblings who reside together are usually economically independent as far as their rights to property are concerned. They are, in a sense, coresident because of the accident of having had the same parent, who gave to each a share of property in a single house. In the older neighborhoods it is unusual to find adult siblings living together when they are not the heirs of a deceased owner, and thus individually owners of separate parts of the property. In the newest neighborhood, Mossi Zongo, where there are still many empty rooms for hire, adult siblings of houseowners are present (see Table 17) even when these siblings are not joint owners. It is likely that as the commercial value of accommodation rises in this neighborhood, economically independent kin will leave and non-kin will move in. In Zongo and Aboabo, and to a lesser extent in YateYate, kin tend to discourage coresidence of economically independent relatives who do not have individual rights to property.

Case I

Thus, Rahman (26)* asked his younger half-brother (63) to move out, so that he could rent the three rooms this brother occupied or use them to accommodate clients and strangers (see Figures 4(a)–(e)). The younger brother had inherited his own house in another neighborhood, and although he derived

*The numbers in parentheses throughout the text refer to the figures, in this case Figure 4(a)–(e). A single individual, appearing in several figures, is referred to by the same number in each figure. The individuals represented in Figures 4(b)–(d) are numbered in Figure 4(e).

Table 17. *Relationships of residents to houseowners in four neighborhoods*

Relationship to owner	Zongo	Aboabo	YateYate	Mossi Zongo
Owner	32 (7%)	32 (3%)	17 (3%)	26 (6%)
Self	17	14	17[a]	26
Widow of deceased owner	6	4		
Child of deceased owner, inheritance not divided	9	14		
Parent	4 (<1%)	1 (<1%)	2 (<1%)	2 (<1%)
Father or mother	2			
Parent's sibling	2	1	2	2
Sibling	24 (5%)	2 (<1%)	1 (<1%)	13 (3%)
Full or half sibling	8	1	1	11
Father's brother's child	15			2
Father's sister's child	1			
Mother's sister's child		1		
Child	73 (16%)	96 (10%)	66 (13%)	98 (22%)
Own child	46	42	51	85
Stepchild	1	5	1	1
Brother's child	8	8	6	6
Sister's child	3	7	1	2
Son's child		15		
Daughter's child	6	12	2	
Adopted child	2	1		
Brother's grandchild	2	1		
Father's brother's son's child	3			
Father's sister's daughter's child	2			
Sibling's grandchild		1	5	4
Brother's sister's child		1		
Brother's sister's grandchild		3		
Affine	27 (6%)	28 (3%)	29 (6%)	45 (10%)
Spouse	19	13	24	39
Brother's wife	2			3
Sister's husband			1	1
Son's wife	2	13		
Daughter's husband			1	
Father's brother's child's spouse	3			
Father's sister's child's spouse	1			
Mother's sister's child's spouse		1		
Sibling's child's spouse		1	3	2
Affine's kin	17 (4%)	21 (2%)	5 (1%)	6 (1%)
Spouse's sister's child	1	3		
Spouse's brother's child	2			1
Sister's husband's child			4	
Brother's wife's brother's child	2			
Sister's daughter's husband		1[b]		
Sister's spouse's parent	1	7		
Son's wife's sibling	1[c]			
Spouse's sibling's spouse				2
Spouse's sibling		5		1

120

Table 17 (*cont.*)

Relationship to owner	Zongo	Aboabo	YateYate	Mossi Zongo
Spouse's parent		3		
Spouse's mother's brother	1	1		
Brother's daughter's husband	1[d]			
Original houseowner's wife's brother	2[e]			
Original houseowner's wife's brother's wife	2[e]			
Original houseowner's wife's brother's child	2[e]			
Father's wife's daughter	1			
Father's wife's daughter's daughter	1			
Sister's ex-husband's wife			1	
Brother's sister's child's wife		1		
Original houseowner's father's brother's wife				2
Other				
Cowife		3		
No relation, same tribe	98 (21%)	259 (27%)	93 (19%)	96 (22%)
Room hirer	30	90	42	51
Dependent of room hirer	68	169	51	45
No relation, different tribe	189 (41%)	517 (54%)	282 (57%)	156 (36%)
Room hirer	68	189	111	68
Dependent of room hirer	121	328	171	88
Total	466[f] (100%)	959 (100%)	495 (100%)	442 (100%)

[a]Two nonresident houseowners not coded.
[b]Original houseowner's granddaughter's husband.
[c]This is also a brother's daughter due to a cross-cousin marriage.
[d]Houseowner's brother's daughter is the caretaker of the house.
[e]The original houseowner was a Yoruba who sold the house to its present owner. The Yoruba man's widow's kinsmen remain in the house.
[f]Ten people who are deceased were coded in this neighborhood, and were, therefore, not included in this table.

income from this house, he did not pay rent to his older brother. Since he neither worked for the older brother nor contributed to the household economy by providing food, the older brother eventually asked him to move. As long as he remained in the house the older brother usually provided the evening meal for the younger brother's family, although he was ambivalent about whether or not he had an obligation to do so. While he asked this brother to leave, he had no objection to letting a still younger one remain. Although this brother had also inherited a house in another neighborhood, he contributed to Rahman's household economy by teaching in his school. Later, even after he married, he remained in the house and kept contributing to the expenses. A married son (18) also remained, but he, too, worked in his father's tailoring business and contributed to the domestic economy.

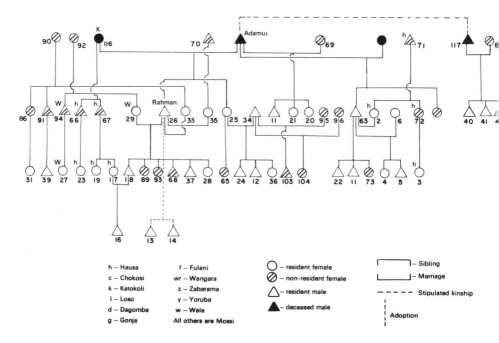

Figure 4(a) Genealogy of Rahman's house.

> Although Rahman was usually referred to as the houseowner, when any
> decision regarding the house was made, he consulted with his older sister (25),
> who owned a third of the rooms in the house. She continued to live in the
> house, while her husband (34) lived in an outside room which had been added
> to the house after it was originally built. Although a co-owner, she formed a
> separate household as far as eating arrangements were concerned. In this
> respect, she was part of a domestic unit including her husband and her two
> co-wives (95, 96), each of whom lived in separate houses nearby. Each wife
> cooked in turn and sent food to the others and to the husband, who visited
> each on the nights they cooked.

Adult sons who are not economically dependent upon their fathers usually move
out and hire their own rooms, while their fathers, if they are owners, rent their
sons' rooms to non-kin. In some cases, when fathers and sons are dispersed in different houses, they may still come together for the evening meal. One father owned
a house in Aboabo but preferred to rent rooms for himself and two of his three
wives in Zongo. His married sons and one wife lived in Aboabo but came to the
father's house in Zongo every evening to eat. The sons' wives prepared food in the
father's house, although they slept in Aboabo. Here, too, this pattern of sharing
food depended upon the fact that the sons worked for their father by caring for the
Aboabo house, looking after the father's strangers who came to trade cattle, and
teaching in his Arabic school.

The above example shows how sleeping in different houses, or even in different
neighborhoods, does not prevent a group of kin from forming a single household in
terms of providing, preparing, and consuming food. Polygyny often has the same

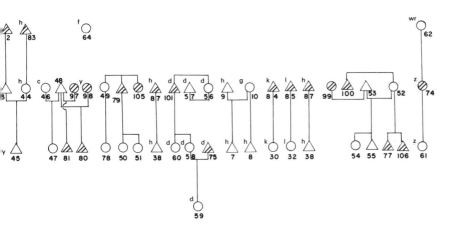

result, since a man and wife or wives may not always sleep and eat in the same house. When a man is not a houseowner, his adult children almost always move out to find their own rooms. Such arrangements are common and lead to daily inter-action with non-kin within houses and between kin living in different houses. The person who sleeps in one house and eats in another has two sets of coresidents, and the residents in any one house are constantly visited by the kin and affines of their permanent members.

The aim of most men who have several wives is to keep them in the same house. It is, however, only houseowners who are invariably in a position to do this. Other men must either live in neighborhoods farther from the center of the city, where rooms are easier to find, or they must keep their wives in different houses, often in different neighborhoods. Although some men say this arrangement is a good one, in that it prevents cowives from arguing, others regret the loss of control it implies. Men with wives in different houses visit each in turn, usually for two-day periods. Similarly, when wives are in the same house, if the husband has no room of his own, he will alternately sleep in the room of each wife. If the husband is wealthy enough to have a separate room for himself, the wives visit him. These alternative patterns symbolize a man's economic status. In only one exceptional case did a man attempt to keep two wives in a single room, but the junior wife had first been the senior wife's ward, had become pregnant by the husband, and had subsequently become mentally ill. These unfortunate events were pointed out as the misfortune that can befall a man who tries to live above his means!

Polygyny is much more common among men who own houses than among tenants, reflecting their better economic position. In the 89 houses in the sample there were 489 married men, 103 of whom (21 percent) had more than one wife. In this sample, 87 of the married men owned houses – although some of these houses were not in the sample – and 59 of these (68 percent) had more than one wife. Among the 65 married male houseowners whose houses were included in the sample, 43 (66 percent) had more than one wife. Thus, men who own houses are about six

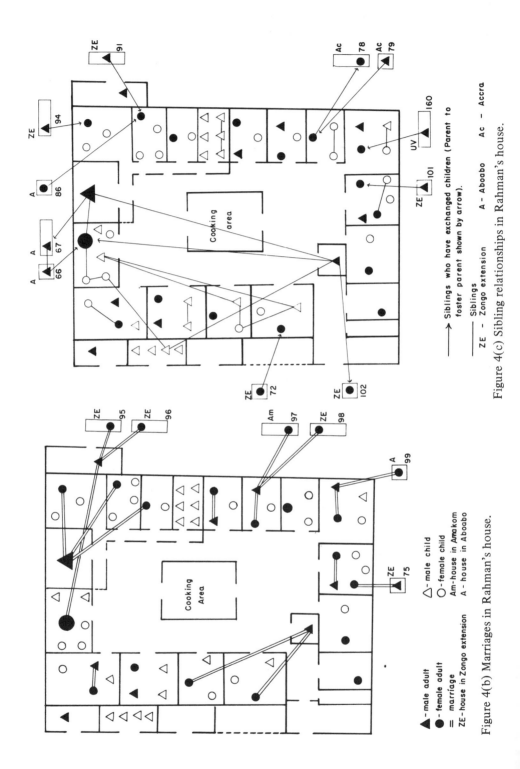

Figure 4(b) Marriages in Rahman's house.

Figure 4(c) Sibling relationships in Rahman's house.

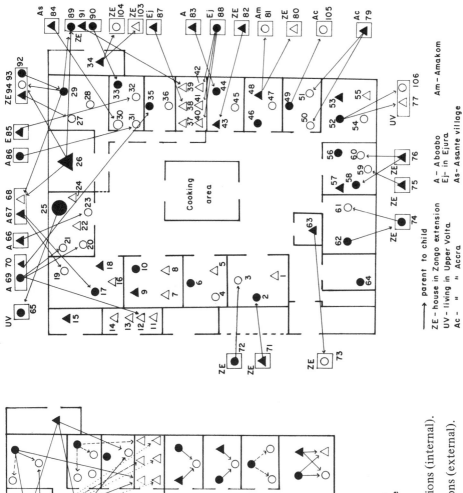

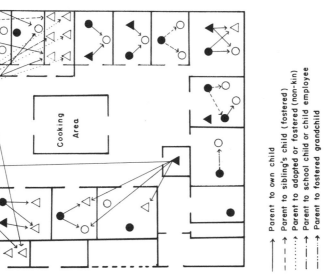

Figure 4(d) (*above*) Parent/child relations (internal).

Figure 4(e) (*right*) Parent/child relations (external).

———→ Parent to own child

– – –→ Parent to sibling's child (fostered)

·········→ Parent to adopted or fostered (non-kin)

–·–·–→ Parent to school child or child employee

·········→ Parent to fostered grandchild

Table 18. *Marital status of adult men in Mossi-owned houses*

	Zongo		Aboabo		YateYate		Mossi Zongo		Total	
	No.	%	No.	%	No.	%	No.	%	No.	%
No wife	22	21	93	31	76	46	56	34	247	34
One wife	49	47	183	61	68	41	86	52	386	52
Two wives	22	21	20	7	20	12	20	12	82	11
Three wives	9	9	3	<0	2	1	1	<1	15	20
Four wives	2	2	3	<0	0		1	<1	6	<1
Total	104	100	302	98	166	100	164	100	736	100

times as likely to have several wives than are men who do not own houses: Houses and wives are both seen as investments and symbols of economic success.

Very few of the houseowners kept wives in different houses: Only seven of the fifty-none polygynous houseowners (11 percent) did so. In these cases there were always factors which led to the choice of this arrangement, such as the fact that the husband had business in the two places and moved between neighborhoods, in any case. In five of the seven cases where houseowners had wives in different houses, the wives lived in more than one neighborhood. On the other hand, among the forty-four polygynous men who did not own houses, a much higher percentage (43 percent) had wives in different neighborhoods, while many more had wives in different houses in the same neighborhood.

I have noted above how virilocal marriage is common among women who own property, but that in many cases the husbands also have wives in other houses. Men never rent rooms for their other wives in houses owned by one of their wives. In only one unusual case, where the second wife was a relative of the first wife, did a property-owning woman give a room to a co-wife.

Table 18, showing the marital status of all adult males in Mossi-owned houses in the four neighborhoods, demonstrates that the greatest number of polygynous men live in Zongo. This reflects the generally higher income level of residents in the older neighborhoods. When only houseowners are considered, the proportion of polygynous men in each neighborhood is higher and, to some extent, equalized.[8]

The composition of the house: kinship

As mentioned earlier, not one house in the sample consisted entirely of kin of the owner or owners. In the eighty-nine houses, 563 (25 percent) of the residents were related to their landlords, while 1,690 (75 percent) of the residents were unrelated tenants. Although the proportion of kin and non-kin varies as families develop, it is difficult to generalize about any kind of developmental cycle in house composition because of the numerous variables which may be involved and because of changes in the pattern of migration. The number of houses a person owns, as well as the number, sex, and place of residence of his children must all be taken into account.

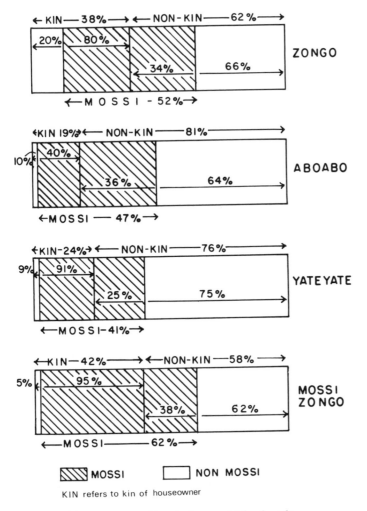

Figure 5. House composition in four neighborhoods.

Since wives and adult sons may live in different houses, rented or owned by the family head, and since heirs may sell their shares to each other, there is no clear relationship over several generations between the size of a family and the proportion of owners' kin in a house.

Nevertheless, it is possible to offer some explanation of the varying proportions of kin and non-kin of owners found in the four neighborhoods. Figure 5 and, in more detail, Table 17, show that of all four neighborhoods, Mossi Zongo has the highest proportion (36 percent of the residents) of owners' kin, including affines. This is mainly because many rooms there are still empty. When a man builds a new house his kin move in first, but as rooms are rented the proportion of non-kin rises.

Houses in Zongo also include a relatively high proportion of owners' kin: 31 percent of residents there are related to the houseowners, compared with only 15 percent in Aboabo and 20 percent in YateYate. This is due to two factors: first, the owners in Zongo Estate are mainly second-generation immigrants who have more extensive kinship networks than do new migrants; second, more of the houses in Zongo are jointly owned by several heirs of an original owner. The presence of kin of two or more owners, whether or not they are related to each other, leads to this high proportion of kin in the oldest neighborhood.

Differences in the neighborhoods also are evident in terms of the categories of owners' kin who live together. In the oldest settlement there are more distant and fictive kin living with houseowners. This is partly because there has been more time for fictive kin relationships to develop among migrants in the older neighborhoods. These ties are reinforced over time by practices such as the fostering of fictive siblings' children. This practice and the fostering of real siblings' children accounts for a large number of cognatic kin in the oldest neighborhood. These children fall into two categories: the children of real and fictive siblings who are also living in Kumasi, but who generally live in different houses, and the children of kin living in Upper Volta. Children described as "father's brother's children" are ones who have been sent by their parents from Upper Volta to first-generation immigrants. Once the original owners have died, these fostered children are described as siblings of the houseowners' heirs, although they rarely are heirs themselves unless the owner has had no other children. In Zongo there is also a higher proportion of fostered siblings' children than in the three other neighborhoods. This is due to the residential dispersal of siblings born in Kumasi and the practice of sending children to live with kin in other houses.

In this discussion and in the tables, the category "distant kin" includes primarily all of a houseowner's cognatic kin, except siblings: parents' siblings, parents' siblings' children, siblings' children, siblings' grandchildren, and all more distant cognatic kin. In Zongo 7.7 percent of the residents fall into this composite category, compared to 2.4 percent in Aboabo, 2.8 percent in YateYate, and 3.7 percent in Mossi Zongo. In Mossi Zongo, siblings' children account for the slightly higher proportion than might be expected if this was correlated more closely with the age of neighborhoods, but in that neighborhood these children are not, on the whole, fostered,[9] for there are eleven coresident adult siblings of owners who are all first-generation migrants. Only parents, siblings, children, grandchildren, and the few truly adopted children[10] have been categorized as close kin. The reason for the relatively high proportion of close kin in Mossi Zongo has been suggested above; that is, the large number of unrented rooms which eventually will be filled by unrelated tenants.

There is a noticeable preponderance of agnatic kin among the owners' co-resident relatives, particularly brothers' children and fathers' brothers' children. This may reflect the maintenance of kinship ties with agnates in Upper Volta, since many of these residents (seventeen) are the children of fathers' brothers who were sent to Kumasi from Upper Volta as children. In the entire sample there was only one uterine relative who had come from Upper Volta; this was a mother's sister's daughter in the house of a female owner in Aboabo. While these figures are small, they lend support to the idea that the principle of agnatic descent can be an important determinant of coresidence in Kumasi for first-generation Mossi immigrants. In the second generation, siblings are not as often coresident, but they maintain their ties by asserting rights to raise each others' children. Many tenants have siblings' children and grandchildren living with them. In some cases this is a continuation of a traditional pattern of fostering (E. Goody 1966, 1970; Oppong 1967), and in others it is a response to the need of urban women to distribute children, so that they can both care for them and trade at the same time.

In all eighty-nine houses, rooms are rented to non-kin of the owners, while there are no owners' kin in twenty-two houses. In eleven houses the only owners' kin are immediate family. In the older neighborhoods, where most owners are urban-born, it would be easy to fill a house entirely with relatives. But owners discourage this, and kin who are not contributing to the household economy are encouraged to move out. In addition to the owners' kin, there are twenty-five room heads, not kin of their landlords, who do not pay rent. Almost all of these are clients of the landlords and render some economic assistance to them.

There are, of course, many other clusters of kin in each house besides the owner's family. Each room head – the person responsible for hiring a room and paying the rent – usually has several dependent relatives.[11] Most rooms are occupied by nuclear families, that is, by men, their wives, children, and, quite often, foster children or children from previous marriages. In the case of polygamous marriages or terminated marriages, room heads are often women. Other rooms are occupied by single men, and in some cases the number of occupants of these rooms fluctuates with the constant arrival and departure of itinerant migrants. The Mossi say, for example, that if you rent a room to a Gao migrant, you can never know how many people will be staying there.

The coresident kin groups of tenants, compared to those of houseowners, are small, even though the tenants may have extensive kin networks throughout the town. Most houses contain a core of kin who are related to the houseowner or -owners. Spouses and children constitute slightly less than half (47.5 percent) of the owners' kin in the sample, and more distant relatives constitute the remainder. The majority of tenants, on the other hand, are small groups of kin, usually nuclear families. The difference in the size and composition of coresident kin groups among landlords and tenants undoubtedly reflects the economically advantageous position of those who own property.

The composition of the house: ethnicity

In the total sample population, half the residents are Mossi, but if one considers just the tenants, only one-third are Mossi (see Figure 5). Thus, most of the owners' kin are Mossi, while the majority of tenants are from other ethnic communities. The high number of Mossi kin is due to the prevalence of in-marriage among the Mossi

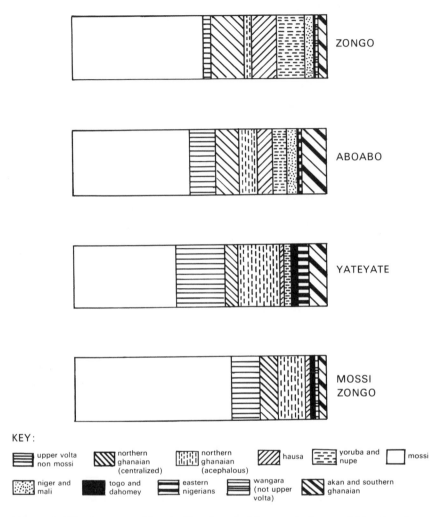

Figure 6. Ethnic composition in Mossi-owned houses in four neighborhoods.

and to the fact that even when Mossi men marry out, the children are counted as Mossi. As far as the tenants are concerned, the Mossi themselves say that it is easier to collect rent from members of different ethnic communities, since if they fail to pay it is not difficult to apply sanctions. Non-Mossi tenants cannot claim a remote or putative kinship bond with their landlord by virtue of being in the same ethnic community, and thus they cannot as easily get away with defaulting on rent. Non-Mossi can be brought directly to court by Mossi landlords, but it is hard to avoid taking another Mossi to the headman's house first. The headman usually attempts to arbitrate a compromise settlement, rather than insisting that the landlord be paid or the tenant evicted.

130

Ethnicity and the domestic context

Figure 6 shows the percentage of Mossi in each neighborhood. Ethnic composition is related to the proportion of kin and non-kin in each neighborhood. The preponderance of Mossi in the newest neighborhood is due to two factors: to the large proportion of kin there amidst many rooms which are still vacant and to the fact that since there are many empty rooms in Mossi Zongo, tenants have a wide choice in selecting landlords. First-generation migrants, on the whole, choose to live with members of their own ethnic communities; second-generation immigrants, living in the older neighborhoods, have less opportunity to make this choice and are less anxious to remain with members of their own group, in any case.

Not all kin of houseowners are Mossi. In all four neighborhoods 10 percent of the owners' kin are not Mossi, but, again, the neighborhoods vary. Landlords in Zongo have the highest proportion of non-Mossi kin, due to the fact that interethnic marriage has been going on among Zongo residents for the longest period. Second-generation immigrants, who are of marriageable age only in the older neighborhoods, marry out of their ethnic community more often than do first-generation immigrants, although in the past, when the male/female ratio was higher, interethnic marriages were also frequent among first-generation migrants. The ethnic identities of the owners' kin are shown in Table 19. Almost one-third of the sixty-seven non-Mossi kin are from northern Ghanaian, centralized groups – Mamprusi, Dagomba, and Wala. Over a fifth are from other groups from Upper Volta – Grusi, Busansi, and Wangara; and another fifth (22 percent) are Hausa.

In analyzing ethnic composition it is instructive to consider all Voltaics as a group. From this perspective, as Figure 6 shows, Voltaic immigrants are found in decreasing proportions in each neighborhood, according to the neighborhood's age: that is, the newer the neighborhood, the higher the proportion of Voltaics in it; or, in other words, the newer the settlement, the greater the correspondence between the ethnic identity of owners and tenants. The Mossi explain these variations in

Table 19. *Ethnic groups of houseowners' kin*

	Zongo	Aboabo	YateYate	Mossi Zongo
Akan	1	1		
Upper Volta, not Mossi	3	7	2	3
Northern Ghana (centralized)	7	5	3	4
Northern Ghana (noncentralized)	2	2	3	
Hausa	9	3	2	1
Togo	3	1	1	
Yoruba	9[a]			
Wangara	1			2
Mossi	144	164	109	179
Total kin	179	183	120	189
Total % of kin who are Mossi	80	90	91	95

[a]These Yoruba are related to an original houseowner who sold the house to the present owner, but they remain in the house and do not pay rent.

ethnic composition by noting that it is only in recent years that many Mossi and others from Upper Volta have acquired property in Kumasi. Thus, first-generation Voltaic migrants had to buy property and settle in newer, less crowded neighborhoods.

Variations in the ethnic composition of Mossi-owned houses in these four neighborhoods can be correlated with the differences that have been described above for the neighborhoods as a whole. In the older areas, there are more members of groups who migrated to Kumasi at an early date – including Hausa, Yoruba, and people from northern Ghanaian centralized states. In the newer neighborhoods, more of the non-Mossi are from northern Ghanaian non-centralized societies. This difference corresponds with a preponderance of more orthodox Muslims, more traders, and more urban-born immigrants in the older neighborhoods and with more wage laborers and recent migrants in the newer areas. These variations are not independent of differences in ethnic composition.

Houses vary considerably in the number of ethnic groups represented and in the size of the groups (see Tables 20 and 21). A comparison of the four neighborhoods shows that ethnic heterogeneity increases as the immigrant settlements in Kumasi develop over time.[12] In all of the Mossi-owned houses, over twenty ethnic categories are represented. Each house has an average of 5.8 different categories represented and, as Mossi Zongo develops, this figure will undoubtedly rise. In the entire sample there is no house containing only Mossi. In the houses in Zongo Estate there are a number of well-represented groups besides the Mossi. There are thirty-seven Dagomba residents, forty-seven Hausas, and fifty-two Yorubas. In YateYate many ethnic categories are represented, but few are found in large numbers. Only one group other than the Mossi, the Busansi, with sixty-nine people, has over thirty-five individuals representing it. In Aboabo there are also a number of well-represented ethnic categories, such as the Busansi with sixty-five, and the Hausa with fifty-seven. The most important differences between the neighborhoods are not so much the number of categories represented, but rather the specific distribution of categories over the four areas. The older neighborhoods are, both socially and economically, centers of immigrant life, partly because of the high numbers of long-term residents there. These tend to be the most orthodox Muslims and are the political and economic leaders for the zongo community as a whole.

Many more residents in the new neighborhood are recent migrants and still involved in varying degrees with traditional cultural values. As Table 22 shows, in Mossi Zongo 10 percent of the Mossi residents have been in Kumasi less than five years; in Zongo this is true of only 3 percent of the residents. In the older neighborhoods there is also a much higher proportion of adults born in Kumasi (Tables 23 and 24). In the new areas most of the second-generation immigrants are children, while in Zongo and Aboabo many children are third- and fourth-generation immigrants. While there is considerable interhouse and interneighborhood mobility, most of this is between Zongo and Aboabo. Kumasi-born immigrants do sometimes move to new neighborhoods, but almost always when they are investing in property and becoming landlords themselves.

Table 20. *Ethnic composition of eighty-nine Mossi-owned houses in four neighborhoods*

	Zongo Estate	Aboabo	YateYate	Mossi Zongo	Total
Mossi	247 (52%)[a]	446 (47%)	203 (41%)	274 (62%)	1170 (49%)
Mossi w.o.s.[b]	152	389	125	271	937
Yarse	66	37			103
Yadiga	27		72	3	102
Yanga		16	5		21
Maroka, Silmi-Mossi	2	4	1		7
Upper Volta, non-Mossi	15 (3%)	96 (10%)	93 (19%)	47 (11%)	251 (11%)
Busansi	5	65	69	27	166
Gurma	5	4	4	10	23
Grusi	1	5	11	9	26
Wangara	2	13	6	1	22
Fulani	2	1	3		6
Samo		8			8
Akan and Southern Ghana	14 (3%)	83 (9%)	35 (7%)	15 (3%)	147 (6%)
Asante	13	46	24	14	97
Fante	1	15			16
Ga		5			5
Ewe		14	6	1	21
Krobo			1		1
Banda			4		4
Kwahu		3			3
Northern Ghanaian, centralized	60 (13%)	83 (9%)	23 (5%)	29 (7%)	195 (8%)
Mamprusi	6	9	9	5	29
Dagomba	37	30	4	16	87
Gonja	8	31	8	6	53
Wala	9	13	2	2	26
Northern Ghanaian, noncentralized	13 (3%)	70 (7%)	82 (17%)	46 (10%)	211 (9%)
Dagati		8	31	1	40
Frafra	3	23	17	22	65
Grusi	3	25	14	7	49
Kanjiaga	5	10	9	8	32
Kusasi		2	5	3	10
Sisala	2	2	6	5	15

Table 20 (*cont.*)

	Zongo Estate	Aboabo	YateYate	Mossi Zongo	Total
Hausa	47 (10%)	57 (6%)	6 (1%)	7 (2%)	117 (5%)
Niger, Mali Groups	12 (3%)	43 (4%)	2 (0%)	2 (0%)	59 (2%)
Fulani	6	6	2		14
Gao		14		1	15
Dendi		3		1	4
Zabarama	6	20			26
Togo and Dahomey	7 (1%)	9 (1%)	15 (3%)	9 (2%)	40 (2%)
Kotokoli	1	8	10	4	23
Basari	1	1			2
Atakpame			4	5	9
Loso	1		1		2
Chokosi	1				1
Togo w.o.s.	2				2
Gurma	1				1
Yoruba and Nupe	52 (11%)	60 (6%)	16 (3%)		128 (6%)
Yoruba	52	47	16		115
Nupe		13			13
Eastern Nigeria	1 (<1%)	7 (5%)	19 (4%)	10 (2%)	37 (2%)
Ibo		4	13		17
Calabar	1	3	6	10	10
Wangara, not from Upper Volta	8 (2%)	5 (5%)		3 (1%)	16 (1%)
Not ascertained			1		1
Total	476 (100%)	959 (100%)	495 (100%)	442 (100%)	2372 (100%)

[a]Percentages indicate percentage of given neighborhood consisting of given ethnic group. Figure 6 shows the same distribution.
[b]w.o.s. – without other specification.

Table 21. *Ethnic groups of adults in Mossi-owned houses*

Tribal group	Zongo No.	Zongo %	Aboabo No.	Aboabo %	YateYate No.	YateYate %	Mossi Zongo No.	Mossi Zongo %	Total
Mossi	99	46	220	42	110	37	148	42	577
Upper Volta (not Mossi)	6	3	54	10	62	21	29	8	151
Southern Ghana	10	5	45	9	22	7	99	28	176
Northern Ghana, centralized	27	12	52	10	18	6	24	7	121
Northern Ghana, uncentralized	10	5	39	7	50	17	34	10	133
Northern Nigeria	25	12	40	8	6	2	5	1	76
Niger, Mali	7	3	32	6	1	<1	2	1	42
Togo	3	1	8	2	13	4	5	1	29
Yoruba and Nupe	22	10	28	5	7	2			57
Eastern Nigeria	1	<1	5	1	9	3			15
Wangara	6	3	2	<1			3	1	11
Total	216	100	525	100	298	99	349	99	1,388

Table 22. *Years of residence in Kumasi of Mossi residents in four neighborhoods*

	Zongo No.	Zongo %	Aboabo No.	Aboabo %	YateYate No.	YateYate %	Mossi Zongo No.	Mossi Zongo %
Less than one year	3	2	1	<1	0	<1	2	<1
One to five years	2	1	3	<1	5	3	25	9
Six to ten years	10	4	43	10	27	13	46	17
Eleven to sixteen years	8	3	39	9	17	9	25	9
More than sixteen years	53	21	57	13	34	15	46	17
Born in Kumasi	171	69	303	67	119	60	130	47
Total	247	100	446	99	202	100	274	99

This comparison of the four neighborhoods has been made in order to show certain trends in the development of the heterogeneous stranger community. The structure of these neighborhoods and of typical immigrant houses, incorporating in the same domestic context individuals of varied cultural backgrounds and varying lengths of urban residence, leads to social interaction and, eventually, to cultural integration in the immigrant community. The effects of this process are, of course, most apparent among urban-born immigrants, and some of the trends can be observed by comparing neighborhoods settled at different periods. At the same time, since houses are built as economic investments, so that rooms are rented to non-kin, and since strangers from many ethnic groups are found in many neighborhoods, kin and members of the same ethnic community are dispersed in different houses and

Table 23. *Birthplaces of residents in Mossi-owned houses in four neighborhoods*

Birthplace	Zongo				Aboabo				YateYate				Mossi Zongo			
	Adult[a]	Child	Total	%	Adult	Child	Total	%	Adult	Child	Total	%	Adult	Child	Total	%
Kumasi	80	230	310	65	185	414	599	62	60	189	249	50	19	166	185	43
Ashanti (not Kumasi)	8	8	16	3	11	2	13	1	23		23	5	10	3	13	3
Southern Ghana	9	1	10	2	16	2	18	2	11	1	12	2	4		4	1
Northern Ghana	29	3	32	7	118	2	120	13	76		76	15	68		68	16
Upper Volta	54	11	65	14	128	3	131	14	102	3	105	21	151	1	152	35
Nigeria	26	7	33	7	34	6	40	4	17	2	19	4	2		2	
Togo	2	1	3		8		8	1	4	1	5	1	2		2	
Dahomey			5						3		3	1	2	1	3	1
Niger and Mali	5			1	25	1	26	3					1		1	
Ivory Coast			2													
Other	2		2			4	4		2	1	3	1		2	2	
Total	215	261	476	99	525	434	959	100	298	197	495	100	259	173	432	99

[a]These are not necessarily the parents of the children listed in the adjacent column.

Table 24. *Second-generation immigrants, by age and neighborhood*

	Zongo	Aboabo	YateYate	Mossi Zongo
Percent of total population born in Kumasi	65	62	50	43
Percent of adults born in Kumasi	37	35	20	7

neighborhoods. The affective bonds of kinship and ethnicity are nevertheless maintained, and associations and relationships – outside the domestic context – are based upon them. This means that the very dispersal of kin and ethnic communities throughout the town leads to social integration on another level, transcending the boundaries of residence units.

6

Ethnicity and the idiom of kinship

Kinship was considered in the last chapter, but only in terms of the composition of houses and the dispersal of kin. In chapter 9, the political aspects of the metaphorical use of kinship terms within the Mossi group will be considered. Here, links of kinship and affinity are discussed, with the aim of contrasting the way these operate within the ethnic community and between members of different communities. Both internal and external relations of members of an ethnic community are in many contexts conceptualized in terms of kinship and affinity. These categories provide complementary models which are used to contrast two sets of interpersonal relationships – those with one's own people, on the one hand, and those with members of other ethnic communities, on the other.

Before developing this idea, it is necessary to clarify my use of the terms *specific kinship, generalized kinship,* and *affinity.* Specific kinship is what the immigrants in Kumasi refer to as "real" kinship. It refers to the relationships which people can describe in genealogical terms, accurately specifying each link between the persons concerned, regardless of whether these links derive from biological kinship or, as they sometimes do, from fictive kinship ties. In Kumasi zongo, specific kinship means close kinship, for it obtains almost always between people who have, at most, a common great-grandparent or, even more often, only a common grandparent or parent. There are very few (if any) adult immigrants in Kumasi zongo who are related through a common great-grandparent, at least among the Mossi. Some individuals claim to have a common great-grandparent in the north, but the community has not existed long enough for anyone to have that many forbears in the town. Moreover, it is unusual for migrants to know very much about their precise ancestry "back home," since in Kumasi such genealogical memory becomes irrelevant. Specific kindreds in Kumasi are bilateral and consist of closely related kin and the affines of these individuals, who are not necessarily all members of a single ethnic community. Since migration to Kumasi was, at most, three generations back from living adults, there are no kindreds with lengthy genealogies, although there are families whose networks of kinship and affinity are extensive on the basis of only a few generations. But everyone in these networks can, if necessary, explain his or her genealogical connection to everyone else.

Ethnicity and the idiom of kinship

In the zongo, according to this definition, because of the short duration of most genealogies, the term *'classificatory'* is inappropriate to refer to distant kin and affines. Here, distant classificatory relatives – that is, those who are recognized as kin but perform few or no jural kinship roles – are usually people who are related only because kinship terms are applied to them, and sometimes because behavior associated with kinship occurs. They are fictive kin in the sense that no precise genealogical links can be traced to justify application of a kin term or the assumption of the jural roles associated with kinship. In time, however, putative biological links are often claimed and/or affinal ties are developed. It seems preferable, therefore, to speak of generalized, rather than classificatory, kinship (the latter often implying a biological link) or fictive kinship (implying only a jural tie and no biological link). I use the term *generalized* to refer to relationships which are, in their inception, metaphorically and behaviorally classified as kinship relationships. All first-generation, and many second-generation, immigrants have many such generalized kin, based upon an extensive use of consanguineal and affinal kinship terms, not upon specific and traceable claims of genealogical relationship, other than, in some cases, a vague notion of having had a common ancestor a very long time ago. However, this notion, vague as it may seem, frequently provides a basis for kinship claims. The idea of descent, unilineal or not, provides a justification for an affective sense of kinship, and although it may seem imprecise to an outside observer, it is nevertheless a crucial component of most kinship relationships among these immigrants. It is the primary means of determining eligibility for recruitment to certain kinship roles, and in particular those roles associated with belonging to the same ethnic community.

Generalized kin, that is, those who cannot trace precise genealogical links, may behave as if they were close kin by assuming the jural kinship roles associated with certain genealogically defined relationships, but they recognize that the obligations entailed in such relationships are voluntarily assumed. As a result, after several generations, the descendants of generalized kin may claim to be specific kin, since they can then trace genealogical links, even if in the first instance these were based on fictions. Among first-generation immigrants particularly, the generalized use of kinship terms and the subsequent adoption of jural kinship obligations is so widespread that it becomes difficult to distinguish biological from fictive kin. In the second and subsequent generations, genealogical kin ties may be derived from relationships that originally were fictive. It is for this reason that I prefer to speak of "specific" and "generalized," rather than "real" and "fictive," to refer to relationships that are genealogically traceable, on the one hand, and not necessarily traceable, on the other hand. Neither category corresponds precisely to "biological" or "fictive" kin, although among second-generation immigrants most specific kin are also biological kin.

The use of concepts of consanguineal kinship and affinity, respectively, to describe and contrast the relations between members of the same ethnic community, on the one hand, and members of different communities, on the other, is one way in which many different immigrant communities are placed within a single

139

conceptual and social framework. There is an essential difference in the way in which members of one's own ethnic community and members of other communities fit into this system. They are placed in complementary categories in much the same way as agnatic and uterine kin are contrasted in societies with a strong emphasis on unilineal descent. Within one's own ethnic community there are many relationships based upon the metaphorical use of terms associated with membership in a common descent group. There are, besides, links of specific kinship and affinity created by intragroup marriages. When kinship terms are used metaphorically to refer to members of other ethnic communities, the terms that are used refer to relationships based upon affinity, rather than descent. Given the patrilateral emphasis of most of the Voltaic peoples, these terms are the same ones that are used in a general way to refer to uterine kin. This contrastive use of kinship terms is one important way in which intragroup relationships are distinguished from those which cross ethnic boundaries.

In order for members of different ethnic communities to be cognatic kin, they must be specific kin, which means that their relationships must be based upon actual marriages between members of two communities. There can be no generalized extension of the idiom of unilineal kinship and descent between members of different ethnic communities, but that does not preclude the generalized extension of affinal terms between certain specific communities. Peoples who are traditionally related historically and culturally often conceive of their relationships as affinal ones. Joking partnerships between them, based upon mythical marriages of their founding ancestors, are given full expression in Kumasi. On the other hand, affinal joking, including joking between mother's brother and sister's son, is not at all stressed among urban immigrants belonging to the same ethnic group. These points will be explained more fully later but may be summarized in the following diagram:

	Kinship	Affinity
Intraethnic usage	G	S
Extraethnic usage	S	G

Here, G refers to the generalized use of the idiom of kinship or affinity and subsumes the presence of specific kinship and affinity, and S refers to specific kinship and affinity only.

In other words, this states that kinship relationships can be generalized within an ethnic community: generalized kinship terms are used, as well as terms expressing specific, genealogically accountable relationships. Kinship relationships which cross ethnic group boundaries are only specific: consanguineal terms are not used in a generalized sense between members of different communities. In contrast, affinal terms are only used specifically within a single ethnic community, while between members of different communities affinal terms may be used in a generalized or metaphorical sense.

For the sake of clarity it is worth reiterating here that specific kinship in the immigrant context is always bilateral; no metaphor of unilineal kinship is used to refer to specific kin, even though the concept of patrifiliation remains the most important means of conferring ethnic identity. Generalized kinship and the generalized use of kinship terms is, on the other hand, invariably involved with the notion of unlineal descent. Since it is used to contrast internal and external ethnic group relations, it distinguishes members of the same "descent" group, or ethnic community, from outsiders, some of whom are, for historical and cultural reasons, classified as affines.

The idiom of consanguineal kinship and intraethnic relations

The Mossi express the idea that they are all one descent group by using the term *budu* to describe the ethnic community, as a whole, or subgroups within it. *Budu,* like the Hausa word *iri,* means "class" or "kind." It may refer to any category of people with some common characteristic, generally one that is inherited. Age and sex groups are not *budu,* nor are occupational groupings, unless these are based on inherited statuses, as is, for example, the blacksmith group in Upper Volta. The term for incest in Moré is *bud pagh gandgho* – literally, to sleep with a woman of the *budu* – indicating again the notion of a kinship connection. All levels of Mossi lineages are described as *budu,* as are the statuses that I have referred to as ethnic communities in chapter 2. Thus, the Yarse, Nakomce, and Talse groups are all *budu,* as are the clans and lineages within these categories. The word *budu,* then, in its most general sense, refers to a category of people in which membership is attained through real or putative filiation. In Kumasi zongo its most common English translation is "tribe," although in many contexts it is used in reference to subgroups within a tribal category, such as the Yarse, or to larger collectivities, such as all Voltaic people.

The most common usage of the term among the Mossi refers to the Mossi community itself, but it is also used to refer to subgroups and to larger groupings which include the Mossi community. These more inclusive units, like the Mossi community, are not necessarily formally organized. However, the recognition of common ancestry is a potential symbol of unity which may be important in particular circumstances. For example, in 1960, the year of Upper Volta's independence, an association known as the Upper Volta Union (UVU) was formed, superseding an association which grouped together all immigrants from former French West African territories. The UVU included Busansi, Gourma, Grusi, Kibisi (known as Chiparse in Ghana), Mossi, Yadse (Mossi from Yatenga), Fulani, and Wangara from Upper Volta. Throughout its history, leaders of the UVU debated about the importance of these ethnic units in the structure of the larger association. At times, they were given no special role and were felt to be detrimental to the unity and functioning of the Union; at other times they were allowed to elect representatives to the local branch of the UVU. During the same period, other unions based upon nationality were formed among immigrants in Ghana, including The Nigerian Community, The Togo Union, and others. These were all referred to as *budu* by the Mossi. Children born of Voltaic parents in Ghana were regarded as eligible for membership in the UVU, and the same rule applied to the other groups. The Ghanaian citizenship laws, which deny the possibility of attaining citizenship simply by virtue of being born in Ghana and require Ghanaian parentage, reinforce the idea that national identity, like other forms of ethnicity, is primarily ascribed at birth.

These *budu* based on nationality emerge only in the context of national politics. Since their activities are focused on the attainment of group goals – for example, protecting the rights of Voltaic laborers in Ghana – the idea that the members are united by kinship bonds is not of primary importance. As a matter of rhetoric the fact that all Voltaics are "brothers" is emphasized to rally support for the Union, but this is not of great significance in the everyday interaction of members acting within the context of the association. However, within the *budu* based upon the traditional ethnic units or "tribes" (what Rouch [1956] refers to as "supertribes"), kinship is much more important, mainly because individuals adopt kinship roles towards one another on the basis of their common membership in these communities.

While the concept of *budu* expresses the idea that Mossi regard each other as "one kind," by virtue of agnatic descent from a common ancestor, within the Mossi community there is an additional concept of *doaghda,* or kinship. This expresses the idea that the Mossi belong to one family – by agnatic or uterine filiation, or both. This concept is usually used among the immigrants to refer to individuals with whom some genealogical tie can be demonstrated. More than the term *budu, doaghda* refers to a person's effective kinship network, to those individuals who not only could be called kin, but to those who also act like kin. For second-generation immigrants the term *doaghda* is associated with specific kin who are not necessarily Mossi. First-generation immigrants sometimes use the term to refer, not to specific kin, but to those members of the Mossi group who assume kinship obligations. All Mossi are potential kin, but a person's effective kinship network includes only those individuals who meet the behavioral expectations of kin.

Fortes (1949: 19) makes a relevant observation when he discusses the idiom of kinship in Taleland and the metaphorical use of kinship terms. In Tale thought, he says, "all social relations implying mutual or common interests tend to be assimilated to those of kinship." Moreover, "a kinsman of any degree is a person in whose welfare one is interested and whom one is under a moral obligation to help in difficulties, if possible" (1949: 203). This is the way Mossi conceptualize intra-ethnic relations in Kumasi. There is still, however, a significant difference in the way kinship relations function in the north and in Kumasi. In Taleland, as in Mossiland, most individuals have a fairly extensive and complete set of kin who are related in varying degrees of genealogical distance. There, it is possible for the rights and obligations implied in the use of a kinship term to vary, according to the genealogical distance between those who use the terms. In Taleland, Fortes states, "the more distant a genealogical tie is, the more does it become a matter of moral and ritual, rather than of jural or economic relations" (1949: 18). Thus, in Taleland, close kin and "metaphorical" kin may be distinguished by different role expectations which are correlated with genealogical distance.

The contraction of consanguineal kinship

Among immigrants, particularly those born in the north who have few kin in Kumasi, genealogical distance cannot be used as a scale to define the rights and obligations of different categories of kin. Consequently, first-generation immigrants are constantly attempting to create institutions and relationships which they can rely upon as they could rely upon kinship relationships "at home." The Mossi headman in Kumasi, whose role is discussed in chapter 9, defines his relationships with others largely in kinship terms, because he so often fulfills the obligations of a kinsman. First-generation immigrants often delegate a member of their own ethnic community to act as a "brother" in making marriage arrangements for themselves or their children. When members of the same community assume the obligations of kin, and when they perform the duties which close kin would perform in the north, they voluntarily contract relationships which may be identical to "real" kinship relationships and may be perpetuated in successive generations among their children.

> *Case II*
>
> Thus, Allassan Mossi wanted to give his daughter to a Zabarama man in marriage. He went to an elderly Mossi man whom he knew to be a Nakomce from Nobere, as was his mother. Allassan asked the man to act as *budkasama,* lineage head, in arranging the marriage. The man agreed and arranged to meet the representatives of the husband. He accepted the *kudin gaisuwa* (Hausa, money of greeting) and agreed to the arrangements. He then negotiated the amount of bride-wealth and told the prospective husband's family that if, in future, trouble should arise in the marriage, he, not Allassan, would deal with it. It is, in fact, considered improper for a man to take a direct role in many affairs concerning his children. This made it absolutely necessary for Allassan to delegate someone to act as a "senior brother" or *budkasama* for him. Allassan's daughter, in fact, had been married before, and on that occasion her mother's half-sister had been responsible for the marriage arrangements. During the divorce case the behavior of this woman was criticized and, as a result, Allassan did not ask her to perform the same role in the second marriage, even though she was the closest relative. Allassan and his wife had no other specific kin in Kumasi and Allassan therefore sought out another Mossi who could act as a kinsman.

Like most first-generation immigrants, Allassan Mossi had come to Kumasi with kinship concepts but without kin. When an occasion arose for which he needed kin, he sought someone to fill the kinship role. Usually, such factors as coresidence in a house or neighborhood, clientage, or common occupation, determine whom a person chooses to be his or her effective kin. But these choices are most often made within the same ethnic community and frequently are based upon the parties having a common town or region of origin or on belonging to a common patronymic group. Once such a relationship is formed by the performance of a kinship role, contact and reciprocity are necessary to maintain it. If it is not actively maintained through visits, gift exchange, and mutual assistance, kinship terms may still be used, but kinship obligations will not be met. In other words, all "tribesmen" or coethnics are potential kin, but close relationships which involve the recognition of the rights and obligations of kin must be voluntarily contracted and maintained. Among first-generation immigrants, then, behavior is what transforms generalized kinship relations into effective ones. Such relationships differ from specific kinship relationships, in that no genealogical link can be traced. When they are maintained, they are equivalent to specific kin ties and, in some instances, they may even be preferred. Unlike specific kinship relationships, in times of crisis these voluntarily contracted kin links can be repudiated. An example from one typical case discussed at the Mossi headman's house illustrates this.

Case III

Two Mossi men from different home towns in Upper Volta were working in a cocoa farming village outside Kumasi. One became seriously ill and delegated the other, Ilyasu, to act as guardian of his wife (a Gonja woman), his two children, and his property in the event of his death. After he died, a "brother" from Upper Volta arrived and tried to claim the man's property and children, leading to a very serious dispute between this "brother" and the wife. During the hearing at the Mossi headman's house, Ilyasu stated that: "Because we are all Muslims we say we are all brothers, and because we are all Mossi we say the same thing. But our home places are different. This brother from Upper Volta comes to me as a stranger, but I am the stranger because I don't know if he and the man who died had one father, one mother, or anything. I don't know my own father's countrypeople, so how can I know someone else's? From the day this man came from Upper Volta and started this case I became annoyed. I told myself that from then I am not his brother."

Still, members of the same ethnic community who are coresident in a house very often do become kin in the sense described above, particularly when a relationship of clientage is added to that of coresidence. In the context of the house, the recognition of a greater obligation to cooperate with and assist members of one's own ethnic community is sufficient to lead to the use of kinship terms and the assumption of ongoing kinship obligations between individuals. Two cases may be cited to illustrate the way in which specific kinship relationships are formed between coresidents.

Case IV

The late Mossi headman, Adamu, built several houses in Kumasi before he assumed office. In his capacity as a *maigida* and kola dealer he also acquired a house in Tamale, about 250 miles north of Kumasi on the road to Ouagadougou. A Mossi man named Timbilla came to Kumasi and was advised by Mossi lorry collectors to contact Adamu. Acting as most *masugida* do with their new clients, Adamu gave him lodging and food, and Timbilla remained in Adamu's house. Timbilla began to work for Adamu, travelling to Asante villages to buy kola nuts at their source. Adamu then sent Timbilla to Tamale to take charge of the northern portion of the kola business, and in Tamale Timbilla became the caretaker of Adamu's house. After several years, when

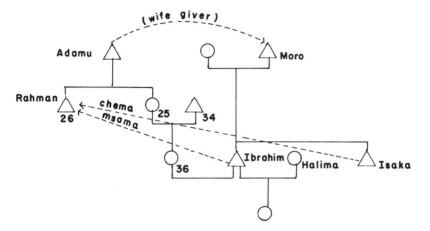

Figure 7. Kinship and clientage: the case of Adamu and Moro.

Timbilla wanted to marry, Adamu provided him with a wife, a Wangara
woman who had been given to Adamu as a *sadaka* by her father, another kola
dealer residing in Tamale. Timbilla and his wife returned to Kumasi
some years later and took up residence in another one of Adamu's houses,
where Timbilla again acted as a caretaker for Adamu. When Timbilla's
daughter grew up, he gave her to Adamu, who, in turn, gave her to his eldest
son as a wife. No bride-wealth was paid, as this was also a *sadaka* marriage.

Case V

Adamu also found a wife for another one of his clients and tenants, Moro.
Many years later, after the death of Adamu, Moro and his children and grandchildren were living in one of Adamu's houses in Aboabo, while some of
Adamu's sons continued to live in his house in Zongo. Several generations
of intermarriage united these people, since one of Moro's sons, Ibrahim, was
married to Adamu's daughter's daughter, Hawa (36). (See Figure 7.) When
Ibrahim's second wife, Halima, gave birth to a son, the naming ceremony was
performed in Adamu's house in Zongo, exactly as if this were the house of
the *budkasama* of his lineage, an analogy made explicitly by those involved.
Ibrahim claims he calls Adamu's eldest son *sama* (Moré, father) for respect.
He considers his marriage to Hawa to be a kinship marriage (Hausa, *auren
gida*) and consequently does not use the affinal term for his wife's mother's
brother. Insofar as he regards Adamu's son as his "father," he has married
his father's sister's daughter. On this reckoning the relationship of clientage
has added a generation "for respect" between patrons and clients and their
families, so that Moro would have been regarded as Adamu's son. Adamu,
it is said, was like a father to Moro, because among other things he gave him
a wife. Adamu's son is still regarded as a member of the generation preceding
Moro's son, although they are the same age and in the same generation in
terms of residence and birth in Kumasi. If Ibrahim did not see the relationship in these terms, his marriage to Hawa would have been a marriage between
members of different generations which, had they been closely related
biological kin, would not have been permitted. You would not marry your
"real" sister's daughter, but in Kumasi you might very well marry your

145

father's sister's daughter. Although in Upper Volta the Mossi avoided marriages between all first cousins, in Kumasi these were increasingly permitted between specific, as well as generalized, kin.

Ibrahim's older brother, Isaka, has not married into Adamu's family, and he calls Adamu's son *chema* (Moré, older brother), "because Adamu was like my father." He explains, "Adamu married my mother for my father (paid the bride price or was given the woman as a *sadaka*), and I grew up in his house." In this case Isaka emphasized that his father and Adamu were in fact of the same generation, although, if they were "like brothers," Adamu was regarded as senior. Isaka then calls Adamu's son "senior brother." In doing so, he is referring to status, and not to age, since he is actually considerably older.

In such situations the use of kinship terms expresses the affective aspect of each particular relationship. Rather than reflecting a set of genealogically defined obligations based on biological reality, they reflect the particular quality of a relationship between two individuals. Thus, two brothers, Ibrahim and Isaka, use different terms for Adamu's son, and each man places him in a different generation, but both use terms that convey some inequality; in both instances Adamu's son is in some respect senior. There need not be any logical or systematic consistency in terms of real genealogical relationships between different individuals' use of terms, since there was no genealogical basis for the original relationship. Nevertheless, as this example shows, kinship relationships which are voluntarily created in one generation may be maintained in the next.

Another example of the way in which kinship terms are used within the house may be taken from the house mentioned earlier, and illustrated in Figure 8, in which all residents are related.

Case VI

Ali (121), the founder's grandson, was married to Sara (123), and she called her husband's father, Malik (120), by the Moré terms for mother's brother, *yasaba,* as shown in Figure 8(a). When asked the reason why she called her father-in-law by the term for mother's brother, she gave several different explanations on different occasions, as did other members of the family. The marriage between Ali and Sara, who was born thirty miles from Kumasi in another zongo community, was considered to be a marriage between kin, although the precise genealogical relationship between them was not clear and was, in fact, quite irrelevant. As was often the case when they were asked, "How are you related?" the answer they gave was a description of the different kinship terms various people used to describe those involved in the relationship. On one occasion someone in the family explained that Adama (124), Malik's mother, had called Sara's mother *chema* (Moré, older sibling), because her mother and Sara's mother's father both belonged to the Zong patronymic group, one of the Yarse *sondere.* Adama's sons, including Malik, Ali's father, claimed that they had simply imitated their mother's usage of kinship terms. Following this logic, Sara had married the son of her *yasaba,* since Malik would have called Sara's mother by a sibling term. Ali also claimed that he had married his father's sister's daughter.

On a different occasion the same person explained that Sara's mother's father's mother was of the Kwanda *sondere,* as was Ali, and, of course, as were all his agnates. Omitting the one male link in this genealogical chain,

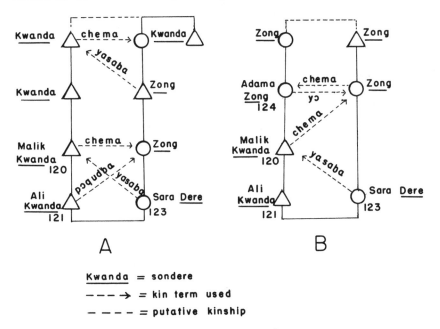

Kwanda = sondere

---→ = kin term used

---- = putative kinship

Figure 8. Explanations of Mossi kinship terminology.

Sara was able to claim that she married her mother's brother, because she married a man who was of the same *sondere* as her "mother's brother," and, therefore, his classificatory sibling, as shown on Figure 8(b). But the main point is that, to the people concerned, the precise genealogies involved in these relationships are irrelevant. A pseudokinship, in this case a sibling bond, was maintained by the consistent use of the sibling term, and this was explained in terms of their possession of a common Yarse patronym. People with the same patronym do not always use sibling terms, however.

This example shows how kinship terms are used pragmatically to describe and structure social relationships within particular contexts. In this case, the wife's integration into a very tightly knit kinship unit was facilitated by her use of a consanguineal kinship term for her new husband's father.

It is common for Mossi residents in the same house to find several kinship terms which can be applied to their relationships. More often than not, if there is a choice between an affinal term and a consanguineal one, they will choose the latter, for these terms have a greater affective connotation of solidarity. In one house in Zongo a woman called the late houseowner *yasaba,* because her mother and the owner had been born in the same town in Upper Volta. This justified calling the landlord *yasaba,* although she also could have addressed him by an affinal term, since her husband was related to him as a "brother's son," having had a common ancestor three or more generations back in Upper Volta. The husband called the houseowner *sama,* while the wife called him *yasaba.* They did not regard their marriage as a cross-cousin marriage, since each one's choice of a kinship term for

147

the houseowner was independent and implied, in this case, nothing about their relationship to each other.

The use of kinship terminology may accompany typical forms of kinship behavior among genealogically unrelated first-generation immigrants. Cases of leviratic marriage and the inheritance of each other's property are common. The story of Seidu Mossi illustrates in another way how coresidence may lead to kinship among first-generation immigrants of the same ethnic community.

Case VII

Seidu (see Figure 9) was one of the first Mossi migrants to build a house in Zongo. He built it with the profits of a successful livestock trade and later, shortly before he died, in about 1945, he became a titled elder, Waziri, to the Mossi headman (whose son his daughter had married). Another Mossi migrant, Braimah, from a different town in Upper Volta, came to live with Seidu, first as a tenant and later as an associate in the livestock trade. It is not clear whether Braimah was at first a client, but he has never been described as such. In retrospect, the two men are regarded as equals in all respects. When Seidu died, he left a widow, Rahmatu, and several young children. Braimah then married Rahmatu and took over the care of her children. He had one more child with her. Previously, Seidu had sold four rooms in the house to one of Braimah's wives, Asetu. When she died, her son from a previous marriage (Mamadu) inherited the four rooms. He then sold two of them to Braimah and two to another man who, like both Seidu and Braimah, was a musician and a trader. After Seidu's death, Braimah became caretaker of the house. He also succeeded to Seidu's title, and although both men are now deceased, the house is still called after the title, that is, "Waziri's house" and "Waziri's children." As might be expected in such a case, the inheritance was not divided. Some people claim that Seidu's son actually sold the entire house to Braimah, but others deny that any sale took place or could have taken place

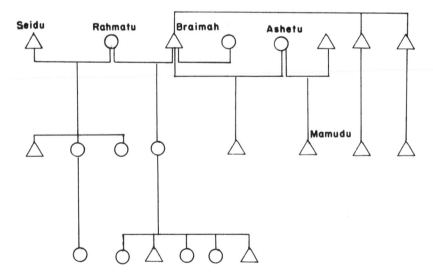

Figure 9. Kinship and inheritance: relationships among heirs to Seidu's house.

under the Islamic rules of inheritance followed in Kumasi. It is generally felt that ownership rights passed to Braimah, as the trustee for Seidu's children, exactly as if he had inherited a brother's wife, title to office, and property. Mahama, Braimah's son by his first wife, who also lives in the house, still has a right to some rooms, even if Braimah never did actually inherit or take over Seidu's share, since two of Asetu's rooms reverted to Braimah. The ambiguity and complexity in the situation may never be resolved or become an issue of contention so long as there is room in the house for those who choose to live there. When there is no longer enough room, this may be a difficult case to settle.

Another example of the same sort of process became apparent one day when an elderly Mossi couple were joking together:

Case VIII

A woman was amusing people by saying that a certain man, Isufu, was her husband, when everyone knew this was not the case. The background to this sexual joking was that the woman's late husband had called the man "brother." They had come from the same town in Upper Volta, and after Isufu came to Kumasi, he had found a room in the same house for his "brother," who then moved to the town. After the "brother" died, Isufu became the trustee of his property and his children. Had he been younger he probably would have been able to marry the woman in what would have been regarded as a leviratic marriage.

Members of the same ethnic community who are not specific kin sometimes exchange children, even when they are living in the same house. In one house a tenant gave her daughter to the female caretaker. The foster mother became responsible for the child's welfare, provided her clothes, disciplined her, and collected enamel dishes for the girl's marriage. Although the girl's real mother continued to live in the same house, she took no direct role in the child's upbringing. All fostering between members of the same ethnic community is felt to be an assumption of a kinship obligation between siblings, so that such fostering may be considered another means of creating kinship relationships. One woman who had several Mossi foster children who were not children of her specific kin claimed that "all my children are my family [*doaghda*]. If they are not family then they are servants [Moré, *yamba;* Hausa, *bawa*]." This reference to servants refers to the fact that many women in Kumasi employ children from different ethnic communities and pay the parents of the child approximately one shilling, sixpence, or two shillings per day. Kotokoli and other Togolese migrants who work in rural areas as farm laborers frequently send their children to town in this way. Like other foster children, these live with their employers and are fed and clothed by the employer. They usually leave before marriage arrangements are made, since their employer has no obligations in this regard, but in other respects they may be treated like foster children. In general, it is assumed that foster children of the same ethnic community are family, while those from other ethnic communities are servants, unless they are specific kin, such as siblings' children. The major exception to this generalization are children who have been sent to Arabic teachers of different ethnic communities. They are neither kin nor servants, but they live in the houses of their teachers and, like all children, may be asked to work for their foster parents – the amount of domestic service expected being somewhat more than in the case of the parent's own children and somewhat less than in the case of child-servants whose parents are paid for their labor. Their own parents usually remain responsible for their marriage arrangements, although it is common for girls to be given to their Arabic teachers as *sadaka* brides. In general, when the parents are not kin and belong to different ethnic communities, the real parents retain the right to remove the child. When the parents are kin or are members of the same ethnic community they retain ultimate jural responsibility although exercising it without deferring to the foster parent is felt to be a violation of the kinship bonds existing between the adults involved.

There is, however, a difference in the way in which immigrants of different generations of urban residence view interethnic fostering. The woman cited above who claimed that foster children were either kin or servants was a somewhat traditional first-generation Mossi immigrant. Orthodox Muslim *'yan k'asa* some-times foster children of other ethnic groups on the basis of friendship or because the child's parents greatly respect the foster parents and express this by entrusting their children to them. Patrons often become foster parents to their clients' children, and neighbors, sometimes even when they are first-generation immigrants, occasionally foster each others' children as a sign of amity and respect. The former Mossi headman fostered the Yoruba headman's son for many years. When the Yoruba boy married and had his own children he remained in the Mossi headman's house. The children of the two headmen describe their relationship as "something like brothers." Had they been of the same ethnic category they probably would have claimed to be distantly related "real" kin.

When Mossi immigrants use kinship terms in a general sense they tend to use certain terms and not others. Epstein (1961, reprinted 1969: 101) has described this tendency in Central Africa:

The further one proceeds beyond the range of immediate kin, the greater is the tendency to regard all kin, whatever their actual genealogical connection, as falling within the same broad category. . . . The deep value which attaches to kinship in the urban context lies in the fact that at its fullest extension kinship becomes synonymous with and gives expression to the fundamental values of brotherhood.

The terms the Mossi use most often among themselves are those for siblings, parents, and children. This choice is significant, particularly when compared to the terms that are used in a metaphorical sense towards members of certain other ethnic categories. The use of the sibling term among the Mossi connotes this general sense of brotherhood and, to some extent, connotes equality. The Moré sibling terms distinguish older and younger siblings (*chema* and *yao*), and these distinctions may be used to express either differences in chronological age or slight differences in rank, as in the case of clients and patrons. This does not obscure the emphasis on solidarity and equality in the metaphorical use of the sibling terms, since these terms are used consciously to express the unity of members of the same ethnic community with members of others.

Ethnicity and the idiom of kinship

When a real distinction in terms of distance or status is required between Mossi immigrants who are using generalized kinship terms, the sibling terms are replaced by those for parent and child, which imply a deference relationship, as well as a close consanguineal bond. The use of these terms is explained more fully in chapter 9, where the role of the headman is described. Although the term for father (*ba, sama,* or *baba*) implies distance and respect, its use between immigrants who are not specific kin implies solidarity, since it suggests that the speakers are members of the same *budu.* In view of the ubiquitous presence of members of other ethnic communities, the consistent use of these terms between members of the Mossi community has added significance. The choice of these particular terms is one way of signifying the boundaries of the ethnic category.

Kinship metaphors and the idiom of affinity

Affinal terms and terms for uterine kin (often interchangeable, in view of the prevailing emphasis on agnatic descent) are rarely, if ever, used between Mossi immigrants in Kumasi in a categorical sense. However, in the traditional Mossi context, ethnic subgroups conceptualized their relationships in terms of affinity. The Mossi population supposedly developed out of marriages between Nakomce men and Talse women, and on this basis the Nakomce call the Talse *yésba* (or *yasaba,* pl. *yésramba*), mother's brother, or simply maternal kin. These relationships are expressed most vividly in the enactment of interethnic joking partnerships. The joking relationship between mother's brother and sister's son occurs between classificatory kin among the Mossi, as in many other African societies, including most of the groups in the Voltaic area (Fortes 1945, 1949, passim; J. R. Goody 1962, passim). In Moré, the joking itself is called *dakiré* (affine), literally a term for one's wife's brother or sister's husband but generally used to refer to all affines. In Kumasi, where the traditional statuses of the Mossi ethnic subgroups are irrelevant, categorical affinity between them is not stressed, and this type of joking does not occur among members of the Mossi community. Joking does occur between Fulani from Upper Volta, Maranse, Yarse, and the Mossi blacksmiths, but this is not in a kinship idiom. Rather, it expresses the distinct non-Mossi origins of these peoples and their sense that they all were less fully incorporated into Mossi society than were the Talse and the Nakomce. During one typical interchange in Kumasi, a Yarse and a blacksmith were telling a Maranse that he was not a "real" Mossi. He feigned anger and replied that they could not call themselves true Mossi, either. It was the tone and the jocular repetition of the arguments that was striking, as if all basically recognized that in Kumasi, at least, the point was amusing, just because it was irrelevant.

The absence of kinship and affinal joking within the Mossi community in Kumasi must be viewed in conjunction with the frequency with which the Mossi joke with members of certain other ethnic communities. This joking expresses a sense of the unity of immigrant Mossi and their feeling that in relation to other ethnic communities they constitute a putative descent group. The interethnic joking that does occur also demonstrates particular historical and cultural relationships between the Mossi and their joking partners. Mossi joke in the idiom of affinity with all Voltaic peoples, but mainly with the Mamprusi and the Dagomba and, to a lesser extent, with the Wala, Gourma, and noncentralized peoples, such as the Tallensi, Kusasi, Dagati, and Builsa (Kanjaga). Joking with Mamprusi and Dagomba is most common in Kumasi and is always explained in kinship terms. The Mossi regard the Mamprusi as their maternal kin, since their putative ancestress, Nyennenga, was the daughter of a Mamprusi king. The Mossi sometimes describe the Mamprusi as their "mother's brothers" or as their "grandparents" (*yabramba,* s. *yaba*), since the mother of the Mossi royal ancestor was Mamprusi. Both the maternal grandparent/grandchild relationship and the mother's brother/sister's son relationship justify joking in the idiom of affinity in this patrilineal context (Schildkrout 1975b).

The Dagomba are sometimes described as cross-cousins of the Mossi, since Nyennenga is said to have had a brother who founded the Dagomba kingdom. On this basis, some of the older first-generation Mossi immigrants say that marriages between the two communities are forbidden, because, "Mossi and Dagomba are the same, like brothers and sisters." Others deny this extension of the incest taboo and say that, although they hesitate to marry Dagomba women, "because they bring bad luck," such marriages occur. This negative attitude on the part of the Mossi is associated with an idea that Mossi men married to Dagomba women encounter many types of misfortune, including losing money, becoming ill, and dying prematurely. Many of the older first-generation immigrants believe that witchcraft is prevalent among Dagomba women. As one man said, "If you have a child with a Dagomba woman, and it is a good child, she will kill you and take the child, and the child will also become a witch by drinking its mother's milk."

Joking between the Dagomba and the Mossi is much more hostile than between the Mossi and the Mamprusi. The respect accorded to the Mamprusi as "grandparents" is not shown to the Dagomba, who are perceived as members of the same generation. In other words, Dagomba/Mossi joking is symmetrical and reciprocal, while Mamprusi/Mossi joking is asymmetrical. When a Dagomba and a Mossi meet, the first to ask can demand money from the other, who then usually rudely throws a few coins at the other's feet. When a Mossi jokes with a Mamprusi it is always the Mossi who ingratiatingly "begs" a gift from his "grandfather." Joking between Mossi and Dagomba also includes such hostile acts as trying to put red pepper in the eyes of mourners at funerals, stealing from each other, and making insulting sexual remarks. Although the Mossi account for variation in the way in which they joke with these two peoples in terms of the different types of genealogical linkages between their ancestors, it is likely that the particular emphasis placed on the more or less hostile aspects of joking is related to real differences in the socioeconomic relationships between these groups in the urban context. Joking in the context of Kumasi zongo can be viewed as one way of expressing competition for status and advantage among culturally related groups. Thus, the different joking patterns can be related to demographic and economic factors in the Kumasi environment. While there were, in the 1960s, at least five thousand Mossi and three thousand Dagomba immigrants in Kumasi, there were only about five hundred settled Mamprusi in the town (*1960 Ghana Census*). This means that economic competition, particularly in the cattle and kola trades, is much less intense between the Mossi and the Mamprusi than between the Mossi and the Dagomba. The ambivalence expressed in joking derives from the fact that, while they are in economic competition with each other, the main other ethnic community contending for trade in these domains is the Hausa, with whom neither share close traditional cultural bonds. Independent corroboration for this interpretation derives from an analysis of the 1969 mosque dispute (Schildkrout 1974a), in which the Dagomba and the Mossi were strongly opposed in support of different candidates for the Imamate, while the Mamprusi basically supported the Mossi but attempted to remain as neutral as possible.

However, all joking varies considerably, depending upon the context, and can be used to express temporary alliances and enmities. On one occasion, when the Dagomba headman was visiting the Mossi headman to discuss politics, he criticized the Mamprusi headman for getting involved in the internal affairs of other ethnic communities. The conversation opened with joking, but the Mossi headman expressed a view of Mossi/Dagomba relations diametrically opposed to the more common one noted above. The Dagomba leader said, "If any Mossi man sees a Dagomba girl he wants to marry, just let me know, and I will give her to you." The Mossi headman replied, "As for the Dagomba, we will be pleased if we get them to marry, but Mamprusi girls bring bad luck. If a Mossi man married a Dagomba girl, he will get rich." Joking, then, is flexible and can express a variety of political postures.

Kinship myths relating their respective ancestors are also cited to justify joking between the Mossi and the Wala and the Gourma. An ancestor of the Wala is said to have come from the Mamprusi area around Gambaga, while the Gourma are said sometimes to be "grandfathers" of the Mossi. This relates to the ambiguities in the ethnic identity of some of the characters in the Mossi origin myth, as discussed in chapter 2. On the basis of these kinship claims, the Mossi claim to be able to sell the Gourma as slaves. This is a common form of joking which is often found in conjunction with the kinship idiom, since traditionally certain categories of kin had rights to pawn other kin (Goody 1962: 72; Fortes 1949: 138). The Mossi are even less explicit about how their myths tie in with those of the Wala, but they are usually regarded as "siblings," since they, too, claim descent from the Mamprusi royal line. All of this joking, whatever the precise content, is explained in kinship terms. I refer to it as affinal joking (as do the Mossi themselves), since it expresses the disjunction between a putative agnatic descent group – an ethnic category in the urban context – and others related to it through putative affinal and uterine links. The joking is between people who are, socially and culturally, closely related but who are, at the same time, members of different ethnic communities.

Sometimes, through marriage, an individual from a community with whom one does not ordinarily joke can be turned into a joking partner. For example, the Mossi do not joke with the Gonja, but one day, Usuman, a second-generation Mossi immigrant, met a Gonja man along the road. Usuman started teasing the Gonja man, who then asked him for some money. Usuman gave him a few coins and told him he was a foolish old man. This was justified, Usuman later explained, by the fact that the Gonja man "is married to my father's sister's great granddaughter. Therefore, she is my granddaughter and she jokes with me, and I joke with her husband because he is also now my grandchild." But it is important to note that in a case like this, although the individuals belong to different ethnic communities, the joking involves only individuals linked by a specific marriage. It is, in J. R. Goody's terms (1962: 68ff.), a joking relationship between individuals occupying kinship statuses, rather than a joking partnership between groups. Since there is no putative genealogical tie between the Gonja and the Mossi based on historical or mythical marriages between their ancestors, there is no basis for a joking partnership between them, although individuals linked by a specific affinal bond may joke in the same idiom.

Other ethnic communities, besides the Moré-Dagbane–speaking peoples, also have joking partnerships.[1] All of these partnerships are given full expression on one night every year, called *zambende* by the Mossi and *jifan wuta* (throwing fire), *wowo* (play), or *daran cikin ciki* (night of the full stomach) by the Hausa. This is the occasion of the Muslim New Year and in Kumasi the orthodox Muslims fast for two days before 'Ashura, the tenth night of the month of Muharram. Some people keep the head and feet of a sheep sacrificed at the last major festival, the *'id al-kabir,* and eat it at this time.[2] After the two-day fast, before the night of 'Ashura, there is a feast, followed by a ritual which shows a mixture of traditional rituals involving water and fire, and the interethnic joking so important in the town.[3] *Zambende* is an important ritual of integration in the zongo, for, although ethnicity is symbolically expressed, participation in common Islamic rituals overrides ethnic differences. Members of the same ethnic community who are in the correct joking categories tease and harass each other. Among the Mossi the most important relationship acted out on this occasion is that between grandparent and grandchild, and then that between cross-cousins. Classificatory mother's brothers and sister's sons joke, but, "You cannot joke with your [real] mother's brother. That is like playing [joking] with your mother. If you need something you may ask him . . . but you could still take a sheep or a cow, or get his daughter to give to a friend of yours in marriage," one Mossi remarked, apparently expressing the idea that familiarity, but not joking, characterized this relationship. Among the Mossi in Kumasi, specific kin in the appropriate categories do joke with each other. They throw water on one another and demand money, *kudin shara* (Hausa, the money of 'Ashura), from one another.[4] Members of ethnic categories which have joking partnerships do the same thing, and children go from house to house begging for money from the appropriate kin, threatening to harm them or tie them up, until they are given some small gift. Formerly, people went around the town with torches, and members of one ethnic community would seek out members of others to demand money and harass them. It is said that this ceased when "politics came," around independence in 1957, when people feared that joking, particularly between ethnically based political factions,[5] might turn into real fighting. At that time the government did, in fact, ban drumming and required permits whenever dances were held. Since real hostilities were in fact intense at that time, joking was perceived as potentially dangerous and something the government would be most likely to punish.

Joking partnerships are also acted out during many marriage ceremonies. Although the most orthodox Muslims do not allow dancing and joking at their marriages, since they claim this confuses Islamic and pagan ritual, most first-generation immigrants encourage it. After the Muslim ceremony, before the bride is taken to her husband's house, guests congregate in the bride's father's house. While the bride sits sullenly inside with her girlfriends, women dance and sing in the courtyard. They perform their customary dances and tease members of other ethnic communities about their performances. Joking partnerships are obvious, since women from the appropriate categories imitate and mock each others' dances.

Joking can serve a very important jural function in the urban context. The following story was related by a Mamprusi migrant:

One Mossi man killed a Mamprusi man in Kumasi, but there was no court case. The Mamprusi chief went to the court and explained that this was "play," because the Mamprusi were descended from a man, and the Mossi were descended from his daughter – so they are all one family. The court didn't do anything to the man; they just told him to leave the town. If a Mossi man kills a Mamprusi, and the Mamprusi dies, you have to say it was an accident, because the Mossi man didn't intend to kill him, and it was just his time to die. It is the same with the Dagati, who also joke with us, and some others. If we fight, the court will say there is no case.

The alliances expressed in joking among first-generation immigrants may assume political importance insofar as these groups are likely to appeal to each other first when they need allies. Thus, in 1967, when a committee was established to plan the expansion of the central mosque, the headmen of the Muslim Moré-Dagbane-speaking communities met together to plan common action against the Hausa faction, who, they felt, were discriminating against them by filling the committee with many Hausa members. However, since these alliances are based on common cultural heritages, rather than on patterns of persistent economic and political cooperation, they are not necessarily stable. This was again illustrated in the dispute over the mosque, when divergent political and economic interests led the Dagomba to repudiate their association with the Mossi and to form an alliance, based on common nationality, with Ghanaians from very different cultural backgrounds.

The categories of people with whom joking is permitted are very clearly defined. No matter how provocative, joking is never insulting between members of groups that are joking partners. When applied to members of other groups the same behavior is highly offensive. This was illustrated one day, when a young Mossi man went to the market and saw some Dagomba and Mossi migrants arriving from the north. The Mossi man recognized them by their facial markings and their speech. He spoke Hausa and insulted them by saying that they were all *kafiri* (Hausa, pagans) and that they had no business coming to a Muslim town such as Kumasi. The strangers became upset, and one of the men prepared to fight. At this point an elderly man intervened and identified the Kumasi-born young man as a Mossi. The strangers immediately relaxed and apologized for their anger, and the Mossi man from Kumasi began to joke with them in Moré, instead of Hausa. The jibes were still insults, but in the newly defined context they provoked an entirely different reaction.

Interethnic joking in the urban setting is, as Mitchell (1956, 1966: 52) has pointed out, a way of placing strangers in familiar categories and, to some extent, of structuring interaction, at least during initial encounters. According to Mitchell, joking in Central Africa occurs between groups which traditionally had hostile relations but are forced to cooperate in town. Likewise, a Hausa man in Kumasi claimed that joking involved peoples who formerly fought one another; however, the specific groups he mentioned, the Mossi and the Dagomba, did not exemplify this at all. For the Hausa man, the content of the joking implied its origin, but mistakenly.

In West Africa, affinal joking of the type we are discussing here exists independently of the urban context, and in town, people who know each other very well continue to joke if they are in the proper categories. Joking is not only a means of categorizing individuals and strangers, it is a way of expressing intragroup solidarity, of symbolizing the social distance between groups, and of making statements about the relative status of different ethnic categories within the zongo. The changes that occur in the urban context involve the delimitation of the boundaries of the groups which joke and the frequency with which joking occurs. Also, the degree of hostility emphasized in joking may change as economic and political relations change.

It is possible to relate the occurrence or absence of joking between specific communities to the cultural and status differences between them in the zongo context. Urban Mossi seldom joke among themselves unless they are specific kin and affines, and they do not joke to emphasize traditional cultural or status differences within the category of Mossi. They unite in the idiom of consanguineal kinship to joke with certain outsiders. These are peoples with whom the Mossi recognize cultural ties, and they express these in the idiom of affinal kinship. Joking between Moré-Dagbane-speaking peoples affirms their solidarity in opposition to peoples who are culturally more distant, such as the Hausa or the Asante, with whom such categorical affinal joking does not occur.

It is possible to look at joking in terms of a series of levels on which cultural and status differences are expressed. On what could loosely be called the "lowest" level, that of the single ethnic community, descent, rather than affinity, is emphasized; consanguineal kinship terms are used to express relations of the greatest solidarity; and categorical status differences such as those between the sub-groups of the Mossi in Kumasi are not recognized. Joking partnerships within this unit are not emphasized. On the middle, or second, level one finds culturally related groups who see themselves as equals in relation to culturally more distant groups but express competition among themselves through joking in the idiom of affinity. This is the joking typical of Moré-Dagbane-speaking peoples in Kumasi, of ethnic subgroups among the Mossi in Upper Volta, and of distantly related clans among the Tallensi, as

Table 25. *Correlates of interethnic joking*

Joking	Categorical kinship	Cultural differences	Status differences	Example
Absent	none	present	present	Hausa/Mossi Asante/Mossi
Present	putative affinity	ambiguous	ambiguous	Mossi/Dagomba Nakomce/Talse in Upper Volta
Absent	putative consanguinity	absent	absent	Nakomce/Talse in Kumasi

described by Fortes (1945: 91ff.). On the next level, typified, for example, by relations between the Mossi in Kumasi and the Asante or the Mossi and the Hausa, joking, again, does not occur, but for a different reason. At this level, no idiom of kinship or affinity unites members of these communities. (See Table 25 for a summary of these points.) At least for first-generation immigrants, clear and unambiguous ethnic boundaries and, in most cases, ideas about status differences are correlated with marked cultural differences. It is apparent, then, that when members of a community perceive themselves as having a common culture and as being a single-status category, the idiom of consanguineal kinship is used to express solidarity in relation to outsiders. The idiom of affinity is used among related but separate groups to express both a recognition of common but not identical cultural heritages and status differences or other forms of disjunction. Where there is no recognition of common culture, this particular idiom cannot be used to express status differences or intergroup competition.

Joking and the use of the kinship idiom which has just been described is apparent in the behavior of first-generation immigrants. Among urban-born immigrants there is often conflict between the desire to act in this traditional non-Islamic cultural idiom and the pressure to conform to the behavioral code adhered to by successful second-generation Muslims in the zongo. This code, based upon universalistic Islamic norms, precludes this type of joking, as it precludes many other forms of "tribally" specific, non-Islamic, behavior, according to the interpretations of the most orthodox and influential Kumasi Muslims. For second-generation immigrants this conflict of values can cause serious difficulties in decisions about social action, as was illustrated during the funeral of an elderly Mossi man in Kumasi.

Case IX

Karim had been in Kumasi many years, and his adult sons were among the most prominent of the educated non-Hausa Muslims. Hundreds of people, including all the immigrant headmen and most of the important second-generation Muslim leaders, attended Karim's funeral. Like other funerals in Kumasi, this one was to be performed in several parts: the burial and Muslim prayers immediately after the death, the three-day, the eight-day, and the forty-day funerals. This ritual schedule was a combination of Islamic and traditional West African rituals but it has become the standard form of zongo funerals (Trimingham 1959: 182). It was expected that this funeral, like others, would combine elements of both ritual systems, for, while Karim's sons were important members of the Kumasi Muslim elite, he had been only a nominal Muslim. He usually had spoken Moré, not Hausa or Arabic, and it was said that he had continued to perform sacrifices privately, in the traditional Mossi manner. Moreover, he had always joked with his Mamprusi and Dagomba friends. Consequently, while the Mamprusi, Dagomba, and Mossi first-generation immigrants viewed the funeral as an occasion to express their solidarity through joking, the second-generation guests viewed the funeral as an event of the utmost solemnity and orthodoxy. This led to a serious quarrel between immigrants of different generations, which placed Karim's sons in a difficult situation wherein they were asked, in effect, to choose between various aspects of their own identity.

At the burial ground, just before the body was lowered into the grave, an old Dagomba man jumped into the pit and refused to move. He claimed that he would not allow them to bury his "brother" and that, moreover, they would have to pay him if they expected him to move from the grave. The Mossi, Mamprusi, and Dagomba first-generation immigrants found this highly amusing, although the Mossi feigned annoyance at the interruption, just as they should have in response to the Dagomba man's provocative joke. The Hausa and Yoruba malams present were enraged at this act, which they felt was insulting, since it interrupted the solemnity of a most serious ritual. These men were leading members of the Muslim organization which had delegated to itself authority to frame the "Kumasi constitution," in which they had laid down rules of behavior for Kumasi Muslims. These rules explicitly forbade joking and dancing at funerals. First-generation Moré-Dagbane–speaking immigrants were annoyed at the interruption and criticism of what they regarded as the traditionally correct way of performing a burial service for a Mossi man. When Karim was finally buried, and people returned to his house to pray, the malams sat down but refused to allow the first-generation migrants to pray with them. These people then went aside and held a meeting to discuss what they would do to perform the funeral in the customary manner.

The sons of the deceased were in a dilemma. They did not want to lose their standing in the Islamic community, yet they knew that the first-generation immigrants were their father's closest friends. Eventually, they decided that for one week, between the day of burial and the eight-day funeral – when they would normally receive visits from friends and relatives, who would pray or perform traditional rituals – they would allow daytime activities at the house to take place in accordance with the wishes of the malams. In the evenings, they decided, they would let the first-generation immigrants dance, sing, and joke inside the house. What eventually happened was that, both day and night, the malams sat solemnly outside, while the first-generation guests joked inside the house. Dagomba women stood at the entrance of the house and threatened to put red pepper mixed with water in the eyes of any passing Mossi – that is, in the eyes of the deceased's "kin." The malams scornfully avoided the inside of the house, and the deceased's sons pretended not to notice the joking in the house and did their best to keep it quiet. Dancing occurred only during the night, to the disdain and annoyance of those who sat outside praying.[6]

The generalized use of consanguineal kinship terms between members of the same ethnic community and of affinal terms between members of different communities is much more frequent among first-generation immigrants than among their urban-born children. *'Yan k'asa* only rarely use consanguineal terms in a generalized way to address other Mossi, and when they do they do not expect this to lead to the assumption of kinship obligations. They very rarely apply affinal terms in the absence of specific marriage ties and, consequently, the type of interethnic joking which has just been described occurs infrequently. There are several reasons why this should be so. First, *'yan k'asa* have networks of specific kin whom they can depend upon to perform kinship roles, while first-generation immigrants must often rely upon the members of their ethnic community with whom they have voluntarily contracted kin relationships. Unlike first-generation immigrants, *'yan k'asa* are able to distinguish near and distant kin living in Kumasi on a genealogical basis. Most of their relatives in the town are closely related, due to the shallow depth of their genealogies. They have affines among the Mossi and in other ethnic communities, and these are not necessarily the same communities with whom first-generation immigrants joke in the idiom of affinity. When *'yan k'asa* do joke with members of different ethnic communities and when they use kinship terms metaphorically within their own ethnic community, it is usually because they are able to trace some genealogical connection, however remote. When Malik called Sara by a kinship term (Figure 8) he claimed that, in selecting a particular term, he was simply imitating his mother's behavior. Still, he applied this term only because his son had married Sara and because his mother was also able to trace a vague linkage between the individuals involved.

Interethnic affinal relationships among *'yan k'asa* can also be politically significant, but this is because they involve actual marriages between living members of the community. Categorical, or stipulated, affinity, based on reputed marriages among various groups' ancestors and demonstrated in joking, can be used to express the perceived status relationships between ethnic categories. Actual interethnic marriages, on the other hand, often significantly affect the political relationships between ethnic communities. As the next section demonstrates, many leaders are careful to arrange such unions strategically. In contrast to categorical affinity, these affinal links are, in Fortes' terms (1949: 18), more a matter of jural and economic relations than of ritual and moral relations. Because they involve individuals in relationships that entail very specific rights and obligations which are difficult to repudiate, they may be ultimately more important politically than are the metaphorical affinal links between individual members of different ethnic communities. They do not merge different ethnic units into more inclusive moral and ritual communities, but they create strong personal bonds between key persons in different groups.

'Yan k'asa do sometimes use consanguineal kin terms, particularly the term for "brother," to address other Mossi with whom they cannot trace a genealogical link. But this is a deliberate effort to maintain the solidarity of the community in the face of a loss of cultural identity. This is demonstrated in their formal associations, such as the Mossi Youth Association, where they pass "laws" to encourage members to use these terms of address. *'Yan k'asa* associations formally re-

quire their members to contribute to naming ceremonies, marriages, and funerals; they do not expect these obligations to be fulfilled simply because they call each other by kinship terms. First-generation immigrants, on the other hand, are not concerned about their loss of cultural identity. Rather, they need members of their community to perform specific roles, many of which are defined in terms of traditional Mossi values. Thus, among the rural-born, the generalized use of consanguineal kinship terms and the accompanying behavioral expectations create an informal ethnic association, or community, that does not require printed membership cards, regular meeting times, and other formal mechanisms to perpetuate itself.

The loss of Mossi cultural identity among the urban-born also accounts, in part, for the infrequency of affinal joking, except among specific kin. Mossi *'yan k'asa* do not feel closer in cultural or linguistic terms to other speakers of Moré-Dagbane than to members of groups that traditionally were much more distant. To them, the most significant cultural distinctions are those between Muslims and non-Muslims and between rural- and urban-born immigrants. Since interethnic joking partnerships are culturally specific, in terms of their manifest content and symbolism, they are meaningful ways of expressing social distance for first-generation immigrants, but not for their urban-born children, who rarely evaluate the status of individuals or groups according to traditional cultural criteria. To many rural-born Mossi, for example, the centralized Moré-Dagbane peoples are culturally superior to the non-centralized peoples who, some Mossi will say, "lack respect and shame," because they lack chiefs. Joking is a way of applying such evaluations in the urban context and also of emphasizing the persistence of traditional values and symbols. Since *'yan k'asa* rank individuals and ethnic categories according to achieved criteria which are not rooted in traditional cultural values, for them such joking is an inappropriate means of making statements about social status.

In this chapter I have discussed the different ways in which first- and second-generation immigrants use the language of kinship to express solidarity with members of their own ethnic group, on the one hand, and separation from members of other ethnic groups, on the other hand. Because ethnicity in Kumasi is conceived in terms of descent, the traditional kinship idiom, with its distinction between consanguineal and affinal relations, is an appropriate way to symbolize internal and external ethnic group relations, respectively. This contrastive usage has been described through the presentation of a number of examples which show how consanguineal terms are used intraethnically, while affinal terms are used, particularly by first-generation immigrants, to describe relationships with members of other ethnic groups. Throughout this chapter I have been concerned with the metaphorical extension of the idiom of kinship over the domain of ethnicity. In the next chapter kinship relations based upon actual marriages and demonstrated genealogical links will be discussed.

7

Kinship and marriage in the second generation

The extensive use of the idioms of kinship and affinity among first-generation urban immigrants is intrinsically involved with affirming the significance of ethnic identity. Moreover, as the discussion in chapter 6 suggests, it is the persistence of the ideology of unilineal descent among most northern immigrants which makes this idiom so appropriate for generating corporate ethnic categories in town.[1] Individuals can claim eligibility in the same ethnic category on the basis of common paternal ancestry; and some ethnic categories are related, affinally, because of putative marriages between their founders. Other ethnic categories in town are not related to each other in this way at all, and some do not emphasize unilineal descent as a principle of inclusion. But those which do – those with a traditionally strong emphasis on this principle – conceive of the relationships between certain ethnic categories in terms of affinity, while relationships within the ethnic community are conceptualized as though they were relations between agnates. It is a person's ethnic identity, based on descent, that determines the possibility of activating such generalized affinal and agnatic ties.

What I have referred to earlier as specific kinship differs from this in the urban context, in that there is less emphasis on unilineal descent. Although ethnic identity is still primarily determined by patrifiliation, for the immigrant Mossi the ideology of unilineal descent does not lead to corporate kinship groupings in the sense of joint residential or propertyowning groups. As far as specific kin are concerned, uterine relatives can be as important as agnates. In some families, paternal kin may be able to make greater claims on one another, but no ideology of unilineal descent justifies or necessitates this. When it occurs, it represents a choice based on the status of particular kin, rather than the operation of a principle or rule. The importance given to both uterine and agnatic kin is partially due to the small number of specific kin that many immigrants have and to the necessity of making the most out of all relationships. It also reflects the operation of Islamic inheritance laws, which disperse property among children of both sexes, and the tendency for brothers, as well as brothers and sisters, to live separately, so long as they are economically independent.

As I have tried to show above, in the absence of specific kin, individuals attempt

161

to turn generalized kinship relationships with members of their own ethnic community into the behavioral equivalent of specific ones. That is, they attempt to add jural content to relationships that are defined as kinship relationships only terminologically and affectively. For many first-generation immigrants, informal ethnic associations are important, because they provide a pool of potential kin. In the same way, patron/client relationships are very significant for first-generation immigrants and are often seen as though they were kinship relationships or potential kinship relationships. This explains the power and influence of landlords: since they are able to provide housing, jobs, wives, and all of the assistance of a *paterfamilias* to new migrants, they gather clients around them. There is a constant search for kin on the part of first-generation migrants, be they potential leaders or simply migrants in need of temporary assistance. This chapter, then, is an attempt to answer the question of what makes specific kinship so important in Kumasi zongo that people continually seek ways to maintain it, to augment relationships with fictive kin, and to reconstitute their kinship networks when they fragment.

Town-born immigrants are just as aware as first-generation immigrants are of the importance of kinship. They very conscientiously maintain relationships with almost all their relatives. While they consider themselves fortunate in having more specific kin than first-generation immigrants, they have to overcome a number of centrifugal forces which continually threaten to fragment their kinship networks to the point where these lose their effectiveness. Among these forces are the Islamic inheritance laws, which emphasize individual ownership and lead to the fragmentation of estates; the residential dispersal of kin, due to virilocal residence after marriage; and the economic value of property and the consequent tendency for people to rent rooms to strangers, rather than to give them to kin. For people who do not own property, the difficulty of finding several rooms in the same house is a contributory factor. In cases where relatives belong to different ethnic communities, the phrasing of political conflict in ethnic terms can sometimes threaten kinship relationships.

People make considerable effort to counteract these disintegrative forces. In order to understand why they do this it is necessary to look at the perceptions they have of the value of kinship in the urban setting. For one thing, kinship is associated with power and influence. In the zongo context, leadership, or the ability to control and influence the actions of others, is a matter of attaining prestige and followers. Theoretically, and in actuality, any migrant can attain wealth, education, and followers. The greater a man's clientele, the greater his prestige and power. In such an open system, when the attributes of prestige and influence can be achieved, a man with kin is believed to have an advantage. It is, of course, recognized that kin quarrel and compete with one another, but such behavior is never sanctioned, and great effort is made to prevent it, to patch up differences, and to give at least the appearance of solidarity. Just as people attempt to solve disputes within the ethnic community, so that "its name won't spoil," they also try to keep family quarrels quiet for the same reason.

People who do not have political ambitions also value kinship relationships.

Kinship and marriage in the second generation

Young migrants born in the north are often heard expressing envy of the *'dan k'asa* whose family finds him a wife, pays his marriage expenses, gives him a room to live in and a business to inherit. Those with kin can get loans from relatives, while others must rely upon their headman, a *maigida,* a friend (who may be called by a kin term), a revolving credit society,[2] or a money lender. A man or woman with kin has someone to bestow a name upon his children – to choose the name, buy the sheep for the naming ceremony, distribute kola, to invite the guests, and act as the child's guardian or foster parent. He has someone to pay his marriage expenses, and to "stand for him" when he marries, as Ahmadu's "brother" did when his daughter married. He has someone to bail him out of the police station if he's in trouble, to wash his body when he dies, to arrange his burial and funeral, and to perform many other roles which kin cannot easily refuse but which others often hesitate to assume.

There are many different ways in which people maintain contact with kin and keep their relationships active and effective. Of course, they do not do this with all recognized kin. Relationships with siblings and more distant kin who have moved away from Kumasi fade, although when the opportunity arises, they usually visit each other and, in times of crisis, they meet or appeal to each other for help. Relationships with genealogically more distant kin who live in the same town tend to be closer than those with immediate kin in distant towns. The former will usually be brought into a person's effective kinship network, while immediate kin who live far away may not.

Visiting and gift-giving are two crucially important obligations through which people maintain their kinship relationships. Siblings in different neighborhoods in Kumasi visit each other regularly, usually at least once a week. To cease visiting causes suspicion and friction. At the end of Ramadan, kin and affines send gifts of food to one another – usually boxes of sugar and milk, packets of tea, or sacks of grain. These gifts are especially important among affines and among second-degree cognatic kin. A man and his wife's parents should always "greet each other" with small gifts after Ramadan. Parents' siblings and siblings' children also receive boxes of sugar and tins of milk at this time. First cousins exchange comparable gifts, while full siblings usually send larger presents to each other if they can afford it. Whenever an animal is sacrificed at a Muslim festival or ceremony of status passage, such as a naming ceremony, marriage, or funeral, siblings are sent portions of uncooked meat, and somewhat more distant kin are sent bowls of cooked food. Children can be seen going on foot or in taxis, carrying food from one neighborhood to another, at the end of Ramadan, during the other Muslim festivals, especially *'id al-fitr* and *'id al-kabir,* and whenever an animal is killed. On these occasions siblings are also expected to contribute money, animals, or bags of rice. All of these exchanges of food may, perhaps, be interpreted as a kind of compensation for the dissolution of these kinship groups as domestic units.

There are many things which the very closest kin – parents and children – are expected not to do for each other, necessitating reliance on more distant relatives. This seems to be true of all ethnic communities in the zongo, and it is sometimes described by the zongo immigrants as "all Africa law." As in the rural context, it is considered arrogant, selfish, and disrespectful to one's kin, particularly to one's siblings, to overtly take a direct role in bringing up one's own children (E. Goody 1966, 1970; Oppong 1967; Schildkrout 1973). This is the rationale for the very frequent exchange of children among kin in Kumasi. Even when children do not leave their own parents' house of residence, they are said to be "for" someone other than the actual parents. This transfer of responsibility for the child's upbringing begins with the naming of the child and lasts throughout the child's life. A man's sibling should choose his child's name, pay all or some of the expenses of the naming ceremony, and act as the child's guardian. If the child gets in trouble, a sibling of the parent who has been delegated as a guardian or the eldest of the parent's sibling group takes some responsibility for the child. He attempts to get him out of legal trouble, he administers discipline, and he helps make decisions about what must be done. Marriage arrangements are partially made by a sibling of a parent, usually by the father's brother or sister; bride wealth is paid and received by them, and a girl's dowry is more often provided by her father's sister than by her mother. Funeral arrangements also are not arranged by the very closest lineal kin, but by siblings or by more distant kin.

In some cases this does not adequately describe what really happens. However, the man who does not at least make it appear that his sister has been informed of his decision to give his daughter in marriage to a particular man before his wife hears the news gets himself in serious trouble with his sister and his other siblings. The marriage arrangements may have to be cancelled, and hours of dispute in front of relatives and close friends will take place, until the man offers an acceptable apology to his sister. There is a particular order of precedence among kin which favors siblings and must be adhered to, in order not to offend one relative or another. In fact, it is not only relatives who are offended by violations of these norms. At a wedding of a Wangara man and a Mossi girl, the Mossi headman reprimanded the bridegroom's father because he, the headman, had not been sent kola to inform him of the wedding. "Even if the girl's father gave you the girl, it is not he alone who controls her. One man is her father, but he is not her family, and she is not for him alone," he argued. In the absence of an extensive network of specific kin, generalized kin assume the roles of family members, of parents and siblings particularly.

Among the urban-born as well, although corporate propertyholding kin groups are not recreated in town, kinship networks are extremely important, and many roles traditionally delegated to kin are preserved. In the urban, as in the rural, context, these relationships serve an important function. Although kin rarely preserve corporate rights to property – that is, to material resources – they nevertheless preserve some notion of corporate identity by stressing their rights to control each other, as shown particularly in the exchange of the responsibilities entailed in childrearing and in the arrangement of marriages.[3]

Urban migrants in Kumasi zongo not only take an active role in arranging the marriages of their kin, they also sometimes arrange marriages among themselves.

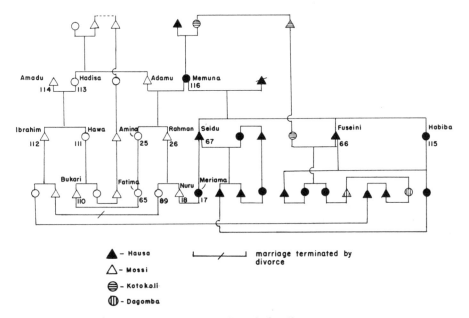

Figure 10. Ethnicity and marriages in Adamu's family.

In the cases of the very wealthy families in the zongo this may be a way of consolidating wealth; nevertheless, since wealth in the form of property or cash is not, strictly speaking, ever jointly owned, what is emphasized is the exchange of gifts between kin. The exchange of gifts between affines who are also kin is inevitably more elaborate than the exchange between members of the two unrelated families.

Conservative first-generation Mossi immigrants sometimes complain that those Mossi who arrange marriages between first cousins are violating Mossi custom and do this because they have become "Hausaized." Still, these and other forms of kinship marriage (Hausa, *auren gida;* literally, marriage of the house) are sanctioned in Islamic law and do take place. The genealogy in Figure 10 shows the marriages known to me in a single well-established Kumasi zongo family, and the description of the marriage of Nuru and Meriama which follows shows the importance placed upon such unions in this family. As Figure 10 also shows, these marriages perpetuate affinal links between members of a number of different ethnic communities. Although most of the *auren gida* have been contracted by the Hausa section of this family, the Mossi increasingly participate in such arrangements. While similar genealogies could not be drawn for all Mossi families, among many who have been resident in town for several generations, are well established, and have financial assets, this pattern is common.

Among other things, these marriages among the urban-born indicate that parents maintain considerable control over their children's marriage choices. In fact, in many second- and third-generation families, marriages are increasingly arranged by parents or parents' siblings. Arranged marriages, although not particularly those between kin, seem to end in divorce at least as frequently as other marriages. Having failed once, most parents let their children choose for themselves the second time. Girls who protest their parents' attempts to arrange their first marriage are often ostracized from their families. The more orthodox and wealthy a family is, the more it is concerned with contracting advantageous marriages to outsiders and with consolidating its status and its assets by arranging marriages between kin. In this sense, control over urban-born children's marriages is an indicator of success, as the immigrants define it.

Another form of marriage arrangement which perpetuates an alliance between two families is known by the Hausa term, *auren musaya*. These are "exchange marriages" arranged between first cousins and other cognatic kin. Figure 11 shows three such marriages between children of Adamu, who appears also on the preceding genealogy (Figure 10), his sister, Hadisa, and another Mossi elder, Umoru. Figure 10 also includes examples of exchange marriages between Dagomba and Hausa migrants. These arrangements are sometimes preferred to *auren gida* by more traditional Mossi migrants, since, in the first generation at least, they do not involve close kin.

Both of these examples concern important first-generation Mossi elders who held titled offices in the Mossi community. Figure 12 shows marriages among the kin of Mossi elders who have held titled offices. If marriages among other prominent Mossi immigrants who did not hold office were also included, this genealogy would be greatly expanded. In some of these cases the brides are given as *sadaka*. In Figure 12 this is true of Naba I's brother's daughter, given to Naba II, Naba II's daughter, given to the Imam, Waziri I's daughter, given to Naba II's son, Naba II's daughter, given to Sarkin Fada's son, and probably some others not known to me. It is impossible in most cases to determine whether the affinal alliances or the political associations come first, but the fact is that the two are very often connected, so that relationships between community leaders are complex, involving many different kinds of interpersonal obligations. In many cases in this particular genealogy, as in many others, patron/client ties existed among the men involved before the client gained an office. Relationships between patrons and clients are simultaneously political, in that they build up the leader's assured support; economic, in that the client often works for and is supported by the patron; and social, in that affinal ties often become superimposed upon patron/client relationships. Among men of approximately equal status, relationships are just as complex, although often more symmetrical.

Interethnic marriages

In much the same way, marriages are often arranged between the children of important leaders of different ethnic communities and between the children of such men in different zongos. In one sense, all interethnic marriages are politically significant, since conflict in the zongo is often conceptualized in ethnic terms and since

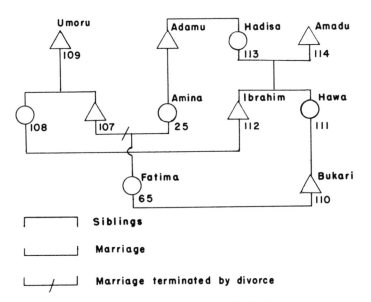

Figure 11. Exchange marriages in Adamu's family.

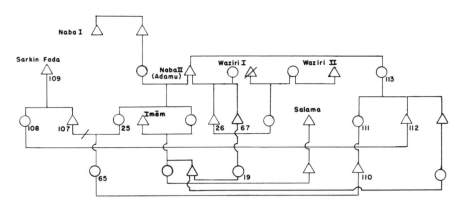

Figure 12. Marriages among Mossi elders and their children.

ethnicity is frequently used to create and justify political alliances. The children of interethnic marriages very often act as mediators between members of different ethnic communities. When these children are community leaders, they perform the same function but on a larger scale. For example, the interpreter whom the Asantehene uses when he deals with the zongo Muslims is a man who had a Banda (Akan) mother and a Wangara father. Since he is a Muslim, he theoretically is a member of his father's ethnic community, but, according to Akan customary law, he is a Banda. He spent many years in the Asantehene's household as a child but has also lived in the zongo as an adult. He advises the Asante leaders on zongo affairs, is trusted by zongo immigrants, and interprets and mediates when the two groups meet. In the 1950s, when the Muslim Association Party (MAP) formed an alliance with the Asante National Liberation Movement (NLM) against the CPP, such individuals were key figures in maintaining cooperation and communication between the parties.

Almost all zongo leaders – headmen, wealthy *masugida,* important malams – have made sure that some of their children are married into leading families in other ethnic communities. They themselves also marry women from other communities, often the daughters of men of their generation and status. These affinal links extend not only throughout Kumasi zongo, but into zongos in other towns. Important traders, Arabic teachers, and political leaders in different towns arrange marriages, often *sadaka* marriages, among their children and for each other. Thus, the Hausa headman in Kumasi was married to the daughter of a very wealthy Mossi cattle dealer in Accra, a man who had supplied Kwame Nkrumah with meat and cattle for many years. Prominent Islamic teachers, such as al-Hajj 'Umoru of Kete Krakye, gave their daughters to their esteemed students – in 'Umoru's case, for example, to the former Sarkin Zongo, Malam Salaw, and to a son of one of the most educated Mossi Arabic teachers in Kumasi.

Many other examples of such marriages could be cited, and only a few can be noted here. The daughter of the Mamprusi headman in Kumasi is married to the son of one of the most important Dagomba leaders. Besides the marriage mentioned above, the Hausa headman also married the daughter of the principal leader of the Kumasi Zabarama community. Two of his daughters were also married to Zabarama traders, and one was married to a son of the former Mossi headman in Kumasi. The brother of Sarkin Zongo Salaw was married to the Hausa stepdaughter of the Mossi headman. One Mossi headman married Kotokoli, Hausa, and Kanjaga women, as well as Mossi women, and his sons, between them, have married into the Mossi, Wala, Zabarama, Mamprusi, and Hausa communities. Besides these marriages there are many others between the children of equally prominent, non-officeholding immigrants. What is perhaps most significant about the marriages mentioned above, however, is that during the period between 1950 and 1960, when political party conflict was most intense, these sets of affines were all on the same side (against the CPP). On the CPP side, political alliances were also reinforced by marriage ties. Mutawakilu, for example, the CPP Sarkin Zongo, had one sister married to a leader of the Kumasi branch of the pro-CPP Muslim Council, a man who also held the office of Chief Butcher (Sarkin Fawa) under Mutawakilu. Another of his sisters was married to a Mossi CPP representative in the Kumasi City Council. Marriages were known to break up in this period, when political disagreements could not be resolved, and spouses pressured each other to avoid having their natal families and their affines on different sides. When fights between kin of the same or different ethnic categories involve politics, they are particularly bitter, and people make great efforts to avoid them. If there is clearly a family head, the others usually follow his political lead. If there is no such person, or if consensus is not reached, so that kin and affines divide along political lines, kinship obligations lapse, at least until the political situation changes.

Many detailed cases could be described to cite ways in which interethnic marriages affect the internal political life of the zongo or the way in which politics affects kinship relationships. One which has more or less become public history in the zongo illustrates this.

Case X

In 1945 the Hausa headman, Malam Ali, quarreled with al-Hajj Yahaya, the leader of the Zabarama community. He accused the Zabarama leader of having five wives. The case was brought before the Asantehene, who decided in favor of Yahaya, since he was able to show that one wife was, in fact, a concubine, a *sadaka,* whom he had obtained in Niger. Before this case arose, one of Yahaya's daughters had married a young Hausa man, Ahmadu Baba. During the dispute between Yahaya and Ali, Ahmadu Baba brought a further charge against Ali, accusing him of violating Qur'anic law by insisting that marriage ceremonies be performed in his house. Ahmadu Baba did not succeed Ali as Sarkin Zongo immediately, because it was felt that he was too young, but after four years, when the next headman, Adamu, died, Ahmadu Baba obtained the office. While his marriage to al-Hajj Yahaya's daughter was not the only, or even the primary, factor in his success, people in the zongo today often tell this story when they describe the succession to the office of Hausa headman. Ahmadu Baba's strategic marriages, of which this was only one, are often related to his political success.

Children of interethnic marriages are known in the zongo as *shin kafa da wake* (Hausa, literally, rice and beans). They belong by descent to their father's ethnic community, according to the interpretation of Islamic law followed by Kumasi immigrants, but to some extent they have a choice of the ethnic community, if any, with which they wish to identify. Ethnic identity is a matter of behavior as much as one of categorization by descent, or even a concept of self, and to make ethnic identity meaningful a person must act in the interests of his ethnic community. This becomes all the more important among urban-born immigrants who cannot be readily categorized in terms of ethnic identity by virtue of any objective cultural criteria. Among them, particularly, action must validate ethnic identity. In Kumasi zongo, children of mixed marriages on some occasions do choose the ethnic community with which they want to associate, and some are able, at times at least, to move from one to another, even though membership through a mother is usually seen as only partial membership in this patrilineal context. Some of these children find themselves in a difficult situation, since the identities from both parents coexist on the same conceptual level: that is, a Hausa is a kind of Nigerian, not a kind of Mossi. Those who attempt to identify with two groups which are potentially or actively in competition risk being mistrusted. Some choose to solve this dilemma by clearly opting for one identity or the other or by remaining marginal to both and serving as a mediator between them.

The choices such children make are important to their parents and to other members of the parents' ethnic communities, since the sheer size of a community is felt to have some bearing on its bargaining position in the zongo. The Mossi are actively concerned with the ethnic identity of their daughters' husbands, because they feel that their grandchildren will be "lost" if their daughters marry into another ethnic category. They then make attempts to win these grandchildren back. For example, in 1967 the Mossi Youth Association, an association mainly composed of town-born Mossi, decided after considerable debate to admit members who had Mossi mothers but non-Mossi fathers. This may very well reflect the bilateral nature of kinship and the weakening of ideas about unilineal descent among *'yan k'asa.* Yet they also decided to allow the non-Mossi wives of Mossi men to join the organization, on the ground that their children would become Mossi; thus, they argued, the women were giving birth for the Mossi community.

Interethnic marriages are also significant in terms of cultural change. The children of these marriages almost inevitably speak Hausa and, although they may sometimes identify themselves with one group or another politically, culturally they represent "zongo culture" most clearly. From the time these marriages are arranged, a common ritual idiom must be found. This is true for the actual marriage ceremonies, as well as for the duration of the marriage. The marriage of Nuru and Meriama clearly illustrates the ritual idiom of social relations in the zongo. As Figure 10 shows, both the bride and groom come from a family in which interethnic marriages have occurred frequently. Their marriage ceremony was more elaborate than the typical one in the zongo, because of the family's prominence, but because of this it may be regarded as a model which other marriage celebrations approximate. It is also of interest, because it is an *auren gida* and a marriage between a Mossi man and a Hausa woman.

The ritual of kinship and affinity: the marriage of Nuru and Meriama

Part of the history of this family has already been presented (Figures 4(a)–(e), 10, and 11). The Mossi branch consists of the children and grandchildren of Adamu and his sister, Hadisa (113), whose origins have already been described. When Adamu came to the Gold Coast, two years after the Yaa Asantewaa War in 1902, he first went to Cape Coast, where he worked as a carrier (*kaya kaya*) for Europeans. He then moved to Kumasi, where he cut and sold timber. He lived in the neighborhood of Amroom but later moved to Zongo Estate, where he built the first of six houses. He became a kola *maigida* and was selected as Waziri to the first Mossi headman, Dawda. In 1932, after Dawda was deported, following his fight with Malam Salaw, Adamu succeeded to this office.

During the course of Adamu's life he married five times. His third wife, Memuna (116), was a Hausa woman born near Accra. She had come to Kumasi with her first husband, a prominent Hausa malam. She had three children with him: Fuseini (66), Habiba (115), and Seidu (67). The last, Seidu, was born around the time of his father's death, soon after which Memuna married Adamu. All three children were Hausa by descent, since their sociological father was Hausa,[4] but all of them grew up in their Mossi stepfather's house. Since he was so active in the Mossi community, as children they learned to understand and speak Moré. However, it is significant, in terms of the status of the Hausa in Kumasi, to note that, although their stepfather was a wealthy and respected Mossi leader, as adults these three people identified themselves very strongly with the Hausa community. Habiba, now widowed, lives in Fuseini's house, and Meriama (17), the bride, also lived there under Habiba's care, although she is Seidu's (67) child. Both Seidu and Fuseini moved to their own houses in Aboabo after their stepfather died in Upper Volta, following his deportation by the Nkrumah government.

Adamu's children living in his house in Zongo Estate in 1966, at the time of my fieldwork, included his eldest daughter, Amina (25), his three sons Rahman (26), Abdul (63), and Usuman (11), and his two youngest daughters, who were under the care of their older sister, Amina, as illustrated in Figure 4(c). All of the brothers became important and active members of the Mossi community, as well as taking part in many multiethnic zongo associations. One other member of the Mossi branch of this family should be mentioned, since he also took an important part in the marriage. This is Malam Aboubakr (117), Adamu's distant kinsman, whom he called "brother." The two men were both members of the same patronymic group, and although they met only in Ghana, when Malam Aboubakr died, Adamu's children planned the funeral and later fostered his young children.

The marriage between Nuru (18) and Meriama (17) was one of the first major events in this family since the 1966 coup. During the CPP period, politics had divided this family, as it had many others. The marriage between the two branches was taken by many people to be a sign of reconciliation, both in terms of politics and ethnicity – for in this case these cleavages coincided, with the Mossi side being strongly anti-CPP, and the Hausa side supporting the Nkrumah government. Although many other interfamilial marriages had occurred among this group, only one other had linked the Hausa and Mossi sides together.

The decision to give Meriama to Nuru was made jointly by Fuseini (66), Seidu (67), and Habiba (115), with the consent of Amina (25) and Adamu's sister, Hadisa (113), who was by then very old. Amina then called Rahman and told him the decision, and he told his wife, Hawa (29), the prospective groom's mother. The key figure in this, as far as the bride was concerned, was her father's sister, Habiba, just as Amina was the key figure on the Mossi side. The fathers' siblings, not their wives, were most closely involved with these decisions.

One month later the wedding took place. It was a double ceremony, since another daughter of Seidu (67) was married at the same time to a Hausa friend and age mate of Seidu's – that is, to a wealthy and respected man her father's age.

The Islamic ceremony which legalized the marriages was scheduled to take place on a Friday. On the Monday before, some of Meriama's (17) dowry was already assembled in Habiba's (115) room. Since this was a *sadaka* marriage, Seidu himself had bought the brightly colored cotton cloths (Hausa, *lefe*) that Nuru (18) was required to give the bride; there were piles of shiny new enamel pots which Habiba had bought the bride, since her own collection had been inherited by her own daughter when she was married; and there were two necklaces, two bracelets, two pairs of earrings, and some head scarves. Fuseini (66) had also contributed a large quantity of new clothes to each bride.

On Tuesday morning the girls had their hands and feet stained with henna. The hands and feet are wrapped in cloth while the henna is absorbed into the skin. As Trimingham describes (1959: 198), "Henna usage is a characteristic of Islamic civilization which has spread widely because of a prophetical recommendation. It purifies, it is known to mollify *jinn* and neutralize their urge to harm." The henna (Hausa, *lalle*) was applied again on Tuesday afternoon and twice again on Wednesday. During this time the girls remained in Habiba's (115) room. Women from their prospective husbands' houses came to see them, and they would respectfully hide their heads in shame (Hausa, *kunya*) under their cloths. Meanwhile the women from Fuseini's (66) house washed all the new pots and showed the dowry to a stream of admiring female visitors. Nuru (18), meanwhile, remained at his house; his male friends visited and prepared a nightly dinner (roasted meat, salad, and soda pop – salad being something rarely eaten, although often served to Europeans or to Westernized visitors). The young men would dance to high-life music late into the night. It was interesting to observe the relatively Western aspect of the young men's dress and activities, in contrast to the orthodox Islamic ritual of the senior generation.

On Wednesday, kola was sent around to invite people to the wedding. Fuseini (66) and Seidu (67) were responsible for guests in Aboabo, Sabon Zongo and Asawase, while Rahman (26), Abdul (63), and Usuman (11) covered Ashanti New Town, Zongo, and Suame. Rahman bought 1,200 kola nuts, at four shillings per hundred, and sat down with his brothers to divide them. They kept a careful record of whom they had included but did not note the amount of kola sent to each. This varied from as many as a hundred nuts for people with many followers to as few as four or five nuts.

The main categories of people who received kola from Rahman included various tribal headmen living in Zongo, who were then expected to distribute it on Rahman's behalf to their elders, who, in turn, would give it to other members of their ethnic communities; the Imams of the various ethnic communities represented in the zongo and resident in the three neighborhoods which they covered; the heads of the main trading and occupational groups who lived in these three neighborhoods, including the Sarkin Baranda (the head of the sheep market) and the chief collectors of the various lorry stations; the heads of all Mossi craft groups in Kumasi; important malams, especially those who ran Arabic schools (as did Rahman himself); neighbors, including the Mossi headman under the CPP who, until then, had been in conflict with this family; friends of Seidu's and Fuseini's who lived in the three neighborhoods; Rahman's friends, or men he considered important in his immediate neighborhood; the families of Rahman's sisters' husbands and brothers' wives; the bridegroom's sewing teacher; and others. Rahman's very closest friends, such as one Hausa man living in Aboabo, did not receive kola. "He passes kola, like my brother," he explained. A few people received personal letters written in Arabic, since, for one reason or another, they were considered to deserve special treatment. It is on such occasions that one can observe individuals' evaluations of their own social networks. Rahman was careful to include zongo leaders from all ethnic categories, Islamic leaders, neighbors in a number of ethnic communities, affines, former enemies, leaders of trade and occupational groupings, and individuals who had various personal ties to his family. His evaluation of the size of an individual's following was also demonstrated in his decisions about how many kola nuts to send.

The evening before the religious ceremony, the two brides were washed by a Hausa woman known by the title Aluwanka ("the one who washes"). Before the washing Aluwanka prayed for the girls and then bathed them in the courtyard of Fuseini's (66) house. Only women from the house attended, and there was none of the dancing and teasing which occurred in less orthodox families, for Seidu (67) himself had been one of the malams who had preached against such behavior.

The next day, before the ceremony, Fuseini's (66) wives cooked large quantities of rice - *abincin auren,* food of the marriage. A large bowl of rice was sent to Rahman's (26) house. After eating, most members of Rahman's house went to Aboabo for the ceremony, but Nuru (18) stayed behind, wearing old clothes and looking unconcerned. In Aboabo the brides sat in their rooms laughing and playing with girlfriends while their hair was braided. Seidu (67) ᴧnd Fuseini (66) prepared trays of kola and coins which were to be distributed among the attending malams and important guests.

About three hundred people attended the ceremony, which was performed (for both daughters) in the mosque outside Fuseini's (66) house. Almost all of the headmen came or sent delegates. The principal malams and the Imams of every ethnic community came. The Mossi elders arrived conspicuously late and sat together. The ceremony was performed by the Hausa Imam, who explained the terms of the marriage contract. Since this was a *sadaka* marriage, no bride price was recorded. Fuseini offered to give the *sadaki,* the formal payment legalizing the marriage, but Malam Aboubakr, Adamu's "brother," had already sent fifty shillings for this from the village where he lived, sixty miles from Kumasi.

After the Aboabo ceremony the bridegroom's friends went back to the Zongo, drumming and dancing, led by Nuru's closest friend, the *abocin ango* (Hausa, friend of the groom), a Yoruba youth who had grown up in Adamu's house. The older Mossi immigrants returned to the mosque in Zongo known as the Mossi mosque, which Adamu had built near his own house when he was headman. The Mossi Imam led them in prayer, first for Adamu and his family, then for the people of Ejura, the town where Rahman had lived for the past seven years, after having been served with a local deportation order by the government. The Ejura people had sent a sack of corn worth fifty Ghanaian pounds for the marriage. Then they prayed for Malam Aboubakr, who had paid the *sadaki.* All of the Mossi young men were dressed in identical gowns, made of the cloth they had selected for the past year's Maulude (the Prophet's birthday) celebration. Even in this ritual merging of ethnic communities, then, there were expressions of the distinct identity of the Mossi.

173

In the evening Habiba (115) and one of Fuseini's (66) wives brought Meriama and the other bride to greet Fuseini and Seidu (67). Both men made brief speeches to the girls, stressing the dominant position of men and describing their duties towards their new husbands. They were reminded of their Islamic education and told that this should have taught them that women went to heaven[5] because they followed their husbands there. They were to obey their husbands and the senior women in their new houses. They were told by Fuseini that they should behave themselves better than they had in his house as children. He stressed that Meriama would have to be especially cautious, because it might be hard for her to suddenly behave as a wife in a house full of relatives: "The place you are going is your house, and all the women there are your mothers. We don't want to hear any bad report of you. Just because your husband is your brother, if he calls you, don't frown [literally, squeeze your face] and say this and that." After these speeches the two girls visited their maternal grandmothers, one of whom was the Hausa Magajia (chief of women).

Having said goodbye to their kin in Aboabo, the two girls were ready to go to their husbands' houses. Nuru's (18) *abocin ango* had come in a taxi to get Meriama, and she reluctantly went with him, accompanied by a younger sister and a friend. After greeting Amina (25), Rahman (26), and other members of Nuru's household, she sat down in the room of Rahman's second wife, Adjara (33). She cried quietly for several hours, while Nuru and his friends danced and talked outside the house. Later, Adjara took Meriama (17) across the courtyard to Nuru's newly decorated room. He came to see her after everyone else had gone to bed and he left before dawn, before the others awoke for morning prayer. For three days, Meriama remained inside the house, surrounded by children and her girl friends, but with little contact with her new husband.[6]

The first day after the marriage ceremony, when Meriama was in this state of semi-seclusion, everyone else celebrated. In Fuseini's house one sheep sent by Amina and another sent by the husband of the other bride were killed. This occasion, in which gifts (Hausa, *kari*) are sent from the groom's family to the bride's, resembles a Yarse ceremony performed after the wedding night, in which the husband's family celebrates the bride's virginity by sending a sheep to the wife's kin. The women in Fuseini's (66) house cooked rice, millet porridge, and the sheep and sent this around to all the kin, including the members of Rahman's (26) household. By mid-morning they had finished and then sat around admiring the marriage gifts. About two hundred women, including the relatives of the two new husbands, came to see the gifts. Nuru's (18) mother (29), however, was absent. Like her son, she could not take an active part in the ceremony; she also had to observe the strict avoidance required, particularly by the Hausa, between a mother and her oldest son. While the other women were elaborately dressed on all these days, when she appeared she wore her usual everyday dresses.

The gifts the girls received were exceptionally elaborate. Fuseini (66) and Seidu (67) had each given a large number of cloths, head scarves, sandals, and jewelry. The brides' mothers and their kin sent cloths and more jewelry, and the grooms' family sent more cloth. All of the cosmetics, jewelry, baby toys, and other items each girl had collected for her own marriage were also displayed in the courtyard for the admiration and comments of visitors. Outside, instead of dancing, which occurred at many Mossi marriages, the children from Seidu's Arabic school sang passages of the Qur'an.[7]

Six days after the ceremony the women from Aboabo came to Zongo to bring the gifts. Again, they displayed these for the admiration of guests and relatives. There were at least thirty cloths, fifty pots, pillows, towels, sheets, cooking utensils, soap powder, thermos bottles, cosmetics, and basic food items, including onions, rice, and handmade macaroni (Hausa, *taliya*). The Aboabo women were joined by relatives and friends who began to arrange the bride's room. Rahman's wife prepared food. When they had eaten and enjoyed themselves, they left Meriama in her not-very-new house.

Although this marriage is typical only of prominent and relatively affluent immigrants, it illustrates a number of points. Among the most important are: the large number of people involved and the care with which many sections of the community are included; the persistence of some actions symbolizing Mossi identity amidst a strikingly Hausa ritual; the assimilation of these ritual patterns by non-Hausa; and the importance placed upon family solidarity, even though the family is ethnically heterogeneous.

A quantitative analysis of interethnic marriage

In the sample of 89 houses described above, there are 560 current marriages, involving 1,017 people (457 men and 560 women – 103 men were polygamous). Approximately half of the people whose marriages were studied (554) are Mossi, while the rest belong to many different ethnic categories. Both first-generation and urban-born immigrants are represented. On the basis of these marriages it is possible to analyze the marriage choices of members of different ethnic categories and generations in relation to variations between the four neighborhoods discussed earlier. Since marriage choices are the focus of this study, the marriages themselves have been taken as the units for analysis. This means that some individuals who were married more than once were counted several times. The patterns that emerge from the study of actual marriages can then be compared to statements of first- and second-generation Mossi immigrants about their marriage choices.

It should be noted that the immigrants themselves often discuss ethnicity in terms of marriage choices. They make many statements about the strength or weakness of ethnic groups, or about how they regard different groups, by discussing interethnic marriage choices. This would lead one, at first, to suspect that strong statistical evidence might be available to support or reject these claims about ethnicity. In fact, however, there are many variables which affect an analysis of this data and make the interpretation of the statistical evidence difficult. For example, the availability of marriageable women in each ethnic category varies over time, so that, while a second-generation man may marry out as a matter of choice, an older migrant may marry out by necessity. The data, then, mean something different for each generation. Among the second generation many factors must be considered which do not push the trend in any one direction. For example, since ethnicity is culturally less significant, and Islam emphasizes the irrelevance of traditional ethnic categories, out-marriage is encouraged. On the other hand, ethnic associations still exist and discourage it, as do many elders, who sometimes exert considerable influence on their children's marriage choices. The multiplicity of such factors, and their changing importance, means that we are unlikely to end up with a very clear picture of trends if we rely on the quantitative evidence alone.

Nevertheless, an examination of the total marriage sample shows that, on the whole, there is a definite preference for ethnically endogamous marriage. That is, had the selection of spouses been entirely random within this sample population, the number of in-marriages would have been 140, or 25.5 percent of the total (Mitchell 1957: 16n.).[8] In fact, there are 413 in-marriages, or 73.7 percent. Approximately one marriage in four is between members of different ethnic groups, while, had the selection been random, one in four would have been ethnically endogamous. But, given this overall pattern, there are still variations in the rates of interethnic marriage in different neighborhoods, generations, and ethnic groups. These variations correlate with changing attitudes among immigrants of different generations, and therefore can be taken as indicative of certain trends in the changing pattern of interethnic relations.

As the discussion of the proportion of non-Mossi kin in each neighborhood has already indicated, neighborhoods vary somewhat in the frequency of interethnic marriages among their residents. In Zongo, 40 percent (59 of 149) of all the marriages in the Mossi-owned houses were between members of different ethnic communities; in Aboabo, 29 percent (65 of 224), in YateYate, 30 percent (35 of 117), and in Mossi Zongo, 21 percent (22 of 106) were mixed. In comparing these data, the variations are statistically significant between Zongo and Aboabo (χ^2 = 4.0487, p < .05, df = 1) and highly significant between Zongo and Mossi Zongo (χ^2 = 9.2949, p < .01, df = 1).[9] The total of 596 marriages is due to the fact that in this count some marriages which were subsequently terminated were included.

That there is a higher rate of interethnic marriage in the oldest neighborhood can be accounted for, in part, by historical and demographic factors. In the beginning of the century, when the Zongo was being settled, there were fewer immigrants in all groups and almost no women in some. Most Mossi informants agree that there were far fewer Mossi women in Kumasi at that time than there are now. Today, the majority of marriageable Mossi women in Kumasi were born there, while a much higher proportion of the men (who are marriageable longer) are still born in the north (see Table 26). Consequently, in the beginning of the century many marriages and consensual unions were between members of different ethnic communities; the preference for in-marriage that is still evident could be met only by importing wives from the north. Migrants often married local women, rather than returning north for wives (particularly when ignoring obligations to kin was a reason for settling in town in the first place), and, in terms of ethnicity this often meant marrying out. Elderly

Table 26. *Birthplaces of spouses in the marriage sample*

	Husbands		Wives	
	No.	%	No.	%
Kumasi	125	21	227	38
North	417	70	285	48
Elsewhere in Ghana	48	8	73	12
Not ascertained	6	<1	11	<2
Total	596	100	596	100

Mossi men say that their first spouses in Kumasi were most often Asante, Kotokoli, and Hausa. Both Kotokoli and Hausa women often came alone, while others did so less frequently.

The offspring of these heterogeneous unions are now adults, and in many cases they are still living in Zongo or Aboabo in houses their parents built. They are more likely to marry out of their ethnic communities than are children of ethnically endogamous marriages. It is very common for people to marry into their mother's ethnic group, and, as arranged marriages become more common, the tendency to reaffirm alliances of this type also increases. This pattern is common among the Yarse in Upper Volta, who try to arrange marriages into their mother's patronymic group (*sondere*); it is continued in Kumasi, where ethnic categories are seen as equivalent to *sondere*. Thus, when the offspring of mixed marriages marry into their mother's ethnic categories, they often claim to have married their *yasaba*.

Among some families out-marriages have taken place for several generations. Some can be traced to the trading towns of northern Ghana, and some to the pre-colonial contacts between different groups in the north. Among these families the preference for in-marriage seems to be considerably weakened. This does not mean that ethnicity plays no part in the selection of spouses, but merely that preferences are not necessarily directed toward one's own group.

However, since in-marriage does, on the whole, seem to be preferred, one might expect that the more nearly equal sex ratio among town-born immigrants would make the rate of in-marriage higher among them. This does not happen, however, and in fact the rate of out-marriage increases among *'yan k'asa*. Taking men of all ethnic groups as our sample, this shift is significant. Seventy-six percent of all the marriages of first-generation men are ethnically endogamous, while only 60 percent of those involving men born in Kumasi are endogamous (see Table 27).

Among the Mossi men there is also an increase in out-marriage, when measured in terms of percentages (28 percent in the first generation and 37 percent in the second). This, however, is not significant ($\chi^2 = 1.3560$, p < .30, df = 1), probably because of the pressure toward endogamy exerted by Mossi elders (including their ability to control their daughters' marriage choices) and by the Mossi ethnic associations. The overall trend, however, is that among both men and women the likelihood of out-marriage is greater for those born in town.

Table 27. *Ethnicity and marriage patterns of first- and second-generation immigrants*

	First generation[a]		Second generation[b]	
	No.	%	No.	%
All men				
Number of marriages	465	100	125	100
Number of in-marriages	353	76	75	60
Number of out-marriages	112	24	50	40
$\chi^2 = 11.7398$, p < 0.001, df $= 1$, $\emptyset = .146$				
All women				
Number of marriages	358	100	227	100
Number of in-marriages	293	82	143	63
Number of out-marriages	65	18	84	37
$\chi^2 = 25.0134$, p $< .001$, df $= 1$, $\emptyset = .164$				
Mossi men				
Number of marriages	249	100	71	100
Number of in-marriages	178	72	45	63
Number of out-marriages	71	28	26	37
$\chi^2 = 1.3560$, p $< .30$, df $= 1$, $\emptyset = .073$				
Mossi women				
Number of marriages	132	100	101	100
Number of in-marriages	129	98	91	90
Number of out-marriages	3	2	10	10
$\chi^2 = 4.9552$, p $< .05$, df $= 1$, $\emptyset = .210$				
Yates correction for continuity: $\chi^2 = 5.052$, p $< .05$				

[a]Those born in the north and elsewhere in Ghana.
[b]Kumasi-born.

In evaluating this generational tendency it is important to note the importance of cultural differences between first-generation and town-born immigrants. Those born in town are generally more orthodox Muslims, and Islam denies the significance of ethnic differences, while it stresses the importance of marrying a cobeliever. When first-generation immigrants marry outside the ethnic community they must make a considerable adjustment to cultural differences. The spouses often do not speak the same language, they come from different areas, and, in general, they have little in common in terms of cultural backgrounds. *'Yan k'asa*, on the other hand, have a great deal in common, regardless of their ethnic affiliation. In cultural terms, therefore, unions between *'yan k'asa* of different ethnic categories are not out-marriages at all. From the *'yan k'asa* viewpoint, a marriage to a member of the same ethnic community who was born in the north generally requires much more adjustment than a marriage to a member of a different ethnic community who was also born in Kumasi. It is possible that if all marriages were intragenerational, out-marriage among *'yan k'asa* would be more frequent than it is. However, the frequency of out-marriage among town-born immigrants is reduced by the control which first-generation migrants exert over their daughters' marriages.

Because of an imbalance in the sex ratio among first-generation immigrants in many ethnic communities, including the Mossi, first-generation men seek wives among Kumasi-born women. Since fathers are able to exert control over the selection of spouses for their daughters, they frequently choose to give their daughters in marriage to men of their own generation and ethnic group. This explains, in part at least, why almost all the second-generation Mossi women in the sample who are married to non-Mossi men were first married to Mossi men of their father's generation. This is not to say that town-born Mossi women never choose to marry first-generation Mossi men, but it does imply that the frequency of such marriages is increased by the arrangements first-generation men make for their daughters.

The marriage sample clearly shows that women born in Kumasi marry men who are born elsewhere, mainly in the north, much more frequently than Kumasi-born men marry women born elsewhere. Among all the marriages in the eighty-nine Mossi-owned houses, 83 percent (104 of 125) of those involving urban-born.men were to urban-born women. Only 45 percent (104 of 227) of marriages involving women born in town were to men born there. Only 18 of 358 women (5 percent) from outside Kumasi married Kumasi-born men, while 102 out of 465 marriages (22 percent) of men from the north, or elsewhere in Ghana, were to Kumasi-born women. Of the Mossi, Table 28 shows that 75 percent (53 of 71) of marriages of Kumasi-born Mossi men were to Kumasi-born women (47.7 percent, 34 of 71, were to Kumasi-born Mossi women), while only 44 percent (44 of 101) of Kumasi-born Mossi women married Kumasi-born men (34 were to Kumasi-born Mossi men). Among the rural-born Mossi, 92 percent of the women married men born outside Kumasi, while only 67 percent (168 of 249) of the men married rural-born women. All of these comparisons are significant beyond $p < 0.001$.

These figures must be interpreted in light of the total number of husbands and wives born in town in the marriage sample. Table 26 shows that in the sample there are over three times as many first-generation husbands represented as there are husbands born in Kumasi, while among the wives the proportions are nearly equal. Assuming that the birth rate for men and women is approximately equal, this difference could be due either to different migration patterns for men and women or to the earlier marriage age for women and the monopolization of wives by first-generation men. In fact, Table 18 shows that there are 247 adult men without wives, while there are practically no women who are not presently married.

While both men born in the north and men born in Kumasi still do show a preference for marrying within their own group, and while among the Mossi this proportion also decreases in the second generation, the decrease is not statistically significant (see Table 27). This may be due to the success that the Mossi have had in encouraging their young men to marry Mossi women and to the control which older Mossi men exert over their daughters. Nevertheless, among those who have married non-Mossi there are some interesting differences in terms of their choice of wives.

179

Table 28. *Provenance of spouses in Kumasi marriages*

	Men		Women	
	No.	%	No.	%
Urban-born (all ethnic groups)				
Spouses born outside Kumasi	21	17	123	55
Spouses born in Kumasi	104	83	104	45
Total	125	100	227	100
x^2 = 45.0729, p < 0.001, df = 1, $\emptyset$ = -.364				
Rural-born (all ethnic groups)				
Spouses born outside Kumasi	363	78	340	95
Spouses born in Kumasi	102	22	18	05
Total	465	100	358	100
x^2 = 45.0783, p < 0.001, df = 1, $\emptyset$ = -.238				
Urban-born Mossi				
Spouses born outside Kumasi	18	25	57	56
Spouses born in Kumasi	53	75	44	44
Total	71	100	101	100
x^2 = 15.1411, p < 0.001, df = 1, $\emptyset$ = -.309				
Rural-born Mossi				
Spouses born outside Kumasi	168	67	125	92
Spouses born in Kumasi	81	33	11	08
Total	249	100	136	100
x^2 = 27.5659, p < 0.001, df = 1, $\emptyset$ = -.274				

[a]There are four marriages in this count of first-generation Mossi women not included in Table 31.

Immigrants from different generations select spouses from different ethnic categories, and this reflects the change in cultural orientation that takes place in the zongo. Thus, Table 29 shows that 11 percent of marriages involving Mossi *'yan k'asa* are to Hausa women, while only 4 percent of marriages involving first-generation Mossi men are to Hausa women.[10] Mossi men born in town marry Yoruba women, while first-generation immigrants, according to this sample, do not. There is also a slight drop in the percentage of *'yan k'asa* marriages contracted between members of culturally related groups, that is, between spouses who are both from Upper Volta or northern Ghana. A study of marriage preferences described later shows the same selective pattern as do the actual marriage choices, even though the sample for the two studies was different.

Despite the fact that Kumasi-born women marry men of the same ethnic category who were born outside Kumasi, thereby increasing the rate of ethnic in-marriage over what it would be, had they married randomly within their own generation, there is still an increase in out-marriage among female *'yan k'asa,* when compared to women born in the north. The differences in rates of in-marriage between

Table 29. *Marriages of Mossi men, according to ethnic group and birthplace of wife*

| Ethnic group of wife | Birthplace of wife | | | | |
	Kumasi	North[a]	Ghana[b]	Total	Percent
First-generation men					
Mossi	56	108	14	178	72
Upper Volta (not Mossi)	5	12	1	18	7
Northern Ghanaian, centralized	7	15	2	24	10
Northern Ghanaian, uncentralized	2	3		5	2
Hausa	6	1	4	11	4
Yoruba and Nupe	1			1	
Akan	2			2	1
Togo	1	5		6	2
Wangara (not Upper Volta)	1		3	4	2
Total	81	144	24	249	100
Percent	32	58	10	100	
Second-generation men					
Mossi	34	4	7	45	63
Upper Volta (not Mossi)	3		1	4	6
Northern Ghanaian, centralized	2	2	1	5	7
Northern Ghanaian, uncentralized	2			2	3
Hausa	6		2	8	11
Yoruba and Nupe	3			3	4
Akan	2			2	3
Zabarama	1			1	1
Ga			1	1	1
Total	53	6	12	71	99
Percent	75	8	17	100	

[a]North means the home area of the group in question. For example, for Hausa this means northern Nigeria.
[b]Ghana means anywhere except Kumasi, or the Northern Region, in the case of people from groups which originate in the Northern Region.

men and women of different generations of urban residence are summarized in Table 27. Both men and women born in Kumasi marry out more frequently than do people born in the north. Almost all (98 percent) Mossi women born in Upper Volta are married to Mossi men, while 10 percent of the Mossi women born in Kumasi are married to members of different groups. In this respect, Mossi women are still more conservative (or less able to exercise free choice) than Mossi men, but the rate of change between the generations is similar among men (a 9 percent decrease in ethnic endogamy) and women (an 8 percent decrease in ethnic in-marriage).[11]

Since the marriages studied were among residents in Mossi-owned houses, they cannot be assumed to be representative of the general marriage pattern of all ethnic communities in Kumasi. This is mainly because virilocality, which is still the most common postmarital residence pattern – except among some property-owning women – affects the ethnic composition of houses. Comparing the rate of out-marriage among men and women of the major ethnic categories in this sample, it appears that only among the Mossi do we find men having a higher rate of out-marriage than women. In all other groups, with those exceptions noted, [12] the proportions are equal or reversed. This confirms what the Mossi themselves say about their marriage policy in general – that they do not like their women to marry out, since their children will not be identified as Mossi. It also lends support to the argument presented by Capron and Kohler (1975, 1976) that the basis of Mossi political power is control over women. In this respect the Mossi in Kumasi seem to be maintaining a traditional pattern. In Kumasi, at least in the Mossi-owned houses, Mossi men are "wife receivers," just as they claim they should be, while other men are "wife-givers." This is shown in Table 30, a summary of data from Table 31, which, in turn, shows the composition of all marriages in the sample.

Ethnicity and marriage preferences

There is a noticeable difference between immigrants of different generations of urban residence in their attitudes about out-marriage. The relative merits of one group over another as spouses are a frequent topic of conversation, and one can often hear men and women of different generations comparing and contesting their views on this subject. In order to quantify some of these differences, a questionnaire was administered to 130 Mossi men, 108 of them born in Upper Volta, and 22 born in southern Ghana and Asante, mainly in Kumasi. They were asked whether they would permit their daughters to marry persons of specified groups. The responses to these questions are an index of ethnocentricity insofar as the adherence to patrilineality means that a woman's, more than a man's, marriage determines the ethnic affiliation of the children. People often say that they do not mind what group their sons marry into, while they care a great deal about the marriage choices of their daughters. Analyzing the responses of the 103 men in the sample, who were themselves married (27 were not), the percentage of positive responses out of the total number of responses can be stated. Each man was asked seven questions, which appear on Table 32. The responses of men who married only Mossi women themselves and of those who married others can be compared. The groups about which they were questioned were chosen to represent the main ethnic categories in the zongo. The Dagomba were included, in order to represent another centralized Moré-Dagbane-speaking people, but since there were some very particular attitudes distinguishing them from others, the Mamprusi were also included. The Frafra (Tallensi) were selected to represent a noncentralized Moré-Dagbane–speaking people; the Asante represent a culturally distant, matrilineal, and generally non-Muslim group. The Hausa were selected because they seemed to be a significant reference group for Mossi immigrants, and it seemed that a study of marriage preferences might bear this out. The Fulani represented a group that the Mossi traditionally did not marry.

It should be noted that although the Busansi were not included in the questions, several Mossi noted, in answer to the first question, that the Busansi were "just like

Table 30. *Out-marriage rate of residents of Mossi-owned houses, by sex and ethnic group*

	Men				Women				Percentage difference between male and female out-marriages	x^2	∅
	No.	Married in	Married out	Married out (%)	No.	Married in	Married out	Married out (%)			
Mossi	339	234	105	31	250	237	13	5	+26	58.0639, p < .001	-.316
Upper Volta, non-Mossi	57	46	11	20	71	45	26	37	-17	3.8116, p < .10	.190
Northern Ghana, centralized	40	33	7	18	74	30	44	59	-41	16.8321, p < .001	.402
Northern Ghana, uncentralized	49	46	3	7	59	47	12	20	-13	3.4130, p < .10	.205
Hausa	38	22	16	41	46	19	27	58	-17	1.6764, p < .20	.165
Niger, Mali	12	8	4	33	13	9	4	33	0	0.0851, p < .98	.027
Togo, Dahomey	7	5	2	28	18	5	13	70	-42	2.3892, p < .20	.400
Yoruba and Nupe	26	23	3	11	28	25	3	11	0	0.1135, p < .80	.013
Akan	29	29	0	0	33	28	5	16	-16	2.9542, p < .10	.224

Table 31. *Ethnic groups of spouses living in eighty-nine Mossi-owned houses*

Men \ Women	Mossi	Busansi	Gurma (U.V.)	Wangara (U.V.)	Grusi (U.V.)	Fulani (U.V.)	Samo	Asante	Fante	Ga	Ewe	Banda	Kwahu	Mamprusi	Dagomba	Gonja	Wala
Total	233	44	4	8	10	2	1	18	4	2	5	1	1	11	28	21	7
Wangara (I.C.)																	
Calabar																	
Ibo																	
Nupe	1																
Yoruba																	
Gurma (Togo)																	
Chokosi																	
Atakpame																	
Basari																	
Kotokoli				1													
Dendi																	
Songhai															1	1	
Fulani (Nigeria)																	
Hausa	5	1														1	2
Dagati																	
Sisala																	
Builsa																	
Kusasi														1			
Frafra																	
Grusi (Ghana)	1															1	
Wala																1	3
Gonja															4		
Dagomba															12	3	
Mamprusi	1	1												4			
Kwahu													1				
Banda																	
Ewe											5						
Ga										1							
Fante									3								
Asante								16									
Samo							1										
Fulani (U.V.)						2											
Grusi (U.V.)	1				5											1	
Wangara (U.V.)				2												1	
Gurma (U.V.)		1		1	1										1		
Busansi	3	31	1														
Mossi	221	10	3	5	4			2	1	1		1		6	10	12	2

Group		Total
Grusi (Ghana)		13
Frafra		16
Kusasi		3
Builsa		7
Sisala		5
Dagati		6
Hausa		45
Fulani (Nigeria)		2
Songhai		6
Dendi		3
Kotokoli		9
Basari		1
Atakpame		2
Chokosi		1
Gurma (Togo)		4
Yoruba		24
Nupe		2
Ibo		3
Calabar		2
Wangara (I.C.)		6
Total		560

Column totals: 321, 35, 4, 4, 7, 3, 16, 3, 1, 5, 0, 7, 17, 5, 4, 11, 15, 3, 7, 2, 6, 32, 3, 9, 1, 4, 0, 2, 0, 0, 22, 4, 3, 2, 0 — 560

Table 32. *Marriage preferences of Mossi men*

Question and response	2nd-genera- tion men		1st-genera- tion men		Total average		Percent- age dif- ference in two gen- erations
	No.	%	No.	%	No.	%	
What tribe would you prefer your daughter to marry into?							
Mossi	10	45	58	54	68	52	−9
Any tribe	1	5	14	13	15	12	−8
Any Muslim	10	45	26	25	36	28	+20
Mossi or closely related tribe[a]	1	5	9	8	10	8	−3
Would you allow your daughter to marry an Asante?							
Yes	1	4	22	21	23	18	−17
Yes, if Muslim[b]	16	73	36	33	52	40	+40
No	5	23	50	46	55	42	−23
Would you allow your daughter to marry a Hausa?							
Yes	15	68	56	52	71	55	+16
Yes, if Muslim	7	32	13	12	20	16	+20
No	0		39	36	39	29	−36
Would you allow your daughter to marry a Fulani?							
Yes	3	23	14	18	17	18	+5
Yes, if Muslim	2	15	15	19	17	18	−4
No	8	62	50	63	58	63	−1
Would you allow your daughter to marry a Frafra?							
Yes	3	14	29	27	32	25	−13
Yes, if Muslim	10	48	29	27	39	29	+21
No	8	38	50	46	58	46	−8
Would you allow your daughter to marry a Mamprusi?[c]							
Yes	15	66	75	70	90	69	−4
Yes, if Muslim	7	33	22	20	29	21	+13
No	0		11	10	11	9	−10
Would you allow your daughter to marry a Dagomba?							
Yes	10	45	69	64	79	61	−19
Yes, if Muslim	7	32	16	15	23	18	+17
No	5	23	23	21	28	21	+2

[a] Answers filled in here included Busansi (4); Wala (1); Mamprusi, Dagomba, or Busansi (2); Mamprusi or Dagomba (3).
[b] Includes seven who were very reluctant.
[c] Fewer men were asked about the Mamprusi.

186

Table 33. *Marriage preferences of married Mossi men: statistical analysis*

	Men married only to Mossi		Men married to non-Mossi	
	No.	%	No.	%
First generation				
Number of men	49		40	
Total number responses	343	100	280	100
Number positive responses	117	34	137	49
Number negative responses	226	66	143	51
Second generation				
Number of men	8		6	
Total number responses	56	100	42	100
Number positive responses	39	69	29	68
Number negative responses	17	31	13	32

Statistical analysis
Responses of first-generation men married to Mossi and non-Mossi women:
$\quad \chi^2 = 13.4098, df = 1, p < .001, \emptyset = -.150$
Responses of second-generation men married to Mossi and non-Mossi women:
$\quad \chi^2 = 0.0250, df = 1$, no significance $(p < .98), \emptyset = .006$
Responses of men married only to Mossi women by generation:
$\quad \chi^2 = 24.0545, df = 1, p < .001, \emptyset = -.253$
Responses of men married to non-Mossi women by generation:
$\quad \chi^2 = 5.1408, df = 1, p < .05, \emptyset = -.136$
Responses of men married to Mossi and non-Mossi women by generation:
$\quad \chi^2 = 26.9133, df = 1, p < .001, \emptyset = -.197$
Responses of men of both generations by marriage to Mossi or non-Mossi women:
$\quad \chi^2 = 10.6864, df = 1, p < .01, \emptyset = -.125$

us." Formerly having the same headman in Ghana, inhabiting some of the same areas and recognizing the same chiefs in Upper Volta, the Busansi are often regarded as part of the Mossi group of Kumasi, even though their language is different (although many speak Moré, as well as Hausa) and they now have separate headmen.

Table 33 shows that, out of 323 possible responses by men born in the north to the question of whether they would allow their daughters to marry into any one of the other groups mentioned, 117 responses (34 percent) were positive among those who had married only Mossi women. Out of 280 possible responses for men born in the north who had married out, 137 (49 percent) were positive. Among first-generation Mossi immigrants, those who have married non-Mossi are more tolerant of their daughters marrying out than are those who have not married out themselves. On the other hand, among the urban-born men, those married only to Mossi women were no more willing to have their daughters marry out than were those who had married out themselves. But the data (Table 33) indicate that generation is, in fact, more important than the ethnic affiliation of a man's spouse in determining a man's attitude. Second- and third-generation men, regardless of the ethnic identity of their wives, were more tolerant of out-marriages among their daughters than were the first-generation men.

There is also a change in the specific ethnic preferences of men of different generations, in accordance with the process of Islamization. When asked an open question about their preferences, almost half (45 percent) of the *'yan k'asa* said they would allow their daughters to marry any Muslim, while only a quarter of the first-generation immigrants gave this reply. The *'yan k'asa* also gave a greater proportion of positive responses for every group asked about, except the Dagomba, about whom there was a difference of only 2 percent. However, they often qualified their positive statements with the comment that the marriage would be permitted only if the husband was a Muslim. In analyzing the responses in Table 33, the answer, "Yes, if he is a Muslim," was interpreted as a qualified positive answer. Frequently among *'yan k'asa,* and occasionally among men born in Upper Volta, this qualification was also added to positive responses about marriages to Mossi. Among the urban-born, the number of unqualified positive responses rose only when they were asked about the Hausa (a 16 percent rise) and the Fulani (a 5 percent rise), but it dropped for all other categories including Mossi, for which the qualification, "if he is a Muslim," was added. It is assumed by most Mossi in Kumasi that Hausa and Fulani men are Muslims.

More than 60 percent of the first-generation immigrants would, without qualification, allow their daughters to marry Mamprusi and Dagomba, that is, other peoples with whom they have traditional linguistic and cultural bonds. More than 60 percent of urban-born immigrants will agree to marriages with Hausa and Mamprusi without qualification, but will agree to other marriages only if they are sure that the spouse is a Muslim. Once this is ascertained, they are more permissive in their choices than are the first-generation migrants. If the percentage of positive responses, including those qualified by demanding that the spouse be a Muslim, is ranked for each generation, it appears that the first-generation immigrants respond positively in the following order: Mamprusi, 90 percent of responses positive; Dagomba, 79 percent; Hausa, 64 percent; Asante, 64 percent; Frafra, 54 percent; Fulani, 37 percent.

As for negative responses, for every category asked about, the urban-born had fewer unqualified negative answers about all groups except the Dagomba. The hostility to marriages with Dagomba is not easy to explain. Some of the attitudes of the Mossi toward them have already been described. It is probable that among second-generation immigrants economic and political competition are major reasons for these negative answers. In the areas of kola and cattle trade, economic competition between Mossi and Dagomba is considerable, and this seems to extend to competition over women. In political affairs, as in the dispute over the imamate of the central mosque, the Dagomba and the Mossi often go separate ways. As noted above, their joking is reciprocal, often hostile, and frequently over women, each group accusing the other of monopolizing its women and refusing to let members of the other group marry them. In the marriage sample there are ten Mossi men married to Dagomba women, but there are no Mossi women married to Dagomba men. This may be partly because the sample includes only those living in Mossi-owned houses, but it may also indicate that the Mossi effectively do prevent the Dagomba from marrying their women.

This should not be taken to mean that the Dagomba are among the most socially distant groups from the Mossi in Kumasi zongo. For northern-born immigrants the lowest number of negative responses was given for the Mamprusi (10 percent), but the next lowest was given for the Dagomba (21 percent). The Hausa, Asante, Frafra, and Fulani ranked lower, in that order. The urban-born respondents gave no negative responses for the Mamprusi or the Hausa; they ranked the Dagomba and Asante next, with 23 percent negative responses each; and they followed these with the Frafra and the Fulani. The great number of negative responses to the Fulani is due to traditional attitudes. In Upper Volta the Fulani, particularly the pastoral Fulani, are endogamous, and the attitude against inter-marriage is reciprocal. In Kumasi, however, some orthodox Muslim *'yan k'asa* now say they will marry Fulani women, and even allow their daughters to marry Fulani men, while some first-generation immigrants say they will agree to these marriages if the Fulani are from Upper Volta and, preferably, also from Mossi country. Despite this qualification, the more positive evaluation of the Fulani in the context of Kumasi zongo may be an aspect of the "Hausaization" of the Mossi.

The rise in unqualified positive responses about the Hausa among urban-born Mossi can be correlated with a rise in the actual rate of intermarriage with this group. While the Mossi, as a whole, married Hausa women more than they married women from any other non-Mossi group, for *'yan k'asa* they constituted the largest single group of non-Mossi wives. Of the twelve Mossi women who married out, five were married to Hausa men. Since the samples of actual marriages and marriage preferences were different, this provides further support that the Hausa form a reference group for Mossi *'yan k'asa*. Among second-generation Muslims, the marriage of one's daughter to a Hausa is sometimes seen as a way of raising one's status in the next generation, for when a man's daughter has married a Hausa, his grandchildren belong to that group. Affinal connections with the Hausa are also felt to be valuable by some, although certainly not all, Mossi. It is interesting that if one questions most Mossi immigrants directly about the Hausa, or if one listens to casual conversations and unsolicited remarks, both first-generation migrants and urban-born immigrants express a range and variety of extremely negative attitudes. They say, for example, that the Hausa are wicked, cannot be trusted, that political fighting in the zongo is due to the activities of the Hausa, and so on. This resentment against a group that many Mossi clearly emulate in many ways may be regarded as an attempt by the Mossi to assert their own status within an environment which is strongly dominated by Hausa values and Hausa leadership. It should also be noted that there does not necessarily seem to be any direct correlation between the frequency of such negative evaluations and actual social conflict between members of these groups. Those who in one context express their Mossi identity by negatively evaluating the Hausa, in another way emulate the Hausa or identify with them as Muslims.

189

Kinship and community

In summary, then, what I have referred to as generalized and specific kinship and affinity both are important integrative mechanisms in zongo life, structuring relationships between immigrants living in different houses and different neighborhoods. Generalized kinship and affinity provide idioms in which relationships between members of the same ethnic group and between culturally related groups are expressed. Generalized kinship and affinity is most important among first-generation immigrants; and because it is based on a traditional cultural model, it expresses the persistence of cultural differences between ethnic categories in the zongo. Specific kinship and affinity, on the other hand, links individual members of all ethnic categories and all generations of urban residence. It transcends cultural boundaries between ethnic categories and generations.

Part III

Politics and change

8

The political history of
the zongo community: 1900-1970

Although there was a precolonial settlement of Muslim strangers in Kumasi, now incorporated into Asante society and known as the Asante Nkramo, the present zongo community dates back only to the beginning of the colonial period. The development of the zongo community was made possible by the British government's encouragement of the settlement of strangers. Consequently, the growth of the zongo political system must be considered in the context of the development of colonial administration in Kumasi and in Asante, as a whole. Changes in administrative policy, even when these did not refer specifically to the zongo, affected internal political development there. For this reason, it is impossible to discuss politics in the zongo, or in the Mossi community itself, in terms of either the development of political structures, or in terms of specific events, without referring to an external system. For the purposes of this chapter, "external system" refers to all personnel, policies, and actions which form part of or emanate from the larger political system in which the zongo exists. This includes the traditional and modified political system of Asante and the colonial and postcolonial governments on local, regional, and national levels. Political parties, as organizations which affect a wider community than the zongo alone, are also part of the external system. Obviously, the external system is defined from the vantage point of the zongo. The concept is used heuristically here only to define the subject of this discussion: the relations between the zongo and external political forces and the effects of these relations on political life and on ethnicity in the zongo community.

This chapter is intended to show first how administrative decisions and the development of local government in Kumasi, as a whole, have affected politics in the zongo. Second, it is intended to give the necessary background and contextual setting without which the case study of Mossi politics presented in chapter 10 is incomprehensible. The main contention is that the politicization of ethnicity occurs partly because of policies and events which emanate outside the zongo. Particularly because zongo residents are strangers, they are at times much more vulnerable than indigenous Ghanaians to events in the external political system. Developments in the zongo, as a whole, and within each ethnic community, are

193

deeply embedded in the changing context of national political life, and it is impossible to understand interethnic political relations within the zongo without taking this context into account.

As the traditional capital of Asante, Kumasi is the center of the traditional political administration. The Asantehene's palace is near the Zongo, and the Asantehene and his officials are in positions which enable them to form close personal relationships with the strangers and their leaders. The external system also includes representatives of the Ghanaian government on all levels of administration: local government is today handled mainly by the City Council, whose representatives, in the form of tax collectors and sanitary inspectors, come in frequent contact with the strangers. Moreover, Kumasi is the center of the district and regional (formerly, provincial) administration. The regional administration – housed in the same building where the British Chief Commissioner had his offices – acts as the local representative of the ministries of national government. Officials of government on all these levels are present in Kumasi, and the strangers have had close personalized contact with them since the zongo began. When they have a request or a petition, they send copies and pay personal visits to a great number of officials, including the Asantehene and city, district, and regional officials. This point should be kept in mind when patronage is discussed below, for the plurality of government representatives makes it possible for the strangers to manipulate the external political system in many ways, as it also makes them subject to many different external pressures. In attempting to gain support for their positions, immigrant leaders may appeal to different sources of power outside the zongo. At the same time, authorities and aspiring leaders outside the zongo use their ties in the zongo to gain local support. Moreover, as power has changed hands nationally, the locus of responsibility for the administration of the zongo has changed many times. With each change, shifts occur in the pattern of patron/client relationships which link the strangers into the external political system. These changes have had significant effects on the pattern of internal conflict within the zongo.

The zongo under colonial rule, 1896–1924: the politicization of ethnicity

In considering colonial administrative policy towards the zongo, one must necessarily consider the changing pattern of British/Asante relations, for in the colonial period the zongo was always seen as a part of a larger polity, that of Kumasi and of Asante, as a whole. In Kumasi itself, the changing relationship between the British and the Asante leaders had repercussions on the administration of the zongo, and these, in turn, affected the relationships between the zongo leaders and the traditional Asante authorities. There was never any consistent policy of administration referring to the zongo alone. Decisions affecting the strangers were made pragmatically, in response to events in the zongo, or in the British administration, or in Asante.

This is so, despite the fact that by 1930, when the theory of indirect rule had been formulated, Rattray, the government anthropologist at the time, expressed the idea that the administration of Kumasi zongo was, in fact, modeled after that of the Hausa emirates. Discussing a conflict in Gambaga, a town in northern Gold Coast where the Hausa Imam was claiming to be chief of the entire town, Rattray commented (*Report of the Anthropological Branch, 1930*):

As a possible solution of this alien problem, which might arise in big cosmopolitan towns such as Salaga, I should like to suggest, as I believe has been tried with success elsewhere [presumably Kumasi], that these communities be run on their own lines which would naturally follow the Nigerian model, as being more in keeping with their pseudo-Islamic characteristics.

In actuality, the most important single determinant of policy towards the zongo was the changing relationship between the government and the Asante chiefs. While the British were attempting to subdue the powers of traditional authorities, they were willing to countenance, and even encourage, the rise of strong leadership in the zongo, so long as the authority of the stranger leaders depended for its legitimation upon the patronage of British officials, and not upon traditional criteria. This was the policy until the mid-1920s, during the period when the Asante king was in exile.

Until 1935, when the Ashanti Confederacy was formed and the Asantehene was returned to what the British considered to be his precolonial office, the British attempted to break up the traditional organization of the kingdom and to weaken the power of the chiefs. Asante chiefs were given limited powers in the 1902 Administrative Ordinance, including the right to hold tribunals, with jurisdiction up to one hundred pounds. These powers were somewhat augmented in 1924 with the passage of the Native Jurisdiction Ordinance. Nevertheless, the cumulative effect of British policy until 1924 was to weaken the chiefs, to break up the centralized organization of the kingdom, and to replace the Asantehene by the British Chief Commissioner (Tordoff 1965). In formulating the 1902 Administrative Ordinance it was suggested that the Chief Commissioner should be regarded as a replacement for the Asante king, Prempeh I, who in 1896 had been removed from Kumasi and in 1900 was deported to the Seychelles Islands. In 1901, Bradford Griffith, the Chief Justice, wrote to the Colonial Secretary on the subject of the Ashanti Draft Ordinance, stating that, ". . . what one wants is large veiled powers, . . . Without definitely stating it in the Proclamation, I think the Government should assume that he has over the headchiefs the powers of the Paramount chief." (No. 3, in No. 13, *Draft Administrative Ordinances,* C.O. 879/67, P.R.O., London.)

The Chief Commissioner was given the power to install and depose chiefs, regardless of their traditional areas of jurisdiction or status. Many chiefs were supported by the government on the basis of their loyalty to the British in the 1900 rising. This led to numerous conflicts between chiefs and their subjects and the consequent impossibility of administering Asante effectively through the chiefs. The Chief Commissioner held a court which handled all serious cases and in 1905 he became head of the newly formed Kumasi Council of Chiefs, which was the only representative organ of local government until 1924, when the Kumasi Public

Health Board was formed. All council members were given the status of head chief, but there were no non-Asante members.

No provision for strangers was made in the 1902 ordinance. Asante chiefs were empowered to hold courts with limited jurisdiction, but theoretically they were supposed to be operating according to traditional principles. The ordinance specified that they "shall exercise the jurisdiction heretofore exercised by them in the same manner as such jurisdiction has been heretofore exercised" (*Administrative Ordinance, Ashanti, 1902*). The contradictions in the law, between the limitation on jurisdiction and the reliance on traditional legal principles, are obvious but do not directly concern us here. What is important is that, according to Asante tradition, strangers would have come under the jurisdiction of the Asantehene himself. In his absence they therefore came under the direct authority of the Chief Commissioner. In some ways their relationship with the Chief Commissioner resembled the relationship which formerly had obtained with the Asantehene. In both periods any authority a stranger leader had was derived from the king or the Chief Commissioner. This led to the development of a system of patronage under the British which was similar to that which existed in the precolonial period. The stranger leaders performed certain services for the rulers and were, in turn, given limited authority within the zongo. Since they had neither traditional nor legal rights to formal office, the headmen in the zongo depended upon this patronage. Moreover, since many of them were from French territories, they were subject to deportation if they fell into the government's disfavor.

The system of patronage which characterized relations between the migrants, their headmen, and the British did not obtain to the same extent between the Asante and the British. The stranger leaders were able to promise jobs and housing to migrants and, in return, they received services, including voluntary labor, which they were then able to offer the colonial authorities. British officials, in return, accorded recognition to the headmen, protected their positions, and permitted them to hold informal courts to deal with internal disputes within their particular ethnic communities. This policy clearly encouraged the growth of ethnic politics, in that it encouraged each migrant group to develop a formal political structure, it set different immigrant groups in relations of competition with each other, and it encouraged zongo leaders to use ethnicity in mobilizing local support.

Most Asante chiefs, on the other hand, were in a much more tenuous position than were the zongo headmen. Their subjects often expressed resentment against demands for labor made by the chiefs or the British. Lacking traditional royal status, but attempting to rule indigenous communities, many of these government-supported chiefs were not respected and had great difficulty enforcing their limited authority. As a result, until 1932, when the policy of indirect rule began to alter the relationship between the British and the Asante, the headmen in the zongo were in a relatively strong position.

The first leader who was formally recognized by the British as Sarkin Zongo was the Hausa leader, Malam Gardi. He is said to have been the Imam of the Hausa force in the British army. However, he was not supported by many of the traders and, some time between 1900 and 1902, he left Kumasi. Once the strangers moved from the neighborhood of Mmoromu to the site of the present Old Zongo, or Yelwa, a wealthy cattle dealer from Kano, called Maigida, became known as Sarkin Zongo. To his misfortune he was not supported by the British, who engineered his deposition and expulsion from Kumasi. He was deposed in 1905 because, according to an Arabic account written by al-Hajj 'Umar, "He ran up many debts with the cattle traders because he wasted their money by squandering it. His creditors brought a suit against him before the colonial authorities. He was jailed, then deposed and expelled" (quoted in Ahmed Baba al-Wa-'iz, *Kanz al-Mufid,* IASAR 410, 1965).

Until 1905 there were no other officially recognized headmen. In 1905 Maigida was succeeded by Malam 'Uthman, who was recognized as Sarkin Zongo until his death in office in 1919. Also in 1905, Sir Francis Fuller became Chief Commissioner of Ashanti. While in office, until 1920, he accorded recognition to headmen of the Yoruba, Mossi, and Wangara communities. During Fuller's term each headman was selected by his own community and, after being recognized by the Chief Commissioner, regarded himself as an autonomous leader with control over the internal affairs of his own community. It was, in fact, a bid for autonomy on the part of a number of ethnic communities which led to the recognition of more headmen. The Mossi, for example, claim that competition with the Hausa over trade, and the Hausa practice of calling them *kafiri* (pagans), led them to appeal to Fuller to recognize their own headman. The Chief Commissioner, like the Asantehene before him, upheld the authority of each headman to govern his own community. However, since the jurisdiction of the headmen was not formally defined, ambitious leaders often attempted to augment their authority by drawing their clientele from other communities and by performing more and more services for their subjects. In 1924, for example, the Yoruba headman complained that the Hausa headman was hearing Yoruba cases. His complaint was supported by the Chief Commissioner, who told the Sarkin Zongo that he could arbitrate only in Hausa disputes (Police Magistrate's Order, 21 Feb. 1924, Kumasi, NAG, Kumasi).[1] The Chief Commissioner and the Police Magistrate, who in Kumasi had the status of Provincial Commissioner, referred cases back to the various headmen, thus relieving the government of considerable court work. There were no rules for the conduct of these tribunals. Each headman was able to increase his jurisdiction until a complaint was brought against him. The personality of the headman, as well as his relationships with the Chief Commissioner and the Police Magistrate, as much as anything else, determined the extent of his jurisdiction. For example, when, in 1919, a complaint was made about the fact that the Sarkin Zongo, 'Uthman, was summoning people from the Gold Coast Colony to his court, the Police Magistrate commented (Acting Police Magistrate to Acting Chief Commissioner, Ashanti [ACCA], 18 Mar. 1916, NAG, Kumasi):

I am of the opinion that this should be jumped on, and that he has no jurisdiction real or implied except in petty cases in his own Zongo. His jurisdiction is not defined, nor is he such a person that the government can allow him to interfere in matters beyond this town.

Although the government seemed to recognize the autonomy of each headman, a principle of hierarchy was nevertheless accepted. This was demonstrated in 1924, when the matter of fees chargeable in zongo courts was raised. The Yoruba headman informed the Police Magistrate that a scale of fees had previously been established, although it apparently had not been enforced. According to this scale (Suley Lagos to Police Magistrate, 1 Mar. 1924, NAG, Kumasi), the Sarkin Zongo was theoretically allowed to issue summonses and charge fines between one and two pounds; the Yoruba headman, from eight shillings, sixpence, to one pound; and the other headmen, from five shillings, sixpence, to eleven shillings, sixpence.

Kumasi under colonial rule, 1924–1932: Asante versus Hausa hegemony

The period between 1924 and 1932, during which the British attempted to restructure their relations with the Asante rulers, was one in which major changes occurred in British relations with the zongo leaders. The position of the Asante traditional rulers was becoming stronger, while, at the same time, in order to balance this, the British adopted a policy of deliberately strengthening the position of the Hausa Sarkin Zongo. However, the British, having encouraged political activity based on ethnicity up to this point, met with serious opposition when they strengthened Hausa hegemony in the zongo. The conflicts this policy provoked, British reaction to these conflicts, and the government's new reliance on the reinstated Asantehene, were factors which combined to weaken the position of the stranger community in the late 1930s through the 1940s – that is, until party politics began in the decade before independence.

The consolidation of power in the hands of the Sarkin Zongo was well under way by 1924. This coincided with two important events in the history of Kumasi: the return of Prempeh I from exile and the epidemic of plague which struck Kumasi in 1924.

In 1919 Malam 'Uthman was succeeded by Malam Salaw, a Hausa born in Yendi of a Katsina Hausa father (actually born in Salaga) and a Dagomba (royal) mother. His election was opposed by certain Hausa, on the ground that his mother was Dagomba; nevertheless, his knowledge of Islamic law and divination had gained him a high reputation, as well as considerable wealth. Salaw had been a student of the well-known Islamic scholar, al-Hajj 'Umar, in Kete Krakye and came to Kumasi as an adult after completing his studies.

After his election as Sarkin Zongo, Salaw proved to be of great assistance to the British administration. During the plague epidemic he gathered the labor to clean the zongo and build the new housing estate, Sabon Zongo. It was Salaw who organized the weekly town cleaning sessions after the plague. Although it was at least partly these services which won him British favor, people today sometimes claim that his success was due to the fact that he gave British officials gifts of chickens which had been fed with holy water – water in which Qu'ranic inscriptions had been dissolved.

Salaw became the first headman in the zongo to gain a formal place in the Kumasi administration. The Public Health Board, formed in 1924, consisted of the Chief Commissioner, the Assistant Chief Commissioner, four "official members" appointed by the Chief Commissioner, and five "nominated members." Of the latter, two were chosen by the Asante traditional rulers, two were members of the Chamber of Commerce, and one African member was selected by the Chief Commissioner. In 1925 Malam Salaw was nominated as the "non-native" African member.

In this period major changes were taking place in the administrative structure of Kumasi. In 1924 Prempeh I returned to Kumasi as a private citizen and two years later he was recognized as Kumasihene. In 1924 also, the Native Jurisdiction Ordinance was passed, marking the beginning of renewed attempts to apply indirect rule to the administration of Asante. The Asante chiefs, however, were still not in high favor with the British. The chiefs did not provide labor for public works, their tribunals were said to be badly run, and they were often in conflict with their subjects, leading to their frequently being deposed, or "destooled." The first attempts to apply the Native Jurisdiction Ordinance in Kumasi were unsuccessful, and not until 1926, when Prempeh I was recognized as Kumasihene, did the legal reorganization of the Kumasi Division take place (Tordoff 1965). The volume of work faced by the Kumasihene's tribunal, which was established as a Head Chief's Tribunal under the 1924 ordinance, was so great that a system of clan tribunals was started. Seven were formed in Kumasi, with three Asante chiefs serving as magistrates on each.

In the same period, an amendment to the Native Jurisdiction Ordinance was passed (Section 41, Sub-section 5) which granted the Sarkin Zongo a tribunal. This was regarded as a unique experiment, for it was the first court established for "nonnatives." The District Commissioner recommended establishing the tribunal, stating, "I have no difficulty in recommending him [Salaw] a Tribunal as a 'chief.'. . . He would function only in Kumasi Zongo and have no jurisdiction from or to any other Zongo." (DC to Chief Commissioner No. 431/20/24 of 1927, NAG, Kumasi.) Of all the chiefs who were granted tribunals at this time, he was the only one who already had a trained staff. Court records were kept in Arabic, and accounts were carefully made. The Sarkin Zongo, the British noted, paid himself a fixed salary (*Annual Report 1930:* 36).

No rules for the conduct of the zongo tribunal were set out when it was established in 1927, but the other headmen's informal courts became illegal, and the headmen were told that they were to serve as jury members on the zongo tribunal. They were to be paid a share of the court revenue, but these rules were not put into law, and the headmen later complained that the Sarkin Zongo did not give them their share. Salaw was empowered to hear civil and criminal cases and to issue fines up to twenty-five pounds. As well as hearing cases regarding the criminal

offenses of assault, stealing, extortion, or defamation, he could also summon people to court for insulting a chief or disobeying his orders. He could imprison, fine,
or banish his subjects. Appeals from the zongo court went to the Kumasihene's
tribunal, where fines up to one hundred pounds were charged. The Sarkin Zongo
used the Kumasihene's prison and he had a staff of *dogari* (Hausa body guards)
who acted as messengers and as a police force.

The establishment of this tribunal initiated a period of intense conflict in the
zongo. While the British praised Salaw and regarded the tribunal as the "best run
court" in the district, the other headmen, deprived of an important source of revenue and authority, became increasingly resentful of the tribunal and the Sarkin
Zongo himself (DC to Chief Commissioner, 19 June 1930, NAG, Kumasi). In the
tribunal, Muslim law, albeit a Hausa version, was applied, and there were no longer
any courts in the zongo where customary law was upheld. As the number of non-
Hausa *'yan k'asa* was relatively small in this period, there were many first-generation immigrants who regretted the disappearance of the tribal courts, where a
combination of Muslim and customary law had been applied.

The autonomy of the non-Hausa communities was also curtailed in other ways.
The Sarkin Zongo assumed the power to "recognize" the headmen of the different
communities. He informed the British that the normal procedure through which
headmen were recognized was for a community to bring its candidate to him for
approval, after which he presented the headman to the Chief Commissioner (Salaw
to DC, 23 April 1928, NAG, Kumasi). This policy soon led to conflicts, the most
famous case being when the Sarkin Zongo would not recognize the new headman
selected by the Yoruba community after the British had deported their headman.)
He had similar conflicts with other groups, such as his refusal to recognize as
headman of the Dagati community a man who had been successfully leading his
people for many years. The reason given was that the man had appealed to the
Chief Commissioner for recognition before appealing to the Sarkin Zongo. A further
reason was probably that the man was not a Muslim. Such cases occurred re-
peatedly and intensified resentment against the Sarkin Zongo in many different
immigrant communities.

The Kumasihene also resented the power the British had given to the Sarkin
Zongo. Between 1929 and 1930 the government agreed to grant the Sarkin Zongo
increased jurisdiction. This had been continually opposed by the Kumasihene,
who complained, among other things, that the Sarkin Zongo was judging cases
involving Asantes and southerners (DC to CC, 19 June 1930, NAG, Kumasi). The
government regarded this as "politically unfortunate" but also maintained that it
reflected the popularity of the zongo tribunal. In 1932 the Sarkin Zongo was
granted an increase of jurisdiction up to fifty pounds and, to placate the Kumasihene, the government warned Salaw not to hear cases involving Asantes and
southerners.

The British invariably sent the other headmen's complaints about the Sarkin
Zongo to him, maintaining that all communication with the government had to pass

through him. Unable to approach the British directly, the other headmen then appealed to the Kumasihene, who at first looked favorably upon their requests. In 1928 he recommended, unsuccessfully, that they be granted tribunals, with jurisdiction up to twelve pounds. The government refused, claiming that this was a plot by the Yoruba headman, who for some years had opposed Malam Salaw.[2]

As conflict in the zongo increased, and as more and more petitions complaining about the Sarkin Zongo's abuse of power were sent to the government, the Kumasihene was warned to remain out of the dispute. His own political position was delicate at this time, given Asante attempts to form a confederacy, and after 1930 he was forced to abstain from directly supporting opponents of the Sarkin Zongo. Had he not done so, it could easily have appeared that he was attempting to augment his own authority by subverting the Sarkin Zongo through the other headmen.

While the government had increased the jurisdiction of the tribunal in April 1932, by July, opposition to the Sarki and the tribunal reached the point of violence. Officials described this as a "sudden manifestation of violence" (CCA to CCA, 20 Sept. 1932, NAG, Kumasi), despite the fact that complaints and petitions had been coming to them for over three years. This first incident occurred after the Sarkin Zongo arrested the Mamprusi headman. A Mossi informant described for me the precipitating event:

Isaka, Chief Mamprusi, took a woman from a Mamprusi man. The woman had gone to the chief to ask for a divorce, and the chief, being like her father, since they were all from one country, took her from the man and gave her to a different man to marry. The first man went and reported Isaka to Malam Salaw, and Salaw sent his *dogari* to Isaka's house to get rid of him [summons him?]. The people bailed Isaka and brought him to his own house and then they began to make a campaign against Salaw.

The British regarded the Mamprusi headman as the "ringleader of the riotous mob" and as head of a "private army of zongo scalleywags" (Sr. Commissioner of Police to Asst. CCA, 16 Aug. 1932, NAG, Kumasi). After several demonstrations outside the District Commissioner's office and the Police Magistrate's court, Isaka was arrested and sentenced to six months' imprisonment with hard labor. This promptly led to further "riotous demonstrations."

The British believed that dissatisfaction with the tribunal was the main source of discontent. Rules for the conduct of the tribunal were formulated, and it was expected that this would pacify all parties. The rules clarified the role of the other headmen on the tribunal. There were now nine headmen in the zongo, for headmen of the Dagomba, Mamprusi, Grusi, Kotokoli, and Frafra groups had been added since Salaw took office. The nine headmen were to sit as panel members on the tribunal and were given increased authority in the judgment of cases involving members of their own groups. The headmen were to serve as a jury in criminal cases, but in both criminal and civil cases sentence was to be passed by the Sarkin Zongo. The headmen had no authority to enforce their judgments, and the Sarkin Zongo had to ratify all recommendations of the headmen. Explicit rules for the division of death duties and court fees were set out (*Rules for the Conduct of the Zongo Tribunal*, NAG, Kumasi). The new regulations would have become law if protests had not led to the closure of the tribunal two months later.

Since the leaders of the protest were the heads of different ethnic communities, and since they were generally followed by large constituencies, the British, and some of the participants as well, were able to describe this protest against government policy as an interethnic conflict based upon the jealousy of the other headmen against the power given to the Hausa Sarkin Zongo. The main opponents of the Sarkin Zongo were the Yoruba headman, who had been deported to Accra in 1929, and the Mossi headman, whose deportation had been recommended by the District Commissioner in 1929, on the ground that he would "never give real service to the Sarikin" (DC to Commissioner, Eastern Province, Ashanti, 30 Aug. 1929, NAG, Kumasi). The Mamprusi, Grusi, and Kotokoli headmen were also strongly opposed to the Sarkin Zongo. The Wangara and Dagomba headmen said they would support any Sarkin Zongo the government appointed, while the Frafra headman, who had been appointed by Salaw and also had been raised in his house, supported the Sarkin Zongo.

Although the Sarkin Zongo had some supporters among the Mossi and other groups whose headmen opposed him, the leaders opposed to Salaw claimed that the conflict was based on the unacceptability of Hausa hegemony in the zongo. They argued that their separate ethnic identities and their different languages and customs made it impossible and unacceptable for the Sarkin Zongo to rule the entire immigrant community. They regarded members of their own groups who supported Salaw as traitors, and among the Mossi, if not among others, these people were accused of attempting to "become Hausa."[3]

Malam Salaw and some of his supporters, including a number of Mossi malams, did not regard the conflict in terms of interethnic hostility. To them it was a conflict between an educated and orthodox Islamic leadership and a backward, ignorant mass of illiterate "semipagans." The fact that they used stereotypes which described whole ethnic communities in these terms intensified the conflict but did not alter the fact that they regarded it primarily as a dispute between high- and low-status Muslims, ranked according to their orthodoxy and their level of education.

The British had another interpretation of these events. They regarded the conflict as an expression of disloyalty or opposition to their authority, as represented by the Sarkin Zongo. They looked upon the Mossi, Yoruba, Kotokoli, and Grusi headmen as political opportunists who thought they would gain power by the removal of the Sarkin Zongo. *The Annual Report of Ashanti* for 1932-3 summarized the administration's attitude toward the situation:

The ex-Sarki was a great personality and a very loyal supporter of Government; he earned the respect of all who came in contact with him and his failure to make a success of the difficult position to which he was appointed must be attributed to the immense difficulties of his task rather than to any misconduct on his part. A cousin to the Emir of Katsina, he was accustomed to autocratic rule and was intolerant of opposition from illiterate and unintelligent foreigners. The movement

against him personally was not a spontaneous one but was fomented by agitators
in the service of persons who stood to gain by his removal.

The events which led to the closing of the tribunal are of interest, for they show
how the government dealt with the zongo and also reveal the emergence of a new
attitude towards the balance of power in Kumasi, as a whole. In August 1932 there
were several minor confrontations between opponents of Malam Salaw, his supporters, and the police. The Chief Commissioner refused to remove Salaw from
office, on the ground that the charges against him would not have justified deposing
an Asante chief (ACCA to DC, 23 Aug. 1932, NAG, Kumasi). The dissenting headmen were asked to approve the new rules for the conduct of the tribunal. They
did so, but continued to refuse to submit to the authority of the Sarkin Zongo.
Nevertheless, on August 25, 1932, Malam Salaw was allowed to reopen the tribunal,
which had been temporarily closed after the July riots. The Mossi, Grusi, and
Kotokoli headmen then refused to accept letters from the District Commissioner
informing them of the opening of the tribunal, on the ground that the letters had
not "passed through the Kumasihene" (DC to ACCA, 26 Aug. 1932, NAG, Kumasi). The District Commissioner was infuriated, complained that the headmen
were being grossly discourteous, and claimed that upon leaving his office these
"objectionable people" went to see the Kumasihene (ibid.).

The Chief Commissioner ordered the headmen to apologize to the District Commissioner and agreed to see them a few days later. By this time he admitted that
it had been unwise to open the tribunal before making peace between the Sarkin
Zongo and the headmen, whose complaints of personal assault by the *dogari,* if
true, warranted that they be pacified by the Sarki. After seeing the dissenting
headmen, the Chief Commissioner admitted that Malam Salaw had been handling
the tribunal as if it were his own. The Chief Commissioner felt that the new rules
might help but still maintained that the Mossi headman should be deported (CCA
to ACCA, 21 Sept. 1932, NAG Kumasi).

In the next few weeks the government gave the appearance of granting the headmen's demand that the administration of the zongo be made the responsibility of
the Kumasihene. The government attempted to make it appear that the Asante
chiefs were responsible for letting the conflict go as far as it had and increasingly
held them responsible for zongo policy. The conflict between the factions in the
zongo became a matter for settlement by the Kumasihene, although he was given
little autonomy in his actions. The issue became a test of his loyalty to the government and the burden of passing judgment against the Sarkin Zongo or the headmen
passed formally to him. Thus, the Chief Commissioner wrote to his Assistant:

It is a test of the loyalty of the Head Chiefs and of the fitness of the Tribunals to
be entrusted with such powers that they do not hesitate to use them when the
necessity arises. In the present case I desire you to inform the Kumasihene of the
above and to request him to send for the Moshie headman and to order him to make
his peace with the Serikin. . . .

If the Mossi headman refused to obey the Kumasihene he was to be charged
under the Native Jurisdiction Ordinance with disobeying a lawful order of the

Kumasihene. Decisions were, in fact, taken by the British, but the responsibility
for them was delegated to the Asante chiefs. The Chief Commissioner's position
regarding the Mossi headman, expressed in the same document, was explicit (CCA
to ACCA, 26 Aug. 1932, NAG, Kumasi):

If the Kumasihene's Tribunal agrees with me that the Moshie headman's continued
presence in the Zongo is likely to be followed by further disorder I would advise
that . . . an order of deportation outside the Kumasi Division be also imposed. Any
police assistance required by the Kumasihene will of course be furnished to him.
Action against the Kotokoli and Grunshie headmen can be taken later if necessary,
but I think that the punishment of the Moshie headman will be sufficient.

The following day, the headmen were ordered to sign a bond to keep the peace,
but they refused and were imprisoned with three-month sentences. When this was
announced, "pandemonium broke loose among the crowd of Moshies, etc., outside
the court" (CCA to Colonial Secretary, 20 Sept. 1932, NAG, Kumasi). An attack
on Salaw's house followed, and the police, joined by a company of the Gold Coast
Regiment, went to fight the attackers. The Chief Commissioner applied the Peace
Preservation Ordinance (an act later declared to have been outside his authority),
to enable the police to search the Zongo for arms. By the next day there were
eighty-one people wounded, one dead, and over three hundred arrested.

The changed attitude on the part of the government to the Asante authorities,
as well as to the strangers, was evident throughout these events. The British were
particularly concerned, lest some prominent Asante be wounded or killed. No
Asantes were directly involved, however, and the Chief Commissioner noted that
"their attitude throughout left nothing to be desired" (CCA to Colonel, Gold
Coast Regiment, 17 Sept. 1932, NAG, Kumasi).

Two days after the riots the Asante chiefs in Kumasi requested an audience
with the Chief Commissioner. He told them that "had they come forward earlier
and assisted the Kumasihene in his efforts to compose the differences in the Zongo
matters would probably not have gone so far as they have done" (CCA to ACCA,
20 Sept. 1932, NAG, Kumasi).

On the advice of the Asante chiefs the Chief Commissioner recommended that
the zongo tribunal be closed. The chiefs pointed out (CCA to ACCA, 20 Sept.
1932, NAG, Kumasi):

. . . the policy of compelling all Northern tribes as well as the Yorubas to be sub-
servient to the headman of the Hausas . . . had always led to disputes and discussion
and [the chiefs] suggested that there should be no Sarkin Zongo in future but that
each tribe should be represented before government and before the Kumasihene
by its own headman.

In the same document, Newlands, the Chief Commissioner, mentioned four
"causes" for the dispute (ignoring, however, the effect of the vicissitudes of colonial
policy): the unpopularity of the institution of the Sarkin Zongo; severe unemploy-
ment (related to the drop in cocoa prices caused by the depression); abuse of his
position by the Sarkin Zongo in matters affecting private lives of people; and
the influx of "undesirable characters" from neighboring French colonies (ibid.).

As soon as wider powers of deportation were granted to the Chief Commissioner, the Mossi, Kotokoli, and Grusi headmen were deported, although no general policy of restricting immigration followed. Salaw was persuaded to resign and went to Katsina. The tribunal was closed, and, for the time being, the office of Sarkin Zongo was abolished.

The zongo under British/Asante rule: 1932–1950

After the riots the administration of the zongo was revised. It was in this period that indirect rule most clearly subordinated the strangers to the local "native authorities." The *District Record Book–1933* stated that, "In future foreigners and strangers alike should be made to conform to general usage, and be administered by the indigenous race on whose land they live" (ADM 51/5/6, NAG, Accra). Although they continued to hold their own unofficial courts, as they had done before the zongo tribunal was created, the headmen now sent appeals to the Kumasihene's court. The Kumasihene, Sir Nana Agyeman Prempeh II, who had succeeded his uncle in 1931, mainly judged political cases, such as disputes over succession to the offices of headmen and disputes between leaders of factions within the zongo. The strangers accorded the Kumasihene recognition as "owner of the land" and acknowledged that he had some measure of traditional authority over them. He attempted to maintain peace in the zongo by remaining outside of the affairs of the stranger communities and opposing the rise of a single strong leader. He acted as an intermediary between the strangers and the government and advised the British on the administration of the zongo.

After 1932 the number of headmen in the zongo increased, as one group seceded from the authority of the headman of a larger group. Thus, the Kumasihene, who had taken over the task of according official recognition to zongo headmen, recognized headmen of the Fulani, Busansi, Yadse, and Chiparsi (Kibisi) groups, all of whom had formerly been under the jurisdiction of the Mossi headman. He also recognized headmen of the Kusasi and Kanjaga communities, both formerly under the Mamprusi headman. A group of southern Togolese seceded from the authority of the Kotokoli headman; a group of Dahomeyans appointed a headman, and several others followed. In 1932 new headmen of the Mossi, Mamprusi, Grusi, Kotokoli, and Hausa communities were recognized, and the previously deported Yoruba headman returned to Kumasi from Accra and reassumed his office. Once a headman was selected by a majority, or a powerful minority, of his own ethnic community, he was accorded official recognition by going through a formal installation ceremony at the palace. The headman brought gifts of schnapps for pouring libation in the Asante manner and formally greeted the Asante ruler with an installation fee.[4] After this, the Kumasihene (who became Asantehene in 1935) presented the new headman to British officials in Kumasi. Although there were inevitable succession disputes and power struggles within each ethnic community, there were no large-scale conflicts in the zongo until the era of political parties began in the late 1940s.

Politics and change

In 1943 the structure of the administration in Kumasi was altered, for the Public Health Board was abolished and the Town Council was formed. Kumasi was divided into six electoral wards, and the first elections were held.[5] Until political parties became important there were two main institutions of local government in Kumasi: the elected Town Council and the Native Administration. The Kumasi Divisional Council, which was then the main organ of the Asante traditional leadership, appointed two members to the Town Council. They were two of the six "nominated members" who served on the Council along with six elected members. Three nominated members were appointed by the Chief Commissioner, and one was appointed by the Chamber of Commerce.

Although a few strangers voted in the Town Council elections, many felt that they should be represented within the Traditional Authority. In 1948 the Divisional Council was reorganized, and representatives from each ward were appointed, but the Asantehene was unwilling to appoint a non-Asante to represent the zongo. (ADM 51/5/6, NAG, Accra).

In 1952, on the eve of the passage of the Local Government Act of 1951, the zongo headmen petitioned the Asantehene for a seat on the Divisional Council. They stated in their appeal (al-Hajj Ahmadu Baba and zongo headmen to Asantehene, 19 Jan. 1952, Kumasi Traditional Council: Stranger Communities) that they

... hold no office at all in the administration of the Kumasi Division to have a say when our people are in need of an assistance [sic].... A great many of us are not lettered but they have been informed of the forthcoming LOCAL GOVERNMENT and its meaning, which has put them into great confusion as well as ourselves as headmen of the community.

At the same time, they requested the Kumasi Divisional Council to consider them for a place in the local government, "in order that we can know our place in the said Local Government." They were not granted a seat but they were asked to submit the names of headmen who would sit as panel members on one of the Asantehene's courts.[6]

Ultimately, the failure of the headmen to become incorporated into the Ashanti Divisional Council was of little political significance, since by 1954 the representatives of the Traditional Authority, as such, were excluded from membership in the Municipal Council.[7] Moreover, political parties opened new avenues through which zongo leaders could participate in local and national politics.

The preindependence decade: party politics and the breakdown of ethnic polities

The participation of immigrant leaders in party activities may be regarded as an attempt to acquire patrons in the changing national power structure.[8] As the authority of the British and the Asantehene waned, leaders in the zongo attempted to form relationships with those now coming to power. This had several implications. First, it meant a new national orientation to politics, which was important for the strangers, both in terms of their relationship to Ghanaian politics and in

206

terms of their identification with their countries of origin. Second, by opening up new channels to political power, the opportunities presented by party activity intensified certain cleavages in the zongo by giving a new group of leaders, other than the headmen, access to external support. Third, political parties weakened ethnically based political units, at least within the zongo. Although party conflicts were often described in the idiom of ethnicity, party alliances in the zongo cross-cut ethnic cleavages, and party leaders sought broader, non-ethnic bases of support.

Rival leaders in the zongo, sometimes in the same ethnic community, supported different, often opposed, politicians outside the zongo, in the hope of gaining external support for their local authority. The virulence of many of these internal contests was intensified by the uncertainty of the immigrant leaders about their relationships with the external power structure and about the nature of that structure itself. In contests over the offices of headmen, for example, uncertainty about who now held the authority to legitimize their position prolonged conflict in many communities. The CPP, of course, eventually replaced the colonial government as the single hierarchy which eventually incorporated all those who held political authority. Before its ascendency, there was a great deal of friction between rival leaders, who looked to politicians in different parties for support. Moreover, even after the CPP gained control of the government, conflict did not necessarily cease in the zongo between leaders who were incorporated into the party and others who were not party members but who still had considerable local support. Because delegated political authority and grass-roots support did not always coincide, many local political aspirants sought to define leadership roles in new ways, with alternative bases of legitimacy.

In the early period of political parties, from the early to the late 1950s, much of the political conflict in the zongo centered on the question of succession to the offices of the various headmen. New political positions and offices were created during this period, and new leaders and associations emerged, but these never became so important as foci of political confrontation as were the offices of the headmen. Incumbents to these new posts were appointed, and it was clear that these offices were given out by party officials on the basis of patronage. Eventually, after 1957, the CPP actually appointed many headmen who had little legitimacy in the eyes of their constituents. Furthermore, some leaders, such as ward heads of party branches and ward representatives to the City Council, did not represent constituencies that had any sense of political or social unity. In 1954 Kumasi was divided into twenty-four electoral wards. No ward coincided with a neighborhood, since the areas which made up wards were not congruent with meaningful social or political units. These factors minimized the importance of many of the new offices. Headmen, on the other hand, as the leaders of ethnic communities, were grass-roots leaders, although members of their communities were dispersed throughout many neighborhoods.

Another factor which focused political activity on the offices of the headmen in the early period of party activity was the limited participation of the immigrants in electoral politics. One reason for this is that they had few leaders educated in

English who were eligible for office. In 1962 the son of the Busansi headman, an MAP member, was elected to the City Council for the United Party (UP). Several CPP members of the Council, including one Mossi man (who had an Asante mother), were also immigrants, and there were several others occupying nonelective positions in the party. Still, the leaders in the zongo with these qualifications could easily be counted. Moreover, although all immigrants had been encouraged to vote before 1954, when it became apparent that many in Kumasi were voting against the CPP they were disenfranchised. A memorandum to polling officials explicitly requested them to bar immigrants, especially those from the French territories, from voting. Since political activity could no longer be directed to municipal or national conflicts, the effect of this order in the zongo was to intensify internal conflict over those offices which were not formally incorporated into the government. This development may not have been restricted to Kumasi zongo, for after 1954, elections were increasingly insignificant throughout the nation.

In the 1950s the major cleavage between supporters and opponents of the CPP was expressed in disputes over the offices of headmen. Although these conflicts were sometimes related to interethnic rivalries, conflict in each particular community can be explained without reference to alliances and conflicts with other groups. The major CPP/MAP schism which existed within every ethnic community prevented the emergence of factionalism between these units. However, after the 1966 coup, when unity within ethnic communities was temporarily restored, past factionalism within them was explained by many people in terms of interethnic conflict. Then, those who had been members of the CPP – which, immediately after the 1966 coup, appeared to represent the forces of evil – were said to have betrayed the solidarity of the ethnic community by associating with corrupt elements in other groups. This recalls explanations given after the conflicts of 1932.

Most of the headmen and the majority of the immigrants in Kumasi zongo opposed the CPP in the early 1950s. In this, they claim to have been supporting the position taken by the Asantehene, the "owner of the town." The NLM, the Asante party opposing the CPP, had been formed in 1954, and the Asantehene appealed to the immigrants for support. It is said that when the Asantehene was in danger of attack from the CPP faction, the Sarkin Zongo, al-Hajj Ahmadu Baba, sent his men to guard the palace day and night for three months. Even earlier, in 1953, the MAP had been formed as a national party, with headquarters in Accra. It had a very strong Asante branch, based in Kumasi, and it was this group which united with the NLM after 1954. Ahmadu Baba, many of the other headmen, and some of the most prominent and wealthy Muslims in the zongo, including al-Hajj Othman Lardan, a Yoruba who had been educated in Cairo, were among the major leaders of the MAP. These leaders, and many in the NLM, felt that the CPP was opposed to traditional leadership. In fact, chiefs and others representing sectional interests had been identified as "reactionary," and even pro-British, in the late 1940s and early 1950s. The CPP had identified itself as a party of "young men," of the common man, as opposed to elders and others in traditional leadership positions. The zongo headmen identified themselves as chiefs, even though they were not really traditional leaders in the areas where they were living. Like the Asante chiefs, they feared the opposition of "young men" – of those who sought power through channels other than those associated with the institution of chieftaincy. The patrons of the zongo MAP leaders were, therefore, the traditional Asante authorities and the Asante NLM leaders. Since the NLM and the Asante leadership found itself in an increasingly disadvantageous position as the CPP rose to power, the MAP leaders in the zongo also found themselves without patrons when they were most needed.

The CPP leaders in the zongo, on the other hand, had found their patrons in the national party organization. By independence in 1957, when the CPP had clearly gained control of the new government, this was an obvious advantage. Until 1957, conflict between CPP and MAP factions in the zongo was open and often violent. Both sides had their "action troopers," bands of young men whose role was to defend members of one faction against attacks from the other. The troopers had started as a volunteer vigilante force organized to patrol the stranger neighborhoods at night for thieves. When party conflict began, they split into two groups and engaged in what was described in the local newspaper as "guerilla fighting" (*Ashanti Pioneer,* Oct. 9, 1953).

The most important CPP leader in the zongo was a man who had opposed Ahmadu Baba for the office of Hausa headman in 1949, Malam Mutawakilu. Apparently still bitter about his defeat, he joined the CPP early and led an association, the Muslim Youth Congress, in opposition to Ahmadu Baba and others in the MAP. From the early 1950s until independence these two factions fought on a variety of national and local issues. One of the most bitter quarrels involved control over the central mosque, which had been started in 1952 with funds collected by Ahmadu Baba and other MAP leaders. Mutawakilu accused Ahmadu Baba of personally misappropriating mosque funds. The case was eventually taken to the Asantehene and to the Kumasi Magistrate's court, and Mutawakilu lost. There were other issues also, including charges of disturbing the peace, a long-standing dispute over the ownership of the "zongo palace" – a house that had been owned and inhabited by former Sarkin Zongos – and the question of which leader's opinion would be followed as to the timing of the appearance of the moon which ends the Ramadan fast. By independence Mutawakilu had a clear advantage, as he was strongly backed by CPP officials in Accra, including Krobo Edusei, then Minister of Interior, and Nkrumah himself.

Five months after independence, in August 1957, Ahmadu Baba and Othman Lardan were deported to Nigeria. They appealed the deportation orders, on the ground that they were Ghanaian citizens by birth, but during the court hearing an act was passed in Parliament which invalidated the proceedings against the orders (The Deportation [Othman Lardan and Ahmadu Baba] Act 1957, Act No. 19, 1957). These deportations brought out the fact that the citizenship act passed after independence (Ghana Nationality Act, Act No. 1, 1957) did not confer citizenship by birth alone and led to an increasing emphasis on non-Ghanaian national identity on the part of immigrant members of all political parties, including those immigrants born in Ghana.

The deportations of Ahmadu Baba and Othman Lardan coincided with an attempt on the part of Mutawakilu to obtain Ahmadu Baba's office as leader of the Hausa community and the office of Sarkin Zongo. Although he already was Joint Constituency Chairman of a local branch of the CPP, he still was interested in these positions. Even before Ahmadu Baba's deportation the Muslim Youth Congress (MYC) had asked officials in the regional administration about the possibility of recognizing Mutawakilu as Sarkin Zongo. Ahmadu Baba was officially only Hausa headman at the time, since the post of Sarkin Zongo had been abolished in 1932. Officials in the regional administration recommended against reviving the office of Sarkin Zongo, maintaining that there were no legal grounds for recognition of a Sarkin Zongo and pointing out the failure of the institution in 1932 (Regional Office, Kumasi, 8 July 1958, File 0459). After Ahmadu Baba's deportation the question was raised again, and this time the Regional Administrative Officer in Kumasi noted that although there were no legal grounds for recognition, there might be some political advantage in such a move (Regional Office, Kumasi, 8 Oct. 1958, File 2268). Local officials delayed taking action, and were on the whole against recognition, but by late 1957 their authority had diminished, in any case, and decisions concerning Kumasi zongo were being taken and/or verified directly by Nkrumah and his aides in Accra. In December 1957, Nkrumah declared that the Cabinet had appointed Mutawakilu to the office of Sarkin Zongo in Kumasi. A state of emergency was immediately declared in the town, and the Sarkin Zongo's house and the central mosque were listed as "protected places," which meant, in the case of the mosque, that it could not be used without special police permission.

In the next two years Mutawakilu and other CPP leaders controlled political activity in the zongo in close cooperation with the Minister of the Interior. The main concern of the administration was bringing the opposition leaders into line. Soon after Mutawakilu took office all those headmen and many other strong MAP supporters who refused to ally themselves with the CPP were removed from office and, in many cases, detained or deported. The headmen of the Mossi and Gao communities were deported in 1958, the Busansi headman was banned from entering Kumasi by a local deportation order, and a number of others, including the Mamprusi and Dagomba headmen, were removed from office and replaced by CPP supporters. Since these new appointments were announced over the radio, and since many of the leaders had little support in their own communities, these headmen gained the appellation of "chiefs by radio." Among non-Hausa, resentment against the fact that a Hausa was again empowered to rule other ethnic communities was as great as it had been in 1932. Many who opposed the CPP refused to recognize the new headmen, on the ground that they had been appointed by a Hausa, and not by their own communities.

Throughout the CPP period the effectiveness of many of these party appointees was minimal. Those who were appointed by Mutawakilu and the CPP had the support of only a small faction within their communities. Since these headmen were ignored by the anti-CPP immigrants, very few cases were brought to them for settlement, and no large meetings of their ethnic groups were held. Opponents of the CPP emphasized that these headmen had little support and that a headman "without people" was necessarily ineffective, for, even if he had governmental recognition, he still had no official administrative powers. In those communities where headmen had been deposed, deported, or detained, the anti-CPP leaders or their successors continued to have considerable popular support, but their effectiveness in governing their own communities was also greatly diminished. Without official recognition, they were no longer able to fulfill one of the most important roles of headmen, that of mediating between the immigrants and the administration.

Some of the headmen remained in office after they joined the CPP, even when they had formerly been MAP supporters. In these communities factionalism was less violent and less overt than in those communities divided by support for two rival headmen. While individuals in these groups may have been opposed to the CPP headman, without an alternative headman the opposition remained unorganized.

Some immigrant communities, mainly those from traditionally noncentralized societies of northern Ghana, had never installed headmen, and village and clan associations were the most inclusive organized groupings in Kumasi. Their involvement with party politics differed somewhat from that of immigrants whose communities had headmen. The Dagati, for example, had never installed a headman in Kumasi, in the sense that no single leader had ever been formally recognized as such by government officials. They also claim not to have been involved with party politics, and, in fact, there is very little said about them in government records of the period. Although individuals may have supported one party or the other, they did not have a conspicuous leader whose political affiliation was assumed to be representative of the entire community. Because they were not centralized, they could avoid being drawn into party politics as an ethnic unit.

In some other noncentralized immigrant communities, leaders of clan and village associations attempted to use party politics to augment their authority. Among the Kusasi, for example, several leaders claimed that through party support they had become headmen. Those members of their communities who did not support them simply denied the existence of their offices.

The CPP headmen did not really represent a new type of leadership in the zongo. Like most of their predecessors, they were first-generation immigrants. They were usually illiterate in English, and often in Arabic as well. A few were younger than the previous headmen. They were men who, like Mutawakilu himself, had been interested in becoming chiefs before political parties emerged but had been unsuccessful in gaining office before they had CPP support.

As the rise of the CPP headmen suggests, there are no clearly defined procedures for the election or installation of headmen which have been consistently followed over the years. There are also no traditional means for legitimizing claims to offices in the zongo. Consequently, leaders have always needed recognition by some authority outside their communities (usually outside the zongo) to secure their positions, even though external recognition alone cannot make leaders effective. When there are several competing candidates for an office, all of whom claim to have the support of a majority of their people, the recognition of a candidate's claim by authorities outside the community can become tantamount to election. Thus, the question of who has the prerogative to accord recognition is of crucial importance and has been a repeated subject of controversy.

As described above, the locus of authority to recognize leaders in the zongo as headmen changed several times in the colonial period, reflecting structural changes in Kumasi government as a whole. Until 1927 British administrators recognized headmen, but after they officially created the office of Sarkin Zongo, this authority was assumed by the Sarkin Zongo himself, Malam Salaw. After the abolition of the office of Sarkin Zongo, the reinstated Asantehene became responsible for according recognition.

During the CPP period this issue again became important. Controversies arose over both the recognition of a Sarkin Zongo and over the recognition of headmen. After the Nkrumah government appointed Mutawakilu as Sarkin Zongo in 1957, the zongo headmen protested, claiming that the normal procedure for the selection of a Sarkin Zongo was that he was chosen by the headmen of the various stranger communities and then approved by the government.

Despite these protests, Mutawakilu did become Sarkin Zongo and subsequently assumed the authority to recognize headmen. From 1958 to 1960 Mutawakilu controlled the zongo through his power to grant or deny official recognition to other leaders. The main qualification an aspiring headman then needed was loyalty to Mutawakilu and to the CPP. Such loyalty could be expressed by the donation of funds and support to those who then assumed the roles of patrons. Mutawakilu maintained that he was not appointing or installing headmen, but was simply recognizing each community's choice. However, as soon as Mutawakilu became Sarkin Zongo, the Minister of the Interior ruled that it was compulsory for every stranger community to appoint a headman. It was later observed that this conflicted with the CPP's official policy of not recognizing tribal allegiances or groupings. But while the Minister's ruling was in force, recognition was said to consist of registration with the Government Agent (the new title of the District Commissioner) after approval by the Minister of Interior, who acted upon the recommendations of the Sarkin Zongo. Control of these positions went, then, through Mutawakilu to Accra, rather than to local officials, as had been the case before. Within a few months after this policy was set out, all headmen and Imams who refused to support Mutawakilu were removed from office and replaced by loyal CPP supporters.

Protests against Mutawakilu's actions were sent to the Minister of Local Government in Accra, who apparently was not aware of the Minister of the Interior's role in the affairs of Kumasi zongo. The Minister of Local Government then asked the Kumasi Regional Commissioner whether he knew that Mutawakilu was installing headmen, under what authority this was being done, and whether he felt this was conducive to the public peace. The Regional Commissioner replied that Mutawakilu did, indeed, consider his actions conducive to peace and that his authority was merely that of "recognizing the installations made by the different communities" (letters between Minister of Local Government, Accra, and RC, Kumasi, R.O. File B 0459:153-6). The Regional Commissioner admitted that Mutawakilu had no legal power to appoint and depose headmen but he also stated that allegations that he was doing so were without foundation. The "sole job [for which] he had been appointed by government" was to promote peaceful conditions between and within the different communities living in the zongo and to deal with the representatives of these communities (Secretary to RC, Kumasi, to Permanent Secretary, Minister of Local Government, Accra, 17 June 1958, R.O. File 2268). Yet, peace was not really maintained, and many of the headmen who had been appointed and installed by Mutawakilu had almost no popular support and were resented by many members of their communities. They kept a certain degree of order, through the threat of deportation or detention, but because of the hostility they faced they could not perform many of the roles which were normally associated with their offices.

In 1961, for reasons described later, the office of Sarkin Zongo was abolished

Ghana's mood of optimism in February 1966 after the coup deposing Kwame Nkrumah

213

again. The Government Agent became responsible for making recommendations to the Regional Commissioner, who would then approve and officially recognize headmen. Between 1961 and 1966 a number of headmen's offices became vacant, for factions within several of the ethnic communities disputed the succession. Although the Government Agent tried various methods to find out which candidate deserved the office, in many cases he or she (one was a woman) was unsuccessful. By this time all candidates had learned the importance of professing loyalty to the ruling party. Given the difficulty in this period of determining the most popular candidate, in many cases the government was unable to decide who should get the post. These disputes usually involved very small segments of the stranger communities. Most immigrants tried to stay out of politics from at least 1961 until 1966, when interest in holding office as headman was once again openly expressed. As a result of these conflicts, the period from 1961 to 1966 was one in which the institution of chieftaincy became less important in the zongo, as elsewhere in Ghana. Public gatherings of ethnic groupings were banned, given the CPP's policy of discouraging manifestations of "tribalism." Since people could not openly support the headmen of their choice, and since ethnic communities no longer assembled and acted as groups, these offices were simply ignored. While conflicts over them smoldered under the surface of political life, political activity centered around new leaders, leaders of CPP-affiliated associations, rather than leaders of ethnic communities.

Party politics and the zongo: the rise of new associations

The importance of both ethnic and multiethnic associations as political factions in the zongo long antedates the period around independence when national political parties became important. As the description of politics in the zongo during the colonial period has shown, ethnic communities acted as political interest groups from the early part of the century. There were also multiethnic occupational and religious associations in the zongo which petitioned the government on various occasions and took an active role in the internal governance of the zongo. Most of the associations which were formed before the 1950s were local, however, with membership drawn from Kumasi itself and with leadership located there. What is significant and novel about the political associations that were formed in the 1950s is that most of them were formally linked to larger regional and national organizations. As independence approached, associations which formerly concerned themselves with local events began to act in the national arena. It became evident that as the context of political action changed, new ethnic identities based upon national origin became increasingly important. The active involvement of many immigrants in ethnic associations shifted from tribal to religious to national associations.

There were three main types of formal associations formed among zongo immigrants which are relevant to a discussion of this period. All of them were linked to organizations which were bidding for power on the national level. The first of these, the political parties, have already been considered. The second type consisted of religious associations. In many cases these became affiliated with the major political parties, and sometimes they grew out of them. The origins of the third type of association also can be traced to an earlier period, although in the late 1950s and early 1960s, when Ghana and the surrounding states were attaining independence, these organizations grew and took more active political roles. These are the associations based on nationality, such as the Nigerian Community and the Upper Volta Union.)

While the CPP began as a mass party, attempting from its inception to be as inclusive as possible, the MAP began as a religious association, representing the interests of a very small segment of the Ghanaian and foreign population. Its support was mainly in the zongo communities throughout Ghana, but particularly in Accra and in the Asante region. Soon after independence, with the passage of the Avoidance of Discrimination Act of 1958, the CPP government banned parties formed on regional, ethnic, or religious lines. This led to the consolidation of the MAP, the NLM, and other parties within the United Party, a coalition which lasted until 1961, when all opposition parties were banned by the CPP government. Thus, from 1958, when the UP was formed, the MAP was formally dissolved and became a religiously based section of a larger party. At the same time, as the CPP grew, it also encompassed more diverse elements and eventually began to fragment into smaller associations which expressed the more particularistic loyalties of its members. Local and regional branches of the CPP were formed which were just as parochial as the opposition parties based on religious, regional, or ethnic units. However, the CPP branches were tied into a much more inclusive organization which, of course, was itself equivalent to the government on all levels.

Among the subsidiary organizations within the CPP there was an Islamic organization, the Muslim Council, which on the local level became the counterpart of the MAP after 1958, when the MAP had already been disbanded as an autonomous political party. From its inception in 1958, the Muslim Council was associated with the CPP. As the CPP gained power, and as the subsidiary organizations within it developed, the Muslim Council took an increasingly greater role in governing Kumasi zongo. When party activity began in Kumasi zongo the CPP faction had been organized and led by Mutawakilu, but after independence, leadership gradually passed to the Council. The Muslim Council had, in 1958, been active in gaining recognition for Mutawakilu as Sarkin Zongo. He acted as a local leader in the Council and derived much of his support from it. However, by 1960 the Muslim Council was demanding the removal of Mutawakilu and the abolition of the office of Sarkin Zongo. Many of the Council members, particularly some of the influential Hausa, were annoyed by Mutawakilu's concern with his own power and with his attempts to manipulate the appointment of non-Hausa headmen, in order to gain support. In 1958 Mutawakilu had tried to form an association called the National Organization of Zongo Chiefs, with himself as president. This group was intended to secure the position of immigrants in Ghanaian politics by demanding,

215

unsuccessfully, as it turned out, a seat in the Ghanaian Parliament for zongo chiefs. Mutawakilu's concern with chieftainship, and his use of this as a means of augmenting his authority, irritated members of the Muslim Council who felt that he should be working within the Council and not seeking support from ethnic factions. By 1960 the Council was demanding his removal. They referred to his "iron rule" and complained about his abuse of power (Secretary, Muslim Council, Kumasi, to National Headquarters, Accra, 10 Mar. 1960, RO File B 0459). They were successful in demoting Mutawakilu, and from 1961 the office of Sarkin Zongo was abolished again, and the Council virtually governed the zongo. There were, of course, internal leadership disputes within the Council, and there were complaints from other quarters, such as the Muslim Mission, an organization formed in 1958 and composed solely of Ghanaian Muslims, which opposed the Council on the grounds that it was dominated by alien Hausa.[9] Nevertheless, the Council, strongly backed by the upper echelons of the CPP, continued to control zongo affairs until the 1966 coup.

One of the crucial incidents which triggered the Council's attack on Mutawakilu involved the question of national identity. From the time of the deportations of Ahmadu Baba and Othman Lardan, immigrants in Ghana had become increasingly concerned about their status as aliens, regardless of which political party they supported. Since the Muslim Council was so strongly tied to the CPP, the alien element in it was tolerated by the Nkrumah government, which was still willing to countenance the presence of foreigners, so long as they were loyal party members. Mutawakilu also showed concern with the issue of nationality, but he attempted to secure his position by claiming to be Ghanaian, a position necessitated, perhaps, by his opposition to Ahmadu Baba, who had been deported on the grounds that he was a Nigerian. On the occasion of Nigerian independence in 1960 the Nigerians in Kumasi, who by now had formed an association called the Nigerian Community, organized a celebration. Mutawakilu refused to attend, claiming that he was Ghanaian. This angered important members of the Hausa community, who were also members of the Nigerian Community and the Muslim Council. This, among other factors, provoked them to start an active campaign against Mutawakilu's leadership.

Just as the Nigerian Community emerged as an important political association in this period, other immigrants also increasingly sought protection and a means of participation in politics through nationally based associations. The parallel group to the Nigerian Community for the Mossi was the Upper Volta Union. This group became increasingly important after 1960, when the power of Mutawakilu and the other zongo headmen declined, but it also had roots in an organization formed many years earlier. In close consultation with the French consulate in Accra, a group was formed in 1950 called the United French Africa Committee (UFAC). This was composed of immigrants in Ghana from all the French West African territories. Its internal organization was based on territorial, rather than ethnic, units; members from each state (Sudan, Upper Volta, Ivory Coast, Dahomey, Togo, Guinea, Senegal, and Mauritania) sent representatives to an executive

216

committee which elected a president every five years. The aims of the UFAC were to protect "French" immigrants in Ghana and help them to communicate with officials in the various West African governments. As the Mossi founder of the organization explained to me:

We didn't like compulsion. We ran away from that to come to this country; when I started the UFAC it wasn't for money, but it was because if we are a group and we talk to any government they will hear us. When we were in Upper Volta we didn't understand the law there. A man makes a farm, and he couldn't get enough to eat and he was told to get money to pay the tax. Then you sell your small chop [food], and your children die. Then comes customs trouble if you come to Ghana. So the Mossi people stayed here. That is why I made the UFAC – because if someone comes for a year and he wants to go back with some small thing he couldn't do it before. He had to pay so much he went back with nothing in his hand. I wanted to be able to tell the government about all this.

The UFAC ceased to function in 1958, when organizations based on national identity began to be formed. Identification with the colonial powers no longer provided a viable basis for association, and organizations of Malians, Dahomeyans, Togolese, and Voltaics were all formed between 1958 and 1962. The leaders of the Upper Volta Union had gained considerable experience in the UFAC, but when they broke away to form the UVU there was conflict between the two groups. One reason, undoubtedly, was that those who held power in the UFAC did not want to give it up. On another level, a source of misunderstanding was that the new groups were formed on entirely different lines. During the early 1960s the composite units of the UVU were not national, or even ethnic, groupings, but were local branches in each region of Ghana. These branches were found mainly in urban centers and in cocoa-growing areas where there were large numbers of Voltaic labor migrants. Initially, then, the UVU was clearly modeled after the CPP, and many of its leaders were active in both organizations. The old leadership claimed that the leaders of the new group were much too deeply involved with Ghanaian politics and that they were using the new national organizations for individual economic and political gain.

The Upper Volta Union began "officially" in 1960, the year of Upper Volta's independence. In retrospect, it is difficult to determine who started the group. The Upper Volta consulate in Accra was directly involved from the beginning, and officials in the consulate claim to have started the association with the aim of protecting Voltaic laborers from exploitation in Ghana. Its aims, according to official consulate releases and comments of consulate officials, were to keep in touch with Voltaic citizens in Ghana, to get them to register on arrival and to register the births of their children, to help them in difficulty, and to promote "democracy and civil education" among them (*Status de l'union fraternelle des ressortissants Voltaïques au Ghana,* Kumasi, 4 Oct. 1962). Mossi residents in Kumasi claim to have started the organization, on their own initiative, shortly after the Upper Volta consulate organized celebrations for Upper Volta's independence. Having held their preliminary meetings, the Kumasi residents claim that they then appealed to the consulate for recognition and that they asked the Ambassador of the Upper Volta to act as president. Whatever the precise sequence of events, the fact is that officials of the consulate served as patrons of the association from 1960. The rules of the organization were drawn up by the consulate, and Upper Volta government officials acted as advisors to the immigrants who were active in the UVU. These officials toured the country, setting up local branches, and for a while they set up a small consulate in Kumasi. Through this association the Upper Volta government became increasingly involved with the affairs of Voltaic citizens in Ghana; through their connection with the consulate Voltaic immigrants became involved more directly with the diplomatic relationships between the two countries.

The Upper Volta Union was formed as an "apolitical" organization which professsed to support the incumbent governments of Ghana and Upper Volta. When it was founded it claimed to unite supporters of the CPP and the UP and it was unconcerned, at first, with the bitter succession disputes to various immigrant headmanships which had become compounded by party politics. However, almost from the UVU's inception, until 1966, the organization was plagued by conflict. Some of this was over corruption among the leaders, particularly the fact that some of the local organizers were going around the country selling membership cards and not accounting for the money. Some did this by telling people who didn't pay that they were likely to be deported if they did not possess the card. Other conflicts concerned Mossi dominance in the association, for while there were eight ethnic categories incorporated into the UVU in the early 1960s, many of the local leaders were Mossi. Other disputes were over party politics and the fact that most of the UVU leaders were strong CPP supporters who worked for their own interests and the interests of the CPP and against the interests of large sections of the Voltaic community, and especially against those immigrants who had opposed the CPP. Another closely related problem was that, while the UVU professed to be unconcerned with chieftaincy, because of the common tie of the UVU's leaders and the incumbent headmen to the CPP, there was a close alliance between them. What is more, such ties were reinforced by marriages: the president of the Kumasi branch of the UVU and the CPP Mossi headman in Kumasi were close affines. The Mossi supporters of the anti-CPP headman in Kumasi felt, with good reason, that the UVU was using its party connections to strengthen the more unpopular headman. Opponents of the CPP headman were continually harassed by government officials and by the police, who clearly supported the UVU leaders and the CPP headman.

Because of these conflicts the organization was reconstituted on several occasions, each time with the hope of achieving greater unity and more honest leadership. In 1962 the Upper Volta consulate drew up a constitution, *Statuts de l'Union Fraternelle. . .* , which, among other things, gave large numbers of migrants the chance to hold an office in a government-sponsored association. At the apex of the organization was a "Congrès" with a steering committee. Subordinated to this were subsections in each region, committees in large cities, and subcommittees in each village. The steering committee of the Congrès was composed of fifty-one members: an honorary president, a president, two vice-presidents, thirty-six different secretaries, three treasurers, and eight commissioners of accounts. On the regional level the staff consisted of sixteen more such officers; in each large city there were eleven; and in villages there were five. None of these was supposed to be a representative of an ethnic group, since the official policy of the Upper Volta government was to discourage all manifestations of "tribalism," including the whole institution of chieftaincy (Skinner 1964: 203). Nevertheless, on several occasions when the Kumasi group met to discuss the organization, a plan, which was based on a parity of ethnic representatives, was accepted for electing both officials and members of the various committees. Selecting officials on the basis of their ethnic affiliation was said to be "apolitical," while choosing them on any other basis was considered to expose the organization to cleavages based on party politics. Each ethnic community was to select representatives in accordance with its size in Kumasi, and officials would be elected out of this general body. The ethnic categories involved were the Mossi, Yadiga, Gourma, Wangara, Fulani, Busansi, Chiparsi, and Grusi.

Despite protestations that the UVU itself was apolitical, many of its leaders attempted to secure their positions in Ghana through loyalty to the CPP. At the same time, the risk of deportation was always acknowledged, and many immigrants consequently looked for security outside of Ghana at this time. In 1961 the president of the UVU in Kumasi and the Kumasi Mossi headman travelled to Upper Volta, where the headman obtained recognition from the Mogho Naba in Ouagadougou. This was an unprecedented act among immigrant chiefs, and the large faction of the Mossi community which did not support this headman claimed that this merely demonstrated his lack of local backing. In 1964 a very large delegation of officials from the different branches of the UVU visited Upper Volta on a trip arranged by the consulate in Accra. The 160 delegates met with the president of the Republic of Upper Volta, Maurice Yameogo, with many of his ministers, and with the Mogho Naba. Some of the delegates, wearing Western dress for the first time, received medals of honor to commemorate their service to the Republic. When the group turned back to Ghana and reached the border, they found that it had been closed, for at this time relations between the two countries were poor, and the motives of the travelers were questioned. Although the delegates did get back to Kumasi, the organization was suspended in 1964, and some members of the Accra committee were deported. In a sense, the UVU had turned out to be a self-fulfilling prophecy. It gave immigrants a chance to protect themselves from Ghanaian politics but it also intensified their allegiances outside and made them suspect in Ghana.

The UVU was revised again after the 1966 coup. The Upper Volta consulate again took an active role in recreating the Union, while it tried to discourage all manifestations of "tribalism." This position meant that it refused to support the functions of the headmen or to endorse one candidate for the headmanship over another. This angered many first-generation elders in Kumasi who were unable to turn to the consulate for external support and who felt betrayed by this policy.

Politics and change

Nevertheless, in Kumasi, to the consternation of many elders, a group of "young men" formed the Upper Volta Union Liberation Movement which engineered a "coup" to get rid of the corrupt leaders of the earlier organization and to try again to form an effective association based on national, rather than "tribal," identity.

Here too, it is apparent that events on the national level were closely reflected locally and that politics in Kumasi zongo cannot be viewed in isolation from the complex economic and political issues facing the nation as a whole. Organizations in the zongo were modeled on Ghanaian political parties and were closely associated with them. Individuals with local ambitions needed patrons outside the immigrant community as much in the late 1960s as they had throughout the past half-century. This can be attributed, at least in part, to their particularly vulnerable position as strangers. One new factor, however, increasingly distinguished their position after independence from what it had been during the colonial period. Earlier, leaders in the zongo could be politically useful to the colonial authorities in their attempts to curtail the power of indigenous leaders in Asante. After independence, although these immigrants continued to play a very crucial economic role in Ghana, they were less useful politically. It became increasingly obvious that their position was tenuous, for no matter how important they were to the Ghanaian economy through commerce and labor, socially and legally the citizen/stranger dichotomy persisted. This was demonstrated clearly in the 1960s, in an intensified awareness of national identity. Although in many contexts of zongo life ethnic identity based on "tribe" was becoming less meaningful to those immigrants defined as aliens, national economic and political conditions created the arena, and perhaps the necessity, for the persistence of identities based on national origin. In the 1960s and early 1970s it became apparent that the persistence of ethnic – particularly national – identities among Ghanaian-born "foreign" immigrants was in large part a function of the nation's inability to incorporate them within its strained economic and political system. Stated differently, one may look at events such as the expulsion of aliens from the late 1950s to the late 1960s and argue that in a national context ethnic categories in Ghana, as in many other states, were categories of exclusion defined by those in power, or, at least, by those securely incorporated into the national polity.

9

The social organization of the Mossi community

From the point of view of outsiders – government officials or members of other ethnic groups – the Mossi often appear to be a corporate unit represented by their headman and other leaders and capable of acting as a political faction in alliance with, or in opposition to, other ethnic groups. However, when the internal organization of the Mossi community is studied, differences in values and social organization between generations are such that it is difficult to describe simultaneously the communities of Mossi migrants and Mossi *'yan k'asa*. This has been shown in the discussion of kinship, where most statements apply to first-generation immigrants or to *'yan k'asa,* rarely to both. Here, the internal political structure of the community is described, and these variations again must be considered.

The Mossi community

The use of the phrase, *the Mossi community,* presents problems when one looks at the question of participation. Mossi live all over Kumasi, as Table 5 suggests. The main headman of the Mossi community has always lived in the Zongo. That is, there have been four headmen, and these have always lived in the same area of Zongo Extension. Meetings of most of the main Mossi associations take place in the Zongo, sometimes in the mosque known as the Mossi mosque, which was built by the former headman. The present and past headmen have held informal courts in this neighborhood. This is, of course, partly a result of the fact that length of residence in Kumasi is a criterion for leadership, and many of the oldest residents live in Zongo or Aboabo.

Still, Mossi often gather in different parts of the town, and when they do they may be referred to as "the Mossi community of such and such area." Despite this, there is a general feeling that the community, as a whole, is geographically centered in the area of the Zongo. This attitude and the idea that the Mossi headman in Zongo is the head of all Mossi in Kumasi are symbolic expressions of the idea that a Mossi community exists and that it has some kind of center. One never finds *all* Mossi in Kumasi meeting together, although on very special occasions, such as at the installation of the headman, several hundred may assemble (approximately 10 percent of the Mossi population, according to the 1960 census). There are many Mossi who never participate in formal Mossi associations and never go to see the headman but nevertheless identify themselves as Mossi in their day-to-day relationships with other people. This is reflected in their selection of friends and in the choices they make about such things as residence, marriage, or appeals for assistance. Yet, they may not concern themselves with organized Mossi activities and they appear to have no concern with the relative status of the Mossi as a group. Nevertheless, because in some contexts they identify themselves and are identified by others as Mossi they are potential members of a political faction, and Mossi leaders can, and do, appeal to them for support.

Participation in the formal activities of the Mossi community is by no means the only way of establishing Mossi identity. Many people who live outside Zongo Extension, in Aboabo, Asawasi, Sabon Zongo, or more distant neighborhoods, such as YateYate and Mossi Zongo, identify themselves as Mossi in their day-to-day interpersonal relations, although they have very little contact with the Mossi headman in the Zongo or with the leaders of formal Mossi associations. Others who also live in outlying neighborhoods regularly bring cases to the headman in the Zongo and attend meetings there. It is entirely a matter of individual choice and may depend on such things as business connections in the Zongo, the presence of kin there, and other factors.

The few Mossi in Kumasi who have remained or become Christians – probably less than fifty in the whole town, and almost all born in Upper Volta – never participate in Mossi community activities in the Zongo. A number of Mossi Catholics were interviewed, and although some said they knew where the headman lived, none had ever met him, nor could they think of any occasion when they might have an opportunity to see him. Since most of the formal Mossi associations are concerned in one way or another with Islam, the Mossi Christians do not participate in these, either. Yet, these people are still conscious of being Mossi and of being strangers in Kumasi, although they do not consider themselves part of the Islamic zongo community. Within their church groups, they frequently form clubs and associations with other Mossi and with other northerners.

'Yan k'asa whose mothers are not Mossi sometimes participate in the activities of their mothers' ethnic community or they may not join any formal, ethnically based associations. A number of Mossi who have been particularly successful in business remain aloof from community activities; and others who have close business acquaintances or friends in other groups specifically avoid Mossi gatherings, but this is by no means a general rule. Some wealthy Mossi send kola to the chief on the occasions of births, marriages, or deaths in their families but would not bring cases to him for settlement. This is often true of *'yan k'asa.* When one can discover positive functions that the Mossi community performs, such as the settlement of disputes or the arrangement of marriage ceremonies and funerals, one can also find alternative arrangements made among friends, coresidents, coworkers, neighbors, or kinsmen, who may not all be Mossi. But for those who cannot make

other arrangements, and for those who choose to participate, a Mossi community does exist.

Despite the optative nature of participation in organized Mossi activities, there is a structure to the Mossi community. There are definite roles within the community, and subgroupings are formed according to explicit principles of social organization. However, as the discussion below shows, the community is differently organized for first-generation and town-born immigrants. They have different needs and demand different things from the Mossi community. The first part of this discussion pertains primarily to the Mossi community as it functions for first-generation immigrants. The second part, on associations, has greater relevance for *'yan k'asa*.

A number of parallels may be discovered in the organization of the Mossi community in Kumasi and the political system of the Mossi state in Upper Volta. Territorially, if one regards the Zongo and immediately adjacent neighborhoods of Aboabo, Sabon Zongo, and Asawasi as the "capital," comparable to the Ouagadougou district, the outlying neighborhoods correspond to districts in Upper Volta. There is some indication that the Mossi see the community in this way. This is most apparent in the judicial structure and in the system of appointing subheadmen or neighborhood headmen. The Mossi residents in Aboabo, Sabon Zongo, and Asawasi are all theoretically under the authority of the Mossi headman in Zongo, even if they choose not to acknowledge him. Although certain minor matters are settled within these neighborhoods, when a Mossi in one of them has a dispute which he regards as serious, he is likely to bring it to the headman in Zongo, provided that he regards it as something for the action of a "chief." In the "suburbs" there are neighborhood headmen who are chosen locally but are presented to the headman in Zongo for recognition. Thus, the day before the headman was installed in Mossi Zongo he sent several hundred kola nuts to the headman in Zongo, who then sent two elders, the Imam and the Wid 'naba, to attend the installation ceremony. In Tafo there is a Mossi headman, despite the fact that the Sarkin Zongo of Tafo is also a Mossi. In YateYate, as in Mossi Zongo, the Mossi headman acts also as Sarkin Zongo for that neighborhood, while some other ethnic groups have their own neighborhood headmen. In both Mossi Zongo and YateYate the Mossi headmen were the first settlers in the neighborhood. In Amakom and Ahinsan there are also Mossi headmen. These headmen judge cases and arbitrate disputes, as does the headman who lives in Zongo. They also appoint elders who bear the same titles as the elders to the headman in Zongo. But these headmen generally handle only cases concerning people in their own neighborhoods. They send cases involving people from more than one neighborhood to the headman in Zongo, and people in these neighborhoods often appeal to the headman in Zongo after a case has been heard by a neighborhood headman.

But the Zongo headman may refuse to hear a case if he feels that it is a matter that can be settled by a neighborhood headman. For example, two Mossi men living in Mossi Zongo argued when one found the other in his wife's room. The husband summoned the other man to the headman at Mossi Zongo, but the accused refused to go and said he wanted to take the case to the Mossi chief in the Zongo. However, the chief refused to judge the adultery case but found the accused guilty of not answering the original summons issued by the Mossi Zongo headman. The men were told to return again with the adultery case, and the Mossi Zongo headman was called in to judge the case jointly with the Zongo headman. These leaders are not in competition, but rather attempt to define for themselves distinct areas of jurisdiction and a hierarchy of authority. There is, I suggest, an attempt to organize the Mossi community in such a way that it replicates as closely as possible the traditional political organization of the Mossi kingdoms.

Disputes of a political nature are usually brought to the headman in Zongo. For example, a controversy arose in the neighborhood of Ahinsan over the appointment of the local Mossi Imam, involving factions of Mossi from the Yatenga and Ouagadougou districts of Upper Volta. It was brought to the headman in Zongo, who judged the case jointly with the Yadse (s. Yadiga) headman, the headman in Zongo for the Mossi from Yatenga.

The neighborhood headmen are also politically subordinate to the headman in Zongo, in that they do not represent the Mossi in Kumasi, as a whole, to the government. Their jurisdiction is confined within territorial limits, while the boundaries of the Zongo headman's constituency are formed by a social category. Allegiance to the headman in Zongo does not depend only on residence. In some ways, the headman in Zongo is regarded as the headman for all Mossi in Asante. Officials of the Ghana and Upper Volta governments try to contact Mossi all over the region through him, when necessary, and cases which start in outlying rural areas of Asante are very frequently brought to him for final settlement.

Defining precise boundaries around the Mossi community is as difficult in Kumasi as it is in Upper Volta. Although linguistic and cultural factors are important in determining personal identity, political and demographic factors affect the definition of the Mossi community. Thus, until the mid-1930s, the Busansi in Kumasi were under the jurisdiction of the Mossi headman. Many of them were not Moré-speakers, yet traditionally, in Upper Volta, they were under the jurisdiction of Nakomce chiefs and had become culturally very similar to the Mossi. In Kumasi the Busansi used to bring cases to the Mossi headman, and outsiders regarded them as Mossi. However, after their number increased they appointed their own headman and were able to identify themselves as a separate community. In 1966, in both YateYate and Mossi Zongo, disputes were still going on between the Mossi and Busansi, for the Busansi were unwilling to recognize Mossi headmen as Sarkin Zongos, since this would give the Mossi jurisdiction over them, while the Mossi claimed that traditionally they were entitled to claim such jurisdiction over the Busansi.

For many purposes the Yadse, Moré-speakers from the northern Ouahigouya kingdom in Upper Volta, regard themselves as Mossi. Yet, in 1935, they, too, appointed their own headman in Kumasi Zongo. While they still consider themselves Mossi in neighborhoods where the total number of Moré-speakers is small and where there is only one headman, in the Zongo they distinguish themselves as a

224

separate political community. After the Yadse headman was recognized by the Asantehene in 1935, the Mossi headman in Zongo became identified as the headman of the Ouagadougou Mossi – that is, as the headman with jurisdiction over all persons who traditionally paid allegiance, directly or through district chiefs, to the Mogho Naba in Ouagadougou. The Yadse headman has his own Imam and titled elders, who are described as "ministers" in English, and he regards himself as equal in rank to the Mossi headman. Members of other ethnic communities generally assume that all Mossi, including Yadse, are under the authority of the Mossi headman; still, the Mossi headman himself recognizes the Yadse headman's autonomy, particularly in jural matters, and sends cases involving Yadse immigrants to him.

The Yanse (s. Yanga) are another community whose members, although recognizing their cultural and linguistic similarity to the Mossi, are reluctant to regard the Mossi headman as their leader. In Upper Volta, the Yanse are an autochthonous group which, although culturally and linguistically assimilated into Mossi society, is not incorporated into the political system. The Yanse neither accept the rule of Nakomce chiefs nor do they send delegates to the Mogho Naba's court. In Kumasi a similar situation prevails, in that the Yanse claim to have their own headman, while the Mossi headman regards the Yanse as Mossi and will judge Yanse cases as if they were Mossi ones. The Yanse headman has never been formally recognized by any authority outside his own group.

Despite this internal segmentation among Moré-speakers, all these groups are identified as Mossi by outsiders, and in interaction with other groups they usually follow the leadership of the Mossi headman in Zongo. All formal Mossi associations include Yadse and Yanse. When the Mossi Youth Association was formed in 1966 it was assumed that Yanse would join as other Mossi. But a letter was sent to the Yadse headman asking him to inform his people that the organization was open to them. An association of Mossi malams and a Mossi women's association include members of all these groups. During Ramadan, when most ethnic groups meet to read the Qur'an and Tafsir (philological exegesis of the Qur'an) in their own languages, Moré-speakers from all groups meet in the same mosque. At the installation celebration of the present Mossi headman in 1966 the Yatenga and Ouagadougou Mossi formed separate dancing groups and performed different kinds of dances, but no non-Mossi participated.

In Upper Volta the Mossi use kinship concepts to describe the relationships between various subgroupings in their society. As chapter 2 has shown, these subgroupings are related to each other as classificatory kin, because of marriages among their founders. Consequently, within any local area in Upper Volta, members of different ethnic categories will be able to place each other in reciprocal kinship categories. In Kumasi, bonds based on common home locality are important and overlap with this categorical extension of kinship terms to produce the major subgroupings within the immigrant Mossi community. These are no longer the ranked ethnic categories found in Upper Volta; they are theoretically equally ranked categories, each of which consists of migrants from a single part of Mossiland. All the people from a particular area describe themselves as a *budu* and use kinship terms with each other. They sometimes meet together to discuss problems that affect them all, they act as factions within the Mossi community, and individuals from the same group are most likely to adopt jural kinship roles towards one another. Each titled elder in Kumasi is recognized as the head, or *budkasama,* of the people coming from his district. Just as the ministers of the Mogho Naba in Ouagadougou are each responsible for a different province of Mossiland, in Kumasi, too, each minister is the head of people from his home area. The Sarkin Fada is from Koupela, the Wid'naba from Bousma, the Balm'naba from Tenkodogo, the Timboco'naba from Manga, and the Salama from Ouagadougou. The Galadima is from the Yanse area but is not regarded as the *budkasama* of the Yanse people, since they claim to have their own headman. The Mossi headman himself is the representative of the Kokologo people, a status he holds independently of his status as headman. This was shown on one occasion, when the Mossi headman from Zongo was called to a village outside Kumasi to help some Kokologo people. He said he would not go as Mossi headman, since the people in the village had a Mossi headman who had not called him to judge the case, but he would go because he was an elder from the same town as the people who had called him, even though he did not know any of them personally.

Although particular titles are not reserved for people from a specific area, there is a feeling that each titled elder should be from a different place and, if possible, that all major areas should be represented. Immediately after the 1966 coup there was no Balm'naba, since the former one had resigned during the Nkrumah period because he did not want to be associated with the other titleholders, who were known to be hostile to the CPP. After the coup there was a definite feeling in the Mossi community that the title should given to a Tenkodogo person. The Tenkodogo people were asked to present a candidate, and they held several meetings before deciding to nominate the former Balm'naba.

People from a single area often get to know each other personally, particularly if they live in the same neighborhood in Kumasi. If a dispute arises involving two people from the same home locality, they attempt to settle it as a "family matter," without bringing it to the Mossi headman. If cases are not settled within this group, the minister from the area may bring the case to the headman. The minister is sometimes asked by the headman to settle cases among people from his area. As in Upper Volta, the minister acts as a liaison between people from one locality and the chief or headman.

The minister is theoretically the oldest man from his locality. In some cases he is not the oldest, but then the senior man may not be active in Mossi affairs or may lack some other qualification. This elder is usually referred to as the *budkasama* of the local group, while the members conceptualize their relationships in kinship terms, despite the fact that they belong to various traditional ethnic categories, which in other contexts would place them in different *budu.* That is, Nakomce, Talse, and Yarse, among others, often regard themselves as part of a single *budu* in Kumasi if they come from the same district in Upper Volta. The *budu* based on ethnicity cross-cut the *budu* based on local area but they do not usually conflict with them, since groups may be defined differently in different situations. At times anyone from the same locality may be included, while at other times only members of a single ethnic category from a particular locality may be included.

People from the same local area will often go to considerable trouble to demonstrate that there are distant affinal and kinship links between them, particularly when they are not members of the same ethnic category. Then, the classificatory links between the different categories become relevant – not to differentiate one from another, but to demonstrate close relationships. The way in which people trace out these connections is illustrated in the following case, which also shows how the *budu* based on locality functions.

Case XI

Amina, a Yarse woman born in Kumasi of the Zong clan, quarreled with her husband, Yahuza, whom she wanted to divorce. Yahuza was a Nakomce from Bousma, the town where Amina's father was born. Yahuza wrote a letter to Amina's two younger brothers, who were living in their late father's house in Kumasi. He also wrote to the Wid 'naba who had replaced their father as the senior Bousma man in Kumasi. Despite the fact that the Wid'naba was from a different Yarse clan, when Amina's father died, the Wid 'naba, who had been a close friend, took over the role of family head. He not only became the *budkasama* of the Bousma people, but he also acted as *kubiga* (Moré, literally, child of the funeral) for Amina's father. He had become of the guardian of his friend's children; he supervised the division of the inheritance, and he was called *mba* (Moré, father) by the children.

When the divorce case was heard, those present were Amina and Yahuza, Amina's brothers, the Wid 'naba, and five other men from Bousma: two Nakomce, one Yaraga, one Dapore, and one Busanga. Despite the fact that these people were all of different Mossi ethnic categories, one of Amina's brothers described the whole gathering as a *babissi* (Moré, children of one father). In a long speech he demonstrated how they were all children of one father, since, in one way or another, they could all trace relationships to the ancestors of the present Bousma Naba. Many of the links were through women, but the group could still be called a *babissi*, he maintained, since a relationship was traced back to a common male ancestor.

After the case was heard, certain statements were made within the immediate family that would seem to contradict the view that the people from one locality really were one *budu*. Amina's brothers expressed annoyance with the Wid 'naba for letting the case become as big as it had, that is, for letting it involve so many people. They maintained that the Wid 'naba should have informed them of the dispute before calling the other Bousma people, that he should have acted as *budkasama* of their immediate family, not of all the Bousma people. The difficulty here was that the Wid 'naba saw himself as the head of a kinship group of Bousma people. If the Bousma people could be thought of as a *budu*, then the Wid 'naba was acting correctly in calling men from all its sections. However, the brothers felt that in calling so many Bousma people, the Wid 'naba was acting as if he were a Tengnaba (village headman), not a *budkasama*. Despite the speech establishing kinship links, in private they maintained that the Bousma people were unrelated and that the Wid 'naba should have seen himself as *budkasama* of their family, not of all Bousma people. As the family *budkasama*, the Wid 'naba should have waited until they brought the case to him, so that they could solve it among themselves. This difference in the interpretation of the situation was intensified by the fact that Amina and her brothers were all *'yan k'asa,* while the Wid 'naba was born in Upper Volta. While at the meeting, the brothers said what they expected the first-generation immigrants to accept, that they were all a single *babissi,* but they were not really prepared to act on this principle.

It seems that misunderstandings of this kind arise from the fact that in town, for first-generation immigrants particularly, the principles of kinship, descent, and locality are merged. For *'yan k'asa,* they remain much more distinct. Among all generations, however, these principles of organization are manipulated according to the situation and they are used to justify action by small groups of people who are members of the same ethnic community. These people may claim to be related as kin in some situations and not in others. The case above also demonstrates that, although the group which met is described as the Bousma *budu,* certainly not all of the Bousma people in Kumasi were involved. The Wid 'naba called certain people because they were involved in the dispute. He called others because he knew them personally, felt they could help find a solution, and because he wanted to solidify his own relationships with them.

Sometimes the principles of descent and locality are merged in the definition of a *budu* in Kumasi so that certain people can justify meeting together, not just to settle disputes, but to act as a political faction within the Mossi community. During the 1966 dispute over the succession to the Mossi headmanship, described in chapter 10, the Yarse from Rakai met as a faction. They attempted to claim that the office was vested in their group, since the late chief had been a Rakai (Sanfo) man. This claim was not stated openly at first, but the group soon showed that it felt that an injustice had been done to it as a *budu* when the office was given to another man. The group which met to act as the core of a political faction in this case included Yarse in Kumasi who came from Rakai, including members of the Sanfo and Dere clans. It did not, however, include Yarse of these clans from other towns, nor did it include a blacksmith and a Hausa man who came from Rakai and who were both well known to the Rakai Sanfo people. The oldest Dere man had been married to the sister of the former headman and was, therefore, an affine of the Sanfo Yarse. Once decisions had been made within this small group, other supporters of this faction were informed.

The groupings which have just been discussed are all called *budu* in Kumasi and have certain characteristics in common. They are extensions of a concept of social organization found among the Mossi in Upper Volta. In both contexts, political relationships and kinship relationships within the ethnic group are conceptually merged. While there are no lineages among Mossi immigrants, the *budu* of people from the same area functions in some ways similarly to the lineage in Upper Volta, particularly in terms of its jural functions and the social services it performs. Disputes may be settled easily within these groups, and members of the same group help each other substantially in the arrangement of marriages, naming ceremonies, and funerals. The same can be said of the Mossi community, as a whole, but these subgroupings are the ones within the Mossi community which actually provide these services most often. However, the analogy between the groupings in Kumasi and the traditional social organization of the Mossi is a rough one, even if it is one the Mossi frequently refer to themselves. The *budu* in Kumasi is neither a ritual nor an economic unit and therefore cannot be equated with the traditional lineage. The groups in Kumasi are more closely analogous to the social unit of the village, and the role of the *budkasama* in Kumasi is more like that of the Tengnaba in Upper Volta. In both the village and in the Kumasi groups based on locality, members of the unit are not biologically kin, but they use kinship terms with one another. While rigid analogies may not be very useful analytical concepts, they are nevertheless used by the Mossi themselves to describe their urban community.

The Mossi in Kumasi do not form groups on the basis of the ethnic categories which constitute estates in Upper Volta. People from one estate rarely meet together, unless they are also from the same locality, and they in no way constitute corporate groups within the Mossi community. Traditional prohibitions against intermarriage between certain groups, between blacksmiths and Yarse or Nakomce, for example, are ignored in Kumasi. The Mossi, as a whole, constitute a single marriage class in relation to non-Mossi, and attempts to encourage endogamy apply to the community as a whole. Among themselves marriages are simply described as marriages among Mossi, regardless of estate membership, with the exception that Yarse patronymic groups remain exogamous, since these are regarded as marriages between close agnatic kin.

The irrelevance of the traditional status categories for the formation of groups in Kumasi is due to the fact that this level of differentiation is irrelevant for determining status in the Kumasi context. All Mossi immigrants are potentially of equal status insofar as ethnicity confers status at all. In Kumasi, one's ethnic identity is based largely on one's own or one's parents' place of origin. All Mossi are considered by others to have a common home, since origins are reckoned only according to the last major migration – the migration to Ghana, not to Mossi country.

A quarrel which occurred one day in the central market in Kumasi reveals the attitude that Mossi have towards traditional concepts of status.

Case XII

Bila, who claimed to be of Nakomce origin, and Ilyasu, whose father was Dapore, both from the town of Nedigo, were arguing in the cushion market. To help settle the dispute the market leader sent for Malam Hassan, the Mossi Na'ib, and for the Mossi Imam from YateYate (the area in Kumasi where the men lived). The men were arguing about a stolen watch which someone had asked Bila to sell. Ilyasu warned him against accepting the watch and reminded him that the last time he did something like this all his friends had to pay, once the theft was discovered. Bila resented Ilyasu's advice and accused him of trying to show that he was of higher status, as well as more knowledgeable than others. A dialogue followed:

Bila: "Ilyasu is nothing to me. It was my father who drove him away from Nedigo."

Ilyasu: "Does that give you the right to drive me from Kumasi?"

Bila: "Do you forget that your father was under the command of my father?"

Ilyasu: "That might be true, but does that give you power to force me from this place? You should forget about the past and think about the future. Last time we fought you said you would expell me from your *budu* [presumably that of the Nedigo people], didn't you?" Mallam Hassan then intervened and said that Bila did not have power to do any such thing, even in Upper Volta, and that moreover such fights were "spoiling the name" of the Mossi *budu* in Kumasi.

Despite the irrelevance of the traditional status categories in Kumasi, there is still some feeling that the Yarse monopolize positions of power, although this is due, not to any ascriptive allocation of leadership roles in Kumasi, but to their history in the town. When the succession to the Mossi headmanship was contested in 1966, someone remarked that "the Mossi would like to get the chiefship from the Yarse, but they can't, because here in Kumasi the Yarse were first, and they control everything." All the headmen (but the first), the Wid'naba, Sarkin Fada, and Imam are all Yarse, as were many of the previous titleholders. (See Tables 34 and 35.)

Table 34. *Succession to office of Mossi titleholders*

Name of office and incumbent	Home town	Group	Installed by	Remarks
Naba				
Dawda	Thyou	Talse	Chief Commissioner	Installed c. 1908; deported 1932
Adamu	Rakai	Yarse	Chief Commissioner	Installed 1932; deported in 1957; formerly was Waziri
Hamidu	Kombissiri	Yarse	District Commissioner	1957–69 (died in office)
Mamudu	Ouagadougou	Talse	CPP Joint Constituency Chairman (Mutawakilu)	Installed 1957, but not recognized as headman by non-CPP Mossi. Formally in office until June 1966
Yisa	Kokologu	Yarse	Asantehene	1966–74 (died in office; succeeded by Rahman, Adamu's son)
Wid'naba				
Somailya	Bousma	Yarse	Adamu	Still in office
Balm'naba				
Sulemanu	Tenkodogo	Talse	Adamu	Left office in the
Sulemanu	Tenkodogo	Talse	Yisa	CPP period (1958) and was reinstalled in 1966

Table 34 (*cont.*)

Name of office and incumbent	Home town	Group	Installed by	Remarks
Timboco'naba				
Musa	Manga	Talse	Adamu	Still in office
Sama'naba				
Seidu	? (Upper Volta)	Yarse	Adamu	Does not support Yisa, gave up title
Waziri				
Adamu	Rakai	Yarse	Dawda	Became headman in 1932
Hamidu	Kombissiri	Talse	Adamu	Became headman in 1957
Yisa	Kokologo	Yarse	Hamidu	Became headman in 1960
Vacant at time of fieldwork				
Galadima				
Nabiga	Yala	Nakomce	Adamu	Died in office
Mumuni	Yala	Nakomce	Yisa	Still in office (1969)
Salama				
Abudu	Kombissiri	Yalse	Adamu	Died in office
Tennorga	Ouagadougou	Talse	Yisa	Still in office
Sarkin Fada				
Seidu	Bori	Yarse	Adamu	Died in office
Musa	Kombissiri	Talse	Adamu	Left and joined CPP
Rahmani	Kukpela	Yarse	Adamu	Formerly was Majidade, still in office
Majidade				
Rahmani	Kukpela	Yarse	Adamu	Became Sarkin Fada
Vacant at time of fieldwork				
Sarkin Samare				
Maigiamo	?	Yarse	Adamu	
Gundo	Zaurogo	Talse	Adamu	Died in office
Sargeant Norga	Ganzurugu	Talse	Yisa	Still in office
Imam				
Seidu	Ouagadougou (born in Ashanti)	Yarse	Adamu	Still in office
Na'ib				
Hassan	Kaya	Yarse	Adamu	Still in office
Magajia				
?	Tenkodogo	Talse	Adamu	Died in office
Memuna	Manga	Talse	Adamu	Still in office

Table 35. *Present Mossi elders: birthplace, occupation, and property owned in Kumasi*

Title	Birthplace	Main occupation	Property	Years in Kumasi	Ethnic group
Naba	Kokologo	Collector and *maigida*	One house	40+	Yarse
Wid'naba	Bousma	Collector and *maigida*	One house	40+	Yarse
Sarkin Fada	Kukpela	Watchman and trader	Half of a house	40+	Yarse
Salama	Ouagadougou	Collector and *maigida*	Two houses	40+	Mossi (commoner)
Galadima	Yala	*Maigida* and trader	One house	40+	Nakomce
Sarkin Samare	Ganzurugu	Police (pension)	One house	40+	Mossi (commoner)
Timboco'naba	Manga	Mason	None	40+	Mossi (commoner)
Balm'naba	Tenkodogo	Watchman and trader	One house	40+	Mossi (commoner)
Magajia	Manga	Trader	None	40+	Mossi (commoner)
Imam	Ashanti (near Kumasi)	Imam and trader	One house	40+	Yarse
Na'ib	Kaya	"Malam work"	One house	40+	Yarse

The Mossi headman

The Mossi believe that every group of people has a leader. The inhabitants of a compound have a *yirisoba,* a houseowner; the inhabitants of a section of a village (*zaka*) have a *zaksoba*; and the head of a lineage is called the *budkasama, kasama* referring to seniority in terms of age. Any larger aggregate of people in a political unit has a Naba, and allegiance to a Naba does not depend exclusively on either kinship or on place of residence. A Naba has authority over all residents in a particular area, but in Mossiland, as in many other African kingdoms, chiefs are said to have authority over people, not over territory. Their domains do not always form continuous territorial areas. In Kumasi the same concepts apply, in that the Mossi Naba in Zongo has jurisdiction over a category of people, not over an area of the town. Although a kinship relation is not a precondition for establishing the allegiance of subject to chief, the Mossi conceptualize the relationship between ruler and ruled in kinship terms. Thus, the Naba is regarded as the "father" of his people, this being a metaphorical expression of the fact that his subjects owe him respect and that he has authority over them. In Kumasi, first-generation immigrants, more than *'yan k'asa,* tend to emphasize the kinship aspect of the relationship between chief and subject. For many first-generation immigrants the headman performs roles which the *budkasama, zaksoba,* or *yirisoba* would perform in Upper Volta.

The present Mossi headman, born in Upper Volta himself, recognizes this aspect of his role. Speaking to a woman who had come with a complaint against her husband, he said, "Every woman should remember that when she is with her husband, the chief is her family, because if her husband does something bad, she must go and report to the chief so that he may call the husband and advise him." When a marital dispute becomes serious the headman may take the woman from the husband and give her to another man. This right is said to belong to the Kumasi headman when the woman has no biological father there. It is for this reason also that the headman acts as a witness to marriages among immigrants. The Mossi headman went on to explain to the woman,

It was written in God's book that you will become my daughter. What makes me say this is that whenever you have any trouble with your husband you may come to me, and if your husband is still doing bad I may take you from him. . . . There is no family other than the person who will help you when you are in trouble.

The headman sees his job mainly in these terms – as one of helping people in trouble. He says proverbially that the chief is like a garbage heap because, like the garbage heap, he must accept whatever "good or bad thing they throw at him." In fact, since the headman's powers are not defined by law, and since the government expects him to look after the welfare of migrants, he often has to do many jobs which a traditional chief would not do. He is often called upon by governmental authorities or by his subjects to arrange the burial of the dead, take physically or mentally ill patients from their homes or the hospital, send the sick or indigent to relatives in Upper Volta, cover the debts of migrants, care for orphans or women who have run away from their husbands, return runaway wives to Upper Volta, and so on. Employers expect the headman to compensate them for broken labor contracts, while migrants come to the headman looking for jobs, shelter, and food. The headman usually stands bail for his subjects, and the local police ask him to settle many civil and criminal cases which would otherwise go to government courts.

Although immigrant headmen have no official position, in that they are not "chiefs" under present or past ordinances defining native or traditional authorities, the nature of their functions makes it necessary for them to cooperate closely with the government. Besides the services just mentioned, which alleviate much judicial and welfare work that government agencies would otherwise have to do, in the past the headmen have provided "voluntary" labor for construction projects and sanitation. Since the headmen were patrons to new migrants, promising them paid employment in return for their temporary services, they obtained in this way the resource which enabled them to act as clients of government officials and Asante farmers and businessmen. They were the middlemen in a chain of patron/client relationships based mainly on the exchange of labor and political support.

There is also close cooperation between headmen and the local police, with advantages for both. The police are relieved of some work; they are occasionally able to use the headmen to help enforce the law; and they receive gifts from the headmen. Whenever a policeman, a sanitary inspector, or another city official passes the chief's meeting place, he is likely to receive a dash – usually ten shillings or one Ghanaian pound (nowadays, one or two cedis). When new personnel come to work at the local police station they receive gifts from the headmen. The strangers feel that they are protected by these relationships, and vulnerable without them. At the same time, aspiring and competing leaders sometimes accuse each other of doing things to gain the favor of the local police, and the police are sometimes accused of playing rivals off against each other. Nevertheless, the better a headman's relationship with the police, the more useful he is to his subjects. If these relations are good, he is able to handle many cases which might otherwise elicit more severe police and court action, and he may be able to prevent the arrest of his people for minor torts. He has no prison but he is occasionally allowed to use the police cell for brief periods. Thus, one day a Mossi man who had been working as a farm laborer in an Asante village was accused of stealing property and absconding with the wife of another Mossi man. The most senior Mossi in the village sent the case to the Kumasi headman, because he knew that the accused had gone to Kumasi. When the accused was apprehended and appeared before the Mossi headman, he started shouting and acted as though he was about to strike the woman and elders. The elders searched the man on the headman's orders and found a cutlass hidden beneath a shirt covered with protective charms. The knife and shirt were removed, and the man was sent to the local police station. The headman asked the police to lock the man in a cell for one night. The next morning the police were given a dash of one Ghanaian pound, and the case was taken back to the Zongo and settled at the headman's court.

Although the headmen hold courts with government knowledge and approval, these are not legally constituted. The only court in the zongo whose jurisdiction was formally defined was that of the Sarkin Zongo, from 1927 to 1932. With this exception, these courts have no statutory powers. They do impose fines and charge fees but they have no power to enforce their judgments. The main sanction is the informal one of social ostracism, since hearings are open to the public. Also, since they handle many cases which could reach the government courts, they often obtain compliance with their judgments, because their fines and orders tend to be less costly and severe than those imposed by the government. They rarely impose punitive measures, but rather attempt to compensate and satisfy injured parties.

The Mossi headman issues summonses to insure the receipt of money to pay fines. When one person brings a complaint against another, he asks the headman to summon the other person for a certain amount of money and gives the headman this amount. People answer these summonses because they feel they may win the case, because they want to find a compromise solution, because of social pressure to do so, or because they feel the case could end up in court if they did not answer. If the plaintiff wins the case, the money is returned, and the defendant must pay the same amount to him. If he loses, the money goes to the defendant. Some amount (generally at least ten shillings) is given to the headman, usually by the party who brought the case, and the headman shares this with his elders. Some cases do not involve financial suits, but the headman still collects a fee for hearing them.

The Mossi headman hears cases in his "sitting room," outside his house. On assuming office in 1966 the headman transformed his usual resting place into a reception room. In an alley between two houses where he had rooms for each of his two wives, he built an "outside room." While he had only cardboard sheets for a roof at first, after he became headman he added a corrugated tin roof and cement walls. There is no door, and anyone passing can see what is going on or can enter. On one side of the room he added another room for a horse which he also acquired soon after assuming office. The horse was only used several times a year, when the headman rode in procession with other zongo chiefs, at the end of Ramadan and on the other important Muslim festival days. He went to considerable expense to maintain the horse, because he regarded it as an important symbol of his royal status. Several months after his sitting room was completed he added a cement platform, where he placed the chair on which he sat most of the day, alone or surrounded by his elders and visitors.

Cases may be heard at any time, but if they are important or difficult, a time is set when most of the elders, as well as all the parties and witnesses, can attend. On Sundays as many as five cases may be heard, often taking the entire day. Some cases require several sessions, depending on the availability of witnesses and the amount of evidence. None of the elders in the late 1960s had jobs which required regular hours of work during the day, although one, the only one holding a regular salaried job, was a night watchman. They therefore could be assembled at any time, and one or two titled or untitled elders usually sat with the headman during the day. During a case both the plaintiff and defendant sit on mats on the floor with their legs folded beneath them, facing the headman. The headman and elders sit in chairs in a circle around the room. The sessions open and close with the recital of Muslim prayers. No one speaks to the headman directly, but rather addresses the Sarkin Fada or the audience in general. The Sarkin Fada then repeats the statements to the headman, translating into Moré if the person has spoken another language which the Sarkin Fada understands. Most of the time the elders do not interrupt, although they will give opinions and supply information, if asked. The headman asks the parties direct questions relevant to the case. He shouts at them if they bring in extraneous information but gives them time to explain their position in detail. As many witnesses as possible are called.

Cases involving only Mossi are settled in the headman's court. Of fifty-five cases fully recorded in 1966–7, thirty-one were disputes over women, some of these involving only a dispute between spouses, and others involving third parties. Nine cases were about payment of debts; seven were over the inheritance of property and the custody of children. Two were complaints about insulting behavior and implied accusations of witchcraft. Four cases were political – that is, they were disputes over Mossi offices in surrounding neighborhoods. Two cases were the result of public fights between Mossi men, and four were heard in conjunction with police cases that were running concurrently, for extortion and assault.

235

Politics and change

Not one of these cases involved a *'yan k'asa*. This does not attest to their better behavior, but rather to the fact that they do not bring their disputes to the headman. They are settled either by small groups of kin, by respected malams, or by close friends. *'Yan k'asa* claim they send most cases to the police, but, in fact, many are also settled outside court. Many *'yan k'asa* bring disputes to their former Arabic teachers; these, like their friends and kin, may belong to different ethnic groups.

Cases between first-generation immigrants who belong to different ethnic groups are usually heard by both headmen jointly. But if they involve a criminal offense they are less likely to remain outside of the state judicial system than are similar cases involving members of the same ethnic community. Cases of physical assault, for example, if occurring between members of the same ethnic group, may remain matters for the assessment of damages by the parties concerned. When these occur between members of different groups they are likely to go to the police. Civil cases, such as marital disputes, questions about the division of inheritance, and so on, are heard by the two headmen jointly, whenever possible. The decision about who hears a case is up to the parties themselves, although headmen do refer cases to each other, in order not to abrogate authority from one another.

The headman acts as the central point in a communication network which includes most of the Mossi immigrants in Kumasi. On the occasion of a birth, a marriage, or a funeral, those holding the event will announce it and invite guests through the headman. They do this by sending kola to the headman, who then distributes it to the rest of the community through his elders and through the headmen in outlying neighborhoods. The titled elders are responsible for informing people from their home areas who are living in the central neighborhoods, while the other headmen inform all Mossi living on the outskirts of the town. The women are represented by Magajia, a titled elder whose following is not determined by either place of origin or place of residence. She communicates with the women in all neighborhoods through representative female leaders in each one. Certain Mossi occupational groups, including the collectors, the brass-smiths, and the mattress-makers are also organized into informal associations with leaders who are given kola on these occasions. *'Yan k'asa* also give kola to the headman on such occasions, but usually in small amounts, to invite only the important elders. As the example of the marriage of Meriama and Nuru showed, *'yan k'asa* may distribute kola themselves, without the assistance of the headman.

The elders

The essence of leadership, to the Mossi, is the fact that all leaders must have followers, while the effectiveness of a leader can be judged by the number of followers. The Mossi headman appointed by the CPP was said not to be "really a chief," because he had few supporters and few elders. There were seldom more than three or four people with him. He "had no work." A headman must have trusted advisors to help him, to show that he has supporters and to create a certain distance between himself and his subjects. Like the Mogho Naba in Ouagadougou,

236

Mossi elders in Kumasi considering a case

or the district or village chiefs, the Mossi Naba in Kumasi has a court. The roles of the various titled elders in Kumasi are not highly differentiated. Specific titles are, as the Mossi themselves say, "for nothing." Yet, all of the elders do have duties and all are made to account for themselves when they do not perform them. They are supposed to mediate between particular groups of Mossi immigrants and the head-man, to represent these people to the headman, and to speak for them on political matters. They are supposed to attend the headman's court regularly and to advise him when he arbitrates disputes or has political decisions to make. When he goes to a letter-writer to write to a government official, some of the elders must go and sign with him. On the major Muslim holidays the elders accompany the headman to greet the Asantehene and the Regional Commissioner. They also take part in the processions led by the Hausa headman. When a member of the Mossi commu-nity performs a ceremony for a naming, a marriage, or a funeral, the headman and his elders attend or the headman sends some of the elders in his place.

Each elder bears a different title, which may be regarded as the name of his office, although not all titles are the names of offices. During the term of the first Mossi headman, from 1909 to 1932, few of the elders had formal titles. But the older, permanently established immigrants who were close to the headman, or who were or had been his clients, acted as advisors and performed the same roles that the titled elders perform today. The number of offices with formal titles increased during the term of the second headman, from 1932 to 1957. He installed

237

many of the elders who hold titles today, although some individuals have moved from one office to another. Even in the early part of the century the Mossi claim to have referred to the elders by Hausa titles. The principal elder was known as Waziri, and the head or representative of the "young men" was known as Sarkin Samare (Hausa, Chief of Youth). As Table 10, in chapter 4, shows, the Mossi in Kumasi have more offices with Hausa titles than with Moré ones, and even when people speak Moré they still use the Hausa titles, except in the case of the headman, for whom Naba and Sarki are used interchangeably. Mossi are aware that the functions of their traditional offices cannot be transposed to Kumasi, and this is probably one reason why Hausa titles are adopted so easily. The Mossi claim that they use Hausa titles because "no one will understand if we use Moré ones," but, since the functions of the elders are mainly concerned with internal Mossi affairs, this situation must be considered in light of the high status of the Hausa in the zongo.

The term "elder," which English-speaking Mossi use to refer to these offices, is somewhat misleading. The elders who hold formal titles, titles associated with offices, or "chairs," as they are called, are referred to in Moré as "chiefs," Nanamse (s. Naba). First-generation immigrants regard them, with the headman, as chiefs because they hold offices, because they have *nam*, and not because they come from any particular traditional status group. Thus, although they are not Nakomce, they do have royal status in the view of first-generation immigrants in Kumasi. This way of thinking becomes obvious when first-generation immigrants talk about the elders, on the one hand, in contrast to the way they talk about "youths," on the other. "Youths" can be of any age; they are so classified, not because they are young, but because they do not have titles. Analogies are made by the immigrants between the status categories in Kumasi and those in Upper Volta, and in this conceptualization youths are analogous to commoners, in the same way that elders are analogous to royals.

Town-born immigrants, of course, do not think about chieftainship in this way. For them, offices are not necessarily chieftainships, and officeholding has no connotation of nobility. For this reason, while office holders in 'yan k'asa associations can easily be impeached or replaced, elders can be criticized but are rarely impeached.[1]

Offices, and the titles that go with them, are highly valued, particularly among first-generation immigrants. When they are vacant, as were the offices of Sama Naba (Moré, chief of strangers), Waziri, and Maji Dade, during the period of my fieldwork, there are men who try to obtain them and people who concern themselves with the merits and faults of the various candidates. There are several reasons why these offices are highly valued among first-generation immigrants. For one thing, chieftainship, in general, has high prestige among Mossi born in Upper Volta. When a delegate of the Upper Volta embassy spoke in Kumasi in 1966 and said that chiefs were no longer needed in the modern state, many older first-generation immigrants, even those without titles, were affronted. Chieftaincy, they felt, was the basis of their political system; to remove chiefs was to hand the community over

238

to a lot of irresponsible young men. The headman himself spoke angrily about the idea of equality which he felt the embassy delegate was expressing. This, he said, was like the CPP: it was absurd to maintain that one man was as good as the next, when clearly not all men were born to rule.[2] The elders, then, gain recognition in the eyes of many first-generation immigrants as responsible leaders, as chiefs, and much of the respect accorded to traditional Mossi rulers is given to them. But since they are not Nakomce and they have no power backed by force, the hostility that is also often shown towards Mossi chiefs in Upper Volta is not often shown to them. Besides prestige, they also gain influence by holding office. They are part of the small group which makes decisions affecting the community, and their opinions are respected when disputes are heard. It is true that no one has to listen to them, but many people do. A further reason why these titles are coveted is that they carry some financial reward. As elders these individuals get money from the headman when they help him judge cases; when the headman receives gifts, usually money or kola, from new migrants, candidates for titles, or others, the elders get a share. When people approach the headman through the elders they receive a portion of whatever gift is given to the headman.

All of the elders, in the late 1960s, except the Imam, were born in Upper Volta, were over sixty years of age, and had been in Kumasi twenty-five years or more. Some had revisited their homes in Upper Volta, but none planned to return north to live permanently. They were all nominally Muslims, but only the Imam and his assistant, the Na'ib, were literate in Arabic. None was educated in English. During their youth some of these elders worked as laborers and had salaried jobs. Sarkin Samare was a policeman, and several others worked as laborers in the timber and construction businesses. In the late 1960s only one elder, Sarkin Fada, had a salaried job – as a night watchman. Most of the elders were traders and *masugida.* The Imam was a cattle dealer; the former Waziri was a sheep trader; the former headman and the present Na'ib were kola dealers. Almost all of them were land-lords for itinerant traders and for laborers going to mines and cocoa farms. All of them except two – the Magajia, a woman, and the Timboco 'naba, a relatively minor official – owned houses and rented out some rooms, while they kept others for itinerant visitors. It is not coincidental that most of the elders and headmen were collectors and *masugida.* In the latter capacity they built up politically useful support. The more important a man is as a *maigida,* the more followers he has. Also, once he gains a title he is able to maintain, and even increase, his business as a land-lord, since he frequently comes in contact with new migrants.

There are few explicit rules for the selection of elders, and there is no formally defined election procedure. All of the elders who held office after the 1966 coup were selected and installed by the previous headman before his deportation in 1957. During the CPP period they effectively lost their posts, since they did not support the CPP headman, and he appointed several of his own elders. The anti-CPP elders were regarded as "ringleaders" by the CPP headman, and in 1965 seven of them were arrested and detained for about two weeks on the ground that they were likely to cause a breach of the peace during the Organization of African

Unity conference in Accra. It was alleged that they had expressed intentions to harm the Upper Volta ambassador, since he had "made the Mossi chief and his followers proud,"[3] a remark signifying their resentment of the fact that he had supported the CPP headman. In the opinion of the anti-CPP elders and many of their followers, they had maintained their offices throughout the CPP period, although "underground." Incidents such as these arrests merely confirmed their view, since it attested to their importance.

After the 1966 coup the anti-CPP headmen and elders immediately reassumed their offices. There was some debate about the selection of a new headman, but once a choice was made, all of the former elders unceremoniously reclaimed their titles. The CPP headman and his elders lost their titles, because they lost the only support they had – that of governmental authorities outside the zongo. The anti-CPP headman and his elders who had held the support of most of the community all along were now able to claim the titles openly and reassume the roles associated with them, since they now could claim that they had the government implicitly behind them.

Several criteria for the selection of elders may be enumerated, although these are apt to change if migration to Kumasi continues to slow down to such an extent that all leaders are born in town. If that happens, both the roles and qualifications may be expected to change. At the present time, when there still is a significant first-generation population, the criteria one can deduce are that: (a) the elder must be born in Upper Volta; (b) he must be a permanent and long-term Kumasi resident; (c) he must be at least fifty years old; (d) he must have some clients and supporters; (e) he must support the headman and the other elders; (f) the other elders must trust him and agree on his leadership qualities and his ability to judge cases fairly, according to the principles of Mossi customary law; and (g) he must have a certain amount of money or property.

The procedure for choosing an elder may be compared to that of electing a village headman in Upper Volta. Skinner (1964: 58) notes that district headmen delay the selection of village headmen as long as possible, in order to receive gifts from contestants. The same is true in Kumasi, and it is therefore impossible to state any fixed price that a man must pay to get a title or the length of time it takes for an office to be filled. Although the headman is the most important elector and is sometimes able to appoint his former clients, he alone cannot appoint an elder. He must gain the support of at least some of the other elders and of some of the untitled immigrants – the "commoners" or "young men."

Since the elders are almost exclusively concerned with the affairs of immigrants born in Upper Volta, the opinions of the *'yan k'asa* are not often heeded. When a new Sarkin Samare had to be chosen in 1966, the candidate favored by the elders was strongly opposed by almost all the *'yan k'asa*. They wanted to install a man of their own generation who was a more orthodox Muslim and was more in touch with the procedures of modern government. The first-generation immigrants, whom the Sarkin Samare ultimately did represent, were mainly over forty, and some were well over sixty, but since for them the category of Samare referred to status, and not simply to age, this was irrelevant. While the debate between the "young men" of different generations continued, the first-generation immigrants held weekly meetings. They were not organized into a formal association, in the sense of an organization with offices, a charter, a membership list, and so forth, but every Sunday for a few months some of them would meet to discuss the forthcoming selection of a new Sarkin Samare. They talked about who they wanted and why only a first-generation immigrant could properly represent them. They discussed the tactics of getting their candidate appointed and general problems facing the Mossi community, including how to raise money to pay off the lawyers who had defended the seven elders arrested during the OAU conference in 1965. They also discussed at great length a forthcoming ceremony of shaving the chief – an installation ritual for the Mossi headman which never took place, because, they claimed, they never raised enough money.

As soon as the new Sarkin Samare was installed this organization of first-generation "young men," which had clearly met for one specific purpose, dissolved. The Sarkin Samare assumed the generalized role of an elder but did not perform special roles to represent the "young men." Almost immediately his position was threatened by the Mossi Youth Association (MYA), a club formed among *'yan k'asa* which became very active in this period and whose members had opposed him all along. His position was also undermined by his own personality and his laxity in attending the headman's court with the other elders. It soon became apparent that he commanded little respect and could not meet the challenge posed by the MYA. What might have been a very important office, had another man been selected, consequently became a very minor post.

The importance of any particular title depends very much upon the personality of the incumbent. However, most migrants consider the most important offices to be those of the Wid'naba, Waziri, Sarkin Fada, and Salama, followed by the Balm'naba, Sarkin Samare, Magajia, and the others. But since their functions are not differentiated, with the exception of the Imam and the Na'ib, there really is no clear ranking. While the office of the Waziri is generally regarded as the most important, and while every man who served as Waziri later became headman, in 1966 there was no Waziri, and things went on as usual. Since the titles are not correlated with distinct roles, the personality and ability of the officeholder and his relationship with the headman are the main factors which determine the importance placed upon a particular office.

Besides Sarkin Samare, there is one other office whose incumbent is not supposed to represent people from a local area. Just as the Sarkin Samare is supposed to represent all the male "youth," the Magajia is supposed to represent all the women,[4] but her role is also increasingly being abrogated by female *'yan k'asa* who belong to formal associations not connected to the chieftainship. And, like the Sarkin Samare, the present Magajia has been criticized for her role performance: for not being available when she is needed, for not organizing the women by holding regular meetings, and for not distributing kola to inform the women of events. In the cases of both the Sarkin Samare and the Magajia the problem is the same – that town-born immigrants are redefining offices and creating new associations to perform the functions that the titled elders formerly performed.

Some titles, especially those which refer to occupations, do not really designate offices, although they are always mentioned by the Mossi when the "chief's elders" are enumerated. These include, for example, the Wanzam, or barber. There are, in fact, many barbers, all called Wanzam, but there is only one, the oldest and longest resident in the zongo, who is associated with the headman and his court. Whenever a naming ceremony is performed the headman sends this Wanzam kola to request him to shave the child and, if it is a boy, to perform the circumcision. After performing these services the Wanzam receives a sheep's leg from the child's father or guardian. After the celebrations of *'id al-fitr* and *'id al-kabir* the headman sends the Wanzam and other elders a portion of a cow or sheep he has slaughtered. However, the Mossi Wanzam is not elected to his title in the same way that the other elders are elected. He attains his title because he has a special skill, but he does not occupy an office just because he has a title.

Bi'naba (chief drummer), Rud'naba (chief violinist), and Warib'naba (chief dancer) are other honorific titles which, even more clearly, are not associated with offices. The men who are called by these titles come from families which traditionally performed these activities or they are known for their skills themselves. These men do not occupy chairs, in that successors will most likely not be appointed to replace them, yet the men who hold the titles often sit with the Mossi headman to judge cases and do many other things the titled elders do. Since the functions of most of the true offices are not associated with specific skills or roles, it is common for first-generation immigrants to behave in much the same way as the titled elders. However, there are certain clear differences distinguishing those who bear honorific titles, used as names, and those whose titles refer to the names of offices. These men – the Rud'naba, Bi'naba, and Warib'naba – are not selected for their titles by the other elders and the headman, they do not pay to obtain their titles, and they do not go through installation ceremonies which consist, usually, of a prayer, followed by speeches and sometimes a dance at the new elder's house. They cannot be called to account for themselves if they do not support the headman or come to his court and, most important, perhaps, they do not represent sections of the Mossi population in Kumasi. They simply have titles because they are known to perform activities which traditionally carried titles or in which they excel. Their titles are names used to designate particular individuals.

Another such title is that of Timboco'naba. In this case, as in others when the first and only holder of a title is still alive, it is difficult to be sure if the title refers to an office. Since everyone who has a title claims that it is the name of a "chair," and since few people would contradict them, this question can often only be answered after the first incumbent has died and the question of succession has had a chance to arise. Timboco'naba is another title, like the ones just mentioned, which has a specific role entailment, although this role is seldom enacted nowadays.

The Timboco'naba claims that before so many people were Muslims he had "plenty of work." He would witness marriages for a two-shilling fee and he would

note the property of each spouse and the amount of the bride price or dowry. If
a divorce occurred, the Timboco'naba would determine the division of property
and the payment of compensation. The husband was not allowed to remove
property from the wife's room without his approval. Today, the Imam and Na'ib
have taken over these duties, since the whole marriage ritual has become Islamized.
The Timboco'naba's role is now identical with that of the other elders. He sits in
the headman's court and represents people from his home area of Manga.

Imam and Na'ib are true offices which do carry distinctive responsibilities. These
officials must perform certain rituals at Muslim ceremonies, particularly at life-
crisis ceremonies, and they are usually called in to lead prayers on important
occasions. They advise the headman on points of Islamic law, although, since
disputes brought to the headman are, as far as possible, judged according to Mossi
customary law, this function is not one of their most important. They keep records
in Arabic of births, marriages, and deaths; they note down the amount of marriage
payments; they are called in on divorce cases. Perhaps most important is their role
in representing the Mossi as a Muslim group within the zongo. There are frequently
occasions, such as at meetings of the Mosque Building Committee or at important
funerals, when the Imams of all the different Muslim groups are represented.

The present Imam is the only second-generation immigrant among the elders.
This is significant, since he represents a kind of bridge between the worlds of the
two generations. As a titled elder, he is incorporated into the institution of chieftaincy, just as the Mogo Naba's Imam was in Ouagadougou. As a second-generation
malam he is able to participate in the religious and political activities of the town-
born Muslims – activities which have nothing specifically to do with chieftainship
or, in other words, with the internal political organization of a specific ethnic
group.

This brings us to a very important distinction which is made among first-generation immigrants but is disappearing among *'yan k'asa* – the distinction between
malams and chiefs. Although many of the Mossi elders are at least nominal Muslims,
this is clearly not an aspect of their role. Since they have chiefs' titles they regard
themselves as royals; and traditionally the royal, Nakomce, estate was distinct
from the Muslim estate. Although a chief may pray and observe other Islamic rules,
he is not therefore a member of the Muslim estate, since his children are royals,
and not Muslims. Moreover, in Upper Volta, although not in Kumasi, he had traditional ritual roles which precluded him from being solely a Muslim. This is a common pattern in all the Moré-Dagbane states, including the Mossi, where being a
Muslim, in the sense that this constitutes the primary aspect of one's identity, is an
inherited status, an attribute of a particular ethnic identity, and not an acquired
set of religious beliefs or practices. In the north, noble status is inherited, so that
nobles may become Muslims, but as members of royal ethnic groups they do
not pass the status of Muslim on to their descendants. In Kumasi, on the other
hand, the statuses of both chief and Muslim are achieved and are quite independent
of ethnic identity. Nevertheless, the first-generation Mossi still talk about chiefs
(the headman and elders) and malams, *as if* this distinction were the same as that

between the traditional royal and Muslim estates. The division between these status categories is reflected in Kumasi in the seating plan adopted on ceremonial occasions. The titled elders, except the Imam and Na'ib, sit with the headman and are referred to as chiefs. The Imam and Na'ib sit with the other malams – those who read Arabic, who "know the book," and who usually were born in Kumasi. The commoners, *samare,* really constitute a residual category – those who neither have titles nor qualify as malams. They sit together in another section, outside the center of ritual activity, and they are often divided into two groups: those born in the north and *'yan k'asa.*

The distinction between malams and chiefs might disappear if there were no more first-generation immigrants in Kumasi. The *'yan k'asa* clearly identify themselves with the malams and, on the whole, show little respect for the elders and chiefs who are not also malams. While chronologically young *'yan k'asa* are classified as *samare,* those who are over thirty do their best to go to Mecca, for which they gain the title of al-hajj, and thereafter are unquestionably classified as malams. Among the Hausa in Kumasi no distinction between malams and chiefs is made, and a man who is not an educated Muslim has little chance of becoming a chief or titled elder. Mossi *'yan k'asa* clearly regard this as the ideal to which the Mossi should aspire. Thus, within the Mossi community in the 1960s the traditional opposition between malams and chiefs was reinforced by intergenerational value differences. For any office, the *'yan k'asa* generally favored orthodox malams, while first-generation immigrants tended to support older men who were familiar with Mossi tradition. For them, restricting the malams to specific offices – those of Imam and Na'ib – was an attempt to preserve the institution of chieftaincy in the face of significant and inevitable change.

Mossi associations

Although the groupings of first-generation immigrants which have been described as *budu* in the previous section can be referred to as associations, they are quite different in form from the associations which are dominated by *'yan k'asa* leaders. The associations of first-generation Mossi immigrants in some ways reflect traditional principles of social structure and to some extent continue to rely upon traditional cultural symbols. *'Yan k'asa* associations, on the other hand, are not based on traditional Mossi cultural idioms and, as a result, are actively concerned with finding appropriate symbols of identity and principles of organization. Much of the time spent at meetings of *'yan k'asa* associations is spent discussing how the group should be organized. While many such groups are formed, once organized they often die out and are replaced by new associations. Devoid of particularized cultural content, the associations of Mossi *'yan k'asa* are organizationally very similar to those of *'yan k'asa* in other ethnic communities.

The most important association which existed in the late 1960s was the Mossi Youth Association (MYA). This was formed after the dispute over the succession to the headmanship, described in the next chapter. In the course of this dispute it

Social organization of the Mossi community

The Wonderful Boys' Club: a multiethnic voluntary association for urban-born immigrants

became clear that first- and second-generation immigrants supported very different types of leaders and that it was difficult, perhaps impossible, to find a single leader who could satisfy the requirements of both sections of the community. The functions that rural- and urban-born immigrants expect their leaders to perform are strikingly different; first-generation leaders essentially help their followers adjust to urban life, while *'yan k'asa* leaders are much more concerned with consolidating a faction which can compete for status and prestige in the Muslim zongo community.

When the MYA was formed in 1966 the headman and elders, especially the Sarkin Samare, were suspicious and resentful of the new group. They accused it of trying "to take the *nam*," while the *'yan k'asa* leaders maintained that they had no interest in anything to do with chieftaincy. Although they had contended vigorously for the headmanship, once their candidate lost he turned to organizing the MYA and to demonstrating the irrelevance for the *'yan k'asa* of the chieftancy itself. The MYA leaders claimed that they were interested in religion, not "politics" – a derogatory term which they then applied to the whole institution of chieftaincy. They devoted a large part of their activity to preparing for the forthcoming Muslim festivals, occasions on which they would be able to demonstrate to the zongo community the educational achievements of the Mossi Muslims. The MYA leaders also stated that they were interested in promoting the solidarity of Mossi youth and in making them proud to be Mossi. These aims were stated explicitly on their printed membership cards:

Objects of the Union shall be as follows: (1) The first aim of the Union is to foster friendship among the Moshie Youth and create a cordial atmosphere among its members. (2) To learn and to speak our own mother tongue (which is Moré) and to be proud of our nationality. (3) Lastly we resolve and fully support the Government of the day.

Although all Mossi men were eligible to join the association, to become a member one had to pay an initial fee of two shillings and sixpence and submit two photographs, one for the member's card and one for the association's records. Dues of sixpence per week were collected, and all payments were recorded in the treasurer's book and on the member's card.

The MYA started with a great burst of enthusiasm from many Mossi *'yan k'asa*. The formation of the group was announced in the national press, and letters were sent to the police, the army, and the regional committee of the National Liberation Council (NLC), informing them of the new association. In a few weeks there were more than 150 members. About 40 regularly attended the general meetings held every Sunday. A core group of 12 people, the members of the executive committee, met every week on Fridays to plan an agenda for the Sunday meetings and to make major decisions concerning the activities of the association. At the same time, these meetings were occasions where events outside the Mossi community – in the zongo, the city, and in Ghana generally – were discussed and where, to some extent, the political positions of a large segment of the Mossi community were determined. When party political activity began, for example, it was at these meetings that many Mossi discussed the relative merits of the various parties; moreover, candidates attempted to reach the immigrants through the leadership of the association. The Mossi position in zongo politics was another topic of conversation – for example, during the controversy over the Imamate of the Central Mosque, when a great majority of the Mossi *'yan k'asa* community strongly supported the Hausa, rather than the Dagomba, candidate.

The first few weeks of MYA meetings were devoted to the election of officers and to the determination of the general policy of the organization. There was also a great deal of discussion about what the structure of the organization should be. Nine offices were created, all with English titles. As Table 36 shows, all officers but two were born in Kumasi, and one of these was from northern Ghana (Tamale).

An executive board of twenty-five members was elected, and the majority of these were *'yan k'asa*. There was an attempt to select those *'yan k'asa* who could speak Moré, but, in fact, only a few were really fluent in the language. A disciplinary committee was planned, to enforce the rules of the association, but its membership was never determined. The age of the members averaged about thirty, and most were born in Kumasi. However, others were invited to join, and several young first-generation migrants played active roles in the association and were elected to the executive board. After much discussion it was decided that Mossi with non-Mossi mothers could become members and, after further debate, it was

Social organization of the Mossi community

Table 36. *Birthplaces and occupations of MYA officers*

Office	Birthplace	Occupation
Chairman	Kumasi	Arabic teacher and tailor
Vice Chairman	Tamale	Clerk of collectors
English Secretary	Kumasi	Sign painter, police service[a]
Assistant English Secretary	Kumasi	Clerk
Arabic Secretary	Kumasi	Arabic teacher
Assistant Arabic Secretary	Kumasi	Driver (unemployed)
Treasurer	Kumasi	Driver (unemployed)
Assistant Treasurer	Upper Volta	Messenger, licensing office
Publicity Officer	Kumasi	Inspector of night watchmen for City Council

[a]A few months after the Association began, this man joined the police service and left Kumasi. They were unable to find another Mossi in Kumasi who was literate in English to replace him.

agreed that people with Mossi mothers and non-Mossi fathers could join, although none did.

The general meetings on Sundays were conducted in Hausa, since many *'yan k'asa* did not speak or understand Moré, but the Friday executive meetings were usually conducted in Moré. At these meetings the activities of the association were planned. For example, the amount of money that the association would contribute to members for births, marriages, and funerals was determined. Many weeks were spent planning the celebration of the Prophet Mohammed's birthday – Mawlid. On that occasion the MYA members all bought the same patterned cloth, known as *yayi* (Hausa, fashion), so that they were distinguishable from other Muslims by their distinctive dress. Although whatever cloth the Mossi select on these occasions continues to be sold on the market long after the celebration of Mawlid, the particular pattern the group selects becomes known in the zongo as "Mossi cloth." Every year this occurs, and these various prints become symbols of Mossi identity, even though they have nothing to do with traditional Mossi culture. During the Mawlid celebrations the MYA also regularly sponsored an evening performance of Qur'anic recitation in which the entire Qur'an was recited in Moré. Mossi malams made speeches, and men announced the *sadaka* marriages they had arranged for their daughters within the Mossi community. What was significant about all these activities, which revolved around the celebration of the Muslim festivals, is that the Mossi quite explicitly were competing for prestige with other Muslim groups. The discussions which took place in the planning stage indicated that the purchase of *yayi* and the Qur'anic recitations were intended to show off the Mossi as an important Muslim group in the zongo. Invitations were carefully sent to members of other ethnic communities, with the hope that they would attend and note the excellence of the Mossi performance of Islamic ritual. In contrast, the activities of first-generation immigrants, which were focused upon the chieftainship, were much more internally oriented; to a far greater extent they were concerned with performing very specific services for individuals who needed assistance of one kind or another. They were much less concerned with their status in the zongo vis-à-vis other ethnic communities.

Another very important association which was active in 1966 was the Mossi Women's Association. This group had been active in the pre-CPP period but dissolved when party politics divided the membership. Before the late 1950s the Mossi women had been organized under the leadership of the Magajia, but in 1966 there was a feeling among many women that the Magajia was not sufficiently concerned with the organization, or even with her duties as Magajia, to reassume its leadership. Consequently, another woman, also a first-generation immigrant, became the leader of the new group. The new leader in some ways typified a very important aspect of the women's association. Although born in Upper Volta, speaking fluent Moré, and extremely knowledgeable about Mossi customs, she also was a devout Muslim. She had been to Mecca and earned the title of Hajia, and she owned two houses in Kumasi, as a result of a very successful cloth-trading business. She thus combined attributes which confer status among both first-generation immigrants and *'yan k'asa*.

Unlike the men's association, the membership of the women's group consisted of immigrants of all generations. In this respect, and also in terms of the way the group's activities were conducted, the group represented a synthesis of the type of association found among first-generation Mossi men and *'yan k'asa*. Among women, differences in birthplace and generation did not produce differences in status that were nearly as significant as among the men. The common interests of the women in trade and their roles as wives and mothers overrode generational differences. Other factors also minimized these differences among women. First, many Mossi women born in Ghana are married to first-generation immigrants and to some extent a woman's status is dependent upon that of her husband; the fact that some female *'yan k'asa* are married to first-generation immigrants, while others are married to *'yan k'asa*, minimizes the importance of generational differences among the women. Among men, generation is very significant in defining networks of friends, business associates, and even kin; among women this is not so, partly because of the marriage pattern just noted, and also because women of all generations basically spend their time in the same way in Kumasi – at home or in the market, where rural- and urban-born women interact closely. Among men, generation to a large extent determines social and business networks. Men's contacts and activities are dependent on their generational status, and their close social relationships, other than those of specific kinship, rarely cross generational lines. As described above, rural- and urban-born men participate in zongo politics and in Mossi politics in different ways. The fact that women are not as overtly involved in political activity also tends to make generational differences less relevant in determining their status or in defining their social networks.[5] Finally, among women, the distinction between those educated in Arabic and others who are not literate is not marked, since women have only recently started attending Arabic schools in significant numbers. Among men educational differences generally correspond to and reinforce generational differences.

When the Mossi Women's Association was organized in 1966, the role of the Magajia as an elder became insignificant, since the association absorbed the functions she had performed, and addressed itself to the needs of women of both generations. The women contributed sixpence per week in dues, and contributions were noted in a membership book. A large part of each weekly meeting was devoted to discussing what to do with the funds collected. As in the men's group, donations were given to women at births, marriages, and funerals, and plans were made to purchase *yayi* for Mawlid. There was also considerable discussion about collecting money to contribute to the Mossi headman for his installation ceremony, the ceremony of shaving the chief's head which never took place. This involvement both in chieftaincy and Islam again reflects the important difference between the women's and the men's association. Unlike the MYA, the women's group did not carefully follow rules of parliamentary procedure. The group discussed the election of officers on several occasions, but none was ever elected. Nor was it ever determined what offices would be necessary. When Hajia replaced the Magajia as leader, it was she who was responsible for keeping records (with the assistance of her daughter, who had been to school), guarding the group's money, and running meetings.

Initially, there was much interest in the association. Several hundred women signed up, and as many as fifty sometimes attended the Sunday meetings. In some cases one woman would attend from a house as a representative of all the Mossi women in the house. Women would encourage each other to come and would even bring non-Mossi women who were married to Mossi men. It was agreed that these women were eligible, because they were giving birth to Mossi children. The general atmosphere of the meetings was very different from that of the men's association. The women were less serious in demeanor; they gossiped, joked, and discussed domestic affairs, conditions in the market, and forthcoming events. Political issues were discussed, but it was not considered important that the women take a unified stand, as was the case among the men. The women, nevertheless, were aware that their opinions counted and they made sure that these would be conveyed to the men.

Meetings continued regularly until 1968, when Hajia became ill and it was no longer possible to meet at her house in Aboabo. At this time the interest of the younger women turned towards the MYA, which had already made overtures to the women to incorporate them into the men's group. The MYA then sought to organize the women through the *'yan k'asa* members of the already existing women's group. They established a women's branch of the MYA and supervised the initial organizational meetings. Female *'yan k'asa* were elected to the posts of president, vice-president, secretary and treasurer. Twenty executive members were elected, as in the MYA, and they were charged with holding weekly meetings, in addition to the usual Sunday meetings. The woman's branch operated under the supervision of three advisors from the men's association. Like the earlier women's group this one collected 6d. a week in dues and contributed £G2.10 to women for births, marriages, and funerals. The new association still included women of both generations, but, under pressure from the young men, the leadership passed exclusively to second-generation immigrants.[6]

Several other Mossi associations have been formed at different times. Some fall into abeyance and are then revived at a later date under new leadership, as in the case of the women's group just described. In 1966 a group of Mossi malams met weekly for three months, with the aim of reconstituting a former group which also had broken into factions during the early 1960s. Several meetings were held, attended by between twelve and twenty men, to plan the activities of the reconstituted group. However, arguments arose over a name for the group, since all the names suggested were associated with political factions. There was also conflict over the activities to be undertaken for the celebration of Mawlid, and the group divided on generational lines. The Mossi malams' association never succeeded in establishing a firm organizational base, so it was unable to create the structure necessary to give it some degree of permanence. Unlike the *budu* described earlier, which exist among first-generation immigrants, the Mossi malam group was not formed as an extension of any traditional type of association, such as home locality or ethnic origin. Its membership criterion, Islamic education, was nontraditional and yet, at the same time, since it included first-generation immigrants, it did not readily look to non-Mossi cultural forms for an organizational model. Moreover, it was too small to support the elaborate hierarchy of officers found in the MYA. Still another problem was that, unlike the MYA or the women's group, it had a narrow criterion for membership, one which would make only a very small proportion of the Mossi community eligible. Consequently, arguments between a few individual members could not be subordinated to the aims of the group as a whole. After a few months of meetings, the malams ceased to meet on any regular basis and gave up attempts to form a formal association.

In contrast, the MYA and the woman's branch of the MYA continued to grow. Their aims were broad, and they were able to gain a wide base of support. Promising to raise the status of all Mossi in Kumasi – "to make the Mossi strong" – they were able to recruit many *'yan k'asa* who had no interest in the ethnically based associations and activities of first-generation immigrants. Their more "modern" organization also made them attractive to some young migrants who regarded the headman and elders as old-fashioned. The MYA thus appealed to immigrants of both generations, although the first-generation immigrants in the group were usually young. The MYA appealed to both literate and non-literate Muslims and to those who could speak Moré, as well as to those who knew only Hausa.

The wide appeal of the MYA drew considerable hostility from the headman and elders. Although the MYA insisted that it had no intention of stealing the *nam*, the threat which it presented was obvious. The headman and elders continued to perform valuable services for many first-generation immigrants, but as the Mossi community grew to include many adult *'yan k'asa*, a new type of leadership and a new type of association were necessary. The period of the 1960s was a period of transition for the Mossi community, when new leaders were emerging but the old ones had not yet become irrelevant.

It is, nevertheless, still impossible to predict that the older leaders will become irrelevant, for this is not simply a matter of time. It depends very much upon the future pattern of Mossi settlement in Ghana, which, in turn, depends upon economic and political developments in Ghana and Upper Volta and the relations between these countries. So long as the immigrant Mossi community consists both of migrants born in Upper Volta, imbued with Mossi culture in its more or less traditional sense, and *'yan k'asa*, who have very little connection with this cultural idiom, a certain amount of intergenerational variation and conflict is inevitable.

However, as a preface to the description of the dispute within the Mossi community in the next chapter, it is important to emphasize that the different value orientations of first-generation migrants and *'yan k'asa* do not necessarily or inherently imply conflict. In fact, there are very few situations in which overt conflict actually occurs. Powerful bonds of kinship, affinity, and common ethnicity unite Mossi of all generations. Consequently, when disputes are simultaneously occurring within the Mossi community and in the zongo, as a whole, the intra-Mossi differences are likely to be either irrelevant or suppressed. There is no definite and inevitable pattern of fission and fusion which invariably enables us to predict the outcome of any particular situation. It is always possible for factions within the Mossi community to appeal to outsiders for support against one another, and therefore to oppose one another in larger disputes as well. Also, ethnicity is not always the primary or only factor determining alliances and oppositions.

If this were not the case, if segmentation were perfect, and if the Mossi inevitably closed ranks against all outsiders, ethnicity would be of little interest to the observer and would be much less useful, politically, to the actors than it actually is. Divisions and alliances within and between ethnic communities are important, precisely because they are complicated and unstable. This is so, because ethnicity, and the segmentary pattern we can discern in it, never operates in a pure form. Other identities and interests always operate simultaneously and affect the relevance of ethnicity in particular situations.

10

Ethnicity, generational cleavages, and the political process

In discussing the structure of the Mossi community, we have so far avoided describing the political process. In this section, through the presentation of a case study, we are able to see how structural changes affect political action – how situations that appear as conflicts in day-to-day political life reflect deeper changes occurring in the immigrant community. The events which took place within the Mossi community after the coup which ousted Nkrumah in February 1966, particularly the contest over the selection of the headman, demonstrated the importance of the generational differences we have outlined. A description of these events shows how the distinct value orientations of first- and second-generation immigrants affect political life and how generational cleavages are handled, so as to prevent the dissolution of the ethnic community. These events are comprehensible only when placed in the context of the multiethnic zongo, for many of the stresses which the Mossi community experienced in 1966 had to do with changes that had affected all strangers in the preceding years. In the period immediately after the 1966 coup there was a great resurgence of overt expressions of ethnic identity among many stranger groups, although these manifestations of ethnicity were completely divorced from national political concerns. In fact, it was the claim that ethnicity was apolitical, and that it implied the absence of conflict, which enabled the stranger communities to reemerge and heal the wounds they felt they had incurred during the period when party alliances had cross-cut ethnic communities. Since the primary symbol of the existence of the Mossi community in Kumasi was the office of headman, it is not surprising that political activity after the coup should have been directed at filling this office – at selecting a leader who represented the unity and consensus which, so many Mossi claimed, had been destroyed by government interference, party activity, and involvement in Ghanaian political life, generally, in the preceding decade.

There are no generally accepted rules of succession to office in the Mossi community, and there is no "traditional" procedure of election. It is assumed that the headman will be the most qualified leader who attains office through the consensus of the entire community. In order that consensus be reached, however, internal conflicts in the community must be resolved. If they are not, the headman may not be able to perform one of his major roles, that of acting to outsiders as a representative of the entire community. Once consensus is reached, principles and values, even rules of succession, are called upon to explain why a particular man has won. But rules which are used to explain the outcome of a succession dispute may be invoked after the event. During the selection process, all sides may appeal to formal rules, but the outcome is determined by other factors, including the balance of power between the generations and the ability of specific leaders to mobilize networks of clients and kin.

In order to understand the dispute which occurred in 1966, it is necessary to review briefly the previous pattern of succession. What were pragmatic choices in the past, sometimes reflecting the political aptitudes of specific individuals, became precedents, even traditions, in 1966, when various factions attempted to appeal to established patterns – to "custom" – to justify claims to power.

The first Mossi headman, Dawda, originally a sandalmaker of Talse origin, was one of the first Mossi landlords in Kumasi. Insistent on Mossi autonomy, he led the movement for recognition of a separate headman in 1909. His insistence on the independence of the Mossi from Hausa leadership led to his deportation by the colonial government after his opposition to Malam Salaw in 1932. He was succeeded by his Waziri, Adamu, of Yarse origin. Adamu also insisted upon Mossi autonomy and, like his predecessor, was deported by the government in 1957, a few months after independence. He, too, refused to recognize the authority of the Hausa Sarkin Zongo, Mutawakilu. After Adamu died in Upper Volta, during the second year of his exile, members of the Kumasi Mossi community selected his Waziri, Hamidu, as successor. Although this man was recognized by the District Commissioner in Kumasi, the current Sarkin Zongo and CPP Joint Constituency Chairman, Mutawakilu, refused to recognize him. Instead, he appointed a CPP member, Mamudu, as Mossi headman. From 1958 until 1966 there was no consensus in the community over the selection, and many Mossi immigrants refused to recognize the CPP appointee. He had been installed even before Hamidu died, in 1961, so that from 1958 until Hamidu's death different factions of the Mossi community claimed to have different headmen, each recognized by different authorities outside the zongo. According to the anti-CPP faction, Mutawakilu's appointee, Mamudu, never was the real headman. He was, they maintained, one of those "chiefs by radio" appointed by the CPP. This faction maintained that when Hamidu died his Waziri, Yisa, became regent. Some maintained that Yisa remained regent, because he could not get government recognition. Others, who also opposed the CPP appointee, claimed Yisa was "sitting on Adamu's chair,"[1] waiting for the time when the anti-CPP faction would be able to regain the office.

There were very close, long-standing relationships between these individual officeholders. In most cases succession has followed patron/client relations of one type or another. When Adamu first came to Kumasi he had lived in Dawda's house and worked for him before becoming Waziri. Both Yisa and Mamudu had been clients of Adamu. It was said that Mamudu resented the fact that Adamu had never given him a titled office, while Yisa had obtained a title. Some people claimed this to be the reason Mamudu "left the Mossi" and joined the CPP. At the time of the 1966 dispute both these men were in their sixties, both had built up businesses as landlords and traders, and both were still sufficiently familiar with Mossi custom to assist rural-born migrants.

Although Mamudu was the official, government-appointed headman from 1958 until 1966, a majority of the Mossi community refused to recognize him. They claimed that headmen could not be primarily government appointees, although they knew that government approval was necessary for them to function, once elected. Hamidu had indeed been recognized by the District Commissioner, although not by Mutawakilu. Therefore, until Hamidu's death, a majority of the community continued to refer to him as headman. Because of these disagreements, during the entire postindependence decade the effectiveness of the office of headman was destroyed by conflicts over the legitimacy of the various leaders.

Besides Mamudu and Yisa there was one other person who played a major role in the 1966 dispute. This was Adamu's son, Abdul Rahman (see Figure 4a), an important *'yan k'asa* leader who had been served with an order of local deportation after a dispute with Mutawakilu in 1958. After seven years in Ejura and Upper Volta, he returned to Kumasi in 1966 and assumed a very important role, both as a potential successor to his father's office and as a *'yan k'asa* leader. He was then in his late thirties and was unusual among the Mossi *'yan k'asa* in his ability to speak Moré, Twi, and Arabic, as well as Hausa, his extensive knowledge of Islamic law and literature, and his knowledge of Mossi custom, gained both from his father and from his experience in Upper Volta. An intelligent and able leader, he had built up excellent connections with leaders of all ethnic groups in the zongo, except those who supported the CPP. He also was more adept than most at working with non-Muslims in the government and in the Asante community.

During his term of office Mamudu had appointed his own set of elders, all of whom were CPP members. His main advisor was the head of the UVU, and, having very little popular support in the Kumasi community, Mamudu attempted to use the UVU to gain income and support. The large number of offices in the UVU were strategically distributed by Mamudu and the UVU's Asante regional head.

Yisa regarded himself as "underground" headman after Hamidu's death and he, too, appointed several elders, while others remained from Adamu's term of office. Those who unofficially retained their offices were frequently in danger of being deported or detained and on several occasions were called to the police station and arrested for alleged anti-CPP activities. Consequently, after the 1966 coup most of these elders appeared as martyrs in the eyes of many Mossi immigrants: their cause had become the integrity of the ethnic community itself.

The dispute which occurred in 1966 involved the three Mossi leaders Mamudu, Yisa, and Abdul Rahman. However, because most immigrants maintained that the headman should not be a former supporter of the CPP, Mamudu could not be considered a serious candidate. Most people operated on the premise that a headman could be selected by consensus, even though there were no procedures for determining how or when this was reached. People also assumed that external recognition of the community's choice had to be attained, but there was general confusion about who now held the authority to confer governmental approval. One other point on which most people agreed was that party politics should be eliminated from the selection process.

Political activity, in the sense of the organization of parties or groups with national political ambitions, was officially banned by the NLC in 1966. Within small communities such as those in Kumasi zongo there was a general feeling that "politics" implied the disintegration of the community. Many Mossi described politics as something which made the group vulnerable to the influence of outsiders, and, likewise, the weakening of Mossi identity was felt to cause factionalism. Thus, the idea that all Mossi CPP members had been under Hausa influence, or were attempting to "become Hausa" was again common. The Hausa were blamed with bringing politics to Kumasi, and after 1966 the CPP-appointed headman was regarded as a man who had sold out to a Hausa (Mutawakilu). Expressions of Mossi solidarity became increasingly important. Loyalty to the Mossi community implied the denial of factional differences within it. It was not surprising, therefore, that the two main contenders for the headmanship, Rahman and Yisa, did not openly admit they were competing for the office.

Although most immigrants regarded these two men as the main candidates, they did not expect either to admit coveting the office. As one man said, "Chieftaincy is like a woman. When you want to court a woman you can't go up to her and just say what you want." In the first days after the coup the two men were united in opposition to Mamudu and agreed on the importance of getting the chieftaincy back from the CPP faction. The headmanship was referred to as Adamu's chair, Hamidu was referred to as the late Waziri, and Yisa as the regent.

Thus, although the deceased Adamu served as the symbolic head of the majority anti-CPP faction, it was divided in support of Rahman and Yisa. Many older first-generation immigrants who had remained in Kumasi during the CPP period, including, of course, the elders he had appointed, tended to support Yisa. Most elders who had been installed by Adamu attempted neutrality and, in the dispute which followed, they acted as intermediaries between Yisa and Rahman. Age, and the fact that these people had all been born in Upper Volta, drew them together into a faction. Although never explicit, there was an awareness, expressed in people's actions, that first-generation immigrants had distinct interests – since many of the older first-generation immigrants were involved in trade with Upper Volta or in channeling Voltaic labor into Asante cocoa farms and other jobs, they recognized that they needed a representative who would help protect these relationships; they felt that the judicial role of the headman necessitated the election of one who could apply Mossi customary law; and, although the Ghanaian citizenship laws did not unambiguously remove second-generation Mossi immigrants from the Voltaic community, these first-generation migrants believed that a leader born in Upper Volta might more easily protect their interests as Voltaic citizens. This was important, for many suspected that they might need the option of returning to Upper Volta, should their status as aliens in Ghana become perilous.

Politics and change

The vast majority of the *'yan k'asa*, on the other hand, tended to support Rahman for similar reasons. They felt that an urban-born Mossi could more easily deal with Ghanaian officials; for, although the participation of the *'yan k'asa* in Ghanaian politics was limited, because they were strangers and aliens, they recognized that the political field in which they had to operate was the Ghanaian one. A man like Rahman with considerable political experience was, given these requirements, an ideal candidate.

In the course of the dispute it became evident that rural- and urban-born Mossi immigrants had different leadership requirements, despite bonds of ethnicity uniting them. While Rahman was prominent in the multiethnic zongo community, Yisa's influence was more limited to the Mossi community. He rarely spoke Hausa and, although Yarse, he was much more familiar with Mossi customary law than with Islamic law.

This generational division of support was not absolute, however. Rahman was able to gather some support among rural-born Mossi, as well as *'yan k'asa.* Besides some younger migrants, who tended to favor him because of his relative youth, he also could draw upon support from his father's former clients. During his lifetime Adamu had established a very large following, and many of these people and their relatives were now bound by ties of specific and generalized kinship to his heirs. On the other side, Yisa could gather some support among *'yan k'asa* – from his own kin, from clients and their kin, and from some traders in Kumasi who relied upon him in his capacity as a lorry collector.

As informal discussion of who would get the chair progressed, it became apparent that conflicting principles of succession were being invoked. Rahman's supporters claimed that the office still belonged to Adamu's family, since he had neither been deposed by the community nor died in office. That is, he had not left the office in any legitimate way – and in a sense, therefore, still occupied it. Yisa, they claimed, like Hamidu before him, had merely been acting as regent, holding the office for Adamu's return or for the succession of his son. They attempted to invoke a principle of filial succession to the chief's office. Those who supported Yisa, however, argued that, like both Adamu and Hamidu, his succession through promotion from the office of Waziri to that of headman should be recognized. Each faction, then, was able to appeal to a different principle to justify the claim of its candidate. Ultimately, neither formal principle had much weight in determining the actual outcome, and people admitted that "things were different in Kumasi," that customary law did not apply, and that precedents were not necessarily equivalent to the traditional "laws." Despite this pragmatic outlook, those who admitted that there were no formal rules still felt that the decision had to be based on consensus. With this in mind, we can now examine how the new headman was actually selected and how people interpreted this decision after the event.

A few months after the coup, a group of zongo headmen who had lost their offices during the CPP period held a meeting and decided to appeal to the NLC for formal reinstatement. This group included: the Hausa headman, Ahmadu Baba, who had returned from deportation to Nigeria; the Hausa chief butcher (Sarkin

256

Fawa); and the Mamprusi, Dagomba, and Busansi headmen. The Mossi were asked to join in writing letters to the NLC with their demands. Representatives of each community prepared a similar letter requesting the reinstallation of the anti-CPP leaders. Among the Mossi, since the deported headman had died, a new name had to be inserted in the letter. Yisa's supporters prevailed, and Rahman and his supporters agreed to insert Yisa's name, on the understanding that this act was simply meant to win the office away from the CPP faction. Once this had been accomplished, it was felt that the question of succession would be decided within that section of the Mossi community which opposed the CPP. As subsequent events showed, it was just this point that became the basis for misunderstanding. While most people agreed to inserting Yisa's name as regent, once the government intervened he appeared to outsiders to be the community's chosen headman.

The NLC sent these letters to the Regional Office in Kumasi and asked the local administration to deal with them. The Regional Administration asked the police to investigate the claims made in the letters. The strangers were unaware that subsequent police actions in Kumasi were related to the letters they had sent to the NLC in Accra and they believed the police were attempting to interfere with the selection of headmen. They began offering gifts to the police inspectors and although some justified this as a traditional practice, different factions accused each other of bribing the police for support.

When an inspector at the Zongo police station decided that the best way to identify the most popular candidates would be to call a series of elections, each group was given an appointment to appear at the police station. Everyone watched the elections in other communities with great interest. Votes were taken by either a show of hands or a count of which candidate had more supporters accompanying him. In one case a candidate arrived with a crowd of supporters, while his opponent came with one. People claimed this was not a mistake – that only one of the candidates had been informed that an election was to take place. When the Mossi heard this, they began to make plans for a confrontation at the police station.

The so-called elections failed in most groups for a number of reasons. The police did not ask people where they were from; no residence qualifications were established; and no date for the election was announced. Given these uncertainties, and the fact that most of the immigrants had had negative experiences with formal elections, it was not surprising that people refused to accept either place of residence or ethnic identity as a necessary qualification for participation. Factions accused each other of bringing in voters from different ethnic groups, or from the same group but from different towns. When elections were held at the police station, conflict, sometimes violent, occurred, and it became obvious that few people accepted this as a legitimate selection procedure.

The day the Mossi were called to the police station, they were turned away before a vote was held. Despite rumors that this was because one CPP faction had bribed the police, the police had received a report from the Regional Administrative Office that violence was about to erupt in the Zongo, due to these elections.

After this, high officials in the Kumasi central police headquarters interviewed contesting candidates from each community to find out the basis for their claim to office. Among the Mossi, Mamudu went with one elder and said that he had been appointed by the Mossi community and installed by Mutawakilu. Yisa went with Rahman and the Wid'naba, the two men who had signed the letter to the NLC. They explained that Yisa had been sitting on Adamu's chair as regent. The police took this to mean that Yisa was the candidate opposing Mamudu.

While these elections and interviews with the police were taking place, the Asantehene was also again becoming involved in zongo affairs. In the period between the police elections and later attempts on the part of administrative officials to regularize the procedure for recognizing headmen, the Asantehene had been requested by Ahmadu Baba to arbitrate a dispute between himself and the Hausa Imam over the membership of a committee supervising repairs to the central mosque. In the course of hearing this dispute it became evident that the basic conflict was the continuing split between factions which had supported the disbanded political parties. The various chieftaincy disputes were also mentioned during this hearing, and candidates who were contesting offices asked the Asantehene whether the "old" (UP) or "new" (CPP) headmen had a right to office. At this time the government's policy with regard to chieftaincy had still not been announced. The Chieftaincy Decree, which removed from office all those who had been appointed by the CPP, was not issued until six months later, in December 1966. The Asantehene was in a delicate position and seemed anxious not to commit himself to the wrong side. Since the NLC government had, so far, said nothing on the matter of chieftaincy, the Asantehene declared that the headmen who were in office during the CPP period were still the legitimate headmen. Arguments broke out in the palace immediately, and the meeting was concluded in tension and bitterness. In the following week it became clear that the strangers looked to the Asantehene for guidance primarily when they expected support from him. When this was not forthcoming they claimed that he had no right to intervene in zongo affairs. Like an unfavorable vote, an unfavorable decision on his part could be ignored. With a number of alternative authorities outside the zongo, the immigrant leaders had the option of following the Asantehene's advice only when it was to their advantage.

During the next week the former UP headmen complained directly to officials in the NLC. An important NLC member (Major General Afrifa) came to Kumasi and held a meeting with the Asantehene. The next week the Asantehene recalled the zongo elders and told all CPP supporters to "get out of my town." People in the UP faction suspected that the NLC had intervened or that the Asantehene had been playing a shrewd political game, forcing the "wolves" to expose themselves.

The Asantehene then requested each ethnic community to name its headman in a petition signed by the group's elders. In some cases two factions brought letters, so that no one was selected. In others the Asantehene dismissed the claim of one candidate who obviously had little support. Some of his decisions angered losing factions, and there were threats and a few outbreaks of violence. Finally, after

258

one such incident in the Gao community, the Regional Committee of Administration intervened and issued a declaration to the effect that the recognition of headmen would henceforth consist of approval by the Regional Committee of Administration, followed by formal installation by the Asantehene.

Immediately after Yisa had gone to the Asantehene, open disputation broke out in the Mossi community. Rahman's supporters, particularly the Sanfo Yarse *budu*, accused him of giving away the *nam* without their consent. He denied this and said that he had been waiting for the question to be discussed in a general meeting. A meeting was subsequently called, and Yisa admitted that he and his supporters had erred in not consulting Rahman and in implicitly taking advantage of opportunities presented by the confusion and uncertainty over electoral procedure. They asked for forgiveness, in the spirit of Islam and for the sake of Mossi unity. They pointed out how dissension would weaken the whole community and how Rahman's actions to that point could have been interpreted as an expression of support for Yisa. Rahman's supporters argued that the *nam* had been usurped. They noted how Yisa had borrowed Adamu's umbrella and had failed to return it. (This, like the horse, is a symbol of the chief's office in Kumasi.) Yisa's borrowing of the umbrella, they maintained, was equivalent to stealing the royal regalia in traditional Mossi society.

Rahman's supporters eventually gave in and agreed to recognize Yisa as headman. They ceased contesting the office, but few of them recognized his authority over them. Few people wanted to admit that the community was still divided, however, and attempts were made to unify the two factions. Yisa asked Rahman to be Waziri. Some people urged Rahman to accept, noting that "the Prime Minister is more important than the King." They also pointed out that Yisa, like the other elders, was an old man without sons, so that after his death Rahman would certainly become headman through two principles of succession – a filial tie to a former headman and promotion from the office of Waziri. Rahman did succeed, eight years later, after Yisa's death. At the time, however, he refused the offer, saying that as a malam he had no interest in being chief and claiming that such offices were antiquated tribal institutions. He was encouraged in his thinking by officials of the Upper Volta Embassy in Accra, who maintained that there were no officially recognized chiefs among Voltaics in Upper Volta or Ghana. Voltaic officials urged Rahman to reorganize the UVU – thereby encouraging him in one of his moves to broaden his basis of support. Yisa and his elders bitterly opposed the UVU and attacked it by claiming it was still a CPP group.

Once Yisa had assumed the headmanship, Rahman insisted on the importance of the distinction between malams and chiefs. He recognized that this distinction reinforced intergenerational differences but maintained that the leader of the first-generation immigrants should properly be a chief, while the leader of the *'yan k'asa* should be a Muslim. He then turned to reopening his Arabic school. To an observer, however, it was clear that his loss of interest in the Mossi headmanship coincided with a renewed interest in expanding his political activities in the wider zongo community. This meant participating in activities which were not associated with the organization of his own ethnic group but were based on national or religious constituencies.

Rahman and others recognized that the distinction between chiefs and malams was one of the few characteristics which still distinguished the Mossi from the Hausa institution of chieftaincy. At times he conceptualized his own ambivalence about aspiring to this headmanship or about accepting the office of Waziri as a conflict between being a Mossi and being a Muslim. He also claimed for a short time that he was embroiled in factional disputes because he had decided to involve himself in Mossi affairs and that if he had remained aloof, as a Muslim, he would have avoided conflict and made fewer enemies. To an outsider it also seemed that his experience had demonstrated to him that involvement in the internal politics of an ethnic community was not really a way of advancing in the broader political arena of the zongo as a whole. Enlarging an Arabic school and enrolling children from many immigrant groups, or including in one's trading clientele migrants of varied backgrounds, seemed more secure ways of advancing one's position in the zongo. For a while, Rahman was prepared to divorce himself entirely from involvement in Mossi affairs. He was not yet prepared to attempt to change the Mossi institution of chieftaincy by claiming that, as a malam, he was particularly appropriate to serve as headman. He seemed to be sufficiently involved with Mossi values to accept that the headman should not or need not be an educated Muslim but he was also prepared to use his abilities in this area to advance in a different and wider political arena.

Many people maintained that Yisa had succeeded to the office "by mistake." They claimed that no one was responsible for having chosen him over Rahman. Obviously, this was not the case; certain individuals had maneuvered events quite consciously during the negotiations with the government. Yet, there were certain cultural factors which determined the outcome and led people, even those on the losing side, to accept this interpretation. Had Rahman succeeded, a number of changes would have occurred in the community – perhaps prematurely, given the ratio of first- and second-generation immigrants that then existed. First, the important Mossi cultural distinction between malams and chiefs would have disappeared; second, a *'yan k'asa* headman would have been elected for the first time, and this would have presented difficulties for many first-generation migrants, who would expect their headman to apply Mossi customary law to their disputes and to assume many roles traditionally associated with a *budkasama*. Moreover, people felt Rahman might have changed many of the appointments to titled offices, replacing first-generation immigrants with *'yan k'asa* who were literate in Arabic, yet who were relatively unfamiliar with Mossi custom and who often could not speak Moré. Their ties in Kumasi zongo outside the Mossi community may have been greater than those of the first-generation elders, but their contacts in Upper Volta were far fewer. The first-generation elders already in office were well aware of this and they were, in fact, the ones who most actively determined the outcome of the succession.

In describing the selection of the headman as a "mistake," the Mossi community was able to maintain an image of unity and to attribute the selection to external forces – to coincidence, misunderstandings, and, ultimately, to the will of God. They were unable to reach an explicit decision because there were too many conflicting principles held by the same people and too many cross-cutting inter-personal relationships. If there had been an open vote, or perhaps even a secret ballot, many people would have abstained. Rahman himself was not able to admit openly that he aspired to the office, since he could not say that he opposed the man who was his father's regent.

However, if people had been forced to choose between the two men, the community would have divided: first, on generational lines and second, according to provenance and ties of kinship and clientage. However, all these cleavages, if openly expressed, would have denied the principle of ethnic unity on which the headmanship was based and which all were so intent on reinforcing after the 1966 coup d'état. Conflict over political parties had led to a situation in which all com-munity activities were suspended, and many immigrants felt deprived by this situation. Thus, after the 1966 coup no one was willing to admit that factionalism existed and no one was able to proclaim support openly for one candidate or the other.

There were other conflicting values which made a formal selection impossible. If an election had been held, individuals would have had to decide whether a malam could be a chief. If he could, the Mossi headmanship would have become culturally indistinguishable from the Hausa office. Also, people would have had to decide whether or not an hereditary principle of succession was relevant in the urban community or if the promotional principle constituted a rule of succession. Each of these possible courses expressed a different value orientation. They pro-vided alternate justifications for particular events, and, although contradictory, these different values existed within the same community. By selecting the head-man by "mistake," rather than by invoking any one principle, all of them could continue to exist and be used when expedient. The coexistence of these different values reflected many of the changes the Mossi community was experiencing; their persistence also facilitated adaptation to change.

Another reason that the selection turned out as it did was that the election of Rahman would have further undermined the seniority principle. Although the Islamic values which Rahman stood for had high prestige among immigrants of both generations, they also represented a threat to Mossi cultural identity. Seniority was both a traditional and a Muslim value; it was one of the few principles which cross-cut generational lines and which could be invoked to support the selection of Yisa.

After the event, people accepted the fait accompli, mainly by emphasizing that the preservation of unity protected the whole community from outsiders' attacks. As has been suggested above, in this period of Ghanaian history, a decade after independence, the metaphor of "politics" was used to describe conflict and to emphasize, by contrast, the community's desire for harmony and ethnic solidar-ity. Thus, none of the events that had occurred were described as "political," since factionalism had not been openly expressed and since it had not become involved with national political parties. After Yisa assumed the office he also maintained that he had no interest in "politics" and that all of the organized associations, such as the UVU and the MYA, were threats to Mossi unity, since they inevitably became involved with national parties. He maintained that all organizations which had nontraditional offices and roles were "political." He turned his attention to arbitrating many cases which people had refrained from bringing to Mamudu when he was headman. Yisa insisted that his office was not a political position, since it was concerned almost entirely with internal affairs which, ideally, were nonfactional and nonpolitical. Conceptually, the Mossi community was a family. In the metaphorical usage then current, it could not, by definition, be political. Had a headman with more interest in the zongo, or even the nation, been selected, the definition of the role might have changed, but it also would have been more difficult to maintain its apolitical image.

A few months later, after Yisa had selected an elderly first-generation immigrant as Sarkin Samare, a group of Mossi youth, mainly *'yan k'asa*, appealed to Rahman to organize the association which became known as the MYA. Yisa then reported to the police that the MYA was a political organization affiliated with the defunct CPP. He also claimed that the MYA was attempting to take the chieftaincy from him. Finally, after months of unsuccessfully campaigning against the group, which had by then successfully established relationships with the authorities outside the zongo, Yisa desisted, although he continued to feel threatened by it. The leaders of the MYA, on the other hand, maintained that they had no interest in his office and that their functions and goals were complementary to his.

Thus, despite the ability of the two generations to act together vis-à-vis non-Mossi, the ethnic community was divided internally on generational lines. This cleavage was reinforced by cultural differences which reflected many of the inevitable changes that migrant communities experience. Rural- and urban-born Mossi recognized different types of leaders and formed different kinds of informal and formal associations. This division was counteracted, however, by common ethnicity and links of kinship and, sometimes, clientship. Because of these ties, the leadership positions of Yisa and Rahman became more and more complementary in the years following the succession dispute. Yisa took care of most affairs involving first-generation immigrants, yet he cooperated closely with Rahman in making decisions which concerned the Mossi community's relations with outsiders. Rahman represented the Mossi on all multiethnic Muslim councils which recognized ethnic representation, and he represented the community in dealing with government officials. Some of the most articulate Mossi expressed the role complementarity that developed, by stating that, while Yisa was formally "president," Rahman was "minister of foreign affairs." Obviously, this, too, is an idealized picture, since Rahman also played a significant judicial role, mainly among *'yan k'asa.*

Similarly, as chapter 9 has shown, the associations formed by rural- and urban-born immigrants are complementary. They are different means of performing similar tasks, and in both a major function is the assertion and maintenance of ethnic identity. The common aim of these very different kinds of association and styles of leadership is, in part, to express and maintain the distinct social identity and strength of the Mossi community vis-à-vis other groups in the zongo and in Kumasi. In the period following the 1966 coup, not only the Mossi, but all immigrants, felt threatened as strangers and aliens. They existed, and still do today, in a rapidly changing, highly complex environment. Jobs were scarce, trade was competitive, there were more migrant men than women, and national politics appeared – at that time, at least – more often as a threat than an opportunity. For these reasons immigrants of both generations attempted to maintain institutions which expressed and vitalized ethnicity, despite the cultural differences emerging along generational lines within the community. This period was significant, in that it illustrated how, despite the changes and divisions within the Mossi community, a facade of unity had to be maintained in the face of what were perceived as possible external threats. The Mossi felt harmed by the divisiveness of the CPP period and felt that if they could recreate internal unity they could use their ethnicity positively to help their individual members, to protect themselves from "politics," and, hopefully, to raise their status in the zongo and in Ghana.

11

Conclusion: ethnicity, cultural integration, and social stratification

The incorporation of immigrant groups into the zongo and the simultaneous persistence of ethnicity are two analytically separable processes of change. In the example presented in this book, incorporation – political, economic, religious, and social – often entails the abandonment of traditional culture and the adoption of new behavior patterns. Nevertheless, this does not preclude the reassertion of ethnic identities based on provenance in constantly changing forms. Through a comparison of Mossi immigrants in two generations, I have tried to show that cultural change does not necessarily lead to the disappearance of ethnicity; not only do new ethnic identities and new cultural patterns emerge, associated with the incorporation of immigrants into larger communities, but older identities persist also, with new symbols being adopted to maintain boundaries.

While the discussion has been restricted to the case study presented here, this situation is by no means unique. It is characteristic of many societies the world over – rural or urban, industrial or preindustrial – where peoples of diverse origins have come together, by choice or not, to create new communities. It is characteristic of all situations where memories of separate histories have been transformed into markers of social, political, or economic status. If one insists, as I have, on looking at ethnicity in time perspective, as a process of social and cultural change, one will probably be struck by how rare are those situations where ethnicity implies the persistence of "traditional" cultural identities. Perhaps what invites further exploration at this point is not so much the inevitable and rapid cultural change which we witness all around us, every day, but the exceptional instances of cultural survival, the cases where cultural patterns persist, despite the pressure of political, economic, and social incorporation.

The Mossi immigrants in Kumasi do not offer such an example, although from another perspective it may appear in time that the persistence of a distinct zongo stranger culture in Ghana is indeed such a case. In the remaining pages I shall turn back to the data presented here, first summarizing the processes of cultural integration, assimilation, and innovation which have been discussed at various points throughout this book. This involves consideration of emergent identities defined on several levels – local, regional, and national. Within the zongo, identities based on provenance persist as a means of allocating political and social status in a context in which stratification is, to some extent, based upon the ideology of ethnicity. At the level of the municipality, zongo identity expresses the opposition (at once, social, cultural, political, and economic) between hosts and strangers, Asante and non-Asante. At the regional level, ethnicity expresses cleavages which reflect an unequal distribution of economic resources, different degrees of Westernization, and differential access to nationally controlled resources. In Kumasi, ethnicity on this level is expressed in the distinction between northerners and southerners. Finally, national identities, based on country of origin, express the increasingly important cleavage between aliens and citizens. At each of these levels, ethnicity is one way of allocating status and attempting to limit or gain access to, and control over, political, social, or economic resources.

The second section of this chapter involves a more detailed discussion of the way in which ethnicity relates to systems of status allocation. These can be referred to as systems of stratification when various statuses entail differential access to economic and political resources. Ethnicity, however, does not necessarily imply stratification. Nor is it simply a synonym for class differences,[1] but rather it may relate to class differences in quite complex ways. In the following pages some aspects of the relationship between ethnicity and status allocation will be discussed in the context of traditional Mossi society, Kumasi zongo, and Ghana. In none of these situations is there a single unilinear scale of stratification. In each, ethnicity coexists with other criteria, including class differences, which are used in allocating status and defining prestige.

The importance of the distinction between prestige and status has been ably considered by Smith (1959b: 251) in his discussion of status systems among the Hausa and, more recently, by Barkow (1975: 558; Bailey 1971; Hutson 1971). While *status*, as I am using the term, can be understood as the totality of rights and obligations inherent in a particular social position, *prestige* refers to the subjective evaluation of status. The relevance of the distinction between status and prestige to the societies described in this book will be explored below.

Processes of cultural integration in Kumasi zongo

From its inception the zongo has been ethnically heterogeneous. Immigrants from many different areas have come to Kumasi and, because of a common identification as strangers, common occupations, and common linguistic, religious, and cultural backgrounds, they have settled in particular areas of the town. Although the distinction between northerners and the Asante has always overshadowed cultural differences between immigrants, these were not insignificant. Nevertheless, northerners have interacted in the zongo for almost a century, sharing not only neighborhoods, but also houses within neighborhoods. In an environment where people spend most of their time outside their dwelling units, and where these dwellings themselves include large open courtyards, physical propinquity encourages interaction and interdependence. People must care for their common living space and must accommodate each other within it. It is impossible not to notice one's neighbors when kitchens, courtyards, latrines, play areas, mosques, and markets are all communally used. These constitute the physical settings where daily interaction takes place.

The ethnic heterogeneity and the physical structure of the stranger community thus necessitate and facilitate the development of common linguistic and behavioral codes. For most migrants, the codes are not abstractions from traditional culture, but rather entail the adoption of new values and new ways of doing things. I refer to these processes of change as "Islamization" and "Hausaization," and to the resultant culture as "zongo culture." Many first-generation immigrants are indeed bicultural. While they may, in some contexts, retain and act in terms of traditional values, they nevertheless quickly become conversant with zongo culture, to the extent that ethnicity does not differentiate modes of behavior. Just as language differences may persist but become secondary to the use of Hausa in many contexts, so, distinct customs either disappear or become relegated to domains that are so private that they do not disrupt interaction and communication. Obviously, assimilation occurs as a process over time, and outward conformity to zongo culture may not always indicate a transformation of values. There is, however, very little social support for the maintenance of traditional behavior patterns, and there is considerable pressure to assimilate into the stranger community. The stereotype of the person from home – the country bumpkin – can be heard at least as often in Kumasi as any ethnic stereotype.

It has been my argument that in Kumasi the heterogeneity of domestic units is one of the most important catalysts for cultural change (chapters 4 and 5 and Schildkrout 1975a). This situation differs from that described in other parts of Africa – particularly East and Southern Africa, where the domestic domain has been seen as crucial for preserving traditional culture. The persistence of traditional linguistic and cultural patterns in the domestic context has been related by observers to manifestations of ethnicity in extradomestic domains (Parkin 1969; Schildkrout 1974b: 190). In Kumasi the domestic context is significant in quite the reverse way: it fosters the abandonment of traditional identities, for it is the main arena for the socialization of children, as well as new migrants. As a consequence of this situation, it has been necessary to look in quite other directions – to political life, to policies of national and colonial governments, and to the status systems operative within the stranger community – to explain the persistence of ethnicity in Kumasi zongo.

Also, because of the great heterogeneity and long history of encapsulation of the stranger community, I have been unable to explain the persistence of ethnic cleavages primarily in economic terms, as did Cohen in his description of the Sabon Gari of Ibadan (1969). While there is, of course, considerable economic competition within the zongo, this rarely becomes consolidated along ethnic lines. Cleavages between big traders and clients, settled residents and newcomers, landlords and tenants cross-cut ethnic lines and lead to both competition and alliances within trading sectors. These cleavages reflect an emerging class structure within the zongo (and within the Islamized sectors of Ghanaian society generally) which is in some ways parallel to the class structure of Ghanaian society, as a whole, even though the cultural expressions of class differences within the zongo are quite different from those within the Westernized sector (Sanjek 1976). The sorts of resources available within the zongo are not identical to those available throughout Ghanaian society, as a whole; nevertheless, there is a division within the zongo between those who control capital (trade and housing), those in skilled and semi-skilled occupations and artisans, and the unskilled laborers.[2] As I will show below, people sometimes attempt to equate these cleavages with ethnic differences. The status evaluations of ethnic categories are not completely independent of class considerations, but the relationship between class and ethnicity within the zongo is by no means such that ethnic groups can be defined simply as classes, or even as economic interest groups in a more limited sense.

Despite the difficulty of explaining ethnicity within the zongo in terms of economic cleavages, there is one important way in which the attribution of ethnicity does coincide with the definition of an economic group. The overriding dichotomy between northerners and southerners, in the distribution of types of salaried occupations and in their differential control over resources, implies that the northern stranger community, as a whole, constitutes an economic sector, with the leaders of the zongo acting as brokers between the sectors. This regional dichotomy is a factor contributing to the emergence of zongo identity, and perhaps also to the minimization of ethnic cleavages within the zongo. Asante and other southerners monopolize professional and white-collar jobs, and indeed hold all jobs requiring knowledge of English, other than the few still held by Europeans, Asians, or Lebanese. Northerners monopolize many areas of trade and predominate in service and unskilled occupations. In the areas of trade where competition between northerners and Asante occurs, this is inevitably phrased in ethnic or nationalist terms. One obvious example of this is the long-standing dispute between Gao men and Asante women over the yam trade; another was the NLC government's economic policy of 1969 requiring the expulsion of all unregistered aliens and the Ghanaianization of small businesses.

Within the zongo, then, it is impossible to explain the persistence of ethnic identities based on provenance as primarily a manifestation of economic interests. There are no really successful ethnic monopolies in trade or in occupations. Where there are partial monopolies, they are mainly in imports and are due to geographic contingencies, and traditional craft specializations. For example, Malians monopolize the trade in a particular type of dried fish from Mopti, Yorubas import cloth from specific towns, and Tuaregs import camel-hair blankets from Mali. In the trade of more generally available and more widely distributed products – and these constitute, by far, the most significant items – no ethnic group has ever been able to establish a total monopoly. This is true, not only of Kumasi, but of most of the zongos in Ghana. Moreover, no group in Kumasi has ever been successful in establishing total control over any sector of the wage economy.

Politics and change

There are a number of reasons why economic competition has not been consolidated along ethnic lines in the zongo. The heterogeneity of the trading community and the diversity in the sources and destinations of long-distance trade are two important factors which have worked against the congruence of ethnic and economic cleavages. This does not mean that ethnicity is never used as an expressive idiom to describe economic competition within the zongo; it simply means that ethnicity has not been the basis of successful economic strategies. The kola trade, for example, is sometimes spoken of as Hausa-dominated, but everyone in Kumasi zongo knows that there are, and have been since the nineteenth century, many major kola dealers who were not Hausa. The same is true of the cattle trade. Outsiders tend to think of cattle traders as Hausa, but, as Hill points out (1970a: 113ff.), most of the major dealers today are not Hausa and do not claim to be Hausa. Ethnicity may sometimes help in establishing networks, but the successful traders do not limit themselves to these opportunities. They utilize ethnicity when this makes economic sense, but they are not limited by it. In Kumasi the heterogeneity of the market, as well as that of the trading community, means that ethnicity can even be a liability. The successful traders emphasize, above all, their commitment to Islam and their identity as men of wealth and wisdom.

Political integration in Kumasi zongo does not imply the absence of politically articulated ethnic communities, but it does express the status and vulnerability of all northern immigrants as strangers and of some as aliens. Although the distinction between citizens and aliens cross-cuts the zongo community, the overriding importance of the north/south dichotomy in some respects minimizes the significance of Ghanaian citizenship for northerners. That is, northern Ghanaians, like aliens, are strangers in the local context. Like aliens, they related to the local political authorities through leaders who are clients of patrons who claim formal political power in the traditional Asante administration and in various levels of the national government. The common status of all the immigrants, as strangers, has facilitated the integration of the zongo into a political community, even though it is segmented by national citizenship and by ethnic cleavages which are autonomous in terms of internal governance.

The political unity of the zongo is symbolically expressed in the office of Sarkin Zongo. The Sarkin Zongo coordinates the political segments of the zongo and represents the zongo polity, as a whole, to outsiders. The incumbent of the office of Sarkin Zongo also governs one segment of the zongo community, in his capacity as Hausa headman. But the strangers understand that these are two clearly separate roles. Unlike the headman, the Sarkin Zongo does not exercise political authority within any stranger community. In the two periods when conflict erupted over the office of Sarkin Zongo, the government had unwittingly extended the authority of the Hausa headman over other communities. The symbolic significance of the office of Sarkin Zongo derives from the fact that he is, in a sense, "above" ethnicity. While this limits his political authority, it enables him to function effectively as a representative of the entire stranger community and as a mediator between ethnic communities.

268

Ethnicity, cultural integration, social stratification

In the domestic, economic, and political fields, as just discussed, ethnicity is minimized as a result of daily interaction. This interaction is itself an inevitable result of certain demographic, structural, and historical facts. The heterogeneity and size of the zongo community, Asante attitudes towards strangers, the British treatment of the zongo community, contemporary citizenship laws, and the nature of long-distance trade in Ghana are among the factors which have necessitated and encouraged interaction and interdependence among northerners. It is in the area of religion, however, that ethnic integration finds its ideological support. While Islam itself is the basis of a new ethnic identity, it has an explicit integrative ideology which tolerates lower levels of cultural diversity and accepts the principle of ethnic categorization. In admitting the principle of unilineal descent, the ideology of Islam accepts ascription into ethnic communities. And, in the notions of *ijma'* (consensus) and *'urf* (custom),[3] Islam tolerates the retention of cultural differences, so long as these are not incompatible with Islamic law.

Identity as a Muslim can either be ascribed at birth or be achieved through conversion. Because Islam is an expansionist and proselytizing religion, conversion is made relatively easy and entails, minimally, as defined in Kumasi, acquiring a Muslim name, making the five daily prayers and the Friday *salla* – the communal prayer – observing certain dietary prohibitions, following certain life-crisis rituals, and observing the main Muslim holidays, including fasting at Ramadan and performing sacrifices at *'id al-kabir* and *'id al-fitr*.[4]

Islamization inevitably leads to cultural integration, even though Islam tolerates, in theory, a certain degree of cultural variation. Islam prescribes and proscribes rules which pertain to almost every aspect of human behavior. These rules constitute part of a set of values which are expressed as behavioral guides, sanctions, and goals. Many of the goals are very explicit and include such things as high levels of Islamic education, including knowledge of Arabic and Islamic texts, performance of the *'hajj*, and the giving of alms. Since all of these can be attained through individual effort, Islam encourages the development of rankings based upon achievement, rather than ascription.

Cultural integration alone, however, does not imply the emergence of a new ethnic identity. In this case there are other factors which allow us to conceptualize Islamization in this way. The ideology of kinship, intrinsic to ethnicity, is metaphorically incorporated into the religious ideology of Islam, despite the fact that Islam also recognizes the validity of ascribed ethnicity through the notion of descent. The notion of descent, and the particularistic ethnic categorization this entails, is not seen by the strangers as conflicting with the Islamic notion of brotherhood, which is more a statement of behavioral and moral obligations than a notion of biological kinship. Nor is the idea of distinctive provenance, also characteristic of ethnicity, seen as conflicting with the idea of the "homeland," as expressed in Islamic religious ideology. Mecca is such a homeland, at least, metaphorically. Through the tracing of *silsilla*, or genealogies of instruction, individuals are linked in pseudofilial relationships to the great founders and teachers in Mecca and elsewhere throughout the Islamic world.

269

Politics and change

Despite the ideological acceptance of ethnic categorization within the Islamic community, the evaluation of prestige according to achieved, rather than ascribed, attributes conflicts in some rather complicated ways with the significance placed upon ethnic identities based on descent. By establishing a prestige scale against which individual accomplishments may be evaluated, Islam creates the basis for an elite whose membership is recruited independently of their ascribed ethnic statuses. This accounts for the political significance of Islamic leaders and Islamic associations in Kumasi. As chapters 8 and 10 have described, these leaders and associations often end up in competition with others whose support is based primarily or solely on ethnicity.

Ethnicity nevertheless persists as a basis for social organization, because, for one thing, being ascriptive, it leads to the formation of communities and support groups with which people may identify, regardless of their individual interests, accomplishments, or even economic status. Insofar as ethnic groups become organized politically and compete for prestige and status in the zongo, they promise benefits to all their members, regardless of these people's individual achievements. However, because they exist within the context of an Islamized cultural community, ethnic associations and their leaders tend to be ranked, particularly by 'yan k'asa, according to the system of Islamic values, which emphasizes behavioral accomplishments and ignores ethnic categorization. This, then, undermines the strength of the ethnic communities and accounts for the dilemma of those leaders who alternate between cultivating ethnic or nonethnic bases of support.

The processes of cultural and social integration which take place within the zongo community must be examined from two points of view. On the one hand, the migrants' loss of traditional cultural values is compensated for by their assimilation into a developing Islamic community with its own value system and its own culture. On the other hand, integration into this community implies increasing alienation and isolation from both local Asante and national Ghanaian culture and society. Not only do the strangers remain culturally isolated from the local indigenous community – in this case, that of the Asante – but their value system also insures that they do not assimilate Western skills and values. Whether this is seen as a response to their exclusion as strangers, or as a cause of their isolation, the fact remains that Islamization and Hausaization are liabilities, rather than assets, when it comes to participation in Ghanaian politics. While education is unquestionably valued in the zongo, since it is in Arabic rather than English, it confers no advantage in any context except that of the zongo and the West African Islamic trading community. Since zongos extend throughout West Africa, incorporation into the zongo community and assimilation of zongo culture do confer benefits for participants in long-distance trading networks. Nevertheless, these Islamic communities still must accommodate to the local and national power structures in which they exist. The values they encourage do not facilitate participation in this power structure or insure the protection which is essential for their continued existence.

The manifestations of ethnicity which have been described in this book can be seen, in part, as a response to, and an expression of, this vulnerability. Ethnicity implies both inclusion and exclusion and, at every level where it occurs, it expresses structural cleavages within the society of which ethnic groups form a part. Ethnicity functions as a positive source of identification, in one respect, but in other respects it is also a defensive strategy. This is so for ethnic groups with power, which attempt to maintain this by limiting membership, as well as for those lacking power. Throughout this book I have examined the emergence of ethnic identities on a number of levels. All of them must be seen as responses to exclusion, to specific government policies which have reinforced ethnic cleavages – in both the colonial and postcolonial periods – and also as positive bases of communal identity.

In Ghana the dichotomy between citizens and aliens is increasingly important and accounts for the emergence of groups based on national identity, such as the UVU and the Nigerian, Togolese, and Dahomeyan associations. Since 1957, the year of Ghana's independence, the possibility of deportation has made immigrants, including *'yan k'asa*, much more aware of national identity than they might have been, had total political incorporation been possible. The national associations which immigrants have formed offer protection by giving them rights to citizenship outside Ghana. Within the context of the Ghanaian state, regional identities become relevant, as they are the basis on which claims may be made on national resources. During periods when political parties have been active in Ghana, regional cleavages have been expressed through party formations. In the context of Ghanaian politics the zongo has, of course, identified itself with the north; nevertheless, within the zongo this identification has, at times, been cross-cut by the cleavages between citizens and aliens and between various ethnic categories. On the local level, the dichotomy between strangers and hosts is phrased in ethnic terms: in Kumasi this accounts for the emergence of zongo identity, just discussed, in structural opposition to Asante identity. Within the zongo, ethnic identities based on provenance persist, despite cultural assimilation, for a variety of reasons which have been considered throughout this book, including, of course, the colonial policy of encouraging ethnicity by supporting the offices of the zongo headmen. The reasons for the persistence of ethnicity are not identical for first- and second-generation immigrants, just as they are not identical for the leaders and the followers of political associations based upon ethnicity; for each, ethnicity and ethnic associations fulfill different functions. For both, however, ethnicity persists, so long as it links individuals into wider communities which are able to offer many forms of social and political (protective or assertive) support.

Ethnicity and stratification

While the dichotomies between alien and citizen, northerner and southerner, stranger and host, Muslim and Christian, Western and Islamic are not, in fact, congruent, they and other binary oppositions[5] are often equated in the paradigmatic models of social structure which people use to conceptualize their society. As Smith (1959b: 250) points out, simplification (or abbreviation) is characteristic of all models of social structure which are ideologically, although not necessarily

271

analytically, useful. Occasionally, the lack of congruence between these dichotomies becomes evident and is the basis of the expression of ambivalence. For
example, southern Ghanaians often think of northerners as poor and uneducated
and think of the zongo as a slum. The wealthy northern trader who owns scores
of houses then appears anomalous. He becomes either the object of a joke, which
expresses this structural ambivalence, and the exception to a "rule," or he is seen
as a threat necessitating xenophobic retaliation. All of these responses enable
people to maintain a working model of their society which expresses observed or
idealized differential access to political and economic resources through the idiom
of ethnicity.

Schematic models of systems of social status occur at all levels of societal integration – wherever it is necessary for people to explain to themselves the relationships between various segments of their society. In the rest of this section I discuss
the way in which these models relate ethnicity and stratification in two contexts:
in Voltaic Mossi society and in Kumasi zongo. The model of stratification which
is most frequently used by observers and actors to describe Mossi society in Upper
Volta has been discussed at some length in chapter 2. In both Mossi and Hausa
society the traditional political structure was based upon an ideology which stated
the relationship between rulers and ruled in ethnic terms. The use of a rule of
descent to ascribe, unambiguously, membership in a ruling elite (which is at the
same time an ethnic category) limits eligibility to political power. Insofar as the
"premise of inequality" (Maquet 1961) is accepted, this model of ethnic stratification will be acknowledged by most members of the society. However, when the
distribution of power or the relationship between ethnicity and role allocation is
questioned, divergent models will be held by different groups or individuals. This
has been well described by d'Hertefelt (1964) for Ruanda and was suggested above
in chapter 2, where Yarse and commoner myths about the Mossi state have been
summarized. In the case of Ruanda, the development of competing models was due
to a number of drastic social and political changes which threatened to reverse the
actual roles of members of different ethnic categories. In Voltaic Mossi society, the
existence of several different models may be explained by the fact that the economic and political structure does not, in fact, stratify the society as clearly as
models of ethnic stratification suggest.

In Kumasi zongo, as in Mossi society, or in Hausaland, people employ schematic
models based upon the stratification of ethnic categories to describe the structure
of their society. However, due to the cultural complexity of the zongo, and to its
brief but complex history, there are many different models, some of which clearly
contradict others. One can describe the multiplicity of ideological, or emic, models
and attempt to analyze the relationships between them, even though one cannot
accept any single model as descriptive of the social structure of the zongo. There
are a number of reasons, which will be elaborated below, for this lack of consensus
in Kumasi. First, although immigrants in the zongo are becoming integrated into a
single cultural system, this process has not been completed. First-generation
immigrants of different ethnic categories still have different value orientations and

272

still conceptualize the status system in terms of these value systems. The second reason for competing models has to do with the distinction made earlier between status and prestige. While statuses based on ethnicity are ascribed, assimilation into the zongo implies the acceptance of values which acknowledge the importance of achievement. When the qualities that confer prestige are not congruent with the ascriptive statuses of ethnicity, a model of stratification based solely upon ethnicity is likely to be questioned. Third, when a single ethnic group does not dominate politically or economically, a model of ethnic stratification based upon a static hierarchy will be unacceptable to many members of the society.

First-generation immigrants from different cultural groups obviously bring many attitudes about ethnicity and about various cultures with them. They do not all evaluate the relative ranking of different ethnic categories in the same way. An ethnocentric evaluation of differing cultural traditions leads to the ranking of groups according to their similarity or difference from one another (Levine and Campbell 1972). Many first-generation Mossi, for example, refuse to compare themselves to the Hausa, saying, "They are far from us." Groups with similar cultural and linguistic traditions are, however, "just like us" or "under us" – referring to their supposed political subordination to the Mossi state. To many Mossi immigrants, and particularly those who accept the traditional Nakomce model of Mossi society, the most important basis of ranking has to do with the nature of political systems. People from societies with chiefs are felt to be superior to those without chiefs. Thus, the Mamprusi and Dagomba rank higher, to these Mossi, than the Frafra or the Kusasi, while the Busansi, having accepted Mossi political hegemony in Upper Volta, are ranked higher than the latter two groups. Nevertheless, in cultural terms, all of these groups are thought of as "one" vis-à-vis culturally more distant groups. However, ideological consensus is lacking, even within the Mossi group; the Yarse, for example, are generally more sympathetic in their view of the Hausa and other strongly Islamized groups than are the Nakomce.

These evaluations have little to do with the distribution of economic or political power in Kumasi, as they are based upon models which are antecedent to the experience of migration. Many first-generation immigrants refuse to acknowledge that there is, in fact, a single-status hierarchy, based upon ethnicity, operative in Kumasi zongo. They insist upon the political autonomy and status equality of all immigrant groups. This is so, even though they sometimes use the valuations mentioned above in their everyday lives – for example, in making choices about marriage partners. Their refusal to acknowledge that ranking based on ethnicity occurs in Kumasi has to do with their resistance to accepting what I have referred to as zongo values and with their ambivalence about the Hausa, the group most closely identified with these values. They also recognize that the acceptance of a notion of ethnic stratification based on zongo values, in which Islam, wealth, and length of residence in Ghana are primary criteria of rank, places them at a lower status level than does an evaluation based upon their traditional value system.

Groups with very few second-generation immigrants or very few Muslims, such as the Frafra or the Dagati, accept their identification as northerners but are also reluctant to accept the notion of a single hierarchy within the stranger community. These groups have maintained their cultural individuality to a greater extent than have the more settled and more Islamized groups. They are thus less concerned than are the latter with asserting their rank, as members of ethnic categories, in a hierarchy which they do not acknowledge in the first place.

While it is possible to speak of "Mossi values," "Hausa values," or "Dagomba values" among first-generation immigrants, and therefore to note a lack of consensus about the stratification of ethnic categories, different questions arise when the values of second-generation immigrants are considered. These, as I have said above, are based upon achieved criteria, including Islamic orthodoxy and education, wealth, and length of residence or generation of birth in Kumasi. There are other behavioral attributes which also confer prestige, such as generosity, community service, polygamy, performing the *'hajj*, wearing fine clothing, and leadership ability. If the change in value orientation simply meant the disappearance of ascriptive ethnic statuses and the substitution of standards of evaluation based on achievement (as defined in terms of the goals specified above), this would be analytically simple. But the evaluation of status in ethnic terms does not simply disappear. It does, however, relate to the prestige rankings based on achievement in quite complex ways.

The emergent zongo identity which has been described above is not without an ethnic component – what has been referred to as Hausaization up to this point. The notion of Hausaization is a generalization based, in part, upon linguistic patterns but also reflecting Hausa cultural hegemony. In the area of the Hausa diaspora, the Hausa have attained prestige through their economic, religious, and political accomplishments. Although members of other groups have also acquired wealth and education and become important religious, economic, and political leaders, the Hausa were more numerous and more conspicuous in the early days of the settlement of Kumasi and other zongos. The long association of the Hausa with Islam and with long-distance trade gave them a kind of "traditional" authority in stranger communities throughout the diaspora. In Kumasi, in the early part of the century, people who identified themselves as Hausa provided many of the educated Muslims and *masugida*, for they were among the first permanent settlers in the town. In analyzing prestige and status in Kumasi, one can establish a hypothetical historical sequence to describe the way in which the Hausa have become a reference group: as the zongo grew and the numbers of non-Hausa increased, the prestige attained by early Hausa settlers became translated into an evaluation of the status of being Hausa. What began as an evaluation of achievement then came to be seen as an aspect of ascribed status. It then becomes possible for the observer to refer to the Hausa as a reference group. One can, in a sense, speak of the operation of a feed-in mechanism from the evaluation of prestige to the creation of the ethnic status system.

Since the high evaluation of the Hausa is associated with qualities which are individually attainable, non-Hausa can always hope to attain prestige by their achievements in these areas. People may quite consciously feel that they are assimilating Hausa culture, yet they can recognize that they are unable to assume membership in the Hausa ethnic category. Confronting this situation, some may attempt to reject the idea that it is ethnic identity which confers high status in the first place. That is, they may reject the idea of a status hierarchy based on ethnicity which establishes the hegemony of the Hausa and, appealing to Muslim ideology, they may emphasize the irrelevance of ethnicity. In other words, they implicitly attempt to demonstrate that there is no difference between the prestige which one can attain through one's achievements and the status based on ethnicity which is ascribed at birth. A status system which ranks groups according to the ascriptive criterion of ethnicity is therefore unstable and unlikely to gain universal acceptance when it develops from an evaluation of the accomplishments of individuals.

Among the Mossi, when an individual becomes an *al-hajj*, attains great wealth, or has many Hausa associates and friends, he may face the charge that he is attempting to "become Hausa." Mossi first-generation immigrants commonly say this of *'yan k'asa* and others whom they regard as traitors to ethnic-group solidarity. When faced with this charge, the *'yan k'asa* may proclaim the irrelevance of ethnicity in the name of Islam or they may attempt to assume leadership positions within their own ethnic community by claiming that they are trying to raise the status of this community, as a whole, within the zongo. This was the dilemma of Rahman when, having lost the Mossi headmanship, he alternated between expressing a negative attitude towards identification with the Mossi community and attempting to create an Islamic ethnic association which would advance the position of the Mossi in the zongo.

A single model of ethnic stratification will also not be accepted if the political or economic system allows universal competition for prestige, status, or power to take place.[6] This is most likely to be the case when the criteria conferring ascribed status and the criteria for the allocation of prestige are different. In virtually all of the states of the Western Sudan in which a ruling ethnic group was recognized and accorded political power, the system of stratification was established by the monopolization of military resources; in the Hausa, Mossi, Mamprusi, Gonja, Dagomba, and Asante states the rulers were able to establish their hegemony by controlling either the passage of armaments or the ownership of horses which were used for cavalry. In Kumasi zongo nothing comparable has occurred. If the Hausa in Kumasi had been able to maintain total monoplies of trade, of housing, of political office, or even of Islamic knowledge and literacy, they might have been able to monopolize political power to a far greater extent than, in fact, they ever did. As events have shown, no single group in the zongo has been able to maintain sufficient control over economic, religious, or political resources to be able to assert its political authority for very long. Political authority has constantly been contested and divided among various ethnic communities. This was demonstrated by the discussion of the two historic periods when first the colonial, and then the Nkrumah, government unsuccessfully institutionalized an ethnically based political hierarchy by giving the Hausa authority sanctioned by force. Governmental policy failed, because leaders in other ethnic groups were able to mobilize support by emphasizing the political autonomy and disparate interests of different ethnic communities.

The lack of consensus about the system of ethnic stratification in Kumasi zongo, and the discrepancies between achieved and ascribed evaluations of status, lead to the rejection of an institutionalized hierarchy based solely on ethnicity. Such a hierarchy not only makes individual or group mobility impossible, but it also negates the Islamic values which emphasize the possibility of achieving prestige in an open system. In social and political terms, institutionalization of the principle of ethnic stratification means that the leaders of one ethnic group are given authority and power over others. Whenever this has occurred the component groups in the zongo have attempted to restore a political system based upon the premise of ethnic equality – a premise which permits open competition among individuals and groups for prestige and status. A major reason for the rejection of Hausa political hegemony is that it prevents the establishment of direct relationships of patronage between leaders of each stranger group and authorities outside the zongo. The attempt to impose such hegemony, rather than purely internal tension, has led to interethnic conflict in the zongo. It is significant that during the periods when there was no Sarkin Zongo there was practically no politically organized interethnic factionalism. Then, no principle of ethnic stratification was embodied in the political structure, and each group was able to build up direct lines of communication with government officials. When the political system within the zongo embodied the premise of the political equality of all stranger groups, internal changes in the status system could occur, and non-Hausa felt that they could make meaningful attempts to raise their position, both within the zongo and vis-à-vis the larger society.

This raises one final question. In looking at ethnicity in terms of levels, or contexts, we are in one sense ignoring the most important question of all. This concerns the relationship between these contexts and the effects which action taken in one context has for participation in others. While ethnicity may be functional on one level of sociopolitical integration, it may be quite dysfunctional on another. Thus, within the zongo, Mossi identity and ethnicity clearly provide many kinds of support for migrants, particularly those born in Upper Volta. In a limited way, it also sometimes provides a strategy for mobility within the sociopolitical context of the zongo; however, it is also a response to the impossibility of becoming socially incorporated into the culturally dominant Hausa community. The Mossi concern with their relative status within the zongo encourages them to ignore those strategies for mobility that ultimately might work in the larger society of Kumasi and Ghana. In their concern with the values of Islamic culture, few have developed those skills which enable them to compete, or even to protect themselves, in the larger political context of which the zongo is a part. The assimilation of zongo culture and the incorporation of migrants into the zongo enable migrants to participate in a religious, social, economic, and cultural community which transcends political and territorial boundaries. At the same time it intensifies the dichotomy between strangers and hosts, and between aliens and citizens, and it does little to lessen the vulnerability of those who remain strangers and aliens. One could, of course, argue that the basis of this adaptation is, in the first place, an emphasis on origins and ethnicity that pervades Ghanaian and African society. This, however, is a spurious argument, in that definitions of origins and ethnic identities change all the time. Exclusion is not based simply on some primordial identity known as ethnicity, but on the ability of one group to control the changing definitions of boundaries, the criteria of inclusion, in such a way as to limit access to power and resources. The immigrants in Kumasi zongo belong to a community which, in social and cultural terms, transcends ethnic, local, and national boundaries. From the political point of view, however, this cannot but be problematic, for the breakdown of territoriality and nationalism are, as yet, barely envisioned forms of world order.

Notes

1. Introduction: conceptual approaches to the study of ethnicity

1 See Paden (1970) for a discussion of the concept of integration. There are three aspects of integration, all relevant to the processes taking place in Kumasi: interaction flow, functional interdependence, and value congruence.

2 Before this there had been, of course, several important discussions of ethnicity in monographs on complex traditional societies, such as Maquet's study of Ruanda (1961), Nadel's work on Nupe (1942, 1947), J. R. Goody's study of the LoWilli (1956), Southall's study of Alur (n.d.), and to some extent Fortes's work on the Tallensi, when he discusses the relationship between Namoos and Talis (1945; 1949). However, see Smith (1969: 105) and Cohen and Middleton (1970: introduction) for a discussion of why relatively little attention was given to this issue in the preindependence period.

3 Cohen (1974: xxiii) has written that the study of ethnicity will "usher social anthropology into the systematic study of the complexity of contemporary industrial society." This, I feel, greatly minimizes the importance of ethnicity in the past and merely reflects the myopia of our discipline, not the nature of ethnicity.

4 A complete bibliography of studies of urbanization which included references to ethnicity would be lengthy indeed and beyond the scope of this introduction. However, besides the above, a number of important works on urbanization published before 1969 may be noted, including: Balandier's 1955 study of Brazzaville, Southall and Gutkind's study of Kampala (1957), and Dubb and Mayer (1962) on the multi-tribal society.

5 Other noteworthy works on urbanization in West Africa, with reference to ethnicity and published before 1969, include Miner's study of Timbuctoo (1965), his edited volume on urbanization (1967), Plotkinov's study of Jos (1967), Fraenkel's of Monrovia (1964), Hilda Kuper's volume on urbanization and migration (1965), and papers specifically on ethnicity by Wallerstein (1960) and Mercier (1965). Davison's 1954 study of migration to Ghana contributed much of the data for Rouch's 1956 publication.

6 Also in that year, a number of urban studies with some discussion of ethnicity appeared, including Pons on Stanleyville, Parkin on Kampala, Meillassoux on Bamako. In 1970 the trend continued with La Fontaine's book on Leopoldville.

7 See Lloyd, Mabogunje, and Awe, *The City of Ibadan*, and Acquah, *Accra Survey*.

8 I use the concept of field as Barnes (1954) defines it.

278

9 This is so, only because social scientists often, for heuristic purposes, construct models of these units which assume a certain degree of boundedness.

10 As Cohen notes (1974: xv), "Ethnicity is a variable. In any socio-cultural milieu this variable is interdependent with many other variables." In Ibadan, Cohen found that economic behavior could not be explained without taking into account the ethnic variable. In Kumasi, where the demographic and economic situation is somewhat different, ethnicity is more important in other areas of behavior.

11 Nevertheless, these distinctions still remain in the two examples cited here: Jews are subdivided according to country of provenance (reckoned from the last major migration), whereas southern Blacks in northern cities are subdivided according to their home states.

12 See Schildkrout 1974a for a case study illustrating the significance of these crosscutting cleavages, and Schildkrout, forthcoming, for a discussion of regional identity.

13 See Paden 1970 for an excellent description and analysis of a similar situation in Kano.

14 Thus fraternities, age groups, the boy scouts, secret societies, and the like are not ethnic communities. Their primary means of recruitment is not ascription at birth. A notion of common provenance and its corollary, the notion of a common cultural heritage – retained or lost – are also lacking.

2. The Mossi: ethnicity in Voltaic society

1 The "ethnographic present" is used here, and "Mossi society" refers obviously to a hypothetical model of traditional society. See also Schildkrout and Finnegan (unpublished ms.).

2 The attributions of different ethnic identities to the main actors in the myth are evident in a comparison of the versions presented in Cardinall (1920: 5); Delafosse (1912: iii, 307); Illiasu (1971); Marc (1909: 130); Ruelle (1904), quoted in Tauxier (1924: 9); Withers-Gill (1924a). See also Schildkrout (1969).

3 See Capron and Kohler (1975, 1976) for an important discussion of the significance of the control over women as the key to the Mossi political system.

4 The daughters of these wives, and sometimes the women themselves, were re-distributed by the chiefs, to lesser chiefs, and sometimes to non-officeholders.

3. Migration and settlement of Mossi in Ghana

1 Slavery could also be considered labor migration but was neither short-term nor seasonal. Since slaves were absorbed into the local economy and society, this ended up being more like permanent, though involuntary, emigration. Amin (1974: 66) makes the distinction between migration of labor and migrations of people.

2 This is absurd. Berg himself notes many heavy tasks that men must perform annually (p. 169). Other studies of the rural economy of Upper Volta also indicate that the labor input of men is far from negligible (Hammond 1966; Kohler 1968). See also Capron and Kohler (1975, 1976) for a discussion of the relationship between limited access to women and migration.

3 Kohler 1968 and the series, *Atlas des Structures Agraires au Sud du Sahara*, ORSTOM, Paris.

4 Throughout, we have used the 1960 census of Ghana, since the 1970 census does not enumerate ethnic identity. Moreover, the 1970 census was conducted immediately after the alien expulsion order, rendering the results questionable.

5 The foreign-origin population was defined as follows, according to the concept of country of origin: "The country of birth of father/mother and of grandfather/grandmother of respondent depending on whether one or both parents were born in Ghana and on whether a matrilineal or patrilineal approach is adopted in determining tribal allegiance" (*1960 Ghana Census, Special Report E: XXV*).

6 This observation is supported in the discussion of Meillassoux (1969: 64).

7 Morris to Secretary of State, 21 December 1900, ADM 56/1/2. Unless otherwise specified, all ADM references are found in the National Archives of Ghana (NAG), Accra.

8 In the Obuasi mine, for example, there were 375 Mossi employed in 1965, 400 in 1966, and 576 in 1967. The increase was due to the reopening of the border in 1966. Approximately 80 percent were underground workers, and 70 percent had been employed at the mine for five years or more. (Communication from personnel officer, Ashanti Goldfields Corporation, 1967.)

9 *Tariqa* are Sufi brotherhoods, the most important of which, in West Africa, are the Tijaniyya and the Qadiriyya (Paden 1973; Abun-Nasr 1965).

10 Tauxier (1912: 445) describes a similar persistence of "pagan" traits among the Yarse in Upper Volta: "Despite their Mohammadanism, the Yarse have not yet adopted the practice of using cemeteries. They continue to bury their dead in the pagan manner by enterring the chief of the *soukala* [compound] in front of the door of the *soukala* and enterring people, including small children, in the maize fields around it."

4. The growth of the zongo community in Kumasi

1 The anachronistic usage *Ghanaian* is used here for simplicity. Unless otherwise stated, *northerner* refers in subsequent passages to northern Ghanaians and foreign immigrants who were regarded as strangers in Kumasi and who became part of the zongo community.

2 With a capital *z*, Zongo refers to a specific geographical neighborhood; with a lower case *z*, zongo refers to the stranger community which inhabits a neighborhood named Zongo, as well as other neighborhoods.

3 After completing this manuscript I had the opportunity to consult Wilks 1975. This work contains a more detailed discussion of the relations between Asante and the north than the references cited here. In another paper (Schildkrout forthcoming) I have drawn upon this book more fully than I was able to here.

4 Kumasi was rebuilt after the fire of 1874, but succession disputes over the Asantehene's stool between 1883 and 1888 delayed reconstruction. It is likely that some Hausa traders came to Kumasi just after 1874, but no documentary evidence of this has been found. See Wilks, 1971.

5 Europeans paid twenty-four pounds per annum for 16,000 sq. ft.; "alien natives" paid four pounds for plots of 5,626 sq. ft.; reservists of the regiment paid one pound for the same plots. Asantes paid two pounds for 2,500 sq. ft. Asante chiefs were charged only nominal rentals. (Annual Report, 1906–7.)

6 In 1943 the Board became the Town Council.

7 A Kumasi native was defined as "a native of Ashanti who by native customary law owes allegiance to the Asantehene either directly or through the chief of one of the Kumasi clans and includes a Head Chief of a Division of Ashanti, but does not include any person serving or owing allegiance to such Head Chief." Kumasi Land Ordinance, 1943.

8 Lovejoy (1973: 634), in discussing the Hausa diaspora, makes the point that,

"In the Hausa case, moreover, ethnicity is a concept which clouds historical analysis. The nineteenth-century Hausa diaspora in the Volta basin, for example, included people who traced their origins to Nupe, Bornu, and elsewhere in the Central Sudan but came to identify themselves as Hausa. 'Ethnicity' was not a static concept but an evolving relationship between immigrants who developed a 'diaspora culture,' as Cohen (1971) terms the process, which supported economic interests." See also Cohen 1969 and 1971.

9 In May 1930 the Acting Chief Commissioner commented on the meaning of the term *native* and referred to decisions taken in the Supreme Court of the Gold Coast. He wrote the Chief Commissioner: "The words 'a native community' are regarded as referring to an indigenous community only and not to every African community. Any question therefore as to whether a person is a 'Native' must be decided on a question of fact, that fact being the geographical situation of the native community of which the person is a member." ACCA to CCA, Kumasi, May 1930, File 12/60; NAG, Kumasi.

10 After the Asantehene's deportation in 1896 he returned as a private citizen, in 1924. In 1926 he was recognized as Kumasihene, or Chief of Kumasi, and in 1935 his successor was recognized as Asantehene.

11 This situation changed in the years following this study. By 1974 the headmen of the Mossi and Yoruba had died, and both were replaced by second-generation immigrants. Both, in fact, were sons of former Kumasi headmen. (See chapter 9 for more on the Mossi case.)

12 Cliterodectomy is still practiced in certain groups, including the Mossi, Busansi, Kotokoli, Mamprusi, and Fulani, but not in others. It is not integrated with Islamic ritual in any way and is done quietly and privately and without prayer, usually by a female practitioner, when the girls are about seven years old. It does not seem to affect interethnic marriage in any way, but if a man whose group performs it marries a woman whose group does not, his daughter will undergo the operation; if the situation is reversed, the daughter usually does not undergo the operation. This follows the straightforward "rule" that ethnic identity is transmitted patrilineally, but it is still interesting to speculate on why one particular ritual should remain so tribally specific. This may be because it is not practiced by the Hausa, but, more important, because it is not in any way integrated into the public, collective Islamic ritual system.

13 Formerly, marriages were frequently performed in the headman's house. One of the Hausa headmen, Malam Ali, was deposed in 1945, after being accused, among other things, of insisting that marriages be performed in his house. The case was taken to the Asantehene, but when it was shown that this was not required according to the Qur'an, Malam Ali lost the case.

14 The group, called Jemiatu Mu'allimini (Arabic, the council of teachers) consisted of eleven members: six Hausa, one Dagomba, one Mossi, one Wangara, one Yoruba, and one other whose ethnic identity I did not ascertain.

15 Similar processes, but with significant local variations, have occurred in many other zongos. For an account of Attebubu, as one example, see Arhin, 1971.

16 The number who do so varies in different groups; northern Ghanaians do this more frequently than do immigrants from further away. In other towns, however, with smaller zongos, a higher proportion of immigrant children go to school. This is true, for example, in Obuasi and in Bekwai.

17 The Ghanaian citizenship laws have changed several times since independence. However, during only one brief period, after the 1966 coup, did birth alone (under NLC decree 191) confer Ghanaian citizenship. This was repealed retroactively in 1969, so that all persons who had gained citizenship in this way lost

it. In order to claim citizenship by birth, a person must prove that one of his/her parents or grandparents was Ghanaian. A person born before 1957 is Ghanaian if one of his/her parents or grandparents was born in Ghana. Therefore, to claim citizenship an immigrant's family must have entered the Gold Coast *at least* two generations before independence, or must have intermarried with someone who was unquestionably indigenous. Under the terms of the constitution passed in 1969, a woman married to a Ghanaian is eligible for citizenship, but no person can become a naturalized citizen unless he/she can speak and understand a Ghanaian language.

5. Ethnicity and the domestic context

1 See Schildkrout 1975a for a general discussion of economic aspects of household ownership.
2 Two Ghanaian assistants helped with the survey, but I interviewed the owners of all houses in Zongo and Aboabo and half of those in YateYate and Mossi Zongo.
3 Before the age of about seven, most children do not differentiate individuals on the basis of ethnic identity and, until about twelve, they often will place people in the wrong categories.
4 See Trimingham (1959: 146ff.). In Kumasi the Muslim tax system has become a matter of voluntary donations. Wealthy and orthodox Muslims give, theoretically, sixpence on each Ghanaian pound of their income, one sheep for every forty they own, and one cow for every thirty. These donations (*zakat*) are distributed among important members of the community whose relationships the donors value for various reasons. There is no specific day for distributing *zakat*, and not every one does so, but such donations, along with the practice of giving daughters as *sadaka*, demonstrate a man's status and reinforce significant relationships between individuals, often across ethnic boundaries.
5 To the angels of the four cardinal points, perhaps. Trimingham (1959: 55) notes that "West-Sudan clergy address themselves to the angels of the four cardinal points in finding out lucky or unlucky times or days."
6 For more quantitative detail on this, see Schildkrout 1969.
7 In a survey of ninety market women, almost all stated that they intended to use the profit of their trade first of all to build a house for their children.
8 The figures are Zongo, 66 percent; Aboabo, 76 percent; YateYate, 71 percent; Mossi Zongo, 50 percent to 56 percent. The uncertainty in Mossi Zongo depends upon the interpretation of six uncertain cases.
9 By fostering, I mean the assumption of parental roles by persons other than a child's biological parents. In Kumasi this usually involved housing, feeding, clothing, and caring for a child, in exchange for the child's services. Biological parents delegate jural rights to foster parents but do not relinquish all their own rights (Schildkrout 1973).
10 A child is only truly adopted if he has attained *all* rights of natural children, including the right of inheritance. This rarely occurs unless an owner has no other heirs or, in a few rare cases, if the child is an orphan.
11 In Zongo Estate there is an average of 1.93 dependents per room head; 2.78 in Aboabo; 1.45 in YateYate; and 1.09 in Mossi Zongo.
12 One way to measure the heterogeneity of the Mossi-owned houses in the four neighborhoods is by comparing homogeneity indices as these are computed by census demographers (*1960 Census of Ghana, Report E:* xxxv). On the basis of such computations all neighborhoods are heterogeneous. According to this

test, a result of 1 indicates total homogeneity, while a result of 0 indicates that each individual belongs to a different group. Mossi Zongo again appears to be slightly more homogeneous than the other neighborhoods, with an index of .282, using the clustered categories and counting only adults (as in Table 21). YateYate appears to be the most heterogeneous on this basis, with an index of .220; Aboabo follows closely, with an index of .222; and Zongo Estate has an index of .257. In computing a heterogeneity index in this way the most heterogeneous areas are those in which the largest number of groups are represented by the smallest number of people.

6. Ethnicity and the idiom of kinship

1 This occurs among various Hausa groups, especially between the Beriberi and others. The Beriberi, who also joke with the Wangara and the Fulani, are described by some as the grandfathers of the other Hausa groups. There are many other partnerships: the Gonja joke with the Chokosi and the Dagomba, the Zabarama joke with the Grusi, the Yoruba joke with the Beriberi, and so on. Some of these, like the Mossi/Dagomba partnership, are symmetrical; others are not, and in these cases it is clear that one group has the right to demand money, insult, or trick members of the other group.
2 Trimingham (1959: 76ff.) describes more or less the same thing: "Peoples of Senegal, Guinée, and Sierra Leone cook and eat the dried head and feet of the ram slaughtered at the Tabaski feast (an animist survival – linking the new year to the old and drawing the blessing of the sacrifice into the new year?)."
3 Trimingham (1959: 77): "With the Islamic lustrations is associated a customary ceremony of purification by fire. Songhay, after ablutions, pass and repass over a small fire shouting *'yesi hirow'* ('The New Year has entered'). After the feast many (Hausa, Nupe, Mandinka, Dyula) have torchlight processions and contests between age-groups." Delobsom (1932: 206) says that the Mossi Muslims light torches and pour cold water on their bodies. See also Bravmann 1974 for a discussion of the Do masking tradition among Muslim Mande, also linked to this occasion. I have been told that, until the Nkrumah government prohibited this in the 1950's, masks – called Dodo – were also used in Kumasi, particularly among the Mande.
4 M. G. Smith (1955: 16) describes how in Hausa society occupational groups give money to each other on this occasion. In Hausa society joking friendships (*abokin wasa*) exist between different craft groups. See also, J. Greenberg 1947.
5 As Chapter 8 shows, the most important cleavages were not between ethnic communities, but within them. Factions within ethnic communities would act as units in joking with factions of other ethnic communities.
6 See J. R. Goody 1962, passim for a relevant discussion of funeral joking in northern Ghana.

7. Kinship and marriage in the second generation

1 See a discussion of a similar phenomenon in Kenya in Parkin 1973.
2 There are many different credit societies in Kumasi, called *esusu* or *adashe*. They vary from small groups whose members know each other personally to very large organizations with professional administrators.
3 This supports Goodenough's notion (1970: 399) that rights in kin should be seen as a type of property right.

4 That is, their mother's husband at the time of conception was Hausa. The last child was born shortly after the father died. The mother's second husband, a Mossi, succeeded to jural fatherhood, once he married the children's mother.

5 *Lahira*, in Hausa. Trimingham (1959: 60) says that the Hausa use this term for "the place of the departed spirits, for the future state in a general sense, and for the intermediate state before the Day of Judgement."

6 See Smith (1954: Chap. V) for a description of traditional Hausa marriage, to which this may be compared.

7 Some months before, some of the Mossi elders and the Imam had told the Mossi community to stop competitive giftgiving at marriages, since this "shamed" the poorer members of the community.

8 This is also typical of the rate for urban Muslim men in Ghana as a whole, which was 30.7 percent, according to the post enumeration survey of the 1960 Census (Vol. VI, Post Enumeration Survey, 1970, Accra). I am indebted to Roger Sanjek for pointing this out.

9 The other comparisons work out as follows: Zongo/YateYate: χ^2 = 2.2819, p < .20; Aboabo/YateYate: χ^2 = .0022, p < 1; Aboabo/Mossi Zongo: χ^2 = 2.1229, p < .30. A comparison of Zongo with the other neighborhoods, on the basis of the phi coefficient, does not reveal a very strong association between changing rates of out-marriage and the age of neighborhoods, although the comparison between Zongo and Mossi Zongo is the strongest. Zongo/Aboabo $\emptyset$ = .110; Zongo/YateYate $\emptyset$ = .101; Zongo/Mossi Zongo $\emptyset$ = .199.

10 Comparing first- and second-generation Mossi men's marriages to women from all other groups, the increase in marriages to Hausa women is significant at the level of p < .05 (χ^2 = 3.4960, df = 1).

11 Comparing the marriages of all Mossi men with all Mossi women, the difference in rates of out-marriage is significant (χ^2 = 50.21, p < .001).

12 The only exceptions are the Niger-Mali group and the Nupe, but the total sample is too small to be significant. The Niger-Mali group includes nine Songhai men, six of whom are married to Songhai women, one to a Dagomba, one to a Gourma, and one to a Gonja. There are only six Songhai women in the sample. Among the Nupe, also, there are more men married out: one to a Mossi, one to a Hausa, and one to a Yoruba. There is one Nupe couple. These do not appear in Table 30, since the numbers are so small.

8. The political history of the zongo community: 1900–1970

1 Unless otherwise specified, all subsequent NAG, Kumasi, references are to the file entitled, "Zongo Affairs" No. 12/60.

2 One of the most important cases the zongo tribunal dealt with was the deposition and banishment of the Yoruba headman. Appealing against the judgment of the zongo tribunal, the Yoruba headman appealed to the Kumasihene's tribunal. The government removed the case to the DC's court, where the sentence of the Sarkin Zongo was ratified. The charge against the headman was that he had refused to obey a lawful order of the Sarkin Zongo to appear before him.

3 The same charge was made in the 1950s, during the period of political party conflict. CPP supporters were accused by MAP Mossis of attempting to become Hausa when again a Hausa was appointed Sarkin Zongo.

4 The fee is not easy to discover, since informants accuse various headmen of offering exorbitant amounts and claim they do not know what the fixed fees are. However, the established minimal fee for greeting the Asantehene – in-

stallation fees of a sort – are about nine pounds for most headmen and double this for the Hausa headman. But these figures are certainly open to question.

5 Although there were 14,613 eligible voters, only 828 voted (ADM 51/5/6, NAG, Accra).

6 The Asantehene had four courts with different domains of jurisdiction. After 1938 he was able to appoint men of his choice to serve as magistrates on the courts for three-month periods.

7 In 1954 the Town Council became the Municipal Council, and in 1962 it became the City Council.

8 See Austin 1964, Fitch and Oppenheimer 1966, and Davidson 1973 for an overview of political change in Ghana between 1946 and 1960.

9 A detailed discussion of disputes which developed in the late 1960s between the different Islamic organizations can be found in Schildkrout 1974a. See also Price 1956.

9. The social organization of the Mossi community

1 In Upper Volta, this was true, except for deposition by death, in battle, or through suicide. According to Skinner (1964: 68), the latter occurred when the Ouidi Naba sent the Mogho Naba a poison arrow, with the message "die."

2 A high-ranking government official from Upper Volta, a Nakomce himself, said, in a moment of anger with the headman for what he regarded as the headman's lack of respect, "And he dares to call himself a feudal lord. In Upper Volta he would be nothing and here he is still nothing."

3 Testimony, dated 17 July 1965. "In the District Magistrate's Court, Kumasi: In the Matter of Section 23 of the Criminal Procedure Act 30/60. The State vs. (1) Issa Kokroko, (2) Tin Norga Moshie, (3) Alhaji Seidu Emman, (4) Wenaba Moshie, (5) Mumuni Moshie, (6) Daramani Moshie, (7) Issaka Moshie." At this time leaders of other West African states were fearful about coming to Ghana, and the government assured them that potentially harmful elements would be controlled. Hence, names were submitted by local leaders, including the CPP headmen, and these people were detained.

4 Magajia is traditionally a Hausa title referring to the head of the prostitutes and the adepts of the *bori* cult. Among the Mossi in Kumasi this connotation is absent.

5 Smith (1959b) discusses the differences in the status systems of men and women in Hausa society and also notes that the status of women is not derived from the political system.

6 These events occurred after I had finished active field work. They were described to me by a man, and I never attended the meetings. It is conceivable that the new group really did not resemble the men's organization as closely as this description made it appear.

10. Ethnicity, generational cleavages, and the political process

1 Despite Hamidu's tenure, the office was still known as "Adamu's chair" – probably because Hamidu had never held it in a period without dispute.

11. Conclusion: ethnicity, cultural integration, and social stratification

1 I am using *class* here to refer to differential control over and relationships to the means of production.

285

2 See Sanjek 1976 for an example of an analysis of female traders in Accra, using comparable categories.

3 Anderson (1970) states, with regard to *ijma*, that "the orthodox view is that this constitutes a valid source of law, for although an individual jurist may err in his deductions from the social texts (*nusus*), the community as a whole is infallible." With regard to *urf* (or *ada*) he notes (1970: 328) that "this is not a formal source of law under the *Sharia*, although in reality a great part of the latter is derived therefrom" (see also Levy 1965, chapter VI).

4 There is, of course, an extensive debate in the Islamic literature on the minimum requirements of being a Muslim, but these are the ones which are generally accepted in Kumasi as the definition of a "real" Muslim.

5 Others commonly expressed are educated/uneducated, civilized/uncivilized, clean/dirty, wealthy/poor, and so on (Schildkrout, forthcoming).

6 The corollary to this, of course, is that it will be quite stable when ethnicity coincides with class. One could well argue here that it is precisely the lack of congruence between ethnicity and class which inhibits consensus about the nature of ethnic stratification.

Bibliography

Abraham, R. C. 1962. *Dictionary of the Hausa Language*. London: University of London Press.
Abun-Nasr, J. M. 1965. *The Tijaniyya: A Sufi Order in the Modern World*. London: Oxford University Press.
Acquah, I. 1954. *Accra Survey*. London: University of London Press.
Adomako-Sarfoh, J. 1974. "The Effects of the Expulsion of Migrant Workers on Ghana's Economy, with Particular Reference to the Cocoa Industry." In *Modern Migrations in Western Africa*, ed. S. Amin, pp. 138–55. London: Oxford University Press.
Africa 1969/70. 1969. Rome: Jeune Afriques Editions.
Ahmad Baba al-Wa'iz 1965. *Kanz al-Mufid*. Trans. B. G. Martin. *Institute of African Studies Research Review* 2(1). University of Ghana, Legon.
Alexandre, G. 1953. *La Langue Moré*. 2 vols. Dakar: Institut Français d'Afrique Noire.
Ambassade de la Republique de Haute-Volta. Undated. "Apercu sur la Vie Sociale, Économique, et Politique; Professions et Activités Diverses de Ressortissants Voltaïques Résident au Ghana." Accra. Unpublished paper issued by The Embassy of the Republic of Upper Volta.
Amin, S., ed. 1974. *Modern Migrations in Western Africa*. London: Oxford University Press.
Anderson, J. N. D. 1970. *Islamic Law in Africa*. London: Frank Cass and Co., Ltd.
Arhin, K. 1971. "Atebubu Markets: ca. 1884–1930." In *The Development of Indigenous Trade and Markets in West Africa*, ed. C. Meillassoux, pp. 199–213. London: Oxford University Press.
Austin, D. 1964. *Politics in Ghana: 1946–1960*. London: Oxford University Press.
Bailey, F. G., ed. 1971. *Gifts and Poison: The Politics of Reputation*. New York: Schocken Books.
Balandier, G. 1955. *Sociologie des Brazzaville Noires*. Paris: Armand Colin.
Banton, M. P. 1956. "Adaptation and Integration in the Social System of Temne Immigrants in Freetown." *Africa* 26: 354–69.
    1957. *West African City*. London: Oxford University Press.
    1961. "The Restructuring of Social Relationship." In *Social Change in Modern Africa*, ed. A. Southall, pp. 113–26. London: Oxford University Press.
    1965. "Social Alignment and Identity in a West African City." In *Urbanization and Migration in West Africa*, ed. H. Kuper, pp. 131–48. Los Angeles: University of California Press.
Bargery, G. P. 1934. *A Hausa–English Dictionary and English–Hausa Vocabulary*. London: Oxford University Press.

Bibliography

Barkow, J. H. 1975. "Prestige and Culture: A Biosocial Interpretation." *Current Anthropology*. 16: 553–72.

Barnes, J. A. 1954. "Class and Committees in a Norwegian Island Parish." *Human Relations* 7: 39–59.

Barth, F. 1969. *Ethnic Groups and Boundaries*. London: Allen and Unwin.

Berg, Elliot J. 1965. "The Economics of the Migrant Labor System." In *Urbanization and Migration in West Africa*, ed. H. Kuper, 160–85. Los Angeles: University of California Press.

Bernus, S. 1969. *Particularismes ethniques en milieu urbain: L'example de Niamey*. Université de Paris, Memoires de l'Institut d'Ethnologie, I. Paris: Museé de l'Homme, Institut d'Ethnologie.

Binger, L. 1892. *Du Niger au Golfe de Guinée par le pays Kong et le Mossi, 1887–1889*. 2 vols. Paris: Hachette.

Bowdich, T. E. 1819. *Mission from Cape Coast Castle to Ashantee*. London: J. Murray.

　　1821a. *Essay on the Geography of Northwestern Africa*. Paris.

　　1821b. *An Essay on the Superstitions, Customs and Arts Common to the Ancient Egyptians, Abyssinians and Ashantees*. Paris: J. Smith.

Bravmann, R. A. 1974. *Islam and Tribal Art in West Africa*. Cambridge: Cambridge University Press.

Capron, J., and Kohler, J. M. 1975. *Migrations de Travail et Pratique Matrimoniale II. Exploitation de l'Enquête par Sondage*. Ouagadougou: C.V.R.S.

　　1976. "Pouvoir et pratique matrimoniale dans la société Mossi." Paper presented to the International Seminar on Family Research, Lomé, Togo.

Cardinall, A. W. 1920. *The Natives of the Northern Territories of the Gold Coast*. London: Routledge.

Cohen, A. 1969. *Custom and Politics in Urban Africa*. London: Routledge and Kegan Paul.

　　1971. "Cultural Strategies in the Organization of Trading Diasporas." In *The Development of Indigenous Trade and Markets in West Africa*, ed. C. Meillassoux, pp. 266–84. London: Oxford University Press.

　　1974. "Introduction." In *Urban Ethnicity*, ed. A. Cohen. Association of Social Anthropologists, Monograph No. 12. London: Tavistock.

Cohen, R., and J. Middleton, eds. 1970. *From Tribe to Nation in Africa*. Scranton, Pa.: Chandler.

Davidson, B. 1973. *Black Star – A view of the life and times of Kwame Nkrumah*. London: Allen Lane.

Davison, R. B. 1954. *Migrant Labour in the Gold Coast: a pilot survey*. Achimota: University College of Ghana.

Delafosse, M. 1912. *Haut-Sénégal-Niger* (Soudan Français). 3 vols. Paris: Larose.

Delobsom, Dim A. A. 1932. *L'Empire du Mogho Naba*. Paris: Domat-Montchrestien.

Deniel, R. 1968. *De la Savane à la Ville*. Paris: Aubier-Montaigne.

D'Hertefelt, M. 1964. "Mythes et Idéologies Dans le Rwanda Ancien et Contemporain." In *The Historian in Tropical Africa*, ed. J. Vansina, R. Mauny, and L. V. Thomas, pp. 219–38. London: Oxford University Press.

Dubb, A. A., and P. Mayer, eds. 1962. *The Multi-Tribal Society*. Proceedings of the Sixteenth Conference of the Rhodes-Livingston Institute, Lusaka.

Dupire, M. 1960. "Planteurs autochtones et étrangers en Basse Cote d'Ivoire Orientale." *Etudes Eburnéennes* 8.

Dupuis, J. 1824. *Journal of a Residence in Ashantee*. London.

Epstein, A. L. 1958. *Politics in an Urban African Community*. Manchester: Manchester University Press for Rhodes-Livingston Institute.

Bibliography

1961. "The Network and Urban Social Organization." *Rhodes-Livingston Journal*, No. 29, 29–62. Reprinted, 1969, in *Social Networks in Urban Situations*, ed. J. C. Mitchell, pp. 77–116. Manchester: Manchester University Press.

Fage, J. D. 1964. "Reflections on the Early History of the Mossi-Dagomba Group of States." In *The Historian in Tropical Africa*, ed. J. Vansina, R. Mauny, and L. V. Thomas, pp. 177–89. London: Oxford University Press.

Finnegan, G. 1972. "Mossi Social Fields." Paper presented at the Fifteenth Annual Meeting of the African Studies Association, Philadelphia.

1976. "Population Movement, Labor Migration and Social Structure in a Mossi Village." Ph.D. dissertation, Brandeis University, Waltham, Mass.

Fitch, B., and M. Oppenheimer. 1966. *Ghana: End of an Illusion.* New York: Monthly Review Press.

Fortes, M. 1945. *The Dynamics of Clanship Among the Tallensi.* London: Oxford University Press.

1949. *The Web of Kinship Among the Tallensi.* London: Oxford University Press.

1969. *Kinship and the Social Order.* London: Routledge and Kegan Paul.

1971. "Some aspects of Migration and Mobility in Ghana." *Journal of Asian and African Studies* 6: 1–20.

1975. "Strangers." In *Studies in African Social Anthropology*, ed. M. Fortes and S. Patterson, pp. 229–55. New York and London: Academic Press.

Fraenkel, M. 1964. *Tribe and Class in Monrovia.* London: Oxford University Press.

Freeman, T. B. 1843. *Journal of Two Visits to the Kingdom of Ashanti.* London: Ghana government.

1964. *1960 Population Census of Ghana. Special Report A: Statistics Larger Towns.* Accra: government printer.

1964. *1960 Population Census of Ghana. Special Report E: Tribes in Ghana: demographic, economic and social characteristics.* Accra: government printer.

1970. *1960 Population Census of Ghana. Vol. VI: Post enumeration survey.* Accra: government printer.

Gluckman, M. 1961. "Anthropological Problems arising from the African Industrial Revolution." In *Social Change in Modern Africa*, ed. A. Southall, pp. 67–82. London: Oxford University Press.

Goodenough, W. 1970. "Epilogue: Transactions in Parenthood." In V. Carroll, ed., *Adoption in Eastern Oceania*, ed. V. Carroll, pp. 391–410. Honolulu: The University of Hawaii Press.

Goody, E. 1966. "The Fostering of Children in Ghana: A Preliminary Report." *Ghana Journal of Sociology* 2: 26–33.

1970. "Kinship Fostering in Gonja." In *Socialization: the Approach from Social Anthropology*, ed. P. Mayer, pp. 51–74. Association of Social Anthropologists Monograph No. 8. London: Tavistock.

Goody, J. R. 1956. *The Social Organization of the LoWiili.* London: H.M.S.O.

1962. *Death, Property and the Ancestors.* London: Tavistock.

1970. "Marriage Policy and Incorporation in Northern Ghana." In *From Tribe to Nation*, ed. R. Cohen and J. Middleton. Scranton, Pa.: Chandler.

Goody, J. R., and K. Arhin, eds. 1965. *Ashanti and the Northwest.* Institute of African Studies, Research Review No. 1, University of Ghana, Legon.

Greenberg, J. H. 1947. "Islam and Clan Organization Among the Hausa." *Southwestern Journal of Anthropology* 3: 193–211.

Gulliver, P. H. 1969. *Tradition and Transition in East Africa.* Berkeley and Los Angeles: University of California Press.

Gutkind, P. C. 1970. *The Passing of Tribal Man in Africa.* Leiden: E. J. Brill.

Bibliography

Hammond, P. B. 1966. *Yatenga, Technology in the Culture of a West African Kingdom.* New York: Free Press.

Hart, J. K. 1974. "Migration and the Opportunity Structure: A Ghanaian case-study." In *Modern Migrations in Western Africa,* ed. S. Amin. London: Oxford University Press.

Hill, P. 1966. "Landlords and Brokers: A West African Trading System." *Cahiers d'Etudes Africaines* 6: 349–66.

1970a. *Studies in Rural Capitalism in West Africa.* Cambridge: Cambridge University Press.

1970b. "The Occupations of Migrants in Ghana." *Anthropological Papers of the Museum of Anthropology,* The University of Michigan, No. 42. Ann Arbor, Mich.

Hodgkin, T. 1966. "The Islamic Literary Tradition in Ghana." In *Islam in Tropical Africa,* ed. I. M. Lewis, pp. 442–63. London: Oxford University Press.

Hodgson, Lady M. 1901. *The Seige of Kumasi.* London: Longmans, Green.

Hutson, S. 1971. "Social Ranking in a French Alpine Community." In *Gifts and Poison: The Politics of Reputation,* ed. F. G. Bailey, pp. 41–68. New York: Schocken Books.

Illiasu, A. A. 1971. *The Origins of the Mossi Dagomba States.* Institute of African Studies, Research Review 7(2). University of Ghana, Legon.

Izard, M. 1971. "Les Yarse et le Commerce dans le Yatenga Pre-colonial." In *The Development of Indigenous Trade and Markets in West Africa,* ed. C. Meillassoux, pp. 214–28. London: Oxford University Press.

Izard-Héritier, F., and M. Izard. 1959. *Les Mossi du Yatenga: étude de la vie économique et sociale.* Bordeaux: Institut des Sciences Humaines Appliquées.

Johnson, M., ed. Undated. *The Salaga Papers.* 2 vols. Institute of African Studies, University of Ghana, Legon.

Kabore, G. V. 1966. *Organisation Politique Traditionelle et Evolution Politique des Mossi de Ouagadougou. Recherches Voltaïques 5.* Paris: Centre National de la Recherche Scientifique.

Kohler, J. M. 1968. *Activités Agricoles et Transformations Socio-Economiques dans une Region de l'ouest Mossi.* Paris: ORSTOM.

1972. *Les Migrations des Mossi de l'Ouest.* Paris: ORSTOM.

Kuper, H., ed. 1965. *Urbanization and Migration in West Africa.* Los Angeles: University of California Press.

Kuper, L., and M. G. Smith. 1969. *Pluralism in Africa.* Berkeley and Los Angeles: University of California Press.

La Fontaine, J. S. 1970. *City Politics: A Study of Leopoldville. 1912–63.* Cambridge: Cambridge University Press.

Last, M. 1967. *The Sokoto Caliphate.* London: Longmans, Green.

Le Moal, G. 1960. "Un aspect de l'émigration: la fixation des Voltaïques au Ghana." *Bulletin de l'I.F.A.N., B.* 22, 3–4, 446–54.

Levine, R. A., and D. T. Campbell. 1972. *Ethnocentrism: Theories of Conflict, Ethnic Attitudes and Group Behavior.* New York: Wiley.

Levtzion, N. 1968. *Muslims and Chiefs in West Africa.* London: Oxford University Press.

Levy, R. 1965. *The Social Structure of Islam.* Cambridge: Cambridge University Press.

Little, K. 1957. "The Role of Voluntary Associations in West African Urbanization." *American Anthropologist* 59: 579–96.

1965. *West African Urbanization.* London: Cambridge University Press.

Lloyd, P. C., Mabogunje, A. L., and Awe, B., eds. 1967. *The City of Ibadan.* Cambridge: University Press, in association with Institute of African Studies, University of Ibadan.

Lovejoy, P. E. 1973. The Kambarin Beriberi: The Formation of a Specialized Group of Hausa Kola Traders in the Nineteenth Century." *Journal of African History* 14: 633–51.

Maquet, J. 1961. *The Premise of Inequality in Rwanda.* London: Oxford University Press.

Marc, Lucien. 1909. *Le Pays Mossi.* Paris: Larousse.

Mayer, P. 1962. "Migrancy and the Study of Africans in Towns." *American Anthropologist,* 64: 576–92.

1963. *Townsmen or Tribesmen.* Cape Town: Oxford University Press.

Meillassoux, C. 1969. *Urbanization of an African Community: Voluntary Associations in Bamako.* American Anthropological Society Monograph 45. Seattle and London: University of Washington Press.

1971 (ed.). *The Development of Indigenous Trade and Markets in West Africa.* London: Oxford University Press.

Mercier, Paul. 1965. "On the Meaning of Tribalism in Black Africa." In *Africa: Social Problems of Change and Conflict,* ed. P. L. Van Dan Berghe, pp. 483–501. San Francisco: Chandler.

Merton, R. K. 1964. "Intermarriage and the Social Structure: Fact and Theory." In *The Family: Its Structure and Function,* ed. R. L. Coser. New York: St. Martin's Press.

Miner, H. 1965. *The Primitive City of Timbuctoo.* Rev. ed. New York: Doubleday.

1967. (ed.). *The City in Modern Africa.* London: Pall Mall Press.

Mitchell, J. C. 1956. *The Kelela Dance.* Rhodes-Livingston Paper No. 27.

1957. "Aspects of African Marriage in the Copperbelt of Northern Rhodesia." *Human Problems in British Central Africa* 22: 1–30. Manchester: Manchester University Press.

1966. "Theoretical Orientations in African Urban Studies." In *The Social Anthropology of Complex Societies,* ed. M. Banton. Association of Social Anthropologists Monograph No. 4. London: Tavistock.

1974. "Perceptions of Ethnicity and Ethnic Behaviour." In *Urban Ethnicity,* ed. A. Cohen, pp. 1–35. Association of Social Anthropologists Monograph No. 12. London: Tavistock.

Nadel, S. F. 1942. *A Black Byzantium.* London: Oxford University Press.

1947. *The Nuba: An Anthropological Study of The Hill Tribes of Kordofan.* London: Oxford University Press.

Nyarko, K. A. J. 1959. "The Development of Kumasi." *Bulletin of the Ghana Geographic Association* 4: 3–8. Legon: University of Ghana.

Oppong, C. 1967. *The Context of Socialization in Dagbon.* Institute of African Studies Research Review 1: 4, 7–18. Legon: University of Ghana.

Paden, J. N. 1970. "Urban pluralism, integration, and adaptation of communal identity in Kano, Nigeria." In *From Tribe to Nation in Africa,* ed. R. Cohen and J. Middleton, pp. 242–70. Scranton, Pa.: Chandler.

1973. *Religion and Political Culture in Kano.* Los Angeles: University of California Press.

Parkin, D. 1969. *Neighbours and Nationals in an African City Ward.* London: Routledge and Kegan Paul.

Pauw, B. A. 1963. *The Second Generation.* Cape Town: Oxford University Press.

Plotnicov, L. 1967. *Strangers in the City; Urban Man in Jos, Nigeria.* Pittsburgh, Pa.: University of Pittsburgh Press.

Pons, V. 1969. *Stanleyville, An African Urban Community under Belgian Administration.* London: Oxford University Press.

Bibliography

Price, J. 1956. "The Muslim Vote in the Accra Constituencies, 1954." Proceedings of the Fourth Annual Conference of the West African Institute Soc. Econ. Res., 160–7. Ibadan: University College.

Rattray, R. S. 1929. *Ashanti Law and Constitution.* Oxford: Clarendon Press.

Richards, A. I., ed. 1955. *Economic Development and Tribal Change.* Cambridge: Heffer, for East African Institute for Social Research.

1966. "Multitribalism in African Urban Areas." *Civilizations* 16: 1–8.

Rouch, J. 1956. *Migrations au Ghana.* Paris: Centre National de Recherche Scientifique.

1960. "Problèmes relatifs à l'étude des migrations traditionelles et des migrations actuelles en Afrique occidentale." *Bulletin de l'Institut Français d'Afrique Noir* 22B: 369–78.

1961. "Second Generation Migrants in Ghana and the Ivory Coast." In *Social Change in Modern Africa,* ed. A. Southall, pp. 300–5. London: Oxford University Press.

Ruelle, E. 1904. "Notes anthropologiques, ethnographiques, et sociologiques sur quelques populations noire du 2^e territoire de l'Afrique occidentale française." *L'Anthropologie* 15: 519–61, 657–703.

Sanjek, R. 1972. *Ghanaian Networks: An analysis of interethnic relations in urban situations.* Ph.D. dissertation, Columbia University.

Sanjek, R., with Lani Morioka Sanjek. 1976. "Notes on women and work in Adabraka." *African Urban Notes.* African Studies Center, Michigan State University, East Lansing, Michigan (forthcoming issue).

Savonnet, G. 1968. *Atlas de Haute-Volta. Carte provisoire des densités de populations.* République de Haute-Volta-ORSTOM.

Schein, M. D. 1975. "When is an Ethnic Group? Ecology and Class Structure in Northern Greece." *Ethnology* 14: 83–97.

Schildkrout, E. 1969. *Ethnicity, Kinship and Politics Among Mossi Immigrants in Kumasi.* Ph.D. dissertation, University of Cambridge.

1970a. "Strangers and Local Government in Kumasi." *Journal of Modern African Studies* 8: 251–69.

1970b. "Government and Chiefs in Kumasi." In *West African Chiefs: Their Changing Status Under Colonial Rule and Independence,* ed. M. Crowder and O. Ikime, pp. 370–93. Nigeria: University of Ife Press.

1973. "The Fostering of Children in Urban Ghana: Problems of Ethnographic Analysis in a Multi-Cultural Context." *Urban Anthropology,* 2: 48–73.

1974a. "Islam and Politics in Ghana: An Analysis of Disputes over the Kumasi Central Mosque." *Anthropological Papers of the American Museum of Natural History* 52(2): 113–37.

1974b. "Ethnicity and Generational Differences among Urban Immigrants in Ghana." In *Urban Ethnicity,* ed. A. Cohen, pp. 187–222. Association of Social Anthropologists, Monograph No. 12. London: Tavistock.

1975a. "Economics and Kinship in Multi-ethnic Dwellings." In *The Changing Social Structure in Ghana,* ed. J. Goody, pp. 167–79. London: Oxford University Press.

1975b. "Ethnicity, Kinship and Joking among Urban Immigrants in Ghana." In *Migration and Ethnicity* (Proceedings of the IXth International Congress of Anthropological and Ethnological Sciences), ed. B. du Toit and H. Safa, pp. 245–63. Paris: Mouton.

forthcoming: "The Ideology of Regionalism in Ghana." In *Strangers in African Societies,* ed. W. A. Shack and E. P. Skinner. Berkeley: University of California Press.

Bibliography

and G. Finnegan. Unpublished MS. "Themes and Variations in Mossi Ethnography."

Shibutani, T., and J. M. Kwan. 1965. *Ethnic Stratification*. New York: Macmillan.

Skinner, E. P. 1958. "Christianity and Islam among the Mossi." *American Anthropologist* 60: 1102–19.

1960. "Labour Migration and Its Relationship to Socio-Cultural Change in Mossi Society." *Africa* 30: 375–401.

1963. "Strangers in West African Societies." *Africa* 33: 307–20.

1964. *The Mossi of the Upper Volta*. California: Stanford University Press.

1965. "Labour Migration among the Mossi of the Upper Volta." In *Urbanization and Migration in West Africa*, ed. H. Kuper, pp. 60–85. Los Angeles: University of California Press.

1966. "Islam in Mossi Society". In *Islam in Tropical Africa*, ed. I. M. Lewis, pp. 350–70. London: Oxford University Press.

Smith, M. 1954. *Baba of Karo*. London: Faber and Faber.

Smith, M. G. 1955. *The Economy of the Hausa Communities of Zaria*. Colonial Research Series No. 16. London: HMSO.

1959a. "Social or Cultural Pluralism." *Annals of the New York Academy of Science* 83: 763–85.

1959b. "Tha Hausa System of Social Status." *Africa* 29: 239–53.

1969. "Pluralism in Pre-colonial African Societies." in *Pluralism in Africa*, ed. L. Kuper and M. G. Smith, pp. 91–152. Berkeley: University of California Press.

Songre, A., J. Sawadogo, and G. Sanogoh. 1974. "Realités et effets de l'émigration massive des Voltaïques dans le contexte de l'Afrique occidentale." In *Modern Migrations in Western Africa*, ed. S. Amin, pp. 384–407. London: Oxford University Press.

Southall, A. W. n.d. *Alur Society*. Cambridge: Heffers.

1961. *Social Change in Modern Africa*. London: Oxford University Press.

Southall, A. W., and P. C. Gutkind. 1957. *Townsmen in the Making. East African Studies*, No. 9 (2nd impression). East African Institute of Social Research.

Sudarkasa, N. (ed.). 1975. *Migrants and Strangers in Africa*. African Urban Notes. Ser. B, No. 1. African Studies Center, Michigan State University, East Lansing, Michigan.

Tauxier, L. 1912. *Le Noir du Soudan*. Paris: Larousse.

1917. *Le Noir du Yatenga*. Paris: Larousse.

1924. *Nouvelles Notes sur le Mossi et le Gourounsi*. Paris: Larousse.

Thomas, R. G. 1973. "Forced Labour in British West Africa: The Case of the Northern Territories of the Gold Coast 1906–1927." *Journal of African History* 14: 79–103.

Tiendrébéogo, Y. 1964. *Histoire et Coutumes Royales des Mossi de Ouagadougou*. Ouagadougou: Chez le Larhallé-Naba.

Tordoff, W. 1965. *Ashanti Under the Prempehs, 1888–1935*. London: Oxford University Press.

Trimingham, J. S. 1959. *Islam in West Africa*. London: Oxford University Press.

Triulzi, A. 1972. "The Asantehene-in-Council: Ashanti Politics under Colonial Rule, 1935–1950." *Africa* 42: 98–111.

Wallerstein, I. 1960. "Ethnicity and National Integration in West Africa." *Cahiers d'Etudes Africaines* 3: 129–39.

Westermann, D., and M. A. Bryan. 1952. *The Languages of West Africa*. London: Oxford University Press.

Wilks, I. 1961. *The Northwest Factor in Ashanti History*. Research Review No. 1, Institute of African Studies, University of Ghana, Legon.

Bibliography

1962. "A Medieval Trade Route from Niger to the Gulf of Guinea." *Journal of African History*, 3: 337–41.

1966. "The Position of Muslims in Metropolitan Ashanti in the Early Nineteenth Century." In *Islam in Tropical Africa*, ed. I. M. Lewis, pp. 318–42. London: Oxford University Press.

1967. "Ashanti Government." In *West African Kingdoms in the Nineteenth Century*, ed. D. Forde and P. Kaberry, pp. 206–38. London: Oxford University Press.

1968. "The Transmission of Islamic Learning in the Western Sudan." In *Literacy in Traditional Societies*, ed. J. R. Goody. Cambridge: Cambridge University Press.

1971. "Asante Policy Towards the Hausa Trade in the Nineteenth Century." In *The Development of Indigenous Trade and Markets in West Africa*, ed. C. Meillassoux, pp. 124–44. London: Oxford University Press.

1975. *Asante in the Nineteenth Century*. Cambridge: Cambridge University Press.

Withers-Gill, J. 1924a. *The Mossi Tribe, A Short History*. Reproduced by the Institute of African Studies, Legon. Accra: Gold Coast Government Press.

1924b. *A Short History of Salaga*. Accra.

Zahan, D. 1961. "Pour une histoire des Mossi du Yatenga." *L'Homme*, 1(2): 5–22.

1967. "The Mossi Kingdoms." In *West African Kingdoms in the Nineteenth Century*, ed. D. Forde and P. M. Kaberry. London: Oxford University Press.

Official publications

The following documents in the Public Record Office (PRO), London, and in the National Archives of Ghana (NAG), Accra and Kumasi, have been cited.

Public Record Office, London:
Gold Coast Colony, Administrative Reports, 1900–1901. C.O. 98/10.
Gold Coast Colony, Departmental Reports, 1902–1903. C.O. 98/13.
Gold Coast Colony, Annual Reports, 1904–1905. C.O. 98/14.
Gold Coast Colony, Annual Reports, 1906–1907. C.O. 98/16.
Gold Coast Colony, Departmental Reports, 1908–1909. C.O. 98/11.
Gold Coast Colony, Annual Reports, 1908–1909. C.O. 98/17.
Letter Book, May–Sept. 1880. C.O. 96/131.
Letter Book, 1900. C.O. 96/151.
Draft Administrative Ordinances, Gold Coast. C.O. 879/67.

National Archives of Ghana, Accra:
Annual Reports of the Northern Territories of the Gold Coast, 1900–1914.
District Record Book, Kumasi, 1926–1951. ADM 51/5/6.
Northern Territories Letter Book, 1900. ADM 56/1/1.
Chief Commissioner of the Northern Territories, Letter Book. ADM 56/1/2.
Northern Territories Letter Book. ADM 56/1/62.
Report on 'Native Labour.' 1914. ADM 56/1/84.
Record Book 42. Northern Territories. ADM 56.
Letter Book, 1879. ADM 1/672.
Half-Yearly Report on the Gold Coast Constabulary, 1880. ADM 1/470.
Report of the Anthropological Branch, 1930.

National Archives of Ghana, Kumasi:
Annual Reports of Ashanti, 1900–1936.
Zongo Affairs. 12/60

Bibliography

Chief Commissioner of Ashanti's Confidential Diary, 1917.

Regional Office, Kumasi:
   File B 0459, 3 Vols. "Stranger Communities."
   File B 2268. "Muslim Affairs."
   File B 2832. "Stranger Communities."
   File B 0856. "Zongo Affairs."

Kumasi State Council:
   File. "Stranger Communities."

Index

Aboabo, 99, 102, 132, 222; development of, 82
absentee landlords, 115–16; *see also* housing; landlord/tenant relationship
abusa, see sharecropping
action troopers, 209
Administrative Ordinance (1902), 195, 196
Adomako-Sarfoh, J., 40, 42, 43
affinity: definition of, 139–40; kinship and, 151, 227
agriculture: among Mossi, 33; subsistence farming, 38; Voltaic, 39
Ahmad Baba al-Wa'iz, 197
Ahmadiyya, 87
Alexandre, G., 35
"all Africa law," 164
Amakom, ethnic breakdown in, 82
Amin, S., 6, 39, 40
ancestor worship, and corporate lineages, 113
apprenticeship, among Mossi, 54–6
Arab culture: influence in Zongo, 94; *see also* education (Arabic); Islam; Muslims
Arabic language, literacy in, 211, 239, 254
Arabic schools, *see* education
architecture, social consequences of, 107
arms, *see* firearms
Asana Moshie, 47
Asante (state): British conquest of, 67–9, 74; campaign against Dagomba, 68; immigration in, 4; investment in Zongo, 77; Mossi in rural areas of, 7; Muslims in, 67
Asante army, composition of, 70
Asante chiefs: British and, 194, 196, 198, 199, 203–4; courts of, 196; land control by, 80; Mossi headmen and, 81; Zongo policy of, 195
Asante forests, 36, 72
Asante National Liberation Movement (NLM): and MAP, 168; opposes CPP, 208, 209; United Party and, 215
Asante Nkramo community, 84, 85, 87, 95, 193
Asante Nkramo Imam, 85
Asante population: *abusa* system, 49; differentiation among, 69; ethnic feelings and, 14; leadership role of, 206, 208, 270; Mossi

laborers and, 50, 72, 114, 233–4; Mossi marriage and, 32, 182; Sarkin Zongo and, 200, 201; strangers and, 12, 94
Asantehene, 97, 167, 169, 194, 209; British rule and, 67, 70, 80, 195, 198; headmen and, 225; immigrants and, 85, 196; local government and, 206
Asawasi, 102, 222
Ashanti Confederacy, 195, 201
Ashanti Crown Colony, 67
Ashanti Draft Ordinance, 195
Ashanti New Town, ethnic breakdown in, 82, 102
Ashanti Traditional Authority, 80
assimilation: economic forces of, 34; processes of, 94, 264
associations: generational differences and, 244–5; among Mossi, 222; rise of, 214–20; types of, 214–15; voluntary, 7, 97, 103, 105, 162; *see also entries for individual associations*
auren musaya, 166
authority: of headmen, 198, 201; Mossi attitudes toward, 50; political sources of, 207, 212; removed from chiefs, 80; stranger immigration and, 67; succession and, 253–4; *see also* power
Avoidance of Discrimination Act (1958), 215

Baba, Ahmadu, 209–10, 216
Banton, M. P., 7
Barth, F., 8, 11, 12
behavior: among immigrants, 86, 100; intergroup and intragroup, 10; kinship and, 142, 144, 169; of migrants, 5; *see also* joking relationships
Berg, E. J., 38
Bernus, S., 8
Binger, L., 23, 34, 36
birth order, in Mossi myth, 23
borders, Anglo-French (1898), 47
boundaries: of community, 89, 224; ethnic categories and, 19; kinship and, 190; problem of, 11
Bowdich, T. E., 36, 68, 70
British: Asanti relations of, 68, 194, 201;

Index

Index

Index

women: cooperation among, 108, 129; as houseowners, 117; housing of, 107; labor of, 39, 106, 126; political rights and, 182, 214, 233; property rights of, 116
women's associations (Mossi), 117, 248-9
World War I, 70

Yaa Asantewaa War (1902), 170
Yameogo, Maurice, 219
'yan k'asa, 90, 93, 163, 200, 221; attitudes of, 100, 104; definition of, 83; ethnic identity of, 222; fostering among, 150; kinship terms of, 159, 179, 228; leadership among, 238, 243, 256; marriage among, 177, 178-9, 180, 188; *see also* first generation, second generation
Yanse, headmen of, 225
YarNaba, rank of, 35
Yarse, 25, 43, 90; crafts of, 53-4; dispersion of, 57; ethnic identity of, 62-3; kinship structure of, 58, 177; myths of, 20; power and, 230; relationship with Hausa, 62; and spread of Islam, 34-5; stratification and, 34-5, 48
YateYate, 99, 132, 222
yirisoba, 232-3
Yisa, as regent, 253, 254, 259, 260

Yoruba, 70; British and, 197, 198; migrants of, 44, 73, 82; Sarkin Zongo and, 200, 201, 202
youth, associations of, 103, 159; *see also* children

Zabarama, 70; slavers, 47, 56
Zahan, D., 21, 27
zaksoba, 232-3
Zionism, 11
zongo: definition of, 67, 85, 280 (n.2); identity in, 14; stranger communities, 5, 14, 69, 98, 193
Zongo (Kumasi): British support settlement of, 69; conflict in, 200; courts in, 199-200; definition of, 280 (n.2); ethnic diversity in, 87, 265; government policy toward, 195, 198, 205; identity in, 88, 94; kinship in, 14, 98, 162; marriage in, 180, 189; migrants in, 6; Mossi headmen in, 221; origin of, 69, 74, 80, 193; political parties in, 215, 255; population sources of, 69, 73, 82; relationships in, 94; revenue of, 76
Zongo (Mossi), 222; development of, 80-1, 99; immigrants of, 132
Zongo (Sabon), 102, 198, 222

DUE DATE